Shaping Your Future

Eddye Eubanks, Ph.D.   Connie R. Sasse, CFCS

Linda R. Glosson, Ph.D.

Contributing Writers

Heather Boggs, Ph.D, CFCS   Patricia Clark, M.Ed., CFCS

Glencoe
McGraw-Hill

New York, New York   Columbus, Ohio   Woodland Hills, California   Peoria, Illinois

Contributors

Gale Cornelia Flynn
Writer/Educational Consultant
Hockessin, Delaware

Christine Venzon
Writer
Peoria, Illinois

Teresa K. Branham
Family and Consumer Sciences Teacher
Eastland Vocational School District
Groveport, Ohio

"Cartography" from THE BLUE ESTUARIES: POEMS 1923-1968 by Louise Bogan. Copyright © 1968 by Louise Bogan. Copyright renewed © 1996 by Ruth Limmer. Reprinted by permission of Farrar, Straus & Giroux, Inc.

Glencoe/McGraw-Hill

A Division of The McGraw·Hill Companies

Printed in the United States of America
Send all inquiries to:
Glencoe/McGraw-Hill
3008 W. Willow Knolls Drive
Peoria, IL 61614-1083

ISBN 0-02-637967-8

4 5 6 7 8 9 10 11 12   003   05 04 03 02 01

Teacher Reviewers

Carol A. Bardon, M.Ed., CFCS
Family & Consumer Sciences
    Teacher
Ludlow High School
Ludlow, Massachusetts

Janet M. Bowen, M.S.
Home Economics Teacher
Edmeston Central School
Edmeston, New York

Marilyn Davis, M.S.
Department Chair
Health/Consumer Home
    Economics
American High School
Fremont, California

Janice Fisher
Family & Consumer Sciences
    Teacher
District #25
Pocatello, Idaho

Diana Geiger
Department Chair
Home Economics Careers &
    Technology
Tulare Western High School
Tulare, California

Bobbie Grassel
Family & Consumer Sciences
    Teacher
Bismarck High School
Bismarck, North Dakota

Anita K. Grier, M.L.S., M.S.
Family & Consumer Sciences
    Teacher
South Colonie High School
Albany, New York

Wanda Guess
Family & Consumer Sciences
    Instructor
Unified District 336
Holton, Kansas

Anne L. Hansen, Ph.D.
Consultant
Walla Walla, Washington

Jane Hassel, M.S.
Department Head
Family & Consumer Sciences
North Platte Senior High School
North Platte, Nebraska

Darlene Hicks, M.A., CFCS
Consultant
New Braunfels, Texas

Rena S. Humerickhouse, M.S.
Department Chair
Family & Consumer Sciences
Elkhart Central High School
Elkhart, Indiana

Donna Jones, M.S.
Department Chair
Family & Consumer Sciences
Blue Valley High School
Stilwell, Kansas

Joyce L. Kennedy
Department Head
Family & Consumer Sciences
Riverton High School
Riverton, Wyoming

Virginia E. Kraft, CFCS
Family & Consumer Sciences
    Teacher
Paw Paw High School
Paw Paw, Illinois

Marilyn C. Lanna
Family & Consumer Sciences
    Teacher
North Catholic High School
Pittsburgh, Pennsylvania

Janet F. Laster, Ph.D.
Ohio State University
Columbus, Ohio

Mary J. Lease, M.Ed.
Family & Consumer Sciences
    Instructor
Wagner Community School
Wagner, South Dakota

Bufaye K. Reynolds
Family & Consumer Sciences
    Teacher
San Juan School District
Blanding, Utah

Barbara A. Robinson, M.A.
Life Management Educator
Flushing Community Schools
Flushing, Michigan

Laurie Ryder
Family & Consumer Sciences
    Teacher
Fairless High School
Navarre, Ohio

Denise Scholl
Life Education Teacher
Keene High School
Keene, New Hampshire

Gloria Taylor, M.Ed., CFCS
Family & Consumer Sciences
    Teacher
Eastern High School
Washington, D.C

Student Reviewers

Gaye Hamilton
Piscataway High
    School
Piscataway,
    New Jersey

Karen Sze Yui Poon
Piscataway High
    School
Piscataway,
    New Jersey

Emily Rhein
Dunlap High
    School
Dunlap, Illinois

Jeff Schubert
Skyline High
    School
Longmont, Colorado

Raquel Tarin
Skyline High
    School
Longmont, Colorado

Contents in Brief

Contents

Unit 1: Building a Foundation for Life . . . 20

Chapter 1: Looking Toward Your Future . . . 22

Chapter 2: Using Problem Solving . . . 36

Unit 3: Enhancing Personal Well-Being . . . 200

Chapter 13: Maintaining Physical Health . . . *220*

Chapter 14: Taming Your Stress . . . *240*

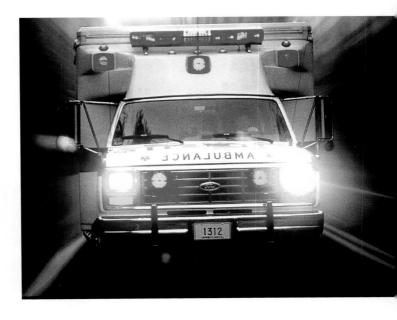

Chapter 19: A Place to Live . . . *332*

Chapter 20: Transportation Options . . . *354*

Unit 5: Developing Your Financial Skills . . . 374

Special Features

REASON Through Life's Problems

FOCUS ON...

MANAGING YOUR RESOURCES

TECHNOLOGY ISSUES

Close-Up

Unit 1
Building a Foundation for Life

Chapters ▽

CHAPTER 1

Looking Toward Your Future

What You Will Learn...

- Opportunities for growth and satisfaction exist in all areas of your life.
- Being an independent adult is easier if you know yourself, have a positive approach to life, and are resilient.
- Goal setting, decision making, management, and problem solving help everyone deal with life's challenges and opportunities.

Terms for Success

interdependence
lifelong learning
resilience

Mark opened a package of cheese crackers and offered some to his study partner, Reese. "Want one?"

"Sure." Reese put down his pen, glad to be distracted from the outline he was supposed to be writing. His thoughts were far from school-work today, anyway. "So your sister is majoring in special education," he commented.

"Yep. Connie called from college last week. Mom and Dad are proud. So am I."

Reese smiled, carefully examining his cracker sandwich. "I wish I knew where I'll be in three years."

Mark stuffed a cracker into his mouth. "I thought we were both heading for Bolton State," he said between chews. "I'm counting on you as a roommate."

"Oh, I'm still planning on Bolton," Reese said. "I mean. . ." He struggled for the words. "I wonder what I'll be doing and what kind of guy I'll be. How will I handle it all?"

"You?" Mark raised his brows. "Worried about grades?"

Reese tried again. "It's not just school. It's paying bills, holding down a job—a real job—and maybe meeting a girl and getting married. . ."

Mark laughed. "Hold on a second! I mean, I think about this stuff, too, but I figure it won't all happen in one day. We've got time. Slow down!"

Reese shrugged. "I know. I guess it just helps to hear someone else worry about the future, too."

"No problem." Mark bit into a cheese cracker as he tilted his textbook forward. "Now *here* we have a problem. It says we're supposed to identify the contributions of Augustus Caesar. Wasn't he the guy who made salads?"

When you're thinking about your future, what types of situations can you plan for and what types might be hard to control or anticipate?

What Does Your Future Hold?

Do you, like Reese, ever wish you could know your future? What job will you have? Where will you live? Will you be happy and successful?

Whether you are eager for the future to arrive or are willing to just let it happen, you have much to look forward to. The next few years will bring many changes and opportunities. What kind of changes would you welcome? Are there any changes you are *not* excited about?

So Many Choices

To begin with, there are job and career opportunities that promise income and work satisfaction. How you spend time off from work can add fun, richness, and fulfillment to life. What opportunities can you imagine in these areas of your life? Think about the following:

- **The challenge of choosing.** Sometimes there are so many options that it's hard to pick the best one. Being able to match your skills to appropriate career opportunities will help you be successful.
- **Which opportunity is best?** Even the best opportunities can clash with each other. When this happens, you will need to make choices. Bob has a job offer on an oil rig hundreds of miles from home. This means he can't take the job and still be with his girlfriend, who is going to school near home.
- **Opportunities may be disguised.** They aren't always easy to recognize. Some come disguised as challenges or problems. Every time you meet a challenge or solve a problem, though, you will learn something that might help you in the future. On the other hand, an opportunity might lead you in a new direction. Being optimistic about turning challenges into possibilities is a good attitude to have.

• When this worker was in high school, she didn't really think about the opportunity to learn welding as a career. Discuss why it is important to be open to new or unexpected opportunities in life. Is this important only in relationship to work? Why or why not?

- **Work toward the best opportunities.** Sometimes the opportunities you see may not be the ones you want at the moment. You may have to look further or just build on what you can do now. For example, if the company you want to work for doesn't have an opening now, take another job—but be ready for the time when you can reapply to your first choice.

Weighing the Outcomes

When opportunity knocks, keep in mind that most choices have consequences. Sometimes you will be able to accurately predict the impact of your choices. At other times, you may find that the positive aspects are less rewarding than you had expected and the negative ones are more overpowering.

For example, if you have the chance to choose which of two movies to see, your choice is not likely to have consequences other than an evening of either boredom or entertainment. However, you need to choose more carefully when opportunities have a long-term impact on your life. Some choices, such as becoming a parent, will affect your life forever.

As you already know, even with thoughtful planning and decision making, your life won't always go as expected. How you handle the unexpected will affect your present and future. If a choice doesn't work out, you shouldn't be afraid of making more choices in the future. Instead you can learn from past mistakes, and your next choice will probably be a better one.

On Your Way to Independence

You have actually been learning how to live independently since you were born. Walking, eating by yourself, and talking were all early steps to independence. What other milestones in your life contributed to your becoming an independent adult?

Independence is only one part of adulthood. Although you may now be independent, you will still interact with and rely on others—family, friends, neighbors, or colleagues—for help, comfort, or companionship. You aren't alone, but are part of a support network.

• Sometimes there are so many opportunities, making a choice becomes difficult. **List at least three situations in which a high school student might face multiple or conflicting opportunities. On what basis would you make a choice in each situation?**

This is **interdependence**—a feeling of mutual reliance. You rely on others and they rely on you, but this reliance does not take away anyone's independence. It does mean that many of your choices will affect the lives of other people, too.

Knowing Yourself—A Lifelong Process

Who are you? You may think of yourself as a student in English class, an employee at work, and a son or daughter at home. These, however, are only roles you play, not the unique individual you actually are. Who you are is more than just the sum of what you do or the roles you fill, but something more. You will probably spend your whole life figuring out exactly who you are.

Your personality consists of all the characteristics that make you unique. Your emotions, your social skills, and your intellectual qualities combine to create the person you are.

People sometimes forget who they are when responsibilities for family, work, school, or community take over. Often it takes a conscious decision to let yourself be you. Daniela said, "If I get busy with work, volunteer activities, and family, I won't take time for myself. When I catch myself being grouchy, I know it's time to take a run or a bike ride."

The Value of Values

Your personal values are one of the important parts of your personality. They are principles or qualities that you find desirable and that guide the way you live. Some values were taught to you by family. Others you learned from friends and life experiences. You take giant steps in understanding yourself when you know what you value and why these values are important to you. Acting on what you treasure gives you a strong foundation for your life. You'll learn more about this point in Chapter 3.

While there are many ways to learn more about yourself, it is important to appreciate your own unique qualities. Of course it's often easier and more comfortable to blend in—you might feel safer knowing you are like everyone else. However, as you learn to appreciate your own worth, value, and talents, it becomes easier to be yourself.

• **Moving into a place of your own is often one step toward becoming independent.** What responsibilities accompany moving into housing of your own? What role might these responsibilities play in your independence?

• Volunteering to work with children is one way to put your values into action. What types of volunteer work could you do that would allow you to put your values into action?

Learning for a Lifetime

Remember when you were 13 and thought you were pretty smart about life and knew what you wanted? Now that you're older, you likely realize how little you really knew. Your whole life should be this way. You won't know "everything" when you finish high school or college. Think about how much more you'll understand about life even after another five or ten years. **Lifelong learning** means taking opportunities to keep your skills and knowledge up to date throughout life. The world and your circumstances are always changing, and lifelong learning skills will help you adapt to new situations.

As you face the opportunities waiting for you, you can make more confident choices if you know yourself—your personality, your values, and your worth.

Keeping a Positive Approach

Regardless of how well you plan your life, it will be filled with ups and downs. You can't protect yourself against every negative possibility, but you can learn how to "weather the storms" with a positive attitude and self-confidence.

For example, if you look at tough times as opportunities for learning, you have a positive attitude. You develop skills for dealing with difficulties. No problem is impossible to solve; some just take more time, effort, and energy. As you become more confident of your abilities, you will feel better about yourself.

Seeing Opportunities

TIPS

Here are some ways to take a *positive* view of challenges and problems:

- A disagreement with a friend is an *opportunity* to make your relationship better.

- Watching your neighbor's children instead of hanging out with your friends is an *opportunity* to demonstrate responsibility.

- Not getting a job you wanted due to a weak interview is an *opportunity* to learn how to better handle an interview and do better next time.

- Getting a poor grade on an assignment is an *opportunity* to show how much you can improve next time.

Bouncing Back with Resilience

Imagine pulling on a rubber band or a piece of paper. What happens each time? The rubber band stretches, but the paper will tear. When you stop pulling, the elastic snaps back while the paper doesn't change. When some people face problems, they are like rubber bands; they snap back and go on with life. Others, like the paper, are torn apart by bad times.

People who are like rubber bands have the quality of **resilience**, the ability to recover from, or adjust to change or misfortune. If you have resilience, you will be better able to handle the unexpected events that may happen to you.

What makes someone resilient? The following factors can help:

- **Problem-solving and communication skills.** If you are both a good listener and a willing talker, you can cope, work with others, and solve problems better.
- **Independence.** Relying on yourself and being self-sufficient can keep you from being overwhelmed by troubles.
- **Spirituality.** Spiritual beliefs often help explain what reasoning and logic can't.
- **Flexibility.** If you can change roles, adjust to rules, and change ways of acting when necessary, you can deal with new situations and problems.

- **Openness.** Being willing to discover and discuss facts and feelings help you solve a problem.
- **Hope.** Being optimistic about the outcome of a problem is essential to resolving it.
- **Family and social support.** Having family members, friends, and others to call on for advice or assistance will help you feel in control of a problem.
- **Routines.** If your family and work lives are predictable, your routine can help you bounce back from problems.
- **Health.** Good physical and emotional health are essential in dealing with difficulties.

• Resilience helps this teen enjoy playing basketball even after a disabling injury. **Discuss the factors that might have helped this teen develop resilience. How resilient are you?**

Some people, because of personality and background, are more resilient than others, but anyone can make choices that help him or her be more resilient. As you mature, you can become more like a rubber band by adding these elements to your life. As Jordan said, "My family never did things together when I was growing up. I want a strong family that will have fun together. I'm going to work for that."

Setting Goals and Making Decisions

Before you can make good choices, you'll need to know what you want. The ability to set goals is important. When you can state what result you want, you will be more likely to act in ways that will bring you closer to these goals. Jenna said, "My parents are divorcing. What I want, when this is all over, is to have a good relationship with both of them. So I try to stay out of their disagreements."

Some goals are short term—such as what do you need to do for tomorrow? On the other hand, many goals are long term, such as the goal of finding a satisfying career. Keeping your goals in mind will help you see beyond current challenges to future opportunities and benefits.

You've already been making decisions since you were very young. Your approach to making choices will affect every aspect of your life, such as where you will live and where you will work, as well as the relationships that you will form and maintain. Some decisions are routine (such as deciding what to wear to school or work) and some are more complicated. Being able to decide by using a logical process can make your choices good ones. To review the decision-making steps, see "Refresh Your Memory" on this page.

• Choosing to study rather than go to a movie with friends reflects this student's goals. **Identify one short-term and one long-term goal that this teen could be meeting while studying.**

Here are the steps to making good decisions:

1. Identify the decision to be made.
2. List your options.
3. Study and evaluate your choices.
4. Make your choice.
5. Act on your decision.
6. Evaluate your choice.

You Can Manage

If you are going to be a success at living independently, you'll need to take control over who you are and what you have—yourself and your resources. In other words, you'll need to be a manager.

Managing your resources means getting a place to live, being smart about spending money, and using your time effectively while trying to meet your goals. It also means taking responsibility for yourself, your well-being, and your relationships and interactions with others. These might be overwhelming without a process to help you through.

This management process is shown below. It's a useful tool in carrying out decisions and reaching your goals.

Managing yourself effectively, however, is more than just following a process. It involves:

- Knowing who you are, including your values.
- Having a strong sense of personal integrity.
- Having the best interests of yourself and others in mind.
- Acting on these things.

Management Process

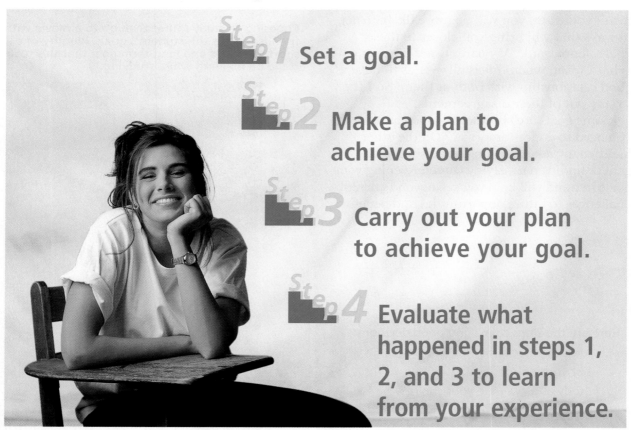

Step 1 Set a goal.

Step 2 Make a plan to achieve your goal.

Step 3 Carry out your plan to achieve your goal.

Step 4 Evaluate what happened in steps 1, 2, and 3 to learn from your experience.

- Using the management process is an organized way to reach your goals. Choose a short-term goal for the coming week and make a plan for achieving this goal. Carry out your plan and then evaluate it. Write a brief report about the success of your plan and what you learned from the experience.

Pulling Your Resources Together

"Some people in my carpentry class are helping a classmate whose home caught on fire," said Mike to a couple of his friends. "We decided to hold a car wash to make enough money to buy them a week's worth of groceries. The father of one of the guys in our class builds houses, so we've asked him to help the family get supplies to fix the damage for a price they can afford. And we're asking everyone in the school to bring in used clothing and kitchen appliances because the family lost that kind of stuff in the fire. We know we can't build them a new house, but we think this will help a lot."

Getting Organized

In order to help a classmate, Mike is calling on a variety of resources. Resources fall into three general categories: human, material, and community.

- **Human resources.** People themselves and all of their talents, abilities, and qualities provide the foundation to human resources. Time, skills, talents, knowledge, abilities, and energy are all human resources that can be used to reach goals, make decisions, and solve problems.
- **Material resources.** Money is often the first material resource that comes to mind. It can buy goods and services that you need. Possessions are also material resources. If you want clean clothes, then a washer, dryer, stain remover, detergent, and fabric softener may be possessions that will help you accomplish your goal.
- **Community resources.** Resources you might find in your community include facilities, such as schools, hospitals, libraries, parks, and museums, as well as services like Head Start and police protection. Community resources usually meet the educational, safety, health, and recreational needs of citizens.

Awareness of the many resources you have is the first step in using them wisely. Often wasted or misused resources can't be reclaimed or aren't available another time. When you use your resources effectively, you will have more of a chance to reach your goals and solve your problems.

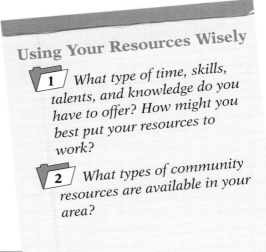

Using Your Resources Wisely

1. What type of time, skills, talents, and knowledge do you have to offer? How might you best put your resources to work?

2. What types of community resources are available in your area?

Using Your Skills to Solve Problems

Solving problems is one way to turn them into opportunities. Being able to solve your problems effectively is a skill that you can learn, and this book can help.

In the end, it's the ability to solve problems that will help you uncover and take advantage of life's opportunities. Being a good problem solver puts you in charge of what happens in your life. It lets you turn negatives into positives. Rebecca said, "When my mom was in the hospital after a car accident, I realized how many things she had done for me. Her accident, bad as it was, made me appreciate what she does for me. I see her in a different way now, and we get along much better. I also have learned how to do a lot of things on my own."

As you can see, setting goals, making decisions, managing yourself, and solving problems are interrelated processes. For example, you need to set goals in order to make effective decisions. Making decisions is involved in both management and problem solving. Sometimes a problem must be solved before a decision can be made.

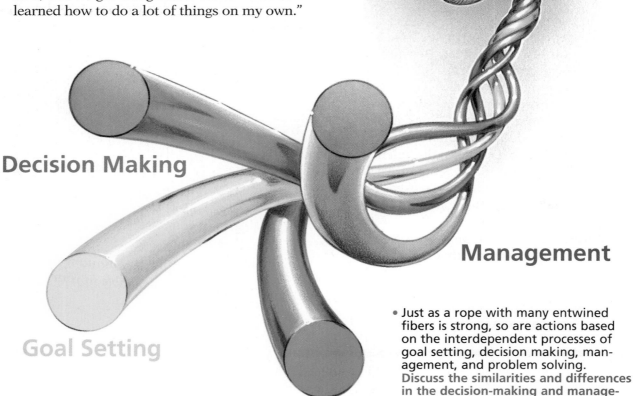

Decision Making

Management

Goal Setting

Problem Solving

• Just as a rope with many entwined fibers is strong, so are actions based on the interdependent processes of goal setting, decision making, management, and problem solving. **Discuss the similarities and differences in the decision-making and management processes. How do goal setting and problem solving relate to these two processes?**

You're on Your Way

In one sense, life is a series of ongoing opportunities, challenges, and problems. Whichever label you tag these situations depends on your:

- Outlook on life.
- Resilience.
- Ability to set goals and make decisions.
- Ability to manage your resources.
- Problem-solving skills.

To see "challenges" and "problems" as "opportunities" is based on your attitude toward life. If you are optimistic, you are more likely to see the positive things that exist even in what appears to be a negative situation. Building your skills and using the opportunities and knowledge available to you can help you shape your future in your best interest.

- Graduation is an outward symbol of an important transition into adulthood. Identify other symbols of adulthood that young adults desire. Is there substance to these symbols? Why or why not?

Understanding Key Concepts

- Your future will bring opportunities in all areas of life, including family, personal, work, and community.
- Taking advantage of opportunities means exploring all possibilities, making choices that are best for you and others, and learning from your decisions.
- Independence and interdependence are both qualities of successful adults.
- Understanding yourself, your needs, your values, and your worth will help you make good choices.
- A positive approach to life means having a resilient, "I-can-do-it" attitude.
- Setting goals and making decisions are necessary skills for capitalizing on life's opportunities.
- Managing yourself means making choices and taking actions that show your values and help meet your goals.
- Effective goal setting, decision making, problem solving, and management are interdependent processes that help you lead a successful life.

Checking Your Knowledge

1. Why do you think some teens feel they don't have many opportunities, while others believe they have a lot? Explain.
2. Describe a time when you had to choose among conflicting opportunities. How did you make a choice?
3. Why is it important to be careful when considering opportunities that may have a long-term impact on your life?
4. Describe the characteristics of an independent person. Does this person ever rely on others? Explain your answer.
5. Identify the similarities and differences between "who you are" and "what you do."
6. Why is understanding and acting on your values important in knowing yourself?
7. Explain why resilience is a quality needed by independent adults.
8. Give examples of a short-term goal and a long-term goal. Why are both types of goals important?

Making TRANSITIONS

Are You Ready?

Leaving high school is one of the major transitions to adult life. Factors that make this transition easier include supportive family and friends, making money, finding satisfying leisure activities, achieving your short-term goals, and educational success. Those who have problems with the transition tend to experience relationship problems, career confusion, financial difficulties, unemployment, lack of satisfying work, lack of educational opportunities, or difficulty adjusting to the educational demands of college or vocational training.

Think about which factors describe your life. Write at least three specific suggestions for actions you could take that would help smooth your transition to adulthood.

STRENGTHENING *Life* SKILLS

Building Support Networks

Imagine that you have found out your best friend has leukemia and has asked for your help in building a support network. Make a list of people your friend might talk to about this situation. This list might include friends, relatives, and community resources. Place a check mark by the names of those people who would give her help if she asked. The people on the list and especially those names checked are her support network.

Answer the following questions:
• What could she do to increase the size of her current support network?

• If she moved away from the support network, how could she replace it with another?
• Could you keep a support network functioning, even if you were away? How?
• What do you think are possible consequences if a person does not have a support network?

Applying Thinking Skills

1. **Predicting consequences.** Make a list of ways people can communicate with one another using technology. For each method on your list, describe one way that the method can help build and maintain relationships or support networks and one way it might harm relationships or support networks.

2. **Seeing relationships.** How does resilience apply to jobs and careers? Describe a work situation in which resilience would be a useful quality.

3. **Recognizing assumptions.** The following statement is based on an assumption: Whether you describe a situation as an opportunity, a challenge, or a problem depends on your personality and approach to life. What is the assumption? Do you agree with it? Defend your answer.

4. **Drawing conclusions.** What conclusions can you draw about the benefits of being an effective problem solver? How could this help you in all walks of life?

Practical Applications

1. **Opportunity and risk.** Every opportunity you face also carries some risk. Identify at least one risk that might accompany the following opportunities: a chance to go on a vacation with a friend; receiving a scholarship for college; being accepted into the armed services; being promoted at work; building a relationship with the person you'd like to marry. Why are these opportunities worth the risk?

2. **Developing your resiliency factors.** For each factor that helps make a person resilient, give an example showing how you are developing it.

3. **Resource management.** Because Shari has decided that she values a good education, she has decided to go to a community college. In order to meet this goal, she's been saving money, but she will still have to find out about and apply for scholarships and work part-time. She's concerned about juggling both work and her studies. What resources will Shari have to manage in order to meet her goal? Give three suggestions that could help her manage effectively.

CHAPTER 2

Using Problem Solving

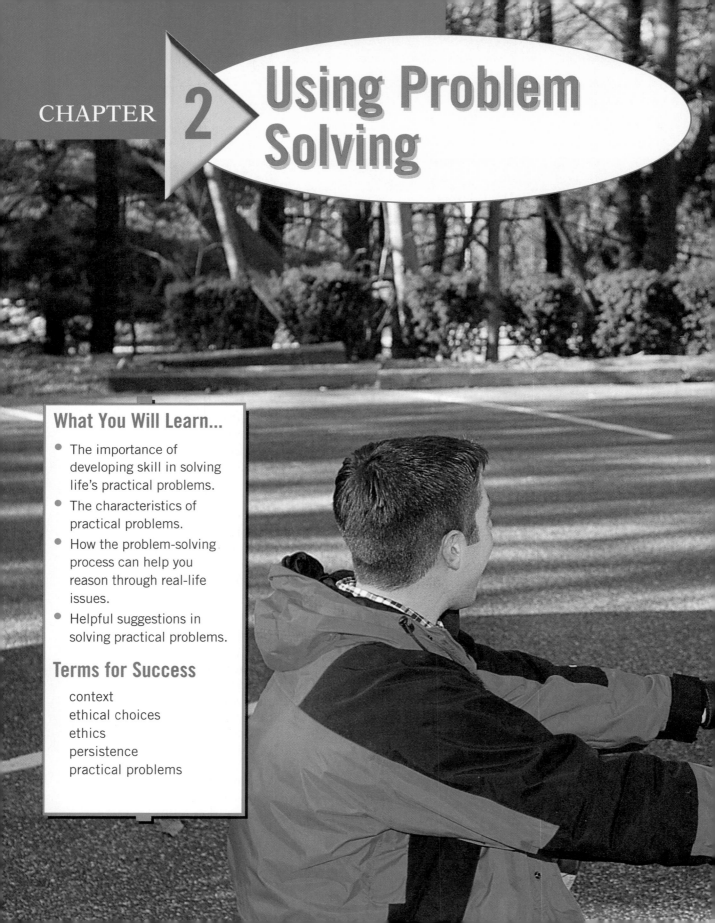

What You Will Learn...

- The importance of developing skill in solving life's practical problems.
- The characteristics of practical problems.
- How the problem-solving process can help you reason through real-life issues.
- Helpful suggestions in solving practical problems.

Terms for Success

context
ethical choices
ethics
persistence
practical problems

As he waited for Jana to unlock her car doors, Ben couldn't help staring at the car a few spaces over.

"Oh, I can just see your mom letting you buy something like that," Jana teased.

"I'd let her use it whenever she wanted," Ben said, grinning. "Actually she wants me to buy my uncle's car. I don't know, though. It's really old and it's gray—not my favorite color!"

"It may not be great, but it's probably all you could afford anyway," Yoshi pointed out.

"It needs some work—new tires for sure," Ben said, "but at least I know what I'm getting with that car—no surprises."

"It would probably make your mom happy," Jana said.

"Yeah," Ben agreed, "but I'd like to see what else is available. I don't like feeling pressured to buy just because it's my uncle's. On the other hand, I don't want to hurt his feelings, or my mom's.—"

Jana laughed. "You've argued yourself into a corner, Ben. Sounds like you've got some valid points on either side. Now you've got to figure out which side has more advantages than disadvantages."

"I know," Ben nodded. "I need to think it through before making a choice." He grinned again. "I guess that rules out flipping a coin."

> **?** What are some ways that people commonly respond to problems such as Ben's? From your point of view, which ways seem to work and which ways don't?

Why Use Problem Solving?

You, like Ben, are probably finding out that the move toward independence is filled with exciting changes and opportunities. Most make your life richer and fuller. Some changes, however, add challenges or even problems to life. Many of these problems are complex and require using different skills to solve them. They involve making the best choices and taking action on them.

The way you view challenges has a lot to do with how you solve them. Keeping an optimistic outlook allows you to see the opportunities that lie within many situations. As you read in Chapter 1, having a challenge or problem isn't always a negative experience.

This chapter will help you improve your ability to recognize and solve complex, real-life situations. It's a process that takes some time and practice, but the benefits are well worth it. Problem-solving skills can help you:

- **Prepare for the challenges you'll face throughout life.** When you were a child, others solved problems for you or carefully guided you to a decision. As an adult, you will have the responsibility for solving problems on your own.

- **Gain confidence in your problem-solving ability.** The more you use your problem-solving skills, the more positive you can be about taking life's challenges in stride. As you gain confidence, the easier it can be to see the opportunities that lie within the problems.

• Every day you decide what to eat, what to wear, and when to do your homework. What issues do you face that take more than just making a casual decision? What issues about your future seem complicated?

- **Develop a skill that helps strengthen relationships.** By considering the consequences for everyone with each option, you can make more sound choices. Solving problems together can bring people closer.
- **Learn from your actions.** It's easy to just make a choice and forget about it. However, when you look back on what you decided and how it worked out, you'll find yourself handling new problems more skillfully.

Real-Life, Practical Problems

Have you ever been faced with an issue that left you feeling unsettled—an issue *so* complicated that you didn't know where to turn or what to do? You knew the situation was too complex for a simple decision.

You were probably facing a **practical problem**—a complicated situation that often includes ethical choices or moral outcomes. **Ethical choices** involve making decisions about what is fair, right, just, caring, and best for all people involved. These choices are guided by your **ethics**—the principles or values that guide your life. Deciding between going to college or getting a job to help support your family would certainly be a practical problem. The choices that you make have the potential to affect yourself, others in your life, and your future.

How can you tell whether a problem is a practical problem? Look for these characteristics:

- **Practical problems are usually complicated.** Imagine a tangled web of vines that have grown along a fence. Each vine goes in a different direction and it's not always clear which vine goes where. In the same ways, practical problems involve several issues and the way to solve them may not be clear. Finding a solution partly involves sorting, analyzing, and evaluating.

- The real-life problems that people face impact others as well as themselves. What real-life problems do you and your friends and family face?

• Real-life problems generally require making ethical choices about what is fair, right, caring, or best for everyone who may be affected by a situation. Think about some real-life situation you've had to deal with. What factors most influenced your choices?

• **Practical problems have unique circumstances.** As you navigate through life, you'll notice each problem has its own **context**, or set of circumstances to consider. There may be more than one acceptable solution to a problem. Your life circumstances—family and school responsibilities, financial resources, time demands, and personal goals—will generally be different from those of others. Your solutions to the same problem will be different because the context will be different.

• **Solutions to practical problems impact others.** The way you resolve a problem may affect family, friends, classmates, coworkers, or your community. Because your choices will impact others, the solution will involve making ethical choices. Considering the feelings, values, and needs of others leads you to make better choices. See Chapter 3 for more information on ethical choices.

• **Practical problems require taking action.** You will need to anticipate and consider the positive and negative consequences for every choice. How might the actions you take on each choice affect others? By considering these factors, your values, and ethics that impact them, you can make the best choice for yourself and others. Remember that no problem is solved until you take action to set the solution in motion.

• Everyone faces real-life issues that impact every area of what it means to be human. You can approach any problem, regardless how complicated, with effective problem-solving skills. **What are three real-life problems that could be effectively solved by using your problem-solving skills?**

Solving Practical Problems

People solve practical problems in many different ways. You probably know someone who does just the first thing that comes to mind. Others follow habit or tradition, or simply do what they see others doing. These approaches do not usually involve thinking through a problem carefully. With careful thought about a problem, you are more likely to come up with a solution that will be best for you and others.

Practical problems require a reasoning process that helps you think through and solve practical problems. One way to help yourself remember the process is by using the acronym REASON. Each letter in REASON stands for one part of the process.

REASON is not a step-by-step method, but a process that gives you the freedom to move back and forth among its parts as you work to uncover the best solution to a problem. REASON offers you an opportunity to use your values and beliefs in solving problems.

Many of the problems you'll face in life will be practical problems. Making effective decisions and choices require effective reasoning. The more you use your problem-solving skills, the easier the solution becomes.

The next part of this chapter explains each part of the REASON process, its importance, and helpful questions you can use to help think through things.

Get the Facts

T
I
P
S

Use questions like these to determine the reliability of information:

- Is the information recent?
- Is the information presented in a logical way?
- Is the source of information an expert on the subject?
- Does the source have a "vested interest" in providing this information to you? (Someone who is trying to sell a product may be biased.)

REASON

Recognize the Primary Problem

Have you ever wondered how a crime gets solved? A detective begins solving a crime by analyzing the crime scene. You need to approach a practical problem in the same way. Some clues help identify the primary suspect. Other evidence is misleading or turns out to be unrelated to the crime. In problem solving, it's often not clear at first what the primary or core problem actually is.

How can you determine the primary problem in a situation? Here's a way to get started:

- Sort through all the interrelated problems and contributing factors. It often helps to make a list.
- Ask yourself questions to help analyze the situation. See the "Ask Yourself" section on this page.
- Cross items off your list that aren't really related or are caused by another problem you've listed.
- State the primary problem clearly.
- Identify possible solutions and factors that might affect them.

Taking time to do this detective work sets the foundation for a solution.

▶ Michael's Experience

What's the Problem?

As he glanced through the classifieds in the newspaper, Michael's attention was quickly drawn to one particular ad. The park district was looking for counselors for its after-school recreation program. "Working with kids might be kind of fun," he thought.

"I know I need to save money for community college next year. On the other hand, working after school could affect other things that are important—making good grades and spending time with my friends. Besides, Mom counts on me to take care of Austin after school. I wonder if I can handle a part-time job during the school year?

"I guess that what I decide to do depends on:

- How well I can use my time.
- How much money I have and need.
- Whether I can keep my grades up.
- Options Mom has for taking care of Austin."

Through Life's Problems

Evaluate Information

Once you've figured out the primary problem, it's time to gather information. Like the detective, you also need to evaluate the accuracy of the information you collect.

Look for:

- **Factual information about possible alternatives and their consequences.**
- **Your own goals, values, and ethics that apply.**
- **The goals, values and ethics of others who may be affected by the situation or its resolution.**

Ask Yourself

- What information do I need? Where can I find it?
- Can I trust the information?
- Do I have enough information to solve this problem? If not, what additional information do I need?

Decide which sources of information are most appropriate for this specific problem. Remember, not all factual information is created equal; some sources are more reliable than others. See page 49 for checking out the reliability of factual information.

In considering which of your values, goals, and ethics apply to a situation, you may want to talk to your parents, religious leader, or someone else who knows you well.

The more information you have, the better. However, in real-life situations it is often impossible to have all the information you need. You'll have to judge when you have enough information to make a decision and take action.

Digging Deeper

"It looks like I'm going to have to dig for more information to solve this problem." As he grabbed a piece of paper, Michael began to write:

✓ Call the manager of the recreation program and find out the details of the job.

✓ Check the newspaper to compare this job with others.

✓ Talk with Mom. What if I can't help out as much at home or take care of Austin? Could she enroll him in the recreation program?

✓ Ask my friends who work part-time how they get everything done at school, work, and home.

✓ Think about my own goals and values about work and saving money.

REASON

Analyze Alternatives and Consequences

Ask Yourself

- Have I identified many possible alternatives and all the negative and positive consequences for each?
- What are the short-term and long-term consequences for each possibility?
- What are the consequences of each choice for me and everyone else involved?
- Are some choices likely to result in positive consequences for everyone?

Just as a detective analyzes evidence to determine possible solutions to a crime, you need to identify and analyze as many alternatives as possible. Don't limit yourself to those that seem best at first. Think about:

- Both the positive and negative consequences of each choice.
- How each choice might impact the people in your life.
- How each choice matches your values, goals, and ethics.

Once you have a more complete picture of all your options, you can come closer to deciding on a solution.

Michael's Experience

Weighing the Evidence

"I've gathered all the information I can, but it's hard to keep it all straight. Maybe a chart will help me look at each alternative and its consequences."

POSITIVE CONSEQUENCES	NEGATIVE CONSEQUENCES
Applying for the job, and taking it if offered	
• Practice interview skills • Develop job skills • Meet new people • Austin will make new friends • Help other families	• Less time for: family, friends, school work • Less time for help at home • Mom may have to hire a sitter if Austin can't get into the program
Not applying for the job	
• Time for family and friends • Time for: school work, Austin, and helping Mom	• Find other sources of college money • Can't practice interview skills • No job experience
Look for a different job	
• A better job may come along • May find one that wouldn't conflict with Austin's care • If another job, same consequences as accepting this one	• Another job may not come along • If no other job, same consequences as refusing this one • No resources for college

Through Life's Problems

Select the Best Choice

Unlike the solution to a crime, practical problems may have more than one acceptable solution. To make your choice, develop a justification for your most likely option. Your justification—reasons that support your solution—should include why your choice is:

- **Ethical**—in the best interests of everyone involved.
- **Workable** for the situation and for the resources you have available.
- **Relevant** to the situation based on reliable sources of information.

[If you come across a stumbling block, you may need to move back-and-forth between parts of the process to get the solution you desire.]

Deciding What's Best

"After taking a look at all of my options, I've decided to apply for the part-time recreation job. If I get it, I'll earn money for college and get some valuable work experience. I don't have to worry about Austin since Mom has decided to enroll him in the program whether I get the job or not.

"Even though the job will mean extra responsibility, my grades are good and I'll concentrate on managing my time well. This wasn't an easy choice—still this job can help me make it to college and shouldn't have any really negative consequences."

R E A S O N

Outline and Take Action

A detective develops a plan for solving the crime. Once you make your best choice, develop a plan to put it in motion. Developing a plan includes:

- Deciding on the steps you need to carry out your decision.
- Identifying and assembling the resources you need to carry out your plan.

Planning gives your solution the best possible chance at success. Then it's time to get started!

Ask Yourself

- Do the steps in my plan need to be carried out in a certain sequence?
- What resources do I need? Do I already have them?
- Do I need help in carrying out the plan?
- Might there be barriers to my plan? How could I overcome them?

Michael's Experience

Moving Forward

"Next, I need to work on getting the recreation job. I'll contact the manager, and apply for the position. If I get the job, I'll find out what my work schedule will be. With that, I can develop a plan for using my time. It will be a lot to tackle—all the responsibilities and time for relaxing with friends, too—but I should be okay if I keep my goals in mind. After a month or so, I should be able to evaluate whether my plan is working or not."

Through Life's Problems

Note the Results of Actions Taken

After solving a crime, the detective writes a follow-up report carefully evaluating all aspects of the crime and investigation. You, too, need to evaluate the results of your actions when you solve a practical problem. Each problem is a learning experience unto itself.

First, evaluate whether or not the action you took got the results you wanted. What aspects of the problem-solving process did you handle best? Which do you need to work on?

Ask Yourself

- Would I make the same choice again? Why or why not?
- What went well? What would I change if I could?
- Were the results what I anticipated? Why or why not?
- Did my actions keep everyone's interests in mind?
- How have I learned from this experience?

Looking Back

"I got the job! Looking back, it seemed to take a long time to think through the problem before I made a decision. I'm glad now that I did so. Next time will be easier.

"Now that I'm working, I'm really busy, but that's okay. I've realized that balancing responsibilities is a skill I need to learn now. Things won't be any easier when I'm in college. Austin's having a great time in the rec program and I've become the "best buddy" of a dozen kids."

• Commitment and persistence are needed to be an effective problem solver. These people are putting their skills to work in helping protect their town from a flood. **How might persistence in solving problems be a benefit to you?**

Working with Problem Solving

Imagine . . . *you're* the detective hot on the trail of a dangerous criminal—and then it happens! You run out of clues or the evidence leads you in the wrong direction. What do you do? You go back and reexamine the evidence in search of missed clues and other possibilities. In the same manner, you need to examine some of the skills that can help you solve problems in ways that are best for you and others.

Think Effectively

If your goal is to solve problems in ways that will get the results you want, you need to avoid faulty thinking. For example, suppose a crime-scene detective was distracted by unrelated evidence. Would the right solution to the crime be found? In the same way, faulty thinking can divert your attention from real issues and lead you to in choices that don't really solve problems. *Avoid* faulty thinking by:

- **Using more than one or two choices.** When you limit the choices you consider, you are less likely to choose a good solution.
- **Checking the reliability of your information.** Without carefully evaluating the reliability of your information, you could select a choice based on incorrect or inaccurate information.
- **Avoiding oversimplification of the problem.** Practical problems are complex. To avoid a solution that is too easy, take time to carefully define the problem and examine it from different viewpoints, especially those of others affected by the problem.

Be Persistent

At times, solving problems can be very challenging! You may even become discouraged or frustrated. Yet finding a solution and taking action that is best for all involved can be a satisfying reward.

Just as persistence is a necessary characteristic in solving a crime, so is it an important characteristic of an effective problem solver. **Persistence** means being committed to a well-reasoned solution, no matter how difficult the process may be. It also means

using a variety of ways to keep focused. For example, to stay focused you might take a brief break to reenergize your thinking or talk with a friend for another perspective.

Work with Others

Many practical problems involve getting the help of others to find a solution that is best for all involved. When friends, family members, coworkers, or neighbors share a problem, everyone is a part of the solution. To be successful when solving problems with others, remember the following key elements:

- **Respect for others.** Acknowledge each person's unique identity and be committed to understanding each person's viewpoint.
- **Effective communication.** Listen to others carefully and ask questions about their values, goals, and viewpoints.
- **Conflict resolution.** When a variety of viewpoints and opinions are involved, conflict can be resolved by using compromise or negotiation to reach an agreement.
- **Support systems.** When you need extra input, seek ideas from people you trust outside the situation.

Lifelong Problem Solving

Think about a skill that comes easily to you now. It probably wasn't easy at first—it took practice to become comfortable and automatic. In the same way, with practice, solving problems will become second nature. You'll find yourself making better choices and getting more satisfying results.

Learning to solve practical problems is one of the most important skills you can learn. Families, communities, and workplaces all face complex problems. People who can find solutions enrich their own lives and the lives of others.

Understanding Key Concepts

- Making decisions and solving problems give you a chance to shape your future.
- Practical problems have an impact on others, involve prioritizing your values, have a unique context, and require action.
- Solving practical problems requires the use of decision-making and goal-setting skills.
- Start solving a problem by defining it carefully and analyzing the factors surrounding the situation.
- Reliable factual information, as well as information about goals and values, is needed for solving practical problems.
- Charting possible alternatives and consequences can assist in analyzing the impact of possible choices on self, family, and others.
- After choosing a solution to a practical problem, organize a sequence of steps to carry out your solution.
- A practical problem is not completely solved until you have carefully evaluated your solution and the results of the action taken.
- You can get the results you want from problem solving if you think effectively, are persistent, and work with others.

Checking Your Knowledge

1. Why is it important to learn how to solve problems?
2. Name at least two specific benefits to effectively solve practical problems.
3. Describe the characteristics of practical problems.
4. Outline the components of the problem-solving process. Why is each component important?
5. How can you decide if factual information is reliable?
6. What makes a solution to a problem an ethical choice?
7. Describe three examples of faulty thinking when you're solving a practical problem. Give an example of each.
8. If you are not persistent when solving practical problems, what can happen?
9. What elements are key to solving practical problems with others?

Making TRANSITIONS

Increasing Awareness of Problem Solving

Design a bookmark, locker sign, or note card illustrating the steps of the problem-solving process. Include some of the questions you think are most important at each step. Keep this reminder handy when you are ready to face a practical problem.

STRENGTHENING *Life* SKILLS

Identifying Contextual Factors

Identifying contextual factors that influence your choices is an important part of learning to solve real-life problems. Choose one of the following situations. Then identify at least three factors that may influence how you will respond to the situation:

- A group of your friends is gossiping about someone at school.
- Your friends are pressuring you to go to a party where under-age people will be drinking alcohol.
- You need to choose between going to college in your state and going to college out of state.

What values, goals, and ethics apply to your choices?

Applying Thinking Skills

1. **Drawing conclusions.** What do you think might happen if someone solving a practical problem left out the first step: "Recognize the Primary Problem"? What if "Note the Results of Actions Taken" was skipped?

2. **Recognizing assumptions.** In this chapter, Michael is trying to solve his problem about taking a part-time job. What assumption does he make about what his mom might think? Is Michael's assumption right or wrong? Explain.

3. **Comparing and contrasting.** What are the similarities and differences between solving practical problems as an individual and within a group? What are the advantages of group problem solving? The disadvantages?

Practical Applications

1. **Discussing consequences.** Shawana is trying to decide whether she should break up with her boyfriend before she leaves for a job out of state. Discuss what might happen if she uses the following methods for solving her practical problem.

   - She follows an impulse.
   - She does what her friends tell her she should do.
   - She just does what she's done before.
   - She uses the REASON method.

2. **Identifying information.** Choose one of the sample practical problems listed below and identify at least three different sources for factual information for that problem. Make a list of questions you would ask to determine the reliability of the information from each source.

   - What should I do about managing stress?
   - What should I do about finding a roommate?
   - What should I do about buying a car?

CHAPTER 3

Building Character

What You Will Learn...

- How taking action on ethical issues reflects your character.
- The attributes and benefits of sound character.
- The role of values in shaping character and solving problems.
- The influence of common values.
- How values influence ethical choices and character development.

Terms for Success

character
common values
decision test
standard

Nick quickly left the store and headed for his car. If he hurried, he could still make the tip-off of the basketball game.

An older man called to Nick from the bus stop. "Does the Oak Hill bus stop here?"

"Every half hour," Nick replied as he hurried past. As he unlocked his car, it occurred to him: city buses only ran on the hour after 5:00 P.M. It was now five minutes past six.

He looked at the man waiting for the bus. "There's a pay phone around the corner," Nick told himself. "He could call a cab."

Nick sighed. "The guy could have a fleet of limos," he thought. "But if I don't go back and try to help, what does that make me?"

He ran back to the bus stop. "I just remembered that the buses run on the hour after 5:00 P.M. You just missed the 6:00 bus," he said. "Can you call someone for a ride?"

The man shook his head. "I could call my daughter, but she's at work. I also don't have change for the phone, just my bus pass."

Nick asked, "Can I give you a ride?"

"Oh, no. Thank you." Nick sensed the mistrust. "It's a nice night. I can walk."

Nick watched as the older man turned away. Certainly Nick could do something.

He hurried after the man. "I'd gladly pay for the call to your daughter," he suggested.

The stranger stopped. "You would do that?"

"Sure," Nick said as they walked to the pay phone.

"She'll pick me up about 6:45." The man seemed relieved. "Thanks for helping me."

"Ah. . . do you want me to wait? Just in case your daughter runs a little late?"

The stranger smiled. "I wouldn't mind the company, but you must have other things to do."

Nick shrugged. "Other things—but not better things."

? **What do you think motivated Nick's actions in this scenario? How might you have reacted in the same situation?**

Problem Solving and Character

As you've likely figured out by now, Nick's motivation came from within. He was concerned about another person. Nick's solution reflected his character.

People of **character** are most often thought of as being morally strong and having the ability to think, judge, and act with maturity. Think of someone you know who has these qualities.

In the previous chapter, you read that practical problems involve ethical choices. These problems concern the welfare of others. In Nick's case, what to do about helping a person in need was an example of an ethical issue. What to do about a conflict with a friend might be another. Solving problems such as these means answering the question, "Which choice is the most fair, just, and caring for all those involved?" The choices *you* make are a reflection of your character and the underlying values that guide your actions.

Recognizing Character

Most people use personal qualities to describe the character of another person. For example, "Ellen is kind, compassionate, and generous." Most importantly, character shows in a person's actions. Someone who behaves in ways that show respect for self and others is considered to have character.

Thomas Lickona, a psychologist who has studied character development, describes character as having three components:

- Knowing what is right.
- Believing in what is right.
- Doing what is right.

• Principle-centered people display strong character traits. They have the ability to think, judge, and act with moral maturity. What does it mean to you to be a person of character?

Many people know what is best to do, but fail to act on these beliefs. For example, some always put themselves first. Others cave in to peer pressure. How is Luisa's situation different in the following example?

As Luisa was cleaning up the restaurant after work one night, she found a gold bracelet. No one else knew she had found it, but Luisa didn't even consider keeping it. She knew someone must really be upset about losing it.

Luisa vaguely remembered a customer with a similar bracelet. She and her boss checked through the charge receipts to find the customer's name. The boss then made a phone call to the customer, who had lost the bracelet. Arrangements were made to return the bracelet.

In this example, Luisa's behavior shows all three components of good character. First, she's aware that her actions will have an impact on others, especially the owner of the bracelet. She knows the right thing to do. She also believes in what is right and has the self-control to return the bracelet, even though it would be nice to keep it. Finally, she has the courage to do what is right and turns the bracelet over to the restaurant owner. All three components together—knowing what is right, believing in what is right, and doing what is right, are vital to displaying positive character traits.

Your Actions, Your Character

When it comes to ethical issues, deciding what action to take can be the easy part. Since character includes doing what is right, as well as knowing and believing what is right, taking responsible action is your final goal.

Your character develops over time—through the experiences you have, the choices you make, and your ideas about how your actions affect yourself and others. However, the time and effort are well spent! Ralph Waldo Emerson once said, "It is one of the most beautiful compensations of life that no man can sincerely try to help another without helping himself."

• Doing what is right and honest leads to positive results and strengthened character. If you had lost something of value, what would you expect of the person who found the item? What might your response be to the person who does the right thing?

Developing your character will bring personal satisfaction and enrich the lives of others. It will allow you to make a meaningful contribution to the world in which you live.

Values: The Foundation of Character

Your values provide general guidelines for living your life and relating to others. They are based on ideas about what is right and good. When your values have positive consequences for yourself and others, they provide the foundation for sound character. You need the courage to stand by your convictions in spite of conflicting messages from the world. Clearly understanding your values and their consequences allows you to set effective priorities and make good decisions.

Knowing Your Values

Your values reflect who you are, your culture, and your unique experiences and relationships. Children begin learning about values from their families. As they grow older, their religion, their life experiences, and their friends influence their values.

Building character requires becoming actively aware of your values and the reasons they are important to you. When you make choices, you consistently use these values as a guide.

Of course, not everyone has the same values or makes the same choices. Recognizing and respecting value differences can help in making good decisions and preventing or resolving conflicts. Respect for others' viewpoints and values is at the heart of character.

• Contributing to the lives of others benefits all involved. **In what ways do you contribute to the lives of others? How does this make you feel?**

Values Common to All

Some values, called **common values,** are found common to most societies and cultures. They relate to respecting others and treating people fairly. These common values support fundamental human worth and dignity. They are often reflected in school rules, public policies, and workplace regulations because they help people live and work together in harmony. Take a look at the chart on page 58 and relate these common values to your own.

Common values are reflected in everyday actions. How have you seen these values woven into the choices and actions of your family, school, and community? Part of becoming an adult means learning how to balance your own needs and wants with the needs and wants of those around you.

A Matter of Ethics

As mentioned in Chapter 2, ethics are the principles or values that guide the way you and others live. How do ethics relate to character? They help *define* the character of individuals or groups. For instance, many professions such as law and medicine have codes of ethics.

Your values are reflected in the ethics you use to make decisions and take action. Both of these components are part of your character. As you go through life, you will use your ethics to decide how you will respond to ethical issues which are often part of solving practical problems.

Ethical issues occur in all parts of society. For example, Anthony has noticed his younger brother Leon getting into a lot of trouble lately. The friends Leon hangs around with have a reputation for getting into fights. One day, Leon asks Anthony to drive him to a party and tell their parents he took Leon to a basketball game instead. Leon explains that he really wants to go to the party—all his friends are expecting him. Anthony has heard about this party at school and thinks his brother might get into trouble there. What should Anthony do?

• This family values time together and each person in the family. Your values are the cherished principles that guide the way you live. **What values are most important to you?**

Common Values

Value	Description	The Value in Action
Respect	Showing consideration for the rights of self and others	Cheri asks her older sister's permission before borrowing any of her clothes.
Honesty	Being truthful and sincere with self and others	Kevin accurately reports his earnings to the IRS each year.
Integrity	The inner strength to stick to high ethical standards	Tina resists pressure from friends to drink at a party, which is something she feels is wrong to do.
Trustworthiness	Keeping promises and fulfilling commitments	As he promised, Jeff brings his elderly neighbors' mail up to their apartments each day.
Courage	Strength to practice positive character traits	Shanequa stood up for a friend by asking others to stop picking on him.
Fairness	Treating others in an impartial and equitable way	Kyle did all of his sister's household chores in return for her picking him up after play practice for two weeks.
Caring	Showing kindness, consideration, and concern for the well-being of others	Kari takes time to phone a friend who isn't feeling well, just to see how she is doing.
Responsibility	To be dependable and accountable for one's actions	Philip helps his mother by picking up groceries on the way home from work.
Self-discipline	To exercise positive self-control, usually for self-improvement	Brittany works long hours on a school project. She wants to do her best.

• Common values transcend the boundaries of culture, gender, and age. **What might the world be like if people did not have these core values to guide their choices and actions?**

Anthony is faced with an ethical issue. He must decide what is fair and right for Leon and others, including his parents. Anthony's response will depend on his values and ethics. His decision will both reflect and shape his character.

Ethics in Action

If you were Anthony, how would you solve this ethical problem? Many situations in life present opportunities to make ethical choices. Applying a number of ethical standards can help you make the best choices.

Applying Ethical Standards

A **standard** is a rule, principle, or measure for testing the quality of something. Ethical standards help people decide whether a choice or action is ethical. The common values described earlier offer one type of standard. Although these values can guide the resolution of many ethical issues, often ethical choices present a conflict between two or more common values.

For example, suppose a three-year-old girl in your care comes to you with her drawing and asks, "Isn't this a good picture?" Think about the child's feelings, level of development, and her need to take pride in her work. In considering these factors, your initial response would be more likely to involve the common value of caring, rather than honesty. This does not mean acting in a fair and just way in this situation involves being *dis*honest. Instead, it means your first consideration is to behave in a caring way—by praising her work and efforts rather than criticizing her developing artistic techniques. As you can tell from this example, additional ethical standards beyond the common values are sometimes needed.

Testing Possible Decisions

Another type of ethical standard you can use in making ethical choices is a decision test. A **decision test** means asking yourself certain questions to determine whether or not a particular choice is ethical. Here are four types of decision tests you might use:

1. **The universal test.** Ask yourself: "What would happen if everyone made this choice?" If an action or choice is ethical, you would be willing to accept the consequences when everyone, including yourself, took this action or made this choice.

• Acting on what you know is right isn't always easy, but is in the best interests of all involved. When was the last time you know you did the right thing even though it may not have been the popular thing?

2. **The role reversal test.** Ask yourself: "What would happen if I were the person being affected by my choice?" This question is based on what is often referred to as the Golden Rule: treat others as you would want to be treated. If you were the person being affected by your choice and could see it as fair and justified, then your choice is more likely to be an ethical one.

3. **The new context test.** Ask yourself: "What would happen if I were in a slightly different set of circumstances?" This question changes the situation to see if the solution would be justified under different circumstances. If your choice is ethical, it will be one you are likely to make even if the circumstances were slightly different.

4. **The test of best consequences.** Ask yourself: "Which choice will have the most positive consequences for the most people involved? Will it contribute to the well-being of everyone involved?" This test focuses your thinking on what will happen as a result of your choice. The ethical choice is usually the one that has the most positive consequences for the most people.

In a particular ethical situation, you may use one or more ethical standards to help decide which choice is best. For example, using the role reversal test before deciding how to respond to a child's drawing would lead you to a positive comment rather than to criticism of the work.

The decision tests are ethical standards that help guide you to the most important part of ethical issues—the impact of your actions on others. Learning how to use and apply these standards can help you develop character.

• Taking the time to show you care about friends and family adds strength to your character. What should you do when two of the things you value are in conflict?

REASON

Through Life's Problems

Note the Results of Actions Taken

Problem solving can help people make ethical choices. As you read Kevin's situation below, think about how he considers the impact of his choices and actions on others.

Mr. Tanaka, the assistant principal responsible for the school's concession stands, shook Kevin's hand. "Thanks for talking with me about Gary's behavior last week, Kevin."

Kevin walked out of Mr. Tanaka's office thinking, "It sure isn't easy to take a stand against a friend—it really hurts, but I know I did the right thing." Kevin's mind raced back over the events that had led to the problem he faced with Gary.

Last week, Kevin, Gary, and a few others were cleaning up the school concession stand after a wrestling match. Kevin saw Gary take several bills from the money drawer and slip them into his pocket. Kevin was shocked. The concession stand profit funded several senior projects. When no one else was around, Kevin casually approached Gary saying, "Hey, Gary, I saw you put some money from the drawer into your pocket. How about returning it?"

Gary said, "No way! Nobody will ever know this is gone—unless you say something! I need money for my senior pictures and graduation fees. I've done a lot for this school, now it's the school's turn to help me out!"

Kevin wrestled with this problem all weekend. He kept asking himself, "What should I do about Gary's taking the money? Do I ignore it, report it, talk with Mr. Tanaka? . . . What is my best choice?"

Kevin thought about how he might react if the situation were a little different. "What if other students took money from the concession stand? What would happen if I were Gary and my friend reported me . . . or didn't report me? What would I do if this happened at the fast-food restaurant where I work? What choice would be best for everyone?"

Kevin decided to talk with Mr. Tanaka on Monday afternoon. As he walked toward his locker after talking with Mr. Tanaka, Kevin started to think about what he had done. "I hate to think that I might lose Gary's friendship. He'll really be angry that I talked with Mr. Tanaka. I'm sure he'll have to pay back the money and could be suspended from school. I hope this doesn't keep him from going through graduation!"

Kevin stopped in front of his locker and thought, "This was the toughest thing I've ever done, but I know I made the right decision. Friend or no friend, it's just not right for anyone to take money from the school—it's not honest or responsible!"

▶ From Your Perspective

1 At what points in the situation is Kevin faced with ethical choices? How were his actions ethical?

2 Were Kevin's actions in Gary's and his own best interests? Why or why not?

3 What might Kevin do differently if he could solve his problem again?

4 How might this experience affect the way Kevin solves problems in the future?

Out of Thin Air: Plagiarism and the Internet

Have you ever had someone take your ideas or work and use them as his or her own? If you have, you've experienced the effects of *plagiarism*. Any created work is susceptible to plagiarism, whether it be a musical composition or a research paper. This is especially true of items found on the Internet.

Some people are confused by this fact. If you distribute information on the Internet, they reason, you expect it to be seen and used. This argument, however, has two flaws.

The Legal Issues

The first flaw is a legal one. An author can make a work public without losing private control. How can you tell? Check the end of the item for a copyright, which shows that someone has the sole right to publish or profit from a work. Copyrights typically include a date, the name of the copyright holder, and a statement such as, "All rights reserved. Material may not be published, rewritten, or redistributed in any form."

On the Internet, the Digital Object Identifier (DOI) System has been created to discourage plagiarism. This system makes it possible to identify any electronically available material by a single, universal code. The code contains two parts—a prefix and a suffix—separated by a slash. A DOI might also be thought of as a "digital fingerprint" for electronic material. For example, if someone copies a work from the Internet and then uses that work as part of his or her own, the DOI can be used to track where the work went and how it was used. Authors, publishers, librarians, and others can order materials, keep track of inventory, and detect plagiarism more easily.

The Ethical Issues

The second problem is an ethical one. As with most other legal issues, plagiarism involves ethical problems, too. Plagiarism is stealing another person's work. It's the same as copying a classmate's answers while you're taking a test. Plagiarists mislead people. They raise their own standing in the eyes of others, sometimes at the expense of the person who truly deserves the credit. When payment for the work is involved, plagiarism is the selling of stolen goods.

Avoiding Plagiarism

Plagiarism is easy to avoid. You can reference your sources when you write a research paper, with either footnotes, a bibliography, or citations within the paper. Some instructors prefer one method over others. If the information is widely known—for example, the order of planets in the solar system—describe it in your own words. Avoid copying whole sections from a source *verbatim*, or word for word.

Voicing Your Opinion

1. *Why might information on the Internet be more susceptible to plagiarism?*

2. *Debate the pros and cons concerning the use of DOIs on the Internet.*

Taking Responsible Action

If you were to create your own rules for living, what might they be? Setting responsible standards is an important part of taking charge of your life and shaping your future.

Life challenges people with many ethical issues and raises opportunities to use responsible standards. Acting with character can help you meet life's challenges in a way that will help you contribute to the lives of others and reach your goals.

• As you continually develop your character, you'll likely gain the respect and admiration of others. What is your motivation for being a person of character?

Understanding Key Concepts

- A person of character is morally strong and has the ability to think, judge, and act with maturity.
- Character has three essential parts: knowing what is right; believing in what is right; and doing what is right.
- Developing character brings personal satisfaction, makes the lives of others better, and allows you to make meaningful contributions.
- Your values provide a foundation for character when they have positive consequences for yourself and others.
- Common values recognize human worth and dignity. They are often stated in school rules, public policies, and workplace regulations.
- Ethics, the principles or values that guide the way people live, shape character.
- You can use several ethical standards to decide whether a choice or action is ethical, including common values and decision tests.
- Using the problem-solving process can help you make ethical choices.

Checking Your Knowledge

1. Describe a person you know who appears to be a person of character. How does this person display his or her character in real life?
2. How might you benefit from developing your character?
3. Explain how values can provide the foundation for good character.
4. Why is it important to know your values?
5. Identify two of the common values and provide examples of behavior that demonstrates each value.
6. What is the relationship between ethics and character?
7. Identify two types of standards used to determine whether a choice is ethical. Give an example of each type.
8. How might problem solving help you when faced with an ethical issue?

Making TRANSITIONS

Ethical Behavior in the Workplace

Assume you are working in the office of a small business. One day during a break, you hear one of your coworkers complain about the way your senator misused campaign money. Later that day, you notice the same coworker putting several boxes of computer disks into her briefcase to take home for personal use.

- What contradictions exist between what your co-worker says and what she does?
- How might you use the decision tests to determine whether your coworker acted in an ethical manner?
- How would you deal with this situation? What actions would you take?
- If you were an employer, what rules might you have for ethical behavior in the workplace?

STRENGTHENING *Life* SKILLS

Applying Ethical Standards

In a small group, choose a practical problem from your own experiences. Explain why the example you have chosen is an ethical issue and requires an ethical choice. Use the problem solving process to arrive at an ethical solution to this problem. Then:

- Present your ethical issue and the solution to the class.
- Justify your choice by describing how you applied ethical standards in making your decision about what was best to do.

Applying Thinking Skills

1. **Drawing conclusions.** What are the most important characteristics of a person of character? What skills, values, and attitudes does a person need to develop character?

2. **Predicting consequences.** What consequences might occur when a person acts in a way that shows a lack of character? Who might be affected? Why?

3. **Comparing and contrasting.** What are the similarities and differences between an ethical and unethical choice? What are the basic characteristics of an ethical choice?

4. **Recognizing Values.** Choose at least two of the common values described in this chapter. How do you apply these values in your own life? How are these values evident in the life of someone you know?

Practical Applications

1. **Recognizing character.** Make a chart listing at least five people whom you believe to be role models. In your chart, include the first name of each person and specific examples of the actions or behavior that illustrate character.

2. **Ethical standards in real life.** Choose an inspiring document from American history, such as those listed below. Analyze the content of the document and determine how it shows ethical standards. Give an example showing how the ethical standards in the document are used now in our society.

   - Declaration of Independence.
   - Preamble to the Constitution.
   - A Presidential inaugural address.
   - A speech from a great American leader.

CHAPTER 4

Balancing Your Life

What You Will Learn...

- The role of balance in your life and its impact.
- How balance is affected by what you value and the actions you take.
- Ways to achieve and maintain balance.

Terms for Success

balance
boundaries
perspective
priorities

Rikki used the chef's knife like an expert, chopping the pizza into eight even slices. She set the pizza on the counter for the waitress to take to the table. Six quick steps took her to the oven, where she put in an unbaked pizza and checked the one already baking.

Rikki glanced at the clock, eager for her 4:30 dinner break. As usual, she needed the time to finish an essay that was due tomorrow.

Rikki picked up the next pizza order. "Sausage with extra onions," she read. As she began preparing the pizza, Rikki suddenly realized, "I can't write the essay during break! I have to shop for Dad's birthday present." She stopped to remove the finished pizza from the oven.

Rikki returned to the last order. She distributed the ingredients evenly over the sauce. She thought, "Maybe I can shop for Dad's present tonight. No, I've got play practice. I can't miss another one. It's not fair to everyone else."

She eased the pizza into the oven. "Wait a minute," she told herself. I need to think about what's most important and then figure out how I can manage to get it done."

Just then the manager passed through the kitchen. "I've been watching you," he said. "You're really on top of things, Rikki. Nice work."

"You just need a system," Rikki replied cheerfully, but sagged against the counter after he had left. "I knew things would get more complicated when I got older," she thought, "but does it ever end? If I only could manage my time better, it would be easy. Does everyone struggle with trying to decide what is needed next? If this is what it means to become an adult, I don't want to grow up!"

Suddenly she remembered: the pizza! She pulled it from the oven just in time. "That was a close call," Rikki thought. "I don't know how, but I need to get my life under control."

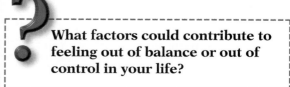

? **What factors could contribute to feeling out of balance or out of control in your life?**

How Does Balance Affect Life?

Do you ever feel like Rikki? Like life is spinning out of control with too many decisions to make, too many problems to solve, or too many things to do? Bringing your life into balance will give you a sense of control and purpose.

People often think of balance as being an equal distribution of weight, amount, or value between two or more things. That's often the case when you're balancing a checkbook, riding a skateboard, or distributing ingredients evenly over a pizza. However, when thinking about balance in regard to life, balance means more than that.

Balance is the internal sense of steadiness that results when all parts of a person's life are in unity with what he or she values. It's when your values and actions work together in harmony as you manage the various roles and responsibilities of your life.

Steady As You Go

Have you ever *really* listened to instruments playing together? The foundation of all music is a rhythmic, pulsating, steady beat that all instruments follow. The beat anchors the music. Balance also provides a sense of steadiness to your life just like a beat provides the steadiness to music. Without that sense of steadiness, life seems a little "off" or out of control.

Think about the many changes you'll experience during the next several years. You will leave the security of high school, friends, and family, and will become more independent and self-sufficient. The steadiness that balance provides is important not only for today, but becomes even more important as you become more independent. Consider some other benefits of balance in your life.

- **Balance brings personal fulfillment.** When what you think, feel, and believe aligns with your actions, you feel happy and satisfied. You will be able to appreciate who you are, what you do, and what you have.

- **Balance supports a healthy lifestyle.** The better your balance, the better you will feel physically, emotionally, mentally, and spiritually. You will have time and energy.

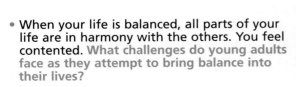

• When your life is balanced, all parts of your life are in harmony with the others. You feel contented. What challenges do young adults face as they attempt to bring balance into their lives?

• Living a healthy lifestyle is one component of living a balanced life. How do your lifestyle activities promote a sense of balance?

• **Balance empowers you.** Life's demands are constantly changing. When life is in balance, you feel strong enough to respond to personal, family, school, and work demands. For instance, you may decide to do your homework as soon as you get home. As you start, you receive a phone call from a friend in crisis. By having balance in your life, you can be flexible to both change what you're doing and accomplish your goals without the added stress that comes from overcommitment.

A Delicate Balance

Balancing life is not easy. Justin said, "Balancing my life is a real challenge as I become more independent. I have to think about how I manage my time, whether what I do matches what I think is important, and how my choices affect others." The following characteristics of balance will help you better understand it.

• **Balance is more than management skills.** Time and resource management skills are necessary, but effectively using these skills does *not* insure balance. For instance, Tanya decided to divide her evening hours into specific times for homework and chores. When she evaluated her plan after two weeks, she found that although she had completed her tasks each night, she was not working on finding a summer job to help pay for college. Tanya was managing her time, but without taking her goals into account.

• **Balance is easy to lose.** One tiny change can throw life off balance, such as breaking a leg, taking on one too many projects, or deciding to add another responsibility that doesn't fit with what you value. It may take days or even weeks to regain that internal sense of steadiness again.

• **Balance impacts others.** The choices you make impact others—both positively and negatively. For example, if you choose to work more hours at your job, then your other relationships might change. Family members may be pleased that you're taking the initiative for new responsibilities but struggle with changing family routines.

When Life Gets Cluttered

Do you ever feel like a circus performer attempting to spin too many plates in the air at once? Or do you look like you have it all together to others, but feel scrambled on the inside because you're overwhelmed with too many things to do? These feelings often reflect imbalance.

People lose balance in the midst of change, when they are overbooked or over-stressed, or when one part of life seems to take over the rest. As Bob practiced his lead part in the school musical, he knew he was consumed with the musical and out of balance in his life. He had let his schoolwork slide, cut back on his work hours, and rarely had time for his family or girlfriend. Bob knew his life would regain balance after the musical. He was willing to give up some balance for a short time to fulfill his dream of having a lead singing part.

However, what happens when being over-stressed or consumed with one part of your life continues for a long time? You probably start unhealthy behavior patterns. Then stress, susceptibility to illness, ongoing fatigue, or distraction from tasks happens. Sometimes people turn to risky behaviors such as unsafe driving, drug and alcohol abuse, violence, or isolation. Either way, long-term imbalance is destructive to your health and well-being.

> Does imbalance affect your life or the lives of people you know? How might it affect your future choices? What might you do to get rid of clutter in your life?

Moving Toward Balance

How do you know if your life is in balance? Kim described it this way: "I have time to do what I need and want to do. I don't feel guilty if I take time for myself. I don't feel like a tautly-stretched rubber band ready to spring loose." Many times the following questions can help you decide if your life is in balance. How do you rate?

- Do you have time for relationships you value?
- Can you complete the daily tasks of living without rushing or skimping on your standard of quality?

- When your life gets out of balance, do you ever feel like the plate-spinner at the circus? What could you do to keep all of your "plates" in balance?

- Are you healthy?
- Do you feel as if you have some control and direction in life?
- Does your life reflect your values and goals?

Even if you answer yes to most of these questions, you may sometimes feel like you have an internal battle going on inside about what you should do with your life. Other times you may feel frazzled because you are too busy and have too many responsibilities pulling at you all at the same time. Either way, you need to separate internal confusion from external disorder.

Values Are Key

One way to move toward balance is to look at your values. When you have analyzed your values, you can separate your internal confusion from your external disorder.

Remember the steady beat in music? What you value is the beat, the foundation for balance to your life. In this sense, what you value is what you prize or hold dear. You might prize family, quality friendships, personal integrity and character, and a faith you believe in. Your values should align with your actions and how you manage your time, energy, and other resources. However, when what you do is in conflict with what you value, your life is not in balance.

Factors That Affect Balance

Several factors affect the balance in your life—some you have control over, some you may not. Your personal needs, the expectations you have of yourself and the ones others have of you, along with your available resources, all influence the balance in your life. These factors can help you either achieve balance, maintain it, or destroy it.

Your Personal Needs

You know how frazzled you feel when you haven't had enough sleep, have been eating on the run for days, and haven't had enough time for your friends. If your physical, mental, emotional, spiritual, and social needs haven't been met, your life isn't balanced.

For example, if you feel a lot of responsibility toward others, you may "do for others" but not take proper care of yourself. You may trap yourself into overcommitment by taking on too much. Sometimes you might even lack the motivation to do much of anything. To maintain balance, you must acknowledge your needs and adjust your life to accommodate them.

Sorting It Out

T I P S

Sometimes it helps to stop and take a look at your life. You might want to check if your values are in conflict with one another, if they are in conflict with your actions, or if you just have too many things to do. Ask yourself:

- Am I confused or satisfied with what I'm doing with my life?
- Does my life reflect my values, goals, and priorities?
- What should I do about managing my activities and responsibilities?

Creating a Buffer Zone

Imagine two boxes that are the same size; each represents your life. One box is crammed full, but you keep adding responsibilities and commitments to it. Eventually the box bulges and bursts. The other box has a smaller box inside of it. Pretend you put some of the same things into the smaller box, except you add only the amount it's designed to hold. Though the smaller box holds your life, there is still room for its contents to spill out into the larger box—without distorting the shape of the larger box. The space between the two boxes is like a buffer zone in your life.

What Is a Buffer Zone?

A *buffer zone* is the space between yourself and your limits. It's the extra time and energy within yourself—emotionally, physically, mentally, and spiritually—saved up for emergencies or unanticipated situations. Everyone needs a buffer zone. Many people don't have one—or at least not enough of one. Instead, they get overloaded with too many commitments, activities, work obligations, expectations, and other things. These people feel starved for time to sit back, relax, and enjoy life. Stress and conflict increase, resulting in physical, mental, and emotional strain.

A Critical Resource

A buffer zone is a critical resource in your life as you become more independent and responsible for all parts of your life. How you manage your responsibilities, balance your life, and make sure you have an adequate buffer zone will help determine your level of contentment and personal fulfillment.

• Creating a buffer zone isn't an easy task—it means making choices about what you do and prioritizing those choices with what you value. **What action might you take in creating your own buffer zone?**

Using Your Resources Wisely

1. *When emergencies or unanticipated situations arise, how do you manage your roles and responsibilities?*

2. *How might a buffer zone help you develop a satisfying and contented life?*

• Failing to meet your personal needs adds stress and strain to anyone's life. **What happens when you don't take care of yourself? What actions could you take to meet your personal needs?**

Great Expectations

People's expectations of themselves and others affect their balance. When you or others place unrealistic expectations on yourself, you may feel overwhelmed. It is frustrating to be unable to do things that align more closely with what you value. Expectations often become more unrealistic as more demands are added to your life or as the importance of the demands increase. Your life will be in balance if you have *realistic* expectations instead.

Your Personal Resources

Your time, money, and energy level affect your balance. The more flex time you have, the more options you have to use that time. This also works for money and energy. By effectively managing your personal resources, separately and together, you can achieve and maintain balance.

Juggling 101

Balance doesn't just happen. Just as a juggler must practice keeping all the balls in the air, life's balancing act takes skill and persistence to maintain. The longer you maintain balance, the more it becomes a way of life.

Establish Goals

Do you have a goal that gives direction to your life? Goals help you maintain balance by focusing your time, energy, and other resources on what is important for you to accomplish. Take Luis, for example. By age 30, he wants to become a licensed electrician, own a pickup truck, and live in his own apartment with his best friend. Luis' goals are realistic—as long as he works toward them. By focusing on what's most important, he will make progress toward his goals. If he doesn't establish goals or chooses not to work on them, his life may seem to be a dead end.

Set Priorities

Setting priorities is another way to help you maintain balance. **Priorities** are those things most important to you. Every day you prioritize your time, energy, and other resources to meet goals and keep from getting bogged down with responsibilities or jobs that are of lesser importance to you. Keisha, who rents an apartment, makes it a priority each day to arrive at work on time so she doesn't lose her job. Much lower priorities for her include cleaning the apartment and writing letters to her hometown friends. By focusing on her highest priorities, she helps herself maintain balance.

• Identifying your goals in life and establishing your priorities in order to meet those goals, is helpful in leading a balanced life. **What are some of your goals for the future? What criteria could you use for setting your priorities to meet your goals?**

There may be times when other people set priorities for you. You need to balance their priorities with yours, especially if the priorities differ. Suzanne said, "My parents tell me that my first priority is getting good grades and then spending time with family and friends. I try to do that, but I also think it's important to work out at the rec center." As you become more independent, you begin to prioritize your time and energy in a way that maintains balance.

Help Yourself

By establishing goals and setting priorities, you are on your way to maintaining balance. However, there are several other things you can do that will help, too. Try the following:

- **Keep a healthy perspective.** Looking at things from a certain point of view is called **perspective**. Some people are optimists; others are pessimists. When life gets overwhelming, humor helps release the tension. Finding the bright side helps you be more optimistic and even realistic.

Having the Time of Your Life

TIPS

Here are some tips for helping you lead a balanced and productive life:

- **Expect the unexpected.** Plan for things to take longer than you predict and for unanticipated situations to arise.

- **Learn to say no.** Saying no allows you to do a few things well rather than a lot of things "average."

- **Reevaluate your activities and commitments.** It's harder to stop something than to start it. Take time to stop activities and commitments you are no longer interested in.

- **Get less done, but do the right things.** Use your time for what really matters to you.

- **Plan for free time.** Create your own way of giving yourself a break—don't schedule anything, but allow yourself to have a few unstructured minutes periodically throughout the day.

- Sometimes stepping back and seeing the humor in stressful situations helps you maintain an optimistic outlook and regain balance. How might changing your perspective contribute to bringing life into balance?

- **Establish boundaries and live within them.** The limits you have set for yourself based upon your values, goals, and priorities are your **boundaries**. Establishing boundaries helps you create order and balance in your life. First, determine what you value. Then when given new opportunities, ask yourself, "What should I do about these opportunities? Do they fit what I value most? Will they help me achieve my goals and keep my priorities?" Consider saying yes to those opportunities that best fit. Then say no thanks to opportunities that don't.

- **Reflect on your life.** Try taking a couple of hours at the beginning of each season or grading period to ask yourself these questions: Are there conflicts between what I value and what I do with my time, energy, and other resources? Am I balancing my personal needs along with the responsibilities and expectations of myself and others?

Sometimes you may need to eliminate activities and commitments or at least cut back on your responsibilities connected with them.

- **Tap into your internal resources.** Internal resources include traits such as determination, confidence, and hope. It may also include skills like management and problem solving. Use your skills and traits to help you maintain balance.

- **Get help from external resources and services.** Family and friends offer encouragement, help you clarify your concerns, and support you in maintaining balance. There are also many available community resources and services such as counseling agencies, intervention hotlines, and support services.

Life's Balancing Act

Balancing your life will be a constant process throughout your teen and adult years. Deciding what you value, and then making sure these values align with your actions, is key. Knowing your needs, resources, and the expectations you and others have of yourself, you can achieve balance.

You will need continually to make a conscious effort to establish goals, set priorities, and help yourself maintain control. As life changes, opportunities arise, and crises occur, you will need to readjust.

• Maintaining balance in life is a continuous process. What can you do at this point in your life to set the stage for a lifetime of balance and contentment?

R E A S O N

Through Life's Problems

Analyze Alternatives and Consequences

Every problem likely has many alternatives. Each has possible consequences–for self, family, and others. Analyze the alternatives and consequences that Lauren has in the situation below.

Lauren's boss wants her to enter an apprenticeship to become an operating engineer for heavy equipment. She ponders, "This decision has so many outcomes for all the other parts of my life!"

Lauren reflected on what she'll gain—operating roadway and vertical construction equipment and getting a journeyman's card. "While apprenticing, my wage will decrease from my current $17.00 per hour. After I earn my card, my wage will be more than $22 per hour!"

"On the other hand," Lauren thought, "If I do this, I would have school every Saturday from 9:00 to 5:00, September through May for four years. I'd also have to decide what to do about coaching and playing volleyball. Mom also needs more help with chores at home since Dad died. I also need to spend time with my boyfriend Tom and my family."

Later, Lauren listed the alternatives and potential consequences for herself and others.

She asked herself, "Are these all the possible choices? Have I identified all possible consequences, both positive and negative, for each alternative?

POSITIVE CONSEQUENCES	NEGATIVE CONSEQUENCES
Enter the apprenticeship program; continue with volunteer and family responsibilities.	
+ Short-term: Still do what I want to do **+ Long-term:** Get car; develop skills to use other places; make more money; work year round	**- Short-term:** Overloaded; tired, busy, stressed; lose Saturdays; reschedule practices **- Long-term:** Might get sick, miss work; less time for Tom & family
Enter the apprenticeship program; drop the volunteer work	
+ Short-term: Not overworked, tired, or stressed; time and energy for everything **+ Long-term:** Get a car; develop skills I can use at many companies; make more money; steadier work year-round	**- Short-term:** Miss coaching **- Long-term:** Company doesn't have operating engineers **- Short-term:** Overloaded; tired, busy, stressed; lose Saturdays; can't make games **- Long-term:** Might get sick, miss work; less time for Tom & family
Not enter the apprenticeship program now; continue with volunteer and family responsibilities	
+ Short-term: Team still has coach; Mom still has help for yard work, etc. **+ Long-term:** Time and energy to work on relationship with Tom, to devote to coaching	**- Short-term:** Boss may not recommend me next time **- Long-term:** More seasonal work; make less money; lack specific skills when called for a job; company lacks operating engineers

▶ From Your Perspective

1 What other alternatives might Lauren have considered? Considering those alternatives, what are the short- and long-term consequences for Lauren and others?

2 How are Lauren's values shown in her alternatives and their positive and negative consequences?

Understanding Key Concepts

- Balance results when a person's life is in unity with what he or she values.
- Balance is more than management, is easy to lose, and impacts others.
- Balance fosters personal fulfillment, supports a healthy lifestyle, and empowers individuals.
- Values and actions align with one another in a balanced life.
- Factors that affect how individuals achieve and maintain balance include meeting personal needs, having realistic expectations of themselves, and effectively managing their personal resources.
- Establishing goals, setting priorities, and other activities help a person maintain balance.
- Long-term imbalance is destructive to a person's health and well-being.
- Anticipating unexpected situations and emergencies is critical in maintaining balance.
- Monitoring activities and responsibilities is a way to help individuals maintain balance.

Checking Your Knowledge

1. In your own words, state what balancing your life means.
2. Give an example of how your decision to balance your life affects others.
3. Compare and contrast the lives of the following two people: someone whose values and actions are aligned with one another and someone whose life does not show that alignment.
4. Explain how the management of time, energy, and personal resources impacts balance, but does not insure balance.
5. What might you say to a friend who was overloaded with too many activities and responsibilities? Explain the importance of balance and some practical ways to achieve it.
6. Discuss the benefits of having a buffer zone. Describe how you can create a buffer zone in your life.
7. Summarize strategies you might use to maintain balance in your life.

Making TRANSITIONS

Balancing Workplace Expectations

Employers may expect or even require employees to put in extra hours on a job—sometimes for overtime pay and sometimes not.

Imagine you are applying for a job. During the interview, the employer says, "As part of your job, I expect you to work beyond the normal work hours. Would you have a problem with this?" Write your response to the question. How would the response change if:
- You had recently been married?
- You were attending school while working?
- You had two young children?

STRENGTHENING *Life* SKILLS

Tapping into Resources

Young adults often move frequently, which creates short-term imbalance in their lives. To get ready for that possibility in your life, create a resource folder of strategies for balance during and shortly after a move. Include in your folder:

- A list of tasks that you might need to do during the move and temporary changes you might need to make.
- A list of your personal skills and character traits that will help you deal with the short-term imbalance.
- A list of other skills that you might need to develop in order to get through a temporary disruption of your life.

Applying Thinking Skills

1. **Developing an analogy.** Compare a person spinning too many plates rapidly in the air with a person whose life seems out of balance. How would the plate spinner control the plates? How would the imbalanced person regain balance?

2. **Predicting consequences.** What consequences might occur when people:
   a) Take on more work responsibilities in an already overloaded work schedule.
   b) Do not set goals or priorities for their lives.

3. **Developing criteria.** Determine how young adults can analyze whether or not their lives are in balance. Decide if and how these criteria change as people get older.

Practical Applications

1. **Developing a plan.** List what you value, your goals and priorities, and your personal resources. Identify your activities, commitments, expectations, and personal needs. Using this information, develop a personal plan of action to balance your life.

2. **Analyzing values and actions.** Read an encouraging story, biography, or personal essay in a magazine. Determine the values, goals, and priorities of one of the characters. Decide if the actions of that character align with his or her values. Defend your choice.

3. **Taking a survey.** Survey young adults in your community about how they balance their lives. Include questions on what affects their balance. Tally their responses. What percentage of them indicated that work affected their balance? School? Family? Friends? Other activities? Personal needs? What conclusions can you draw?

CHAPTER 5

Community Involvement

What You Will Learn...

- Ways of becoming involved in your community and how the community can benefit from your involvement.
- The characteristics of effective leaders.
- The roles of values, talents, interests, and your passions in deciding where to get involved.
- A plan for including volunteer activities in your life.

Terms for Success

apathy
mentor
network
service learning

"**G**eneva!"

The gray-haired woman blinked and fidgeted in her wheelchair. A young woman and a friendly brown dog walked into the room. Geneva's face lit up as Bobbie explained, "He insisted we see you first."

Geneva stroked the dog, who rubbed his face against her fingers. He was so handsome, she tried to say. The slur of sounds she made could hardly be called words.

"Oh, he's a pretty boy, all right," Bobbie agreed. "Don't let him kiss you, though–he ate a cricket this morning." The two shared a laugh. "Speaking of favorite foods," Bobbie went on, "did you see they're serving raisin pie at lunch today?"

Geneva nodded. She described again how she had made raisin pie when she was Bobbie's age. She'd never cared for raisin pie as a girl, but it had been her husband's favorite. So she had learned to make it, and it had become her favorite, too.

Geneva smiled. The dog rested his head on her lap, blinking lazily.

"Well, I guess we should make our rounds," Bobbie sighed as she squeezed Geneva's hand. "See you in two weeks," she promised, and disappeared out the door.

Geneva was still smiling as Bobbie left. She knew Bobbie didn't understand half of what she had said. That didn't matter. To have someone listen and treat her like an adult, and remember that she, Geneva Jackson, had once been young and capable and active—that was what mattered.

> **?** This story tells us what benefits Geneva received from the visit of a volunteer, Bobbie. What rewards and benefits do you think Bobbie received from her experience as a volunteer?

Why Become Involved?

When you think about it, people choose to get involved in their communities in many different ways. Some donate money; others, like Bobbie, give their time and talents to a worthy cause; some become leaders in a community organization. No matter how you look at it, community involvement centers around both service and leadership.

• Participating in events such as this gives you an opportunity to enhance the lives of others in your community. **What are some sources of community involvement that appeal to you?**

Benefits to You

"Why should *I* get involved at this stage of my life?" you might ask. "I don't have much extra time because of my friends and family obligations. I have a job, go to technical school, and even look after younger family members." Looking at the benefits from a number of perspectives may help you answer the question.

Besides the built-in benefit of personal satisfaction, there are many other benefits that come from getting involved in the community. Some of these benefits include:

- **Fun and fellowship.** Community service can be fun. It also provides you with opportunities to make new friends with similar interests and values.
- **Increasing self-worth.** Everyone wants to feel there's a purpose in life. By responding to the needs of others—by lending a helping hand with the Special Olympics or serving meals at a homeless shelter—you can fulfill your own need for a purpose.
- **Learning new skills.** Getting involved provides opportunities to learn and practice new skills. For example, Karen had a first-hand opportunity to practice resolving conflicts when she refereed a basketball game for a local youth center.
- **Networking with others.** Giving time and energy to the community offers many chances to **network**, or make contacts with others. Community involvement might even lead you to future employment opportunities or other forms of community involvement.

Benefits to Others

If you think about it, you've probably benefitted directly from someone else's community involvement. Perhaps your friend's father coached your softball team. Maybe a police officer came during her day off to make a presentation at your school. In these and other cases, these volunteers gave you an opportunity to learn something, do something, or enjoy something new or different.

You've seen first hand how involvement can help others. Do you wonder how your community could be a better place because of *your* involvement? The following examples show ways that people benefit from the actions of good citizens. You probably can think of additional ones.

- **Safer streets and neighborhoods.** Participants in neighborhood crime watch groups help reduce crime.
- **Higher quality of life.** Cleaning up neighborhoods and parks helps make the community better for everyone. So do citizens who write letters to newspaper editors and contact local officials to help solve community problems. Other volunteers sponsor youth groups or donate time or money for schools, museums, and libraries.
- **Increased care and concern for others.** Lilly volunteers at the animal shelter. James teaches English to new immigrants. People who realize they are lucky to have a good quality of life want to improve the lives of others.
- **More informed and involved citizens.** By getting involved in community issues, citizens learn more about where they live. They become more aware of community problems and what resources are available, or needed, to deal with these problems.
- **Expanded community resources.** Involved citizens help community resources go further. One neighborhood group successfully worked to stop vandalism at a

school. As a result, tax money that would have gone toward removing graffiti and replacing broken windows was available to pay for a long-awaited afterschool sports program.

Close-Up

Reaching Out

Are you new in town and haven't made any friends yet? Perhaps you feel lonely in your new surroundings. If so, community involvement is a terrific way to make friends. Here's Tom's story.

"I had been living in my new city about three months when the loneliness hit me. I decided I needed to find a way to make some friends and feel a connection to my new community.

"After I had checked out a number of service organizations, one of my coworkers introduced me to someone who answers the phone for a local teen crisis hotline. I've always been interested in psychology and counseling. My friends tell me that I'm a good listener. The thing that really appealed to me was that I could both use my skills and make a difference in someone's life—maybe even save lives.

"Along with feeling good about helping others, I've met some great people who also volunteer at the crisis hotline. My friendship circle is growing and I'm feeling something I've never felt before—a real bond with the community. I'm finally feeling settled."

Everywhere you look, opportunities for community involvement exist. Brainstorm a list of places in your community that need volunteers.

What areas of community involvement appeal to you the most?

Developing a Sense of Community

Lonnie is a member of the local orchestra. Whenever the group gets together to practice or perform, he feels a part of something important. He likes knowing that the orchestra helps improve the life of his community through entertainment.

Involved people relate to their surroundings both emotionally and physically. They have developed a sense of community—a feeling of belonging to a place accompanied by a sense of responsibility and obligation to all the people who live there.

Unfortunately, many people don't feel a part of a community. They may feel they don't belong. Some may just be insecure or shy, just waiting to be asked to work on a project or join a group. Sometimes feeling left out leads to **apathy,** a lack of feeling, concern, or interest in the lives of others.

Do you think *you* might help bring people together in your community? One way to begin is by broadening your circle of friends to include someone who feels left out. You can also encourage family members, friends, and acquaintances to join groups that you are a member of or know about.

Influencing Community Issues

There are many ways you can be part of your community. One way is to work for changes in public policy and laws. For example, Tanya works for people running for election or to get a law passed. She knows that no candidate can get elected or that no ordinance can pass without the participation of ordinary citizens.

• Communities benefit when concerned citizens take action to improve the lives and welfare of others. How do people make a difference in your community?

Tanya tries to stay well informed about issues that are important to her, such as environmental threats. She reads newspapers and magazines, and she goes to meetings where government officials discuss their stands on these topics. She also tries to teach her family and friends what she has learned. Once she asked them to join her in a petition drive to get tougher water pollution laws in her area.

Making Your Vote Count

Only a very small percentage of young adults who can vote actually do so. Some forget about it; others don't take the time. Still others don't know whom or what to vote for, or they feel their vote won't make a difference.

However, when you become informed about current issues and express your opinion about them by voting, you are very effectively involved in your community. Now is a good time to begin making a difference—in and out of the voting booth.

What Does It Take to be a Leader?

You might choose to make a difference in your community by becoming a leader—someone who takes primary responsibility for organizing people and activities so that change happens. Being a leader could mean heading a committee in an existing volunteer organization, or it could mean starting your own organization.

• **Communities offer many ways to bring people together.** What groups and organizations in your community help meet a variety of needs and interests?

Three months ago, Nancy joined a neighborhood association. The goal of the group was to bring about a greater sense of trust, neighborliness, and safety in her neighborhood.

Even though she's the youngest member of the new association, Nancy is now seen as a leader who gets things done. For example, she persuaded the group to invite city council members to last week's meeting. She wanted the council to learn first-hand about the neighborhood's problems, such as graffiti painting, street-corner loitering, and truancy by teen gangs. Nancy believes that public officials and her group can work together to solve these problems. Her dream is to convince city officials to build a recreation center, providing both sports and tutoring programs.

Without leaders such as Nancy, social problems might never be resolved. Of course, few people are natural-born leaders. Instead, they must learn and practice leadership. Sometimes being a "follower" first can teach you how to be a good leader later. Equally important, you can take an informal leadership role among one or more friends by setting an example.

Styles of Leadership

Not all leaders are alike in the way they get a job done and keep a group together. Leadership styles differ from person to person and group to group. Two of the most common leadership styles are participatory leadership and directive leadership.

- **Participatory leadership.** In participatory—or democratic—leadership, the leader and group members need time so they can set goals and make plans and decisions. Getting ideas directly from group members makes everyone feel enthusiastic and involved. Effective participatory leadership requires responsible, committed followers.

- **Directive leadership.** The directive, or authoritative, leadership style is most effective when a job needs to be done in a hurry—such as when organizing volunteers to assist during a natural disaster. In situations such as this, leaders must tell group members what to do; they have little input in directing group efforts. Of course, this style of leadership may not be effective in nonemergency situations.

• These students are taking a stand against homelessness in their communities. Take a look around you. How many people do you see on a daily basis that have inadequate or no housing? What can you do to make a difference?

Characteristics of Effective Leaders

Good leaders have certain characteristics in common. Read the list that follows and see how these characteristics apply to you. Which do you have? Which ones might you need to develop?

- **Initiative and persistence.** Good leaders get things done; they don't put them off or give up. They assume the group is working *with* them, not *for* them, and they stay with the job until it's successfully completed.
- **Thoughtfulness.** Effective leaders are considerate and aware of the feelings of others. They take time to listen to ideas and concerns of the group, listening not only to words, but to feelings, too.
- **Vision and imagination.** Good leaders keep an open mind. They look to the future for opportunities and challenges. Also, they use their vision and imagination to think of ways group members can use their creative skills.
- **Sincerity and integrity.** Good leaders can be trusted. They are honest and straightforward. They are guided by a set of moral principles and values.
- **Acceptance.** In order to enhance a feeling of belonging, good leaders recognize the worth of each group member and his or her ideas. As a result of seeing their ideas accepted in the group's planning, members become more enthusiastic and effective in carrying out the work.

• Building your leadership skills through community involvement can benefit many areas of your life. **What qualities do you most admire in effective leaders?**

Working Together

Like everyone else, you have special qualities, knowledge, and abilities to bring to a group, regardless of its size. Pooling your personal resources with others means that you can accomplish more together than you could apart.

Working together requires good teamwork. This involves shared values and goals—realized and accomplished by the entire "team," not by just one individual. Interaction with one another, feelings of belonging, and high standards are also important when people work together to achieve common goals.

Follow the Leader

Not everyone can be a leader all the time. You may be a leader in one group and a follower in another—both roles are important. Without good followers, leaders would get little or nothing done, or they would have to do all the work themselves.

Many people prefer to be followers. Hardworking followers contribute greatly to groups. To be successful, groups need the active participation of all members. Unfortunately, some members fail to do their part, simply sitting on the sidelines enjoying the work of their peers. Others are quick to criticize the leader, but are not willing to lead or help out. When you join a group, commit to doing your share of the work. When everybody works together, each person has less to do.

Becoming a Volunteer

Throughout the world ordinary people are doing extraordinary things to improve the lives of others. Jenna helped start a volunteer telephone service to keep in touch with elderly neighbors each day. Carlos spends time at the hospital, visiting sick children. David, a volunteer firefighter, helps save people's lives, homes, and their possessions.

Many teens and young adults would like to improve the life of their community by becoming a volunteer, but they don't know where to start. Alex felt like that last year while listening to a speaker discuss her experiences as a Peace Corps volunteer. The speaker inspired Alex and made him want to help others. What could he do? Where should he begin? You may have the same questions. How do you decide how and where to get started?

• Behind every successful leader there are supportive followers. In what situation are you more likely to lead? In what situations are your skills best used as a follower?

Where in the Web?

The popularity of the Internet has greatly helped the causes of political groups and volunteer organizations. Web pages allow these groups to share information with people all over the world about certain issues or efforts. This technology makes it easy to sign up volunteers, organize and publicize events, and get information to the media and community decision makers.

Getting the Information You Need

You can use the Internet to get information about volunteer opportunities both nationwide and in your community. For local groups, try using one of the major search engines for a keyword search such as:

"volunteer" and "my community." Other keywords to try are "nonprofit" and "charity." Or look for local chapters of some of the large national and international nonprofit organizations you might know, such as United Way, Habitat for Humanity, Big Brothers and Big Sisters, Peace Corps, and Amnesty International.

Once you have become a volunteer, you may want to use any computer talents you have to publicize various worthy projects or organizations in your community, including the one you've chosen to serve. Ask if you can develop a Web page for them.

Voicing Your Opinion

1 *What benefits can you identify for using the Internet to find out more about volunteer organizations?*

2 *What might be some obstacles to look for as you search for information about volunteer or service organizations on the Internet?*

Look at Your Values, Talents, and Interests

One way to begin the process of community involvement is by identifying and ranking what you value. Alex did this and determined that his most important values were caring for others and responsibility to his community. This step helped him begin his search.

Personal interests are also important when you're deciding to volunteer. For instance, if

you like sports, you might become a Big Brother or Big Sister and take your new friend to ball games. If you're an outdoors person, you may decide to work with wildlife or environmental protection groups.

Next, try to be realistic when considering your talents or abilities. If you can't bear to ask someone for money, you may not be an effective door-to-door fund-raiser. Taking an honest look at what you have to offer can save time and frustration on everyone's part.

Match Your Heart with Community Needs

Su Hung knows that she values the time she can spend with children. So she decided to help out at an inner-city day camp. "Working with children is my passion. They make my heart sing," Su says. "Seeing them grow into happy, responsible young people makes me feel so good. Now I recommend volunteering to everyone I know."

Service to children and their families brings a great deal of purpose and pleasure to Su's life. It's also an important need in most communities. Because Su's passion is combined with a worthwhile project for the community, she has a very rewarding experience.

Perhaps you have a similar feeling about something you care very much about. It may be a deep concern for teens who are in crisis or people who are homeless. If so, it's important to listen to your "heart," that part of your inner, caring self, and to be aware of issues that cause concern for your community.

Not only may you find meaningful and rewarding opportunities for service, but also you may discover and develop talents and interests that you did not even know you had.

Start with Realistic Expectations

Some people who volunteer expect to change the world with a single effort. When this doesn't happen, they get discouraged and drop out. If you are new to community service, and don't know what to expect, you may find it helpful to work on projects with people you are comfortable with. This can give you confidence and courage. Also, don't hesitate to ask an experienced volunteer to serve as your **mentor,** or guide, for a while. By serving as a guide or coach, a mentor will demonstrate how to be an effective volunteer.

Get Prepared

Finding enough time and energy for school, family, friends, and a job isn't easy. Add volunteer commitments, and your time and energy

• Organizations such as the Peace Corps offer opportunities to serve others around the world. **Where do your service interests lie?**

gauges may soon be on EMPTY! Balancing all of these elements of your life is possible, but it takes practice. Fortunately, the word *volunteer* means that you do have some control over how much time you will commit. You should keep your priorities in mind, the schedule, and your use of time and energy so that there will be enough for volunteering. Focus on what is most important to avoid wasting limited resources on less important matters. This might mean limiting telephone or TV time.

• Opportunities for service that stir up your passion and commitment are generally the ones to which you are best suited. What issues do you feel passionate about? Are there opportunities to serve?

FOCUS ON ...
Service Learning

Service to your community is so important to adult life that many high schools and colleges ask students to become involved in **service learning**, student action that builds on learning through community involvement.

Most volunteer work doesn't come with an instruction manual. However, Kayla, a sociology major at the local college, felt that a manual would be helpful for new volunteers at the food bank where she worked. First, she interviewed representatives from the food bank and asked what people could do there as first-time volunteers. Afterwards, Kayla used this information to develop a volunteer training booklet.

In this way, Kayla applied what she was learning in sociology class to a real-life situation, helping an organization that was solving a social problem. She not only received classroom credit for her work with the food bank, but she had contributed something worthwhile.

Service learning has become a meaningful experience in many schools and colleges. Service projects can happen within the school walls or out in the community. The possibilities are almost endless; they include creating public service announcements, working for nonprofit organizations, or designing safe playscapes for children. The most successful projects allow students to make major decisions and take a central administrative role.

That's why students who are new to volunteering find it especially effective. They can experience community involvement with plenty of initial support and structure before finding a volunteer experience on their own.

Just Do It!

Many problems in your community may never be resolved without help from community members like you. Unless individuals decide to act, numerous worthy things will remain undone. Fortunately, volunteering doesn't always take lots of time; commitments will range from an hour a month to as many hours as you can spare. Many veteran volunteers advise starting small and working up to a more time-consuming commitment.

So what are you waiting for? A rewarding volunteer opportunity is out there with *your* name on it!

Be a Successful Volunteer

TIPS

Many long-time volunteers suggest you ask the following questions before getting involved in your community:

● **What needs to be done in your community?** Look around, read local newspapers, and talk to community leaders. What problems could you help solve in the community? Which ones are of interest to you?

● **What is already being done in the community?** Maybe existing groups could use your help. For example, in one community, a few members of an auto club sort, shelve, box, and distribute canned goods at a food bank.

● **What can people my age do?** Some people find it easier starting small and close to home. That's why many schools offer service learning opportunities. There volunteers gain confidence to move on to projects or problems involving the larger community.

• Having a mentor to encourage you through the challenges of serving others is important to having successful experiences. Who could you call on to be a mentor?

R(E)A S O N

Through Life's Problems

Evaluate Information

Seeking and organizing information is important in the problem-solving process. In the situation that follows, notice how Jason gathers and evaluates information.

Jason walked out of the coach's office, his mind reeling with questions. The track coach had just asked Jason and several other track team members to think about coaching the local Special Olympics track team.

"The offer sounds interesting, but I have lots of questions," Jason thought. "What's the time commitment? Whom would I be working with? Would I be in charge of, or responsible for, anything? What do I need to know how to do? I've never coached before! What if I decide I don't like it? What's it like to work with kids with special needs? What if I'm uncomfortable with them?

Jason thought about how this commitment might affect his time with friends after school and his track. He reflected, "I love track—it's my life. Something I've always valued is helping others. I realize adding

one more activity to my schedule will be tough. I need to gather and evaluate more information before I think about what I do."

During the next two days Jason talked to others about the Special Olympics. He called the local Special Olympics track coach; talked to his high school track coach and the parents of a Special Olympic participant. Each of them had at least two years' experience working with the Special Olympics programs. They gave him pamphlets about Special Olympics. They also explained the coach training schools he could attend, the ten-week time commitment, his role as a track coach, and other volunteer opportunities in Special Olympics.

The people involved in Special Olympics also told Jason that the participants are mentally disabled and may or may not have physical disabilities. Jason could see how meaningful it is

to work with those taking part and how glad volunteers are to devote their time and energy.

Jason also talked to his neighbor, Joe, who had watched a television program about Special Olympics. Joe told Jason the participants have both mental and physical disabilities. He thinks the program's great but doesn't want to get involved.

Jason thought about the information he had gathered. He reasoned, "I think Joe gave me inaccurate and unreliable information. It doesn't match up with the other information I've received from people actually involved in the program or from pamphlets about Special Olympics.

Jason thought for a moment and then said to himself, "I think I have all the information I need to make a decision. Now I just need to think about my alternatives."

▶ From Your Perspective

1 Where did Jason go for information? Were his sources reliable, credible, and accurate? How do you know?

2 Does Jason have enough information to make a decision? What other information might be helpful?

3 What are Jason's values regarding this opportunity? What are the values of others? What values might Jason use as criteria to decide what to do?

4 Where might you go for information regarding an opportunity you are facing?

Understanding Key Concepts

- There are many personal benefits to getting involved in the community.
- Your actions can make a difference in the quality of life within your community.
- Citizens who feel a sense of community are more likely to get involved in society.
- Effective volunteers consider their values, talents, interests, and passions when choosing volunteer opportunities.
- By volunteering, you help both yourself and others; you can help improve people's lives while you learn new skills at the same time.
- You can overcome barriers to volunteering through family and peer support, mentors, your time and energy management skills, and adequate information about volunteering.
- Effective leaders have characteristics that include initiative and persistence; thoughtfulness; vision and imagination; sincerity and integrity; and acceptance.
- Groups consist of more followers than leaders. Without effective followers, the goals of a group probably would not get accomplished.
- Your involvement in the community can have a positive impact on public policy.

Checking Your Knowledge

1. Summarize the benefits that you may receive from getting involved in the community.
2. Explain how community involvement often helps people develop new friendships.
3. What is the relationship between networking and community participation? Give an example showing how a person's community participation might provide opportunities to network with others.
4. Describe three ways that your community might benefit from your involvement in a project or problem.
5. What are the distinguishing characteristics of strong leaders? Give an example showing how each characteristic might be effective in a situation that required the teamwork of a group.
6. Why is it important to consider your values, talents, and interests when you're deciding how or where to volunteer? Give examples of three of your personal talents that might be helpful while you're volunteering in the community.

Making TRANSITIONS

Developing Your Leadership Skills

Imagine that you are employed at a restaurant that has become the frequent target of graffiti. The owner is worried that business may drop off because of the ugly messages. You notice that the offenders are several young teens who have nothing to do after school. You've talked with the owner about some ideas you have to solve the problem and she asks you to take charge of the solution.

- What do you think might solve this problem?
- How would you work with the restaurant owner to reduce the incidences of vandalism?
- What other community members might be able to help in a positive way?
- How could the teen offenders and their parents help deal with this problem?

STRENGTHENING *Life* SKILLS

Getting Involved

When you develop a volunteering spirit, you can find little ways in everyday life to do things for others. You might volunteer at home or do something for a neighbor occasionally as the need arises. If you have the time, you can get involved in an activity that takes a regular commitment of hours and energy.

With a partner, think of as many opportunities as you can to volunteer in your community. First, write down these opportunities for future reference. Next, write answers to the following questions:

- Which of the opportunities would you find the most enjoyable?
- Which of the opportunities would require a considerable amount of time? Which would require only a minimal amount of time?
- Which of the opportunities seem most suited to your personal qualities and abilities?
- What steps would you need to take to get involved in one of the volunteer activities?

Applying Thinking Skills

1. **Clarifying fact or fiction.** People sometimes fail to take care of their community because they believe that the actions of one person won't make a difference. How would you respond to this position?

2. **Predicting consequences.** What consequences might result if someone vandalizes a public facility such as a school or recreational center in your town? If the individual is not caught, who would pay for the vandalism?

Practical Applications

1. **Taking time to express appreciation.** People often get too busy to remember to express their appreciation to others who have made an important contribution in their lives. When they remember to, it may be too late. Write a note to people you appreciate, stating how they've helped you. How would you feel if you received a similar note from someone whose life you influenced in a positive way?

2. **Exchanging roles.** Role reversals can help people understand another person's feelings and actions. Select a partner who is different from you in some way, such as: gender, race, religion, height, culture, physical ability, or country of origin. While sitting face to face, imagine that each of you is the other person. Carry on a discussion about your school and community experiences, values, goals, and challenges—as if you were the other person. After completing the exercise, write a paragraph describing your feelings about this experience. What did you learn about each other? In what ways did your role reversals accurately or inaccurately reflect the other individual?

3. **Writing skills.** To learn about volunteer organizations, write e-mail letters to national or international organizations, such as the Red Cross or Habitat for Humanity, asking what you can do to assist people in need. Use the results of your inquiry to come up with a written plan for your own volunteer activities.

Unit 2

Improving Relationship Skills

Chapters ▽

Communicating Effectively

What You Will Learn...

- The benefits of improving communication skills for all areas of your life.
- Communication skills you might use and strengthen to improve your relationships with others.
- Common problems in communication and strategies to solve them.

Terms for Success

active listening
affirmation
aggressive
assertive
I-message
passive listening
reciprocal relationship

Gary stepped inside and stamped the slush off his boots. "Man, it's a mess out there," he declared, hanging his cap and coat in the closet. He saw his sister Bettina and her friend Isabel looking at magazines at the kitchen table. He overheard bits of conversation: "Get rid of the fat . . . especially the thighs . . . the legs are okay."

"Exercise," he pronounced confidently.

The conversation stopped. "Excuse me?" Bettina asked.

"Exercise," Gary repeated. "That'll get rid of the fat. Coach had us running up and down the bleachers since we couldn't practice outside. That'll shape the thighs in no time."

Bettina and her friend exchanged glances. Isabel smothered a laugh.

"Of course," Gary went on, "being fit is fine, but neither one of you needs to lose weight. People are so concerned about their weight, especially girls. You shouldn't judge yourself by what you weigh. People are more than a number on a scale."

Bettina approached, grinning and holding open a magazine. "Read," she commanded.

Gary put on his glasses. "Seven Great Chicken Recipes: High in Flavor, Low in Fat."

Isabel began to laugh. Bettina explained, "We need low-fat main dish recipes to evaluate for our nutrition class. We were talking about the *chicken's* thighs.

"But it's nice to know you're so open-minded about people's appearance," Isabel put in.

Gary started to blush, then to laugh. "I just imagined a gym full of plucked chickens in leotards and high tops, doing aerobics!"

? Why is listening just as important to communication (and your relationships) as speaking?

Communicating and Relating

Have you ever walked in on a conversation like Gary did and, after hearing a few words, assumed you knew what was being discussed? In this case, Gary's blunder left everyone laughing. Suppose the conversation had been between his boss and another employee. If Gary had made comments that were misinterpreted, it could have damaged his relationship with one or both of them.

Good relationships usually don't just happen. Most people find that relationships require a lot of work and energy—plus effective communication skills. When messages aren't communicated clearly or understood correctly, the misunderstandings that result can pull people apart. However, when communication is effective, there can be positive results.

Relationships That Work

Everyone wants great relationships with friends and family and at school or work. Getting along brings real satisfaction and pleasure. (Think about the emotions that negative relationships bring into your day!) There's no magic formula for achieving such harmony, but there are proven paths to follow.

Two essential elements of strong, positive relationships are respect and healthy give-and-take. Think about your own relationships as you examine these elements:

- **Showing respect.** When people respect one another, they work out their differences without hurting one another. Sometimes they just agree to disagree. Put-downs, constant criticism, and blaming all show lack of respect—provoking anger and hurt. In a relationship based on respect, words and actions show that each person values the other. Which of your relationships has the highest level of mutual respect?

- At the heart of effective communication, is accurately sending and receiving messages. How could this enhance reciprocal relationships?

- **Building reciprocal relationships.** Have you ever been in a relationship in which the other person always wants you to do things his or her way? In **reciprocal relationships**, the amount of give-and-take is about equal. For example, suppose a friend of yours is having a bad day. You listen and boost your friend's spirits because of your friendship. Your friend, in turn, does the same for you. In contrast, if one person carries most of the caring load, the relationship is not a healthy one.

Almost all relationships fall short of the ideal. Most, though, are worth working on. The most basic tool you can use in relating to others is effective communication. When people can't or don't express their thoughts and feelings honestly but with care and concern, their relationships wither. Better understanding the communication process and its pitfalls can improve and enrich your relationships.

FOCUS ON ...
Communicating Through Writing

The ability to write clearly is a powerful communication skill. Writing skills are useful in all walks of life—with friends, family, on the job, or in community work.

Effective writing involves:

- Getting your message across to the reader.
- Organizing your thoughts, so the message flows logically from beginning to end.
- Using correct grammar, spelling, capitalization, and punctuation.
- Presenting the material in a neat, orderly fashion on the page.

Refresh your Memory

Review these key terms in communication:

- **communication:** The exchange of information, ideas, feelings, and thoughts.
- **message:** The substance of a communication—the point or points conveyed.
- **mixed messages:** Simultaneously sent messages that are contradictory in meaning. Often the verbal and nonverbal messages don't match.
- **nonverbal communication:** Body language, or communication without using words. Includes body posture, facial expressions, gestures, and tone of voice.

Strengthening Communication Skills

By now, you may be thinking, "We studied communication in English" or "I've got friends, so I must already know this stuff." It's true that everyone does communicate, even if no words are spoken. However, when you look at all the life skills you've learned so far, few others have such enormous power to improve *all* areas of your life. By taking the time now to analyze and strengthen your communication skills, you can take positive action toward strengthening your relationships. As you read the paragraphs that follow, think about which strategies might be most helpful to you.

Sending Positive Messages

It's human nature to notice what you don't like rather than what you do. Degrading remarks and complaints often roll off the tongue without much thought about their effects on others. To avoid this problem, practice routing your thoughts through your heart on the way to your mouth. If you wouldn't want someone to make a certain comment to you, don't make it to anyone else. Instead, look for opportunities to offer kindness, understanding, and words of praise.

Of course, not everything you say to others is positive. However, you can frame even negative messages in ways that are encouraging, rather than ways that cause defensiveness. Successful communicators have mastered the art of building others up rather than putting them down.

In spite of your best efforts to communicate positively and clearly, at times, the receiver of your message may become hurt, angry, or confused. Here are some things you can try if this happens to you:

- Ask questions to clarify the points of misunderstanding.
- Apologize if necessary.
- Make another attempt at communicating your message if the receiver agrees.

The Power of Affirmations

Affirmations are positive expressions that smooth the way to mutual respect, understanding, and cooperation. These powerful expressions show kindness, give praise, and build self-esteem. Here are some examples showing how affirmations can be used effectively:

- Say, "I know I was really upset when I came to work this morning. Thanks for calming me down and helping out with the customers. I really appreciated the way you pitched in and helped me," rather than taking a coworker for granted.

- Say, "Thanks for fixing my breakfast this morning, Dad. I'm really worried about my exam today. You're great for helping me out," rather than gulping your food and bolting out the door.

- Say, "I can tell you've really worked hard on this English essay. You've made a lot of interesting points. I wonder if your paper could make an even more powerful statement if you reordered the facts a bit," rather than saying, "This paper is a mess. Your thoughts are disorganized."

• It takes many hours of diligent practice to achieve this level of dance skill. Most people do not spend nearly as many hours practicing communication, a skill they use every day. How might your relationships benefit from practicing effective communication?

As the last example shows, it can sometimes be a challenge to frame your communications in an affirming way. With a little practice, however, using affirmations can become second nature.

Don't confuse using affirmations with insincerity. There is usually something that you genuinely appreciate, respect, or admire about a person. As in the English essay example, every effort shows strengths as well as weaknesses. Putting the power of affirmations to work is as simple as identifying and sharing those positive aspects.

Assertiveness—It's a Balancing Act

How can you get your point across without threatening or hurting others? Learning to communicate assertively can help.

When you're *assertive*, you communicate directly and honestly about what you think, feel, believe, or want without showing disrespect for those of the other's. Assertive messages don't blame or judge others.

In contrast, an *aggressive* message is a verbal attack that judges and tramples on the feelings of others. Insults and threats are examples of aggressive messages.

The difference between assertive and aggressive messages is key because they usually cause very different results as shown in the following examples:

- Rico is *assertive* when he says, "Lauren, I get really frustrated when I have to stay late after the store closes, because I am cleaning up after everyone else. As I see it, if everyone picked up as soon as things got messy, I could get home at a reasonable hour."

- Affirming and constructive messges promote cooperation, allowing these teens to accomplish this job more easily. **What are some ways that affirmations could improve your relationships?**

- In contrast, Rico is *aggressive* when he says, "Lauren, you always make a mess and never clean up after yourself. The others do the same thing. I'm going to report all of you to the manager."

If you were Lauren, would you react differently to the assertive and aggressive messages? What thoughts and feelings could each message generate?

the needs or wants of others. In contrast, statements such as "you should" or "you ought" come across as negative or judgmental, and sometimes aggressive. They often cause the person receiving the message to feel put down and become defensive.

One Message at a Time, Please!

For some people, using gestures while talking is as natural as breathing. Most people simultaneously use different methods of communication to get their meaning across. However, each method actually sends a separate message. Your challenge is to combine these methods in a way that's complimentary.

When all of your messages match, you add power to your spoken message. For example, reinforcing what you say with the same messages sent by your tone of voice, facial expressions, gestures, and body posture, you bring balance to your messages.

Mixed messages may confuse the person you are communicating with. Suppose when you arrived late for work, your supervisor said in a serious voice, "You've been late four times this month. I expect you to be here, ready to work by 5:00 P.M." That verbal message is easy to interpret. What would you think if she winked at you while she spoke and smiled at you as she walked away?

Which communication method is more powerful? One research study showed that only 7 percent of an emotional message was sent verbally. The other 93 percent was sent nonverbally. Based on your experience, which seems more significant to you? See pages 106 to 107 to further study the effects of nonverbal communication.

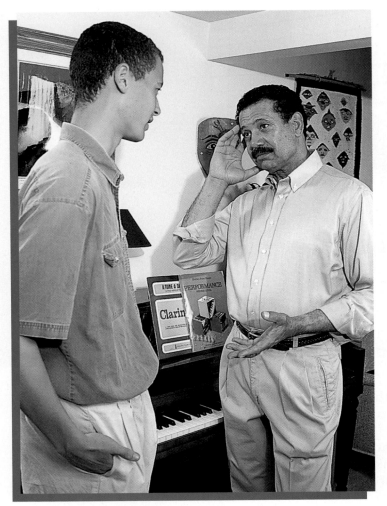

• This dad has just said in an angry tone of voice, "All right, all right, you can go to the party." Does this message match? Why or why not? **Why are mixed messages detrimental to effective communication?**

Messages Can Help!

Assertive communicators find it helpful to use **I-messages.** These explain facts and feelings as you see them and contain such phrases as "from my viewpoint" or "as I see it." I-messages help you assertively set boundaries for your needs and wants without compromising

REASON Through Life's Problems

Recognizing the Primary Problem

Everyone faces opportunities to solve complex problems every day. Sometimes just identifying the problem is a challenge! Carefully read the situation below and examine the process Tasha used to identify her problem.

Tasha plopped into a chair and let out a deep sigh. Her parents had just given her more chores, but when she asked for a later curfew, they wouldn't even talk about it. Tasha's mind churned. "I feel like I am 15 when they treat me that way! Most of the time I'm so overwhelmed with my college classes, working part-time, making dinner every night, and watching the kids, that I feel 28, not 18. I can't go out at night, even to the library, because of the kids. And, there isn't even a place to study at home without constant interruptions. How can I keep my grades up with all this?"

Taking a deep breath, Tasha told herself with determination, "I need to solve my problem," but then groaned, "Which one?" "This situation is so confusing. Each problem seems wrapped up with the other ones." She finally picked up a piece of paper and pen and asked herself, "What's at the root of all of this? What's

really bothering me?" Finally, it dawned on her. "I want Mom and Dad to understand my needs as another adult!"

With a sigh of relief Tasha thought, "Now that I know what the real problem is, maybe I can figure out what to do about it. Jotting down more about the situation would help." She listed the following:

- Mom and Dad work double shifts usually three times a week.

- My 15-year-old brother is home every night after 7:00 and the younger two are home every night by 5:30.

- I have not broken my 11:00 P.M. curfew for three months.

- When Mom, Dad, and I discussed things tonight, no one really listened to anyone else!

- I didn't express myself in a way that would make my parents listen. I wasn't positive, respectful, or assertive, and my points weren't clear.

Tasha checked her watch. It was getting late. She knew there were other factors to add to her list. She also wanted to gather some more information and talk to other people. Thinking about what was really important to her about solving this problem would help, too. Taking the time to analyze the problem and decide what to do—even if it took days or weeks—would be worth it. Right now, she needed some sleep.

Not enough time to study
No quiet place to study
Too much childcare
No time for library
No time to get it all done!

From Your Perspective

1 What other implied factors might affect Tasha's decisions about her problem?

2 Tasha chose her parents' not accepting her as an adult as the primary problem? Why?

3 In a similar situation, would you have chosen the same primary problem? Why or why not?

4 Choose another real-life situation that deals with a complex problem such as Tasha's. Then think about: What is the underlying problem? Why should it be addressed? What factors might affect how to solve the problem?

Respect Counts

Showing disrespect is the fastest road to communication breakdown. Don't you have difficulty cooperating with someone who is rude? Such behavior—whether from tone of voice, choice of words, or nonverbal communication cues—usually initiates a self-protective "fight" response in the other person. Respect has the opposite effect on people. It generates goodwill. Showing respect is one of the simplest ways to increase the effectiveness of your communications. To get started, try the following:

- Check your tone of voice. Aim for a respectful tone, even if you are upset.
- Let others speak without interrupting them.
- Show you are paying attention. Look the other person in the eye as you talk and listen.

Do You Know Your Body's Talking?

The Practical Side of Nonverbal Communication

When was the last time you looked into the mirror as you were talking to someone? Were you surprised by what you saw? Body movements carry many messages. Ideally, these movements should clarify spoken messages instead of adding confusion.

Consider the following items as you focus in on nonverbal communication:

HAND GESTURES.
Hand gestures can be used to emphasize a key point or to indicate size or direction. Your handshake is a powerful communicator, too!

BODY POSTURE. Standing or sitting comfortably upright as you face those you are talking with conveys confidence, professionalism, and interest.

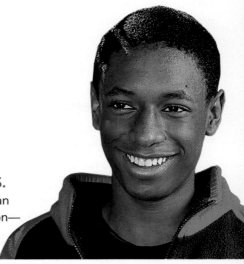

FACIAL EXPRESSIONS.
Just with your face, you can convey almost any emotion—from sadness to surprise.

- Use *please, thank you, excuse me,* and other words of respect. They have been around a long time because they really work!

A Manner to Match the Occasion

Do you talk to your teachers the way you talk to your parents? Are your conversations with friends like those with strangers? Do you talk to males and females the same way? If you communicate effectively, your answers will be "no, of course not." Communication should be very specific to the context—interrelated circumstances—in which it occurs.

Physical environment, age, or a person's mood and energy level all offer different contexts that affect communication. In which context would you choose to talk to your mom about something important—riding home in the car after she's had a frustrating day at work, or after a relaxed meal?

SPATIAL RELATIONS. How close you get to those you talk with usually depends upon the situation. Generally, the closer the relationship, the less distance between people.

APPEARANCE. Studies show that people's reaction to others is based on what they see during the first ten seconds of contact. What does your appearance say to others? What causes you to react positively? Negatively?

ACTIVITY

It's often been said that actions are more powerful than words. How could your relationships change for the better as you learn to coordinate your verbal and nonverbal messages?

EYE CONTACT. When it comes to nonverbal communication, eye contact offers powerful connections with others. Use it to show confidence and caring as you communicate with others.

Other circumstances that may affect the way people communicate include the formality of a situation and the timing of messages. Usually, the less familiar you are with people, the more formal you need to be. Joking and teasing with your friends may be fun, but in a work situation, that same behavior could get you fired.

The timing of your messages, as in the example above, is also important to think about. Choosing a time when others are relaxed and able to talk influences the results of your communication.

Listening to Others

Effective listening skills go hand in hand with effective speaking skills. Both are necessary for effective communication. At first glance, listening seems effortless. Effective listening, however, is more than not talking.

There are two ways to listen—passively and actively. **Passive listening** means listening quietly and attentively. The passive listener may nod or gesture to indicate understanding but does not make comments, or ask questions.

In **active listening,** the listener interacts with the speaker and pays close attention to what the speaker is saying, feeling, and doing. For example, when Sonaya was telling Jade about her job interview, he responded, "How did that make you feel?" and "That was a good answer. What else did you say?"

TECHNOLOGY ISSUES

Email at Work

Email is increasingly commonplace at work, as well as in the home. However, many employees fail to think about the difference. At work, these systems belong to the companies involved. Consequently, employers have the right to set and enforce rules for employees' use of email. Most companies distribute a written document to all employees explaining the company's email policies. The document should include clear guidelines about what kinds of messages may and may not be sent on the office email system. Companies often reserve the right to read all messages.

Today's technology makes it possible for an employer to access all email sent on a company system, including deleted messages. Lawyers who specialize in labor law suggest that employees assume that any email messages sent or received—even deleted ones—could become public. Since misuse of email has been used as grounds for dismissal, it makes sense to avoid messages that might be embarrassing or damaging to you.

Voicing Your Opinion

1. *Imagine that you observe a coworker using your company's email system to send jokes to a friend during regular work hours. How would you handle this situation?*

2. *Should a company be able to fire an employee for sending private messages on the company email system? Why or why not?*

Try using these active listening techniques:

- **Asking for feedback.** Summarize the message and repeat it to the sender, to make sure you understand the intended message. This is sometimes called *reflective listening*.
- **Asking for clarification.** Ask questions to draw out the speaker's thoughts, feelings, and experiences.
- **Empathizing with the speaker.** Show you understand the speaker's message and feelings about a situation through your actions and what you say.
- **Avoiding judgment or giving advice.** Stay neutral about your thoughts while encouraging the speaker to continue.

Effective Listening

T I P S

Here are some helpful reminders to sum up effective listening:

- Maintain eye contact, concentrate with your mind and body, and avoid distractions.
- Listen for main points of the conversation.
- Identify nonverbal and verbal messages.
- Avoid only listening for what you want to hear.
- Mentally process what you are hearing. Ask questions to clarify messages.

How will you know when to be an active or passive listener? The answer is not always easy. You may need to use your best judgment. If you misuse active listening, you may imply you aren't interested in what the speaker is saying. If you use passive listening with someone you've just met, the conversation may never get off the ground. Sensitivity to the speaker and the situation is essential to whether you choose active or passive listening.

- Effective listening takes intense concentration. How does it make you feel to be really listened to?

Increasing Your Awareness

A large part of daily communication is natural and effortless. People talk and listen to what is being said without conscious awareness of everything that is happening during a conversation. That's not all bad, but poor communication awareness is one of the major factors in many relationship problems. When people don't pay close attention to the messages they send and receive, they open the door for misunderstanding.

Reading the Situation

In many ways, monitoring your communication means getting the right "read" or interpretation of an *entire* situation. You can develop your skills in this area by paying careful attention to several factors.

- **Interpreting the signals.** How do others appear to be receiving your messages? Do their verbal and nonverbal cues show disinterest, confusion, or boredom?

- **Interpreting mood.** You also need to consider how a person's present mood might affect communication. For example, what effect could great joy, sadness, worry, or physical pain have on the way a person responds to any conversation?

- **Analyzing your messages.** Are you actually sending the messages you want? How's your body posture and your eye contact? Are your facial expressions and gestures sending the same message? When you are aware of how your messages are received, you can adjust your delivery to be more effective.

Meeting New People

For many people, one of the most difficult communication challenges they face is not knowing what to say when they must spend time with unfamiliar people. Some individuals have a knack for talking casually to people they have just met. For others the art of

casual conversation is an uncomfortable mystery. That's why it's worth making the effort to develop casual conversation skills. You will make use of them in both social and business relationships throughout your life.

Close-Up

Why Communication Fails

When communication breaks down, misunderstandings, loss of trust, and hurt feelings can result. For example, when communication breaks down between parents and teens, parents may feel hurt because their children broke their trust. On the other hand, teens may feel angry and cut off from their friends when parents ground them for lying.

Here are several key factors that contribute to communication failure:

- Making incorrect assumptions. When people talk, they often suppose something is true about the other person, situation, or message.

- Differing viewpoints. Focusing on your own viewpoints, or needs and customs is natural. Differing viewpoints make life interesting, but they can cause problems in getting along with others. How often do you and your parents have differing viewpoints?

- Cultural differences. People from other cultures tend to communicate differently. What is acceptable in one part of the world may be offensive in another—especially with nonverbal communication.

What positive actions can you take to avoid communication failure?

When you are in a situation in which you don't know what to say, try these techniques:

- **Choose topics that are easy to talk about.** Sports, the weather, or current events can be good icebreakers.
- **Play an active part in the conversation.** Willingly answer questions and respond to comments. Remember that one-word answers tend to be conversation stoppers.
- **Avoid talking too little or too much.** Talking on and on or saying nothing tends to turn people away.
- **Be sincere and honest.** People easily catch on to a phony in conversation.

• When meeting new people, showing genuine interest in others' activities and interests is one path to successful small talk. **What are some of your favorite conversation topics? How would you start a conversation with someone new?**

The Challenge of Communicating Effectively

Effective communication involves many skills, some basic, and others more advanced. As you read about the specific skills included in this chapter, were you able to analyze your particular communication strengths and weaknesses? How might you apply each skill to different types of situations involving personal relationships, family members, school, and work?

Of course, improved communication skills can't solve all your personal and relationship problems overnight. In time, however, you will begin to see that effective communication can help make your relationships more rewarding and satisfying.

Review and Activities

Understanding Key Concepts

● Effective communicators use affirmations, send assertive messages, and show respect.

● I-messages help people communicate needs and wants without compromising the needs and wants of other people.

● Sending mixed messages confuses the receiver.

● The context of a situation refers to interrelated circumstances that affect the way you communicate.

● A passive listener is attentive without interrupting the speaker.

● An active listener encourages the speaker through the use of appropriate questions and feedback.

● Low communication awareness is a factor in relationship problems.

● Monitoring communication helps people determine if they are sending and receiving messages accurately.

Checking Your Knowledge

1. Summarize the characteristics of relationships that work.

2. How do affirmations benefit both the giver and the receiver? Write two examples of affirmations.

3. State an assertive, I-message to tell someone that you don't want him sampling food from your lunch. Give an example of an aggressive approach to the same problem.

4. Compare and contrast clear messages and mixed messages.

5. Explain how *context* affects your communication with others.

6. How could an active listener respond to a friend who has just lost a loved one? How might a passive listener respond to the same situation?

7. List the strategies you plan to use to monitor your communication with others.

8. What might you do to avoid circumstances that lead to communication failure?

9. Develop at least four conversation-starting questions (using several topics) you might ask someone you've just met.

Making TRANSITIONS

Workplace Communications

Communicating in the workplace requires more than just using your verbal skills—your written communication skills often share equal importance.

Assume that you are applying for a new job. Part of the job description states written correspondence with clients, in addition to writing detailed reports for the employer. As part of the application process, write a one-page summary of your experiences, achievements, and interests or hobbies related to writing.

STRENGTHENING *Life* SKILLS

Using I-Messages

Using I-messages effectively in communication takes practice. A common formula for an effective I-message is: "I feel (*name the emotion*) when (*identify the action or situation*) because (*state the consequence or reason*)." The formula helps keep the emphasis on your own thoughts, feelings, and reactions.

A good I-message does not contain the word *you*. Working with a partner, identify three situations in which a person might be having communication problems. Then practice writing I-messages that could be used in each situation.

Write a summary of this activity based on the questions that follow. Attach your list of I-messages to your summary.

- How are the I-messages you wrote similar to or different from comments you might make in similar situations?
- What could you expect to happen if you used an I-message in a situation where you have trouble communicating?

Applying Thinking Skills

1. **Recognizing assumptions.** How does appearance affect communication? How might assumptions about appearance interfere with good communication?

2. **Predicting consequences.** What consequences may occur when people gossip in the following situations: coworkers talking about the personal life of another; several classmates discussing the dating experience of another classmate.

3. **Comparing and contrasting.** Think about conversations you've had with males and females. Compare and contrast the ways that males and females communicate. Are there similarities and differences? Defend your reasoning.

4. **Drawing conclusions.** How can frequent ineffective communication affect self-worth? How might it affect a person's adult life experiences?

Practical Applications

1. **Using affirmations.** To observe the effects of affirmations, give them to others as often as possible. Also note the reactions you receive. Write a short paper explaining your observations and whether your behavior has had an effect on your relationships.

2. **Assertive communication.** You believe that you deserve a raise at work. Based on what you've learned about assertive communication, develop a plan for approaching your employer for a raise.

3. **Setting personal goals.** Identify one area in which your communication skills tend to be weak. Write examples of what you plan to do or say to improve these skills. For example, identify a plan of action you can take to become more aware of how your communication affects others. Identify ways in which you will use these skills to improve specific relationships.

Dealing with Conflict

What You Will Learn...

- How to identify and describe the positive and negative results of conflict.
- Why conflict occurs and how it escalates.
- Constructive methods for dealing with and resolving conflict.

Terms for Success

mediator
win-win solution

Behind the music store counter, Devon and Cali were filling supplies before opening. From the stock room doorway, Ed's accusing voice stopped them in their tracks. "Who moved everything back here?"

"I did," Devon said. "The way supplies were arranged before was confusing. My way makes more sense. It's easier to learn."

"The company has rules about arranging the supplies," Ed snapped. "You'll have to put things back like they were." Devon rolled his eyes in Cali's direction and slammed a stack of CD cases on the counter. He stormed back to the stock room.

Watching him leave, Cali commented quietly, "I didn't know we had rules about the supplies."

Ed picked up the scattered CD cases. "We don't," he admitted, "but the guy is always doing that. He makes all these changes without telling anyone."

"I know." Cali said. "Why does he think he's so smart? He's only been here three months."

"Yeah. And because I'm shift manager, *I'm* the one who's supposed to be in charge."

Cali nodded. "I know."

"I don't even care that Devon changes things," Ed went on. "I just wish he'd ask first." By now he was cooling off. "Sometimes Devon even has some really good ideas."

"Yeah, you're right," Cali said as she changed the CD playing in the store stereo. "Sometimes I feel a little stupid that I didn't think of them myself."

"See?" Ed said. "You understand. Why doesn't Devon?"

Cali looked right at Ed. "Well, have you ever told him the right way to make suggestions?"

"I guess not," Ed said, shaking his head. He turned toward the stock room and yelled: "Devon! Hang on a second . . ."

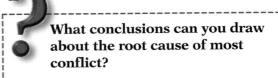

What conclusions can you draw about the root cause of most conflict?

Conflict—A Part of Life

When was the last time you had an argument with someone just because you thought she understood something she didn't? In the situation you just read, Ed assumed Devon knew the rules but just wanted to ignore authority. Devon assumed that Ed didn't appreciate his ideas. Luckily, in this situation, a third person was there to see the conflict differently. Cali helped both Devon and Ed resolve their problem so it wouldn't come between them in the future.

As a unique person, with your own ideas and experiences, you will often see things differently from the way others do. These differences can lead to conflicts. They can cause hurt feelings and relationship problems, so learning to deal with clashes like this one can help you avoid negative results.

Strange as it may seem, conflict can also be a positive force in your life. When you deal with conflict successfully, you can have better relationships and a more solid sense of who you are.

As you learned in Chapter 3, conflict can be internal. You might debate whether or not to buy a new pair of boots because your values of saving money and looking good are clashing. In this chapter, you will learn more about dealing with external or interpersonal conflict. This grows out of and affects your relationships with others.

The most intense conflicts you will experience are probably in your family, in love relationships, among your friends, and with close coworkers. In a close relationship, there are just more issues to disagree about. In addition, when relationships are close, conflict is likely to be more intense and emotional.

Dealing with conflict is never easy. You can, however, minimize the distress that conflict creates and work toward better results. A variety of strategies and skills can help you manage, deal with, and resolve conflict.

• Conflict can take place in any setting. Why is the family likely to be the setting for conflict that is emotional and intense?

It's About Good Health

Learning to manage and resolve conflict constructively can help you feel better by improving your physical and mental health. Unresolved, "underground" conflict can have serious negative effects on health, both mental and physical.

Accent the Positive

Conflict is unavoidable, but when it has been resolved, you can work through your anger and other negative feelings and replace them with positive ones. The positive feelings you experience will then promote health in all areas of your life.

Conflict in the family during the teen years is often caused by issues of dependence and independence. "My dad still thinks he should make my decisions," Amy said. "We have a lot of arguments about my classes, whether I should have a job, and what I'm going to do when I graduate."

Family conflict over freedom and decision making stem from the teen's search for a sense of self—an important part of good mental health. As you work through conflict issues with your family and friends, you begin to clarify your position and outlook.

If you have a sense of what is right for you, you can respect the values of others, but still live up to your own standards. Those without a strong sense of self often do not deal well with conflict because they aren't sure exactly what they stand for.

While conflict itself may help in building a personal identity, learning to manage conflict constructively builds self-confidence. Knowing that you can create positive results from the conflicts with others helps you feel good about yourself.

Minimize the Negative

Conflict often creates negative feelings such as anger, frustration, and hurt. These negative emotions don't disappear automatically.

Controlling Anger

TIPS

Anger is a legitimate emotion. It can also eat at you, make it hard to think straight, and make conflicts worse. So when you feel anger build, try these ideas to keep control:

- Take a deep breath. Count to ten or think of something else for a second. Don't blurt out something or do something you might regret later.

- Think about what's got you steamed. Ask yourself, "Why?" "Why now?"

- Get out—away from the situation or person until you calm down.

- Work out. Sweat off some of those negative emotions.

- Talk, talk, talk—to parents, friends, teachers, coaches, or counselors.

- S-t-r-e-t-c-h yourself to see all sides of the problem.

If these emotions are not dealt with constructively, conflicts can lead to boredom, poor relationships, depression, drug use and abuse, or other physical and mental health problems. As Justin said, "My roommate and I argue a lot over who should do what chores. When that happens, I eat. I've gained almost ten pounds in the last couple of months."

Many people make more self-destructive choices when conflict goes unresolved. Avoiding the negative effects of conflict is one goal of learning to resolve conflict successfully.

• Using a punching bag helps
this teen keep anger under
control to avoid damaging
relationships with others.
**What are some ways that
you could use to keep your
anger under control?**

Building Better Relationships

Imagine that you have a splinter in your finger. If you leave it there, the finger is likely to become infected and sore. Your finger heals only when you remove the splinter.

Conflict in a relationship is like a splinter. If it is not resolved or removed, the relationship can become infected and unhappy. Tanisha and Carl had been going together for three years. They wanted to attend the same college, but Tanisha planned to go to a large out-of-state school. Carl preferred a small local college. Carl said, "The college issue caused so much stress and anger and so many disagreements that we finally broke up—which I guess was one way to take care of the problem."

Resolving conflicts can heal and improve your relationships. It can relieve tension and bring you closer together than before. People who work through their conflicts often understand each other better. They can build a more genuine relationship while respecting each other's ideas and viewpoints.

Looking at Conflict

One key to successfully deal with conflict is understanding it. When you know how conflict starts and how it grows, you are in a better position to resolve it.

Why Does Conflict Occur?

What causes conflict? It happens when people want something that requires the cooperation of others who don't want to or are unable to give it. Conflicts generally focus on three areas: resources, needs, and values.

• **Resources.** Each person has only a limited number of resources—whether the resource is money, time, possessions, or skills. When two or more people are competing for the same resource, conflict results. Time is the resource in dispute if your dad wants you to babysit for your younger brother when you'd like to go out with friends.

- **Needs.** Personal needs and wants are often the basis of conflict. John and Crystal frequently argue because Crystal isn't always dependable. John needs a friend who'll be there when she says she'll be.
- **Values.** Different values are a major source of conflict in many situations. Jocelyn and Brooke argue because Brooke isn't going to go to the mall after school. Brooke's mom needs her home after school and Brooke doesn't want to break her trust. Jocelyn wants Brooke to go anyway, just to have fun.

Identifying the underlying causes of conflict is important. The issues that create conflict also provide clues about what it will take to resolve the problem.

The Conflict Escalator

Imagine you're showing a snake to a group of kids as part of a science project. Think of how they'd react. Some would squeal and move as far away as possible; others might beg to hold it.

Other people respond to conflict in different ways, too. Some withdraw, some approach, some attack. These are natural ways of reacting.

Whatever an individual's response is to conflict, there is always the potential for the conflict to grow or escalate. Visualize this tendency for conflict to expand as an escalator. Each level of conflict is reflected by different behaviors and communication.

- **The first step.** Most people get on to the escalator on a step that reflects their natural reaction to conflict. People rarely move down the steps of the escalator—the normal tendency is for conflict to grow and expand.

• Conflict is common in all walks of life. What do you think would be the most common source of conflict in the workplace—resources, needs, or values?

- **Going up!** As conflict escalates, behavior becomes more emotional, more intense, and the outcome more destructive. The possibility of a violent outcome, either physical or verbal, increases as the intensity of the conflict does.
- **Getting emotional.** Once level 3—the level of reacting emotionally—is passed, the opportunity to resolve conflict constructively becomes much more difficult.

- **Stop! I want to get off.** Most of the steps shown on this escalator do nothing to help resolve conflict. Avoiding the issue may keep a surface peace, but it does nothing to solve the underlying problem. The best opportunity for conflict resolution occurs on the second step of the escalator. This step corresponds with the process of problem solving that you have been studying.

Setting the Stage for Resolving Conflict

Ever wonder why dealing with conflict is so hard? Perhaps the toughest part is figuring out how other people think, feel, and behave. You can't control the way they'll act in conflict. You can only control yourself and create conditions that will help resolve conflicts.

FOCUS ON ...
The Conflict Escalator

Note how conflict intensifies with each step.

Step 6: Fighting by pushing, shoving, hitting, or throwing things, accompanied by extreme verbal abuse.

Step 5: Fighting by yelling, screaming, and making personal insults.

Step 4: Fighting with raised voices, angry looks, and mildly insulting remarks.

Step 3: Arguing intensely and emotionally.

Step 2: Discussing the conflict calmly and rationally.

Step 1: Avoiding each other or subject.

In some ways, resolving conflict is like learning a new dance or a complicated offensive strategy on the soccer field. It's the most fun and successful when your moves are coordinated with everyone else's—when you work as a team. Learning "moves and steps" that deal with conflict set the stage for effective conflict resolution. If you know the routine, you can stay on the second step of the conflict escalator.

Respecting Others

Whether you agree with others or not, it is important to show respect for them. Others have a right to their beliefs and feelings, just as you have a right to yours. The challenge is not only in finding a way to allow for differing viewpoints, but also to prevent differences from leading to or escalating conflict. Respecting each other can help you accomplish this.

Jessica said, "My friend Scott and I disagree all the time. He loves pets—I don't like animals. I'm a jock—he ignores sports. Somehow, it doesn't matter. It's great that we're different. He doesn't try to change me, and I don't try to make him more like me."

One way to show respect and keep conflict from escalating is to understand the position of others. This usually means asking questions and listening so that you know how the other person sees the issue.

Criticizing, blaming, sarcasm, and teasing show a lack of respect. They are also usually ineffective in resolving conflict and solving problems.

Lower the Emotional Temperature

Emotions, especially anger, are sparks that can make a conflict escalate to a four-alarm fire. As people become emotionally charged, they tend to feel threatened. This makes them more attached to their opinions. They show less respect for others, and are less able to think logically. When emotions start running high, there is little opportunity to resolve a conflict.

• Withdrawal, either emotionally or physically, keeps people from finding a solution to the problems that cause conflict. **How would you cope with a situation such as this?**

The sooner you can deal with a conflict situation, the easier it is for everyone to lower the emotional temperature. That's because emotions tend to build on themselves. Christopher says, "Once I get really mad, I think about how angry I am. That just makes me madder. When I get to that point, I can't seem to calm down. Then I might say or do something stupid that I regret later."

Don't Take It Personally

Think about it: when someone disagrees with you, do you often feel threatened and want to strike back? Does striking back escalate conflict? Instead, try saying to yourself, "Don't take it personally." Whether the other person means it personally or not, you can decide not to get trapped into reacting emotionally.

This is obviously not easy. If you can separate your personal feelings from an argument,

however, you are in a better position to refocus the discussion on the disagreement that needs to be resolved.

Resolving Conflict

Effectively resolving conflict requires teamwork. The resolution of a conflict won't make everyone happy unless everyone is part of the solution. This requires a variety of interpersonal skills.

Working It Out Together

In one sense, resolving conflict constructively is a form of problem solving. The conflict is a shared problem, so the people involved need to work together as a team to solve it.

• Respect for others can be shown in many ways, including a handshake after a heated competition. **What are some ways that you can show respect to others despite conflict?**

Take Connor and Brigid, for example. This brother and sister often fight over who gets to use the car they share. One day, Brigid finally explained that she was not upset about getting her turn. She was mad because Connor never filled the car with gas. "First, we had to agree on what the problem really was," Connor said. "Only then could we make a list of ideas and possible solutions that we could both live with. We decided that each of us would put $5 a week into a jar for gas. We agreed that we'd use the money to keep the tank at least half full all the time."

Problem solving in this manner is complicated because there are at least two points of view to consider. When Connor and Brigid agreed that filling the gas tank was the issue, they could find solutions that satisfied both of them.

Negotiation and compromise are processes you can use to turn options into solutions.

Like a recipe, they require certain ingredients or the result won't be appetizing to everyone. These ingredients are:

- Everyone's willingness to cooperate and collaborate.
- The ability to find common interests and goals.
- Flexible attitudes about new ways of doing things.
- Willingness to give and get.

Many people think of negotiating and compromising as bargaining or overtly trading one thing for another. Instead it is better to say things like "Yes, I could live with that," or "That point really isn't that important to me—I can give on that."

If you think about conflict as a mutual problem to be solved, you can settle arguments differently. Practice and use the problem-solving process, and it will become easier.

Can Conflict Improve Relationships?

No one likes to have arguments or conflicts, but it's going too far to think you should never do battle with people you care about. Sometimes families or friends spend many years avoiding the same conflicts. Doing this allows negative feelings to build up, which often cause new conflicts and resentment. It takes even more time, energy, and effort to uncover and then resolve conflicts that have been buried in this way.

"I feel I'm luckier than most other people I know," said Kyle. "My mom and stepdad never fight, and they never yell at me. I think it's because my mom and my real dad fought all the time. My dad used to hit my mom when he got really mad, so they got divorced. My mom says she never wants to live in a house with fighting again. Now, when my older sister and I disagree, she tells us to just drop it. We do.

"So I'm not sure I have a problem. Yet sometimes I get so angry, I want to explode, and I can't. I know my mom gets angry at me, too, because she acts disappointed in me.

"Last summer I decided to work at a hardware store instead of at my usual job cutting lawns. Mom kept pointing out that a guy down the street took all my old lawn mowing customers and made twice as much money as I did. I tried to ignore her. I kept wishing she had told me I was making a bad decision at the time I had made it. Even if we argued. Now it's too late to change anything.

"So every time Mom asks me about my new job, I try to change the subject. Then I get in trouble for not answering her directly. It's like I'll never be good enough."

Using Your Resources Wisely

1 What might happen if Kyle continues to ignore his problem?

2 If you were in Kyle's position, whom would you go to for help? Why?

3 How might good communication skills be a resource for solving this problem?

Spotlight the Problem

Sometimes an argument can quickly turn into an attack on the other person. This happens when it seems easier to pick on someone rather than deal with the mutual problem. For example, you might be tempted to say things to the person you are arguing with such as "You're always late," "You never pay attention to what I'm saying," etc.

If you can focus on the problem and see it as separate from the person you are arguing with, you're closer to a solution. Resolving conflict means looking for a solution, not having a competition.

• Making threats is common during heated conflict, but does little to help create an effective solution. **How do you respond when someone issues a threat?**

Communication is Key

Effective communication is critical in dealing with conflict. The verbal and nonverbal messages people use determine how the conflict will turn out. Messages sent in conflict tend to fall into one of three categories:

- **Offers.** Offers indicate what a person is willing to give in exchange for something else. Example: "I know tomorrow is my day to cook dinner, but I really want to go to my favorite band's concert. How about if I cook two nights next week in exchange for missing tomorrow?"
- **Demands.** This type of message dictates the terms expected of the other. Example: "You'll tell Derrick you lied about seeing me out with another guy," is an example of a demand.
- **Threats.** A threat states the consequence (usually negative) of not meeting a demand. Example: "You'll be home at midnight or you'll be grounded for two weeks," This contains both a demand and a threat.

Notice how demands and threats are not I-messages. Offers are. If you combine offers with careful listening and feedback, you'll come closer to resolving your conflict.

If you can phrase your messages as offers, they will usually be received more favorably. The better your offer meets the other person's needs and wants, the closer you are to a resolution of your conflict.

When people are involved in conflict, and their messages don't "win" the argument, their natural tendency is to do more of the same, more forcefully. Will says, "When we argue, my friend Thomas starts talking very loudly. It seems like he somehow thinks I didn't hear or understand the first time, so he repeats himself. I heard all right, I just didn't agree."

Suppose what you say or do hasn't accomplished what you hoped. Try something else instead of more of the same. If you used a demand message, try an offer instead. If one offer wasn't acceptable, think of another. Use your communication skills to change the direction of the conflict to a more positive path.

Close-Up

When Conflict Turns Violent

Reacting violently in words or actions means the conflict has escalated to the point that emotions are out of control and logic has taken a vacation.

The first step toward avoiding violence is to understand it:

- *Violence is rarely planned or premeditated. It simply occurs as arguments escalate.*

- *Violence doesn't solve problems. It usually makes a situation worse. It can hurt people physically and emotionally, damage property, and can even get people killed.*

- *Violence hurts people, relationships, families, and communities. The widespread existence of violence in society is proof that people need better ways to deal with conflict.*

What suggestions do you have for preventing violence?

Take Time Out

In basketball, when play becomes wild, tense, or uncontrolled, a coach will usually call a time out. The time in the huddle allows players to cool down, relieve tension, and refocus on the game plan. Take your own time out when a conflict starts up the emotional part of the escalator. If you calm down first, reason and logic can take over.

Sometimes humor can be a time out. If you can laugh together for awhile and then come back to solving the problem, you have a good chance of having a positive outcome.

• Humor and laughter can help resolve conflict by relieving tension and lightening the atmosphere. When have you found humor and laughter to be helpful in resolving conflict?

- A win-win solution works because it meets the needs and wants of both parties involved in a conflict. **Share a situation in which a win-win solution worked for you.**

MY GOALS

OUR GOALS

YOUR GOALS

Go For Win-Win Solutions

Many people approach conflict in the same way they play games. Games are structured so that there is usually a winner and a loser.

Conflict, however, is not a game. The goal of conflict resolution is to solve your problem. When it's solved so that everybody has some benefit, you have reached a win-win solution. **Win-win solutions** are created from a collaborative effort to solve a problem so that everyone benefits. Developing a win-win solution means using teamwork as you cooperate, negotiate, and compromise.

In a conflict over an honest difference of opinion, there can never be a winner and a loser. The loser stores anger and resentment that poisons the relationship, so the "winner" ends up losing, too. Which would you choose—a win-win solution or a lose-lose one?

Use a Mediator

Unfortunately, people's differences can be so great and conflict so out of control that there seems no possible way to create a win-win solution. Then using a mediator can often help bring people together. A **mediator** is an impartial person who acts as a go-between for those in conflict. Mediators help others find fair solutions to their problems.

Sometimes people serve informally as mediators. For instance, a family member or a particular friend may be good at helping others resolve conflict.

There are also formal mediation programs. Some schools have peer mediation programs that provide a trained student mediator to help other students when disputes occur.

If your school doesn't have a peer mediation program, talk to a counselor or administrator about starting one. Such programs have good success records in reducing conflict and violence in schools all over the country.

Knowing When to Let Go

One skill in managing conflict is knowing when to "let it go." If the conflict is resolved satisfactorily, move on in your relationship.

Sometimes disagreements are so deep that people can't let go; conflict can't be resolved. For example, some family members may have great differences in beliefs and values. These families can live together harmoniously, however, if they share mutual respect and love. Then they can accept and respect their differences and disagreements. They can learn to "agree to disagree." By letting go of the conflict, they can rebuild loving relationships.

Letting go of conflict can help you. Hanging on to conflict and the emotions it generates takes a lot of energy. Those who harbor bitterness and anger over conflict hurt only themselves. Forgiving others helps release negative emotions. When you can let go, your relationships can improve. So can your outlook on life.

Making Conflict Work for You

Dealing with conflict is a lifelong process. If you can learn effective approaches to conflict now, you will have a skill with a lifetime warranty.

When a conflict arises, ask yourself these questions:

- Why is this happening? What exactly do I want this conflict to accomplish?
- What can I do to keep this conflict from escalating?
- How can I figure out and respect the other person's position? How will that help me solve this problem?
- How can I get the other person to meet me halfway in collaborative, problem solving?

- How will I deal with this situation if the conflict can't be resolved?

If you can answer these questions, you will be better able to manage the conflict and probably more likely to resolve it to your satisfaction.

• These people can let go of their differences to enjoy a quiet walk together. **What do you see as the benefits of letting go of conflict? When is it best to let go?**

REASON

Solving a Problem

Practical problems are everyday problems that involve taking some kind of action. In the situation that follows, note how Taylor uses the REASON process to solve her problem.

Taylor is attending community college as a part-time student this year in the hope of transferring to the state university next year. She wants to major in chemical engineering, but first needs to earn some extra money to help pay for the tuition. For the past year, Taylor's been working full-time for a construction company specializing in home building. The problem is that she dreads going to work! Every day, some of the guys on the crew make sexually-related remarks about her under their breath. Sometimes as she passes by them to get equipment, they intentionally brush against her. She gets so embarrassed and flustered she's been making mistakes on the job.

The male foreman didn't seem to notice. Once Taylor tried to talk to him about it. He told Taylor he would talk to the business owner about the situation, but he never followed-up with her.

One night while trying to study, Taylor realized, "I've really got to do something about this. It's affecting my entire life. I wonder what I am doing to cause the guys to act this way?" As she calmed down, Taylor mentally sifted through her emotions. After thinking about it, Taylor decided it probably isn't her behavior that's the problem. She just does her job. "I am being harassed," she thought, "and it's affecting my work."

"I've got to get more information about sexual harassment." Taylor thought to herself. "Let's see . . . I could talk with my college advisor, check out some articles at the library, and check out the Internet."

During the next week, Taylor spends time talking with the people on her list and checking out other sources. Each time, she takes notes and tries to decide if she can trust each source. She's also making a list of facts about her situation, including who, what, when, where, and how the harassment happened. Next, she compared her situation to the ones her sources talked about.

The more she thinks about it, the more Taylor realizes that she values people showing respect for others and being free to work and learn. "I guess that the guys don't seem to have the same values. If they do, they sure aren't showing it."

While making a list, Taylor analyzes each alternative, and thinks about the short-term and long-term consequences of each. She wonders how each alternative might affect her, the guys who harass her, others on the crew, her foreman, and the business owner.

Considering both her values and the information she's gathered, Taylor makes her choice. "I am going to write a letter to the coworkers who are harassing me and send a copy to my foreman and the owner of the company. "

Having justified her choice, Taylor outlined a plan of action. "This letter needs to communicate factual information about what had happened and how it made me feel," Taylor thought to herself. "I need to clearly say what kind of behavior I expect these guys to have toward me and what future action I'll take if they don't change. I think I'll let my college adviser read my letter since he was such a good source of information. Mom and dad should probably read it, too."

Several weeks later Taylor saw the results of her actions. The foreman and the company owner met with Taylor and the crew, stating expectations for the derogatory behavior to stop.

The guys on her crew aren't harassing her now—they're just leaving her alone. "I did the right thing," she thought. "Maybe when tough situations arise in the future, I won't be afraid to do something."

Through Life's Problems

ALTERNATIVES	CONSEQUENCES FOR SELF AND OTHERS
Not do anything.	+ Short-term: None. + Long-term: None - Short-term: I feel increasing frustration and distraction; don't do well on the job; get lower grades; guys won't change disrespectful behavior. - Long-term: Guys feel they can continue to do this to other females; I become more uncomfortable with men I don't know.
Talk to the guys and ask them to stop harassing me.	+ Short-term: Immediate feedback; can get it over with quickly. + Long-term: Guys may stop. - Short-term: I'll be tense and upset while talking to the guys; all embarrassed by a public scene; guys may not think I'm serious enough by just talking. - Long-term: Word circulates that I'm a "problem."
Write a letter or talk to foreman.	+ Short-term: Get foreman's support; foreman would deal with guys so I don't have to. + Long-term: Not get directly involved; increase foreman awareness of problem. - Short-term: Foreman might not do anything; I deal with foreman liability. - Long-term: Tied up with the situation long after I quit working for the company.
Write a letter to the guys asking them to stop harassing me. Send a copy to the fore-mand and owner of the construction company.	+ Short-term: Tell my needs and expectations without getting flustered; stand up for what I value; don't have to directly confront; no PR hassle; kept quiet. + Long-term: Guys change behavior; others not hurt in future; can continue with next step if no results. - Short-term: Guys don't change behavior; may hassle me more; create revenge; no results until letter delivered. - Long-term: Word circulates that I'm a "problem."
File a formal grievance with the construction company.	+ Short-term: Take a long time to get action. + Long-term: Guys stop the behavior or will leave the company. - Short-term: Picked up by newspaper; bad publicity. - Long-term: Tied up with situation long after I quit working for the construction company.

► From Your Perspective

1 Why was it important for Taylor to address the problem?

2 What other alternatives might Taylor have considered? What were their possible consequences?

3 Would you have selected the same choice as Taylor? Why or why not?

4 What barriers exist that might have prevented Taylor from taking action? How might she overcome these barriers?

5 Did Taylor's actions reflect her values? Did they have positive consequences for herself and others? Were there any negative effects?

Understanding Key Concepts

● Learning to deal with and resolve conflict can help you feel good mentally and physically. It can improve your relationships.

● Conflict most often involves clashes about resources, needs, and values.

● The more emotional and intense a conflict is, the more difficult it will be to resolve.

● Conflict is most likely to be resolved when there is mutual respect.

● Collaborative problem solving is the basis of effective conflict resolution.

● Focusing on the problem, using communication skills, and taking time outs are strategies for dealing with conflict.

● Conflict can be constructive if it is resolved with a win-win solution.

● Skills in communication, teamwork, negotiation, and compromise are all needed for successful conflict resolution.

Checking Your Knowledge

1. Summarize the positive and negative effects of your conflicts with others.

2. Explain how conflict resolution builds strong, healthy relationships.

3. Identify the three major causes of conflict and give an example of each.

4. What are the characteristics of conflicts that escalate? Discuss why, when conflict escalates, the chances for effective conflict resolution decrease.

5. Explain why respect for others is important in dealing with conflict.

6. Describe the "don't take it personally" strategy for managing conflict. How does using this strategy help you keep conflict under control?

7. Explain how problem solving applies to conflict resolution.

8. Identify and give an example of each of the three kinds of conflict messages.

9. How do collaboration and teamwork affect the possibility of a win-win solution?

10. Describe the role of a mediator in resolving conflict.

11. Why does letting go of a conflict sometimes bring benefits to those involved?

Making TRANSITIONS

Workplace Conflict

Conflict on the job can cause hard feelings, loss of morale and teamwork, and a drop in productivity. Poor relationships, often caused by conflict, are a major cause of resignations and firings. Knowing how to deal with conflict in the workplace is important in being successful on the job.

Assume that two coworkers have been arguing over what radio station to play at work. You are an informal mediator in this conflict. Write your responses to the following questions:

• Describe how you would help your coworkers.
• How would you help them identify and evaluate solutions?

STRENGTHENING *Life* SKILLS

Making Offers

Making offers is not easy when conflicts get emotional. However, offers can help resolve conflicts. Working with a partner, think of three situations in which a teen might have conflict. Then together decide what offers a teen could use in each situation. Write down the offers for future reference.

Also write out your answers to these questions:
- How would *you* respond in the conflicts you identified?
- How would making offers help you resolve each conflict?
- Why are offers more effective in resolving conflict than demands or threats?

Applying Thinking Skills

1. **Drawing conclusions.** Would the impact of conflict on relationships be the same for everyone in every conflict? Why or why not?

2. **Predicting consequences.** People sometimes deal with conflict by avoiding it. Would this approach be likely to strengthen or further weaken the relationship? Explain your answer.

3. **Recognizing points of view.** Find an article about some type of conflict. Read the article and identify at least two reasons why the people involved in the conflict disagree. Identify points of view that are presented in the article. Is there any way to know which point of view is right? Explain your answer.

4. **Comparing and contrasting.** Compare and contrast conflict, anger, and violence. What is the relationship among the three?

Practical Applications

1. **Teaching conflict resolution skills.** Working with a group of your classmates, pretend that you must teach preschool or elementary school kids how to resolve conflicts. What would you emphasize? How could you encourage the kids to practice what you've taught them? How could you evaluate the effectiveness of your teaching? Present your lesson to a group of real kids and evaluate its success.

2. **Interview.** Interview a police officer about dealing with conflict and violence on the job. What type of conflict management strategies does the officer use? Communication skills? How does the officer approach domestic disputes, which are considered among the most dangerous types of police calls? What kind of training was the officer given in conflict management? Write a report of your findings.

3. **Investigation.** Find out about any peer mediation programs in your community. Check the library, Internet, or interviews (either in person or via telephone). Investigate how the programs work and how successful they have been. Present your findings in a written, oral, or multimedia report.

CHAPTER 8

Maintaining Family Ties

What You Will Learn...

- The joys and frustrations of new relationships within your family as you move from the teen years to adulthood.
- The importance of lifelong family ties.
- How to apply information from this chapter to your own circumstances.
- How to enhance your family relationships during adulthood.

Terms for Success

adult development
attachment

Jamal and his stepfather walked into the kitchen after dinner only to catch Jamal's mother reorganizing the shelf below the sink.

Rose Williams looked up at the two men and frowned like a child caught snitching a cookie.

"A sophomore in college with my own apartment, and my mother still organizes my life," Jamal said.

"Habit," she said, then immediately put things back where they had been under the sink. "I've organized your life for so long, I see I'm having trouble letting go."

"Actually, Mom, I was hoping that by making you and Bill dinner tonight I could show you I'm doing fine on my own."

"And you are, " his mother said.

"You know, I don't think I even mind if you do rearrange that shelf, but I would like you to ask me first."

"And *that* is exactly how it should be," said Bill.

"You both are right, and I am so sorry, Jamal," said his mother as she put the last item back in place and stood up.

"It's okay, Mom," Jamal said as he reached out to hug her.

"Say, I just remembered, Jamal, your mother packed about three dozen double fudge chocolate chip cookies for you. I'll go get them out of the car."

"You know, Mom, there are *some* things about my relationship with you that I hope never change," Jamal said.

What types of challenges do people face as they work to become independent and still keep their family connections strong?

Understanding Family Ties

Family ties are the most lasting of any connections among people. You are always someone's son or daughter no matter what else happens in your life. If you have siblings, you are forever a brother or sister.

Living in a family involves special dynamics, or causes for change and growth. As you begin to understand the various qualities of family life, it is easier to make sense of what may be going on in your family. By understanding family ties, you can enhance and strengthen not only the family you were born into, but also the one you will likely create someday.

There are three main types of ties in families:

- **Physical.** Biological ties between parents and children and among siblings are permanent ties.
- **Legal.** Created by birth, marriage, or adoption, these ties are permanent unless further legal action is taken.
- **Emotional.** The ties of feeling dedicated to and responsible for one another. These can be positive or negative, and they change and shift throughout life.

A Change in Your Future

As you move toward independence, your relationships with your parents, siblings, or guardians will inevitably change. You have a great deal of influence over not just these changes, but also over the *kind* of long-term relationship you will have with your family.

Changes are seldom easy in any area of life, and it definitely takes time, patience, mutual respect, and love to navigate changing family relationships at this time in your life.

What type of relationship would you like to have with your family throughout the years? Would you like to live close, so you can drop in frequently and have daily contact? Would you prefer to live a distance away so that you have little contact? Is your choice somewhere between these two?

- As you move into your adult life, your relationships with your family change. How do emotional ties with siblings and other family members help create and maintain rewarding relationships?

• Going away to school means a change in the ties these students have with their families. How might leaving home for any reason change the way you relate to your family? What are your feelings about leaving home?

Here are two important things to keep in mind:

- While you will always be a son or daughter, you will begin to move into a new, more equal, role with parents as you become more independent. Some people take on this adult role more quickly than others. You may find it challenging at first to take care of yourself, make your own decisions, and take responsibility for your choices.

- Although relationships change over time, the type of relationship you establish with family members now will likely affect your lifelong relationships. Even if your relationships seem frustrating now, keeping in touch will make it easier to build closer ties in the future. Parents and adult children typically grow closer as the children reach their late twenties. Siblings often become closer when their "children" have grown. If you cut off contact and communication now, you eliminate the chance for more satisfying relationships later.

Family Life on the Stage

In a television drama, film, or stage play, the story line is told through a series of scenes. In a similar way, over time, family life goes through a series of scenes that are called "stages." These stages connect to tell the "story" of a particular family. Stages of family life are shown on page 136.

In general, the stages of family life are based on marriage, and the birth, growth, and launching of children. You can see how life changes as the family enters each new stage. Children have different needs and responsibilities at each stage, and parents have different needs and responsibilities at each stage.

There are many, many different kinds of families, such as single-parent families, childless couples, three-generation families, and stepfamilies. Regardless of family type, most families experience the stages outlined in this illustration.

High schools and colleges offer courses in human development. You could study a toddler's love of Winnie-the-Pooh!™ and a teen's steps toward independence. It's also very important, though, to understand **adult development**, or changes in how adults think and behave as they go through different phases, such as middle age and retirement. Chances are your parents and grandparents could be entering one or more of these stages. See pages 138-139.

Stages of Family Life

Beginning

Parental

Middle Age

Expanding　　**Developing**　　**Launching**

- The age of family members and the presence of children define the different stages of family life.

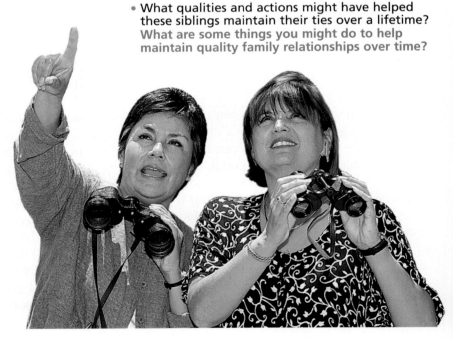

- What qualities and actions might have helped these siblings maintain their ties over a lifetime? What are some things you might do to help maintain quality family relationships over time?

One simple example is the "empty nest" phase, that time when a family's youngest child has graduated from high school and moved out. Parents who have organized all their interests around their children's activities can be left looking for new, meaningful things to do.

REASON

Through Life's Problems

Select the Best Choice

When solving practical problems, it's important for you to select the *best* choice among the alternatives. Read the situation below and examine how Aaron goes about selecting and justifying the best choice to solve his problem.

"Living in the dorm this first year of college, I learned to live with others, manage my time, balance study time and my job, *and* do my own laundry. But now I am back home and facing a new problem—Mom's given me a weekday curfew of midnight and 1:30 A.M. on weekends. I don't get off work until 11:30 P.M. I've talked with my friends, and some of their parents to help figure out what to do. I even wrote down all of the pros and cons of each choice. Now it's time to decide!

"The best choice is to talk with Mom about a new curfew," Aaron says to himself. "I've managed my time pretty well this past year and, with my current work schedule, I can justify my need for more flexibility. I understand Mom's desire to know where I am

and what I am doing—I think we can work that out.

She'll be pleased that I'm taking this approach and not just ignoring the curfew.

POSITIVE CONSEQUENCES   NEGATIVE CONSEQUENCES

Not do anything and just live by Mom's rules.

+ Me: Not much. I'll clearly know what is expected of me.
+ Mom: Knows when I'll be home; she is in control and comfortable.

- Me: Anger and frustration; tension will increase and communication decrease.
- Mom: Won't understand the tension; we won't establish an adult relationship.

Do as I please.

+ Me: I come and go as I want.
+ Mom: None.

- Me: More restrictions, chores, etc.
- Mom: Frustrated and angry; our relationship is tense.

Talk with Mom about negotiating new guidelines.

+ Me: I voice my concerns; living at home is better; talk with Mom as an adult; understand Mom's concerns.
+ Mom: Understands my concerns; accepts my adulthood; we establish an adult relationship.

- Me: Take time to have conversation.
- Mom: None.

►From Your Perspective

1 What information did Aaron have to support his choice? What values appear to have influenced his choice?

2 How was Aaron's choice ethical, workable, and based on relevant, reliable information?

3 How might the situation change if: the roles were reversed between Aaron and his mom; or if Aaron had to use public transportation to get to and from work?

4 If you were in Aaron's place, would you have selected the same choice? Why or why not? How might your values and personal situation have changed the outcome of this problem?

Stages of Adult Development

Although they vary from one person to another, most adults follow these general stages of development.

AN ADULT AT LAST. This stage begins around age 18 and lasts for 10 to 12 years. During this time, most people begin to have their own careers and their own families.

THE BIG 3-0. This is usually a time of serious self evaluation. At thirty, adults look at marriages, careers and parenting skills to see what needs improvement.

MID-LIFE QUESTIONS. Around age 45, adults again go through a stage of self-evaluation, giving serious thought to how to spend the rest of their lives. At the same time, their teen "children" are becoming more independent and leaving home.

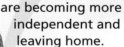

SETTLING DOWN. This period, which lasts until the mid-40s, is one of general stability. Adults tend to focus on family life and careers.

ACCEPTANCE. During their 50s and 60s, most people come to accept that life is too short to accomplish everything, so they concentrate on what is most important.

RETIREMENT TRANSITION. As people retire, they look for meaningful ways to contribute other than through paid employment. They volunteer, travel, spoil the grandchildren, and struggle with growing medical concerns.

OLD AGE. While many adults remain active forever, this stage is marked by intense reflection and, perhaps most challenging, adjustments to the loss of family members and friends.

ACTIVITY

Talk with people you know that have gone through each of these stages. Discuss the major life changes each person experienced in each stage.

At each stage there is a transition, and that means stress, tension, and likely conflict among family members. Whatever happens to each individual can affect the family as a whole.

When you look at the family from all the different perspectives, you can gain a better understanding of what is happening. "When my mom got laid off, I had to get a job and put off going to cosmetology school," said Dianne. "I was really disappointed and upset and I blamed Mom. It took me a while to realize that what had happened was especially hard on Mom because she felt like she'd failed all of us. When I started to see her side of the situation, all I could think about was helping rather than how mad at her I was."

Independent at Last

As teens mature, the family starts through the launch stage of family life. Some teens move out on their own. Others may live at home while they work or attend college or vocational school. A partial transition occurs when teens go off to college, but return home for the summer.

The launch stage brings mixed emotions for teens as well as their parents. You may eagerly anticipate your entry into the adult world, yet be frightened to think of being on your own, relying only on yourself.

Meanwhile, your parents must face up to the fact that they are aging. While proud of teens moving toward independence, they may have trouble gradually giving up parental authority and treating you as an equal.

The launch stage almost always coincides with the mid-life phase of adult development. This means conflict is inevitable. You need to be free and independent. Your parents still need to be needed and to keep things as they are. Understanding this can be very helpful, especially at those moments when you want to scream at each other.

• The conflicting needs of teen and adult development often create conflict in the launch stage of family life? What are some ways teens and their parents could avoid conflict during this stage?

• Graduation is a milestone in the lives of most teens and is sometimes considered the formal beginning of the launch stage. **How do you see your life changing after graduation?**

Attachment in Families

The long-term psychological and emotional ties between people in a close relationship is called **attachment.** You definitely feel attached to your closest friends. You probably feel attached to some people you work with. Over the course of your life, however, the most important attachments you are likely to have are to the people in your family.

There are four main characteristics of attachment:

• **Tolerance.** Tolerance is the ability to put up with a relationship, even though it may be unpleasant at times. In every extended family, for instance, there are people you cherish and people you simply tolerate. In your immediate family, tolerance is best expressed as openness to others' views, even if they are different from your own.

• **Acceptance.** Acceptance means that people recognize their differences without trying to change each other.

• **Respect.** Respect involves admiring others and appreciating their differences. Jarrod talks about his father like this. "I really admire how hard my dad works. He owns a small video rental store, and it is hard to make money with the competition from the big video chains. Personally, I don't like working in the store, but I respect what my dad has accomplished."

• **Affirmation and solidarity.** Affirmation and solidarity involve standing together in a relationship. Families with this quality strongly value the family itself. "There is nothing my parents treasure more than family," said Heather. "Whenever any decision has to be made, the first thing they say is "How will this affect our family?"

Instant Access

Your generation more than any other since the beginning of human kind, understands the impact that the Internet, cell phones, email, and pagers have on communication. From your home in the Midwest you can play chess with someone in England or exchange email with your grandparents. From your car phone you can reassure your parents you are fine (just running late). By wearing a pager, you can be available to your little sister while your parents are at work.

The best advice is this:

• Use whatever communication devices fit reasonably into your budget as a way to increase your communication with those you love and to keep yourself safe. A cell phone in an unfamiliar city can really increase your security.

• Remember not to give out personal information to someone you meet on the Internet. (You've probably heard this often, but it really is worth repeating.)

• Consider surprising your immediate family by creating a Web homepage in its honor.

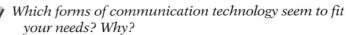

Voicing Your Opinion

1 *Which forms of communication technology seem to fit your needs? Why?*

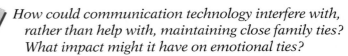

2 *How could communication technology interfere with, rather than help with, maintaining close family ties? What impact might it have on emotional ties?*

In general, the more of these qualities a relationship has, the closer and more meaningful it becomes. When family members work to strengthen each of these qualities in their relationships, they usually gain more satisfaction and support. Family ties become more meaningful and rewarding. What qualities do you think are important in the long-term attachment you'd like to establish with your family?

The Ultimate Support System

Your brother listens patiently as you talk about problems with a girlfriend. Your mother teaches you how to change the oil on your first car. Your granddad packs your lunch just minutes before you have to leave for work. Your older sister sits up with you when you are sick.

Families can be considered the ultimate support system. They are usually available at any time of the day or night.

Not only does your family give you support, but you help them as well by ironing your mom's blouse when she's running late, answering your sister's questions about homework, loaning money to your brother for an evening out, or working with your dad to fix a leaky faucet.

• Attachment is an important quality in maintaining family ties. **What qualities of attachment do you think this family shares?**

Emotional support may be the most important kind of support a family provides. "From the time I was a little girl," Jody said, "my grandmother would say, 'If anybody hurts you, let me know.' I know I have to deal with my problems myself, but I always loved her for that support."

In most families, members expect to help and support each other and usually the stronger the ties, the greater the support.

Strengthening Your Family Connection

Most strained relationships within a family can be improved. If you feel you are completely stuck, consider working with a religious leader or counselor to help yourself and your family. In the meantime here are other steps you can consider.

Transition to Adulthood

Probably the most stressful element in your changing relationship with your parents is learning new ways to respond to each other. Keep in mind that parents often take their cues from teens. This means if you are responsible, trustworthy, and act like an adult, they will treat you like one. Kristi said, "I complained a lot because I didn't think my parents treated me like an adult. One day my mom said, 'When you act like an adult, I'll treat you like one. Do you support yourself financially? Cook your own meals? Keep your home clean? Do your own laundry?' I realized that I wanted to be taken care of like a kid with meals and clean clothes, but that I also wanted the privileges of an adult to come and go as I pleased. I figured out that Mom wasn't going to let me have it both ways."

The great news for you is that your changing relationship with your parents may become one of friendship. You and your parents have a wonderful opportunity to respect and enjoy each other for the special and unique people you are.

T
I
P
S

Whether you continue to live at home after you finish school or return after some time on your own, there are several ways you can increase your chances of living with your family and liking it.

- Show your respect—family members are people, too.
- Be a problem solver—don't let problems turn to conflict.
- Give others the benefit of the doubt.
- Do Not Disturb—everyone needs some place and opportunity for privacy.
- Share in household responsibilities.
- Keep relationships on an adult basis. Avoid the trap of old parent-child roles.
- Make friends, have fun, and enjoy life.

Accept Responsibilities

Adulthood involves a lot of different kinds of responsibility. Accepting these responsibilities willingly, shows maturity on your part. Here are some of the responsibilities you can expect to change:

- **Financial:** By paying toward rent and food you are demonstrating a cooperative spirit.
- **Housework:** Consider really pitching in or even taking full responsibilities for certain chores. Mike is responsible for the laundry for his family. He usually does the wash late at night while he is studying.
- **Going the extra mile:** Running errands for your grandparents, teaching a younger sibling how to cook macaroni and cheese, and driving two hours to see your sister perform in a college musical—these all show that you are a strong contributor in your family's support system.

Plan Activities Together

In most families with children, parents plan family activities. However, one way to build family ties is to plan and organize a family activity yourself. This is especially important if you are living on your own.

Nichole said, "My dad doesn't like sports, but Mom and I do. So sometimes I invite her to go to a game with me or invite her when I'm playing. She always acts grateful for an invitation and I enjoy having her along."

• No matter what hour of the day or night, most parents generally are a source of support. Why is a source of support necessary as you make the transition into your adult life?

• Mutually enjoyable activities offer opportunities for young adults and their parents to adjust to their changing relationships. **How do you see your relationship changing with your parents as you move into your adult life?**

Make A Good Effort

Good family relationships don't happen automatically. They take work and effort. One person alone can't magically create loving and lifelong ties. You can, however, make a really strong effort in maintaining and strengthening your family ties.

Your positive support and help, your appreciation, and your willingness to assume adult responsibilities tell your parents that you value your family. This also sets you on a very solid path toward a rewarding and meaningful future with your family of origin while creating a family of your own.

• Sometimes an unexpected gift is the best way to show appreciation to a parent. **What are some ways that you might show appreciation?**

Show Your Appreciation

You probably know that people tend to take for granted those who are closest to them. Then remember that appreciation can go a long way in strengthening family ties.

Tell your brother how good the meal is when he cooks. Say *thanks* for the new tie your stepmom gave you for a job interview. A hug may be one way to say "I'm glad you are here for me" when your dad listens to the details of a bad day.

No family is perfect. Every family has its weaknesses, but every family has strengths as well. Letting others know you appreciate them is one way to build family ties that will last a lifetime.

Understanding Key Concepts

- Just as a newborn goes through predictable stages, so the family, as a unit, goes through predictable stages.
- Relationships within the family change during different stages.
- Understanding family interactions from the view of both children and adults make a big difference in moving through these stages.
- The launch stage—when teens move into adulthood—is often very challenging. This is because parents and teens have such different (and often conflicting) needs.
- Qualities such as tolerance, acceptance, respect, and affirmation and solidarity, are essential in maintaining family ties.
- For most people, families are the ultimate support system.
- Your future relationship with your parents will be strengthened by simple gestures such as planning events together or staying in touch through email, phone calls, and letters.

Checking Your Knowledge

1. Explain why stages of family life are useful in understanding families even though there are many exceptions to these stages.

2. Summarize how teen and adult development issues can cause conflict in the launch stage of family development. Give an example.

3. Identify the four qualities of attachment. How do these qualities contribute to satisfying relationships in a family?

4. What is the most important type of family support as identified in the text? Do you agree or disagree? Why or why not?

5. How do taking responsibility, planning activities, and showing appreciation contribute to strong family ties?

Making TRANSITIONS

Attachment in the Workplace

An understanding of qualities of attachment can also be useful in the workplace. Developing teamwork on the job is one way to increase employees' productivity. The more qualities of attachment that exist among coworkers, the more they are likely to work together as a team.

Assume you are a shift manager supervising six employees. You have been given a budget of $100 to plan an event that will help employees identify themselves as a team and that will help increase the ties among them. What kind of activity would promote tolerance, acceptance, respect, and solidarity among the employees? What other ways could you encourage these qualities at work?

STRENGTHENING *Life* SKILLS

Building Attachment

Share three affirmations with your parents, your siblings, your friends, or coworkers. You may especially want to share one with someone you are going out with. Use a note, an email message, a phone call, or a face-to-face conversation.

After you've shared your affirmations, respond to the following questions:
- Did sharing your affirmations appear to strengthen your attachment? Why or why not?
- What other things might you do to strengthen your attachments with others?

Applying Thinking Skills

1. **Recognizing assumptions**. What assumptions could cause a young adult, who is living at home, to demand that all parental rules and restrictions be removed? Should parents remove all rules and restriction? Why or why not?

2. **Compare and contrast.** How is an adult-adult relationship similar to and different from a parent-child relationship?

3. **Predicting consequences.** What consequences could occur if a young adult never calls or visits home unless help is needed? How could this impact future relationships?

4. **Drawing conclusions**. What impact might the following have on young adult-parent relationships: postponing marriage until age 30; becoming an unmarried parent at age 15; moving away and back home four times between ages 20 and 25; being sent overseas on the job for two years?

Practical Applications

1. **Taking a survey.** Survey at least three older adults in your community. Ask them to identify their three longest lasting attachments in life. How might this help you in your own attachments in the future?

2. **Analyzing support systems.** Make two lists. Title one "People Who Support Me" and the other "People I Support." Where is your balance between giving and getting support? If there is an imbalance, what could you do to correct it? Where do you give and get the most support—family, friends, or others?

3. **Strengthening family ties.** Identify at least two activities you could do that would strengthen the ties in your family. Put your plan into action. Later evaluate how effective the experience was. Did you feel successful?

4. **Examining the trend of living at home**. The trend is for young adults today to live at home longer than was common in the past. What factors may be causing or contributing to this trend?

CHAPTER 9

Relating to Others

What You Will Learn...

- Relationships inevitably change as you go through young adulthood.
- Positive ways to deal with changing relationships.
- Ways to establish and maintain effective relationships at work.
- The importance of friendship throughout your life.
- The development of friendships between family members and those outside the family.
- Ways to nurture friendships and keep them from ending.

Terms for Success

mobility
values conflict

R ae sat alone in the student cafe, staring at her plate. She blinked back tears from her eyes. She couldn't eat this food. It wasn't edible.

Rae had chosen this University for its excellent drama school. She hadn't thought she'd be this lonely, or that everything would be so different.

"Excuse me. Can I sit here?"

Rae looked up at a vaguely familiar face. "Sure."

The young man pulled out a chair. "I'm Lamar Eaton. I'm in your British lit class. Every time you open your mouth, I tell myself, "I've got to ask where she's from. You can't be local."

Rae smiled shyly and told him.

Lamar looked impressed. "Wow! What made you come here?"

Rae told him about the well-regarded drama school. "They hold a nationally-known performing arts festival here every spring," she added.

"I've heard of that," Lamar recalled. "I didn't realize it was that big. Me, I'm taking just enough English classes to get by. Physics, that's my field."

"Physics?" Rae said. "You understand physics?"

Lamar shrugged. "I guess so far, at least."

Rae shook her head. "I gave up on science somewhere between biology and chemistry."

Lamar laughed. "Well, I'll make you a deal. I'll help you with science, if you'll help me with Shakespeare."

Rae smiled broadly. "It's a deal."

Lamar stood to leave. "By the way, the food here is lousy. Try Manny's Diner on Grant Street. They could help the folks here with their cooking."

Rae felt buoyant and energized. Where was Grant Street? Suddenly, she had plans for dinner.

> **?** What parts of this conversation make you think perhaps Rae and Lamar could develop a friendship on campus? How have these two individuals helped each other in just this brief exchange?

A Lifetime of Relationships

Rae's friendship with Lamar began over bad food in a lonely student cafeteria. Today, you probably will have many opportunities to meet new people—at home, at school, in your neighborhood, in your community, and at your place of worship. Every single day offers you the chance to develop, enjoy, and learn from past, current, and future relationships.

Your relationships with people began as soon as you were born. You probably first learned to relate to immediate family members, other relatives, and close family friends. After awhile, new friends, acquaintances, neighbors, peers, and classmates entered your life. Others, such as coworkers and employers, may have followed.

Life Changes

Wes and Carlos have been best friends for years. Now that Carlos is going away to college, Wes worries that their friendship won't be the same anymore. Wes has enrolled in the local technical school to study electronics. Carlos wants to get away from home and see what college life is all about.

Carlos and Wes have promised each other that they'll get together as often as possible. They also plan to keep in touch with each other through frequent email messages. Both young men value their friendship and do not want it to change.

• You've been relating to others all of your life—family, friends, and community members. **How are your relationships likely to change in your adult life?**

This, though, is very unlikely. Just as surely as day changes into night, relationships with others also change. This happens for many reasons:

- A move to a new community or environment.
- A change at work. Promotions, layoffs, and transfers can affect friendships.
- People change. Think about the kind of person you were five years ago and how you have changed since then. Maybe you traveled to a foreign country and learned about a different culture. Perhaps you went through a serious illness or experienced the death of a loved one. Any of these instances—whether triumphal or tragic—has the potential to affect how you relate to others.

It can be scary or sad when life and relationships change. You may experience feelings of insecurity, fear, loneliness, and even guilt. Olivia is worried about her decision to commute 45 miles to a cosmetology school. She will be sharing a ride with three people she hardly knows. The three are close friends and are already halfway through the program. Olivia fears she will be treated like an outsider whose only purpose is to share car expenses.

Olivia's feelings of insecurity are normal and are often experienced by people going through change. Working to develop a positive attitude about the situation can help. If Olivia envisions herself being accepted by the three, rather than rejected, she can begin to see them as individuals just like herself. In fact, they may be worried that she will not like them.

Another way to deal with change is to be active and involved in daily life. For example, by working hard at school or in the workplace you can help reduce your anxiety about long-

• As you move into your adult roles, you'll find yourself relating to a broader spectrum of people. What opportunities do you see in increasing the variety of people you relate to? What qualities might be most important to developing adult relationships?

distance friendships. You can take the opportunity to learn as much as you can, and at the same time develop new relationships. You can continue to nurture your long-distance friendships by keeping in touch and sharing your experiences.

Unfortunately, feelings of guilt sometimes accompany changes in relationships. Emma is excited about joining the army, but she also feels guilty about leaving her mother and two younger brothers. Emma's feelings of guilt are understandable, even though her mother tries to reassure her that her decision is a good one.

Talking with a trusted adult or counselor may be helpful whenever you experience uncomfortable feelings because of changes in relationships. Friendly support and assurance that you are not alone in your insecurities can be crucial at this stage of your life.

Adult Relationships

Relationships tend to change as people enter young adulthood. Worksites, college campuses, community organizations, and religious organizations are places where many wonderful lifelong friendships begin.

Relationships formed during young adulthood often consist of a broader spectrum of people than those formed during high school. These include individuals who may be different in age, background, and experience. Some will have different cultures, religion, and ethnicity. Accepting diversity in your relationships can add interest and enjoyment to your life.

- There will likely be some people in the world that you'll find a challenge to work with. **How you respond to them can make or break your relationship. What are some approaches you could take in learning to work successfully with others?**

REASON

Through Life's Problems

Outline and Take Action

Problems are not solved until a reasoned decision is put into action. Taking action requires careful planning and implementation. Read the following situation and study how Ryan outlines and implements a plan for action.

"I feel good about the decision I've made," Ryan said to himself as he prepared to go to work. "I know it is in my best interest to try to make new friends at work. I don't see my old friends because they work during the day and I'm working second shift in this new job. Many of my other buddies have left for the armed forces or college. Very few people at work interact. Granted, we're all at different points in our lives with spouses, kids, and other activities, but we all could benefit from being friends with one another. Now I just need to think about how I can make new friends at work.

"First, I can try to strike up conversations during the break at the water fountain or vending machines. It's hard for me to initiate conversation, but I can

do it. The key is getting coworkers involved in a conversation of interest to them.

"Next, I can set the goal of eating lunch with someone three times a week. Most of my coworkers pack their food and eat in the lunchroom. I don't always have to leave the building to eat. I've been using that as an excuse to not talk to people. So I'll just pack my food and eat with them. Maybe I can find out what they like to do.

"Another action I can take is to participate in the company's volleyball league. Though I haven't ever really played volleyball, it would be an opportunity to get to know people and have fun. I need to find out when I must register to be part of the team.

"The toughest thing I need to do is learn to call people I already know by their first names. Some of these people are parents of my high school buddies and I've called them Mr. or Mrs. So-and-So all my life. It seems strange to call them Dick or Helena. They've all told me I need to use their first names, but it sure feels awkward. Maybe I need to just try it someday rather than let my discomfort get in my way."

Ryan thought about the plans he made. "I'm getting excited about this. I might as well start today!"

► From Your Perspective

1 What kind of assumptions might you make about Ryan's work situation? What might Ryan's problem have been?

2 What skills has Ryan identified to carry out his plans? What other skills might he also need?

3 What barriers exist for Ryan that might prevent him from taking action? How can he overcome these barriers?

4 How might Ryan organize the various tasks needed to achieve his choice of making new friends?

5 What similar situation might you anticipate needing to take action in the future? How might you outline and implement a plan of action?

Relating at Work

Whether you are employed at a small business or a large company, you probably will work with others. Most people are happier and enjoy their work more if they are on good terms with those around them. Also, if coworkers enjoy working together, they tend to be more effective, which makes their employer happy. This, in turn, can result in pay raises and promotions.

Accepting Differences

Getting along with coworkers isn't always easy. Because no two people are exactly alike, they may see things differently and react in different ways to the same situation. Different attitudes and beliefs can lead to conflicts at work.

To get along with coworkers, you need to accept them as worthy individuals. Try to understand the other person's attitudes and behaviors. If you do this, you will be doing your part to encourage good working relationships.

If one of your coworkers is extremely difficult to get along with, try to understand some of the reasons for his or her behavior. Perhaps a bad experience had a negative effect on the person, or maybe your coworker has serious problems at home. If challenges with your coworkers continue, you may want to consider some assertiveness training.

Whatever the situation, try to do more than your share to develop a good working relationship. Someday, you may be the one in need of some extra understanding, patience, and cooperation.

Being Professional

When you're new on a job, it's important to avoid spending a great deal of time idly talking to others. Just be friendly and ask questions about your work. Most experienced coworkers will help you get started and offer support. Once you understand your job, do the work yourself. This can't be stressed enough.

Work & Friendship

TIPS

To help keep friendships at work from interfering with effectiveness on your job:

- Learn your company's policy about work relationships, and closely follow the rules.
- Keep friendship and work separate as much as possible.
- Do not break coworkers' confidences.
- Avoid any situation in which a friendship puts you or a friend in a compromised position.
- Avoid gossip at work.
- Be careful that your body language, voice, or words are not too familiar when you're talking to coworkers and employers.
- Avoid name-dropping or bragging.

When you're new at work, it may be hard to determine how formal or informal you should be with your employer and coworkers. A good rule of thumb is to be more formal than informal. This doesn't mean you can't smile and be pleasant to everyone.

Avoiding Disputes

One of the best ways to maintain a good working relationship with others is to mind your own business. No matter where you work, there probably will be disputes between people. It does not pay to get involved in such disagreements. The best thing to do is to remain neutral. Working hard and doing your best can help you stay safely on the sidelines, rather than in the middle of someone else's problem.

Establishing Boundaries

Jasmine knows that it is important to maintain good relationships at work. However, she is careful that the relationships she forms are friendly and casual, rather than too close or personal. The exceptions are several longtime friends of hers who work for the same company but are in other departments. By establishing boundaries or limits regarding her other work relationships, Jasmine avoids getting involved in unprofessional or uncomfortable situations with coworkers and her employer.

Unfortunately, some work relationships turn into cliques or closed groups. Close relationships that develop into office romances can cause all kinds of problems and complications at work—especially if the couple later breaks up and continues to work together.

Learning from Mentors

Many companies have mentors for new employees. These are role models and advisors who introduce you to the coworkers, work environment, and explain company policy. Most mentoring relationships, whether casual or formal, can be helpful to young adults in the world of work.

• Establishing effective boundaries is essential to good working relationships. Getting involved in others' disputes tends to make you less productive. What are some ways that you could distance yourself from problems at work, but still maintain good working relationships?

The Power of Friendship

Friends can be a source of affection and good times; and, in moments of despair, friends can offer hope and solace. Unfortunately, friendship is something many people take for granted.

They are unaware of how powerful and positive friendship can be.

- Good friends can help you feel worthwhile and valued. Several years ago, a group of students in California shaved their heads so their friend and classmate, who was undergoing treatments for cancer, would not feel self-conscious about his bald appearance. His dozen friends kept their heads shaved until they learned their friend's cancer was in remission.

Their friendship, both genuine and powerful, provided support and encouragement rather than hollow offers of assistance.

- In some ways, friendship is more important and powerful today than ever before. One reason is because of the trend toward smaller nuclear families. With fewer members in the family, friends often gain increased importance.

- Another reason for the increased importance of friendship is the **mobility**, or geographical relocation, of individuals and families due to school, work, retirement, or other factors. When people move, family members may not be around for frequent contact, so new friendships are often formed at the new site.

• A mentor can serve as your personal guide in all aspects of your work situation. In what ways could having a mentor help you best?

• Enjoying friendships with a variety of people can help get you through some of the insecurities about moving out into the world. **What changes about moving into adulthood concern you most?**

Making New Friends

Rachel moved to a new city about 200 miles from her hometown after being offered the job of her dreams. When she arrived, she decided to follow a simple plan:

- She visited service organizations like Friends of the Library, hospital volunteer groups, and Junior League to see if she might want to join.
- She began visiting places of worship to see where she might become involved.
- She joined the softball team at her place of work.

Most importantly, Rachel showed genuine interest in her coworkers when her mentor introduced her throughout her division in the company. She made an effort to hold conversations during breaks and lunch.

Family Friendships

Pedro and his brother are very good friends. They like to spend time together, playing ball or working on their cars. Twenty-year-old Amber counts her mom as one of her closest friends. She and her mom have become even better friends since Amber finished high school and got a job in a neighboring town. They enjoy talking to each other on the telephone and getting together on the weekends.

Internet Friendships

Joe was doing research on the Internet at his college library when he decided to take a short study break and enter a chess chat room. Twenty minutes later he'd met people from three different countries and had learned a new game strategy he was eager to try.

After a week Joe had a regular chess partner from Canada, but he also had cut into his valuable study time.

Internet Interference

Even though the Internet is fun, fascinating, and a way to make friends, it can be a potential source of problems for some people. You may know people who find the Net so riveting that they spend vast amounts of time online. In fact, some people may not have much of a life beyond the computer.

Their friends and acquaintances are accessed only on the computer terminal.

Keeping Your Perspective

In general, however, as long as other obligations and personal relationships are not sacrificed, time spent on the Internet can be worthwhile. Nevertheless, it is important not to lose perspective whenever you are tempted to spend time on marathon online sessions. Keep boundaries on your time.

When chatting on the Net, always avoid revealing your residential address, phone number, dates you or your family may be out of town, and other information that someone might use as an aid in theft, fraud, or other crimes.

Voicing Your Opinion

 1 *What advice might you give to a friend who is considering meeting and going out with someone she met on the Internet?*

2 *In your opinion, what are the pros and cons of Internet friendships?*

Ideally, a relative has the potential to be more like a chosen friend than a relationship that is an accident of fate. However, age, differences, and unresolved rivalries—especially among siblings—sometimes get in the way of close family friendships. Often, these obstacles become less important as people approach adulthood.

Extended family members, such as cousins, aunts, uncles, nieces, nephews, and grandparents, frequently become good friends. By sharing family traditions and memories, relatives can develop very special and unique friendships with each other.

Nurturing Friendships

Do you want the keys to nourishing your friendships? Then be a good listener, show sympathy to each other, and have a good sense of humor. Make time for each other. Be honest and trusting with each other. Trust as the cornerstone of a relationship can help friends successfully deal with problems that may come their way. Situations involving jealousy, borrowing or loaning money, and maintaining long-distance relationships are more easily dealt with when both parties trust each other—and are worthy of the other's trust.

Whether you live near or far, there are a variety of ways to improve and maintain friendships. Frequent phone calls, letters, email messages, or personal visits are just a few of them. Make a point to note friends' birthdays and other special occasions on a calendar and follow up with a card, call, visit, or small gift.

• Friendships with your family members can develop and change as you move into your adult role. **What qualities do you cherish most in your family members? In what ways are you friends with your family members?**

Making Friends

T I P S

Whether you live in a small town or a large city, now is the time when you will develop some of the most interesting friends of your lifetime. Try to make friends:

- In your dorm or apartment complex.
- With the people who provide services to you—the mail carrier, your newspaper carrier, the clerks at the shops you frequent.
- In a service organization or volunteer group.
- At work (while keeping in mind the boundaries already mentioned).
- At a local restaurant or at the gym.

Preserving Friendships

An angry word, an ignored phone call, an insult said without premeditation, or plan—all these can trigger the end of a friendship. So can unrealistic expectations about the relationship. If friendships should end because they are harmful or destructive, that is one thing. However, if friendships have value and you want to keep them, there are ways to restore or prevent them from fading away:

- Express to your friends just how much you appreciate them.

- Identify and emphasize similar values. **Values conflict**—different priorities, goals, or lifestyles that clash—tends to threaten friendships. A difference in interests is one thing. A similarity in values is key to a solid friendship.
- Make time for friends during their tough times. Let your friends know how much you appreciate their support when you are down.

Living in a Diverse Community

Just as you want to be understood and appreciated because of the kind of person you are inside, so do others in your community. Even if they worship in a different way, speak with an accent, or have a skin tone that's different from yours, people need to be accepted as valued members of society. In fact, acknowledgment and appreciation of people's diversity can help bring about strong, caring community relations.

Ask yourself:

- "If I were of another race or culture, if I grew up speaking another language, how would I feel here?"
- "What special talents might I contribute to the community if I were of another race or culture? How might these talents benefit others?"

Thoughtful answers to these questions can help you develop *empathy*, the ability to understand what someone else is experiencing. You empathize when you put yourself in another's place and try to see things from his or her point of view.

Close-Up

When Friendships Don't Work

Changes in circumstances often make it difficult to maintain casual friendships. Trigger incidents, such as angry outbursts due to jealousy, can end even close friendships. Value conflicts and unmet expectations often destroy friendships.

No matter who ends a friendship—even if it was your choice—you are likely to go through a kind of mourning that typically follows the end of any significant relationship. Try to incorporate the best memories of your friendship into your collection of memories.

Making new friends and strengthening your commitments to other long-time friends can help tremendously. Participating in activities such as hobbies, travel, volunteer work, or sports are other positive ways to deal with a friendship that no longer works.

Think about a friendship you've had that hasn't worked. What factors affected the break in your friendship? What might you do differently in the future in establishing and strengthening friendships?

Similarities and Differences

People are easily drawn to others with similar interests and lifestyles. This is only natural. However, sometimes people live in such isolation and exclusion that they miss out on opportunities to understand and appreciate individuals who are different from themselves. As a result, they may form a *prejudice*, or an unfair or biased opinion, against others.

Prejudice involves forming an opinion about individuals or groups of people, before—or instead of—getting to know them through personal experience. Prejudice often stems from fear, suspicion, or ignorance. It limits how you see others and how you see yourself. Prejudice comes in many forms. People devalue others based on economic standing, age, race or physical condition.

Any kind of prejudice can lead to discrimination. When people are discriminated against, they are unfairly left out of certain groups, activities, or employment opportunities.

When people discriminate against others, they lose out on opportunities to enrich their own lives. For instance, Julius has a great sense of humor and is fun to be around. Unfortunately, some of his coworkers have let his need for a wheelchair stop them from getting to know him. "Most people know very little about having a disability or how to behave around someone who does. Sometimes they think I'm helpless," Julius sighs.

Prejudice and discrimination are learned, often at an early age, but can be overcome. Learning the real facts about people and groups helps. Then you can begin to identify your own prejudices. When you have done this, it helps to look for positive ways to get to know people for whom you felt prejudice. In time, you may notice that you have more similarities than differences with each other.

• Staying in contact with friends and making it a point to remember special occasions are just some ways to maintain friendships. **What are some ways that you keep connected with friends?**

Understanding Key Concepts

- As soon as you are born, you begin to learn patterns of relating to people.
- Relationships are not static; they change throughout your lifetime.
- Moving from adolescence into young adulthood often results in a greater diversity of relationships.
- Getting along with employers and coworkers increases job satisfaction and work effectiveness while reducing conflict at work.
- Establishing boundaries can help prevent unprofessional or uncomfortable relationships at work.
- Friendships are very important because of trends toward smaller families, geographic mobility, postponement of marriage and child rearing.
- Family members often overcome age disparities or rivalries to become close friends.
- Developing empathy and overcoming prejudice are keys to living in harmony within your community.

Checking Your Knowledge

1. Explain how changes in a person's life may affect his or her relationships with others.
2. Describe some of the changes in relationships that often occur as individuals enter young adulthood.
3. Give examples of how to relate effectively and professionally at work.
4. Give examples of family friendships in people's lives.
5. Think about a relationship you have with a close friend or family member. What actions have each of you taken to maintain and improve your friendship?
6. Describe a situation in which you've observed prejudice. What happened in this situation? Give two suggestions showing how the situation could be improved.

Making TRANSITIONS

Overcoming Prejudice in the Workplace

Prejudice can prevent healthy workplace relationships from forming. Assume you are the team leader in your work area. You supervise several employees. You notice that two of your employees appear prejudiced toward one team member who is from a different country.

- What kind of actions might you take to deal with the behavior of the two employees?
- What might be the positive and negative consequences of your actions?
- How might you help encourage respect and tolerance among your team members?

STRENGTHENING *Life* SKILLS

Seeking Friendship

Finding friendship seems to be easier for some than it is for others. Some people have plenty of friends in the casual acquaintance category, but find getting to know people on a deeper level difficult. Try the following activity and then answer the question.

- Teach family members or friends how to send email messages and how to set up Web pages with their interests or hobbies.

- What impact could this have on their friendships with each other and with you?

Applying Thinking Skills

1. **Clarifying fact or fiction.** People sometimes avoid developing friendships with persons of a different culture, religion, or ethnicity because they believe they have nothing in common. How would you respond to this position?

2. **Drawing conclusions**. Think about young adults you know who are employed or attend school. Which of them seem to balance their lives well, making time for school, work, family, friendships, and volunteer commitments? What suggestions do you think they might give others to help them balance similar parts of their lives? Explain.

3. **Considering consequences.** Think about the job you have—or would like to have someday. What are some possible advantages, and disadvantages, of developing close relationships there? How might the situation change if one or more of the relationships ended because of a conflict between them? In what ways might other coworkers be affected because of the changed relationships? Explain.

4. **Comparing and contrasting.** Think about family and nonfamily friendships you have experienced. In what ways are your friendships with family members similar to your friendships with persons outside the family? In what ways are they different? Defend your reasoning.

Practical Applications

1. **Taking time to reflect.** Older people often have a long history of interesting relationships. Interview an older relative or other senior citizen about his or her lifetimes of relationships. Write a brief report summarizing your findings.

2. **Showing support.** Write a letter, song, poem, or story to give to a friend, expressing what the friendship means to you. After doing this, consider the outcome. How did it feel to show support and appreciation to your friend?

3. **Reversing roles**. Select a partner you do not know well and who is different from you in some way. Take turns pretending to be each other and describe your typical day, your friendships, and your family. What was the most interesting fact you learned about the other individual? In what ways are your values, goals, daily activities, and relationships similar and different?

CHAPTER 10

More Than Just Friends

What You Will Learn...

- How the changing roles of men and women affect relationships.
- Ways to meet the kind of people you'd like to go out with.
- Qualities of healthy dating relationships.
- The myths and realities of acquaintance and date rape.
- Positive ways to deal with feelings from a broken relationship.

Terms for Success

autonomy
platonic relationships

Maria scrambled up the slope, grabbing the bare branches of shrubs for handholds. At the top of the ridge, she caught her breath and gazed across the valley. "So," she turned to her companion, "what do you think?"

Keith cleared the brambles and joined Maria on the path. He scanned the view of meadow and scenic woods with a surprised look. "It's beautiful," he said. "I see why you get back here so often."

Maria beamed. "Let's take the historical tour." She led him down the hill. They came across a pile of large, jagged rocks, sticking up from the soil. "That is an ancient Scottish castle," she explained. "At least, it was when I was twelve years old."

"You had a castle?" Keith said. "All I had was a tree house."

Maria pointed to the forested slope beyond. "I used to go sledding in those woods with my brothers. They'd tell me they heard a tiger, then run off without me."

Keith laughed. "I once left my sister in our basement and told her to look out for the lions."

Maria gasped. "You were awful!"

"I was nine," he protested.

They circled around the clearing and headed back uphill, talking and laughing. At last they returned to the brow of the ridge, and crept down the incline to the road and Maria's car.

"What a great place to grow up," Keith said as they drove to Maria's parents' home for dinner. "I'm glad you showed me that."

Maria felt her face begin to glow. "Well . . . I don't drag just anyone out here, but I thought you might be interested."

"I am," Keith replied. "Very interested."

A minute later, Maria could sense his eyes still on her. She glanced at him slyly. "What are you looking at?" she demanded.

He paused a moment and answered, "You."

In what ways have Keith and Maria demonstrated respect, humor, and caring as they explore a possible romantic relationship?

Developing Your Social Life

Maria and Keith are at very exciting times in their lives. Both are starting their own paths separate from those of their parents. They are learning a great deal about themselves, and now they'll learn about each other through a committed, meaningful relationship.

When it comes to social life, young adulthood can be both exciting and scary. Being on your own, in new situations, is cause for both celebration and concern. You may have questions such as:

- Where is the balance between a social life and work or school?
- How will independence affect my relationships?

Jeff, who moved to a nearby city to attend school, is starting to develop a healthy adult social life. He worried a bit about moving away from home and into his own apartment. He learned quickly that adulthood means having many choices and responsibilities. Some of these choices are different from those his parents and older siblings had faced when they were just starting out.

Jeff has made several good friends and has begun casually going out with a young woman named Deanna. She surprised him one evening by taking him out to dinner and a movie—and insisting that she pay for everything.

On the way home, Jeff thought of how different the evening had been from the evenings his parents had described to him about the first few times they had gone out. Jeff's relationships are more equal with regard to gender and other differences.

Couples today are more likely to share expenses and take equal responsibility for planning their time together. They are also more likely to delay marriage and to delay having children when they are married.

• Finding new ways to develop your social life is an exciting challenge. **What are some ways that you might like to meet people?**

• Young adult relationships tend to be more egalitarian with respect to gender. How might this be different from the experiences of others in your family?

Enjoying Single Life

Twenty-two-year-old Robert is a news reporter in a midwestern city about 300 miles from his family. In his first year at the paper, he developed many friendships in the office with both men and women. Amiable, sincere, talented, and hardworking, Robert has caught the attention of single women who'd like to spend more time with him socially. He's also caught the attention of newspaper management, who want to consider him for a promotion.

One of Robert's best friends is Margo, another reporter who has helped him with interviewing and writing skills. Outside the office, they roller-blade, play on the paper's softball team, and go to plays together.

They talk to each other like any other close friends: they discuss work, family—and people they'd like to go out with. What they share is a **platonic relationship**, one in which there is affection, but no romance.

Refresh your memory about these terms:

- **autonomy:** The ability to direct your own life independently.
- **compatible:** Capable of existing together in harmony.
- **societal:** Relating to society.

- Having time to spend on your personal interests is one of the benefits of single adult life. What interest do you spend your free time on?

Platonic relationships allow individuals to grow in friendship, and to understand and feel comfortable with each other while keeping boundaries regarding dating. This is emotional intimacy without physical intimacy, and its rewards are vast.

While at college, Robert was a resident adviser in a co-ed dorm. Living on a men's unit, he was also responsible for enforcing rules with all residents. He became friends with many of the young women in the dorm. They often sat talking late into the night in the TV room. They talked about classes, campus events, and also about the people they were going out with at the time. In fact, Robert was able to help some of the women with questions about their boyfriends, and the women were able to help him with questions about the young women he was seeing in the residence hall next door.

Meeting People

There are many places and ways to meet people you might enjoy socializing and going out with:

- **In the community.** Co-ed sports teams, dance clubs, environmental organizations, and community service groups are just a few possibilities. Look around your community for activities that interest you. Check out local newsletters and newspapers, and ask friends and acquaintances for suggestions.

- **Blind dates.** Being introduced to others by people you mutually know, or a blind date, is another way to meet people. Blind dates can be interesting and fun. To be more comfortable in such situations, it's a good idea to follow some basic rules: 1) find out about your date, such as workplace, hometown, and personal interests; 2) consider going out with another couple the first time you meet someone; 3) and on additional outings consider meeting at a neutral and safe location until you know each other better.

Overcoming Social Anxiety

Are you an outgoing person who enjoys being around people and making friends? Or are you shy and anxious when you're around others? Perhaps you fit somewhere in the middle, comfortable around close friends but less than outgoing among strangers.

Everyone experiences social anxiety or discomfort at some time. To reduce your own anxiety, try to emphasize the concepts of grace, common sense, and good manners:

- *Mentally take one step back, take one deep breath, and identify something positive about the situation you're in.*

- *Avoid being clever at the expense of the people around you. Avoid anyone who does this.*

- *If you are nervous as you meet someone new, and you need some time to gather your thoughts, simply ask your acquaintance an open-ended question like, "What's your favorite part of work or school?"*

- *There is a wonderful expression: "Never cut what you can untie." If you are thrown into an awkward social event and are having a terrible time, get out of it as quietly as possible. Don't make a scene. The exception is if you feel physically threatened and must act out to get the help you need.*

- *If you are in a comfortable, friendly environment and see that someone is struggling, make every effort to help.*

How have you dealt with social anxiety in the past?

• Meeting people at community sponsored events is one way to begin developing your social life in a new place. **In what types of situations do you most like to meet people?**

- **In groups.** Many young adults enjoy dating in groups. Going with several other people to community functions, sporting events, or other activities can be less stressful than going out as a single couple. Group dating provides a casual environment for getting to know people and establishing friendships at your own pace. Premature romantic attachments are less likely to develop during group dating.

- **At work.** Some people consider the workplace a good place to meet people they might enjoy going out with. Coworkers who share mutual interests and goals often develop friendships that extend beyond work. As you studied in previous chapters, career counselors recommend that working relationships remain neutral rather than romantic.

• Although many successful relationships have developed for people who have met through the personals, it's wise to keep certain precautions in mind. **What might concern you most about meeting someone through the personals?**

Recognizing Healthy Relationships

How can you recognize healthy dating relationships? Start by looking for the same qualities found in close friendships. When these qualities are present, dating partners are free to respect and enjoy each other's companionship. These qualities include:

- **Similarity of values, standards, interests, and goals.** Couples who share basic beliefs are more likely to interact well with each other. They tend to be more compatible and have fewer conflicts in their relationship.

- **Mutual support**. Caring about the other person's successes and failures, well-being, and other aspects of life helps build a strong relationship. Giving each other encouragement during success or failure makes individuals feel valued and special.

- **Honesty.** In healthy relationships, behavior is not based on falsehoods. Instead, each partner's set of ethics allows an openness with the other person. Each can express personal feelings without being ridiculed or rejected by the other person.

- **Autonomy.** Freedom to enjoy time and activities away from each other, as well as time spent together, reflects independence as well as trust. Socially and emotionally mature couples don't limit each other's interests or relationships with family and friends.

- **Through reputable dating services.** Commercial dating services are designed to help adults find persons with whom they may enjoy spending time. Answers you provide on personal questionnaires furnished by a dating service are similarly paired with the answers of other clients. You are then given one or more names or descriptions of people you may choose to contact. If you choose to meet people in this manner, it's a good idea to follow the same safety precautions you would take when meeting a blind date.

T I P S

Knowing the difference between love and lust is a key to having a healthy, successful dating relationship. Think about:

- **Love** is primarily giving, not receiving.
- *Lust* is a strong desire to receive sexual pleasure.
- **Love** takes time to develop.
- *Lust* can develop in an instant.
- **Love** is caring about the other person.
- *Lust* is concern about oneself.
- **Love** is based on respect and responsibility.
- *Lust* is driven by physical desire, not respect and caring.
- **Love** is sharing.
- *Lust* is taking.
- **Love** involves commitment.
- *Lust* is not based on commitment.

Planning for Success

Anita is pleased that Michael has invited her to his cousin's bar mitzvah next week. Although she and Michael have been coworkers at the restaurant for several years, it will be the first time they have gone out together. Anita is unfamiliar with Jewish customs. She hopes to talk with Michael about the event during some of their breaks at work. You can learn from her example:

- **Learn about your partner's interests.** Informal conversations before going out, casual observations, and information from friends and family members often can be helpful in learning about the other person's interests.

Close-Up

Protect Yourself Against Rape

Date rape is a painful reality. The truth about rape is that it usually happens between people who know each other. In acquaintance, or date rape, the rapist and victim may know each other casually, having met through a common activity, mutual friend, or as classmates. Some may have closer relationships.

Date rapes should never be seen as some sort of misguided sexual adventure. Rape is violence, not seduction. People who have become drunk or high on drugs often become targets. When intoxicated, victims' perceptions about what is happening around them become blurred. Their ability to resist an attack is lessened as their verbal and physical responses become sedated.

Not all rapes can be prevented, but these suggestions can help keep you safe:

- *Lock all doors and windows in a car and at home.*
- *Go places with a friend or in a group. If alone, let others know about your plans.*
- *If you are being followed or threatened, go to a public place. If necessary, make all the noise you can.*
- *Avoid the use of alcohol and other drugs. They can make you vulnerable to assault.*
- *When at parties, do not leave your beverage unattended. It's much too easy for someone to put a substance—such as the date-rape drug, Rohypnol (flunitrazepam)—into your beverage. These drugs are illegal and dangerous.*

What are some ways that you might protect yourself against date rape?

- **Learn about new activities.** If you are going to a play, film, or art exhibit, learn as much about it as you can. Read magazine or newspaper reviews of the activity. Ask friends, acquaintances, and coworkers if they are familiar with it. The same advice applies to sporting events, concerts, and other activities.

- **Consider double dating.** You may want to include other couples on some of your outings, especially if you are shy and a bit concerned about keeping the conversation going. It may also help if you want to keep your relationship casual.

An Important Perspective

Will is aware that dating often leads to an ongoing relationship with one person. Although there are some advantages to this type of relationship, Will knows that young adults who go out with only one person may close themselves off from meeting other people too early in this period of their lives.

An exclusive relationship may be convenient and may ensure that people have someone to go out with, but it limits opportunities for choosing a lifetime partner. It may also place undue sexual pressure on one or both partners.

Will is forthright in all of his dating relationships. His honesty and set of values help him choose activities that are fun, but don't lead to serious involvement at this stage of his life.

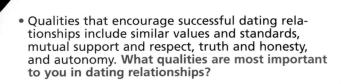

• Qualities that encourage successful dating relationships include similar values and standards, mutual support and respect, truth and honesty, and autonomy. **What qualities are most important to you in dating relationships?**

Creative, Inexpensive Activities

So you've met someone special, and you have the chance to arrange a special evening together. What will it be? Dinner and a movie? A carriage ride through the park? Tickets to a concert? A nice evening no doubt, but it's also an expensive one.

Your goal of getting to know someone better doesn't have to be costly as well. When Evan learned that Joan loved kittens, but couldn't have one because of the no-pet rule in her apartment, he surprised her with an afternoon in the cats' play area at the local animal shelter. "We sat. We talked. I saw how gentle he was with the kittens, and I simply loved getting to know him," Joan said.

If you are looking for inexpensive, creative ideas, consider these:

- Find out your partner's hobbies and interests. If your partner likes coaching junior high soccer, then join him or her for practice. Fix a picnic and have it on the field after the players leave.
- Volunteer together for nonprofit causes you both believe in. Building a home for Habitat for Humanity or visiting the elderly through an outreach program can give you a great opportunity to get to know each other while doing something constructive.
- Find out your date's three favorite films and host a film festival with another couple—complete with popcorn and chocolate-covered raisins if you like.
- Plan a long walk or bike trip in a local park.
- Spend time together in an evening of babysitting.
- Find out your partner's favorite television shows and create a tradition of watching them together.

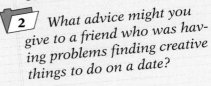

Using Your Resources Wisely

1. If you have limited cash resources like many other young adults, what are some ways in which you might creatively spend time with the "someone special" in your life?

2. What advice might you give to a friend who was having problems finding creative things to do on a date?

• Sharing in and learning about your partner's interests is one way to work toward a successful dating experience. **What are some things that you and your friends could do in preparation for dating?**

based on respect can lead to a genuine closeness, or intimacy. Because it takes time and effort to get to know more about each other, there are no real shortcuts in the process!

Couples in respectful relationships tend to be secure and self-reliant. They are comfortable with—and are able to accept—themselves to the same degree they expect acceptance from the other person. Although they give each other a sufficient amount of attention and appreciation, they also respect the other person's privacy and need for independence.

Sexual Respect

Anna treasures her year-long relationship with Pablo. She feels that the closeness they are forming is more meaningful and long lasting at this stage of their lives than relationships she sees based primarily on physical intimacy.

Anna appreciates the respect Pablo shows to her. He admires and supports her lifelong desire to graduate from college and become a teacher. She respects his goals and understands the time demands of his job. She trusts him when they are not together.

Together they have decided sexual intimacy will not be part of their relationship yet. Health statistics today demonstrate the wisdom of their determination and choice:

● There is an epidemic number of females with unplanned, unwanted pregnancies each year.

Developing Respect in Relationships

Respecting yourself, as well as the other person, is a key ingredient in any successful relationship. Respect for each other develops mainly through honest and open communication. Actively listening to the other person and accepting what is said helps both partners learn more about each other and think about what they want and expect from the relationship. Good communication in relationships

• Good communication puts you on the road to mutual respect in a relationship. What qualities do you respect the most in people you go out with? **What does respect have to do with how you treat your dating partner?**

The growth of sexually transmitted diseases—including the deadly AIDS virus and others that can cause infertility—has been tragic in the past 25 years. Recent studies indicate that one out of every three people who are sexually active will contract a sexually transmitted disease by age 24.

As you consider developing long-term relationships, think about some of these guidelines regarding sexual respect:

• Self-respect and being well defined in your own personal or professional goals will be a great ally for you.

• No major world religion encourages casual sexual encounters. In fact, all warn against these encounters.

• The best love you can experience is to love yourself. Focus on establishing yourself in a good job, training program, or college. Take time to develop your interests; get exposed to a variety of experiences and people.

• Do your own research on the personal cost of unplanned pregnancies and the growth of sexually transmitted diseases.

Note the Results of Actions Taken

Problem solvers need to evaluate the outcome of their choices in determining their success in solving problems. Reflecting on the problem-solving process and noting the results of actions taken can help problem solvers learn from their experiences and improve their reasoning skills. In the situation that follows, study how Marcus and Julia note the results of their actions.

Marcus looked at Julia who was sitting next to him in the car, singing their favorite song along with the radio. He said to her, "I can hardly believe the way our relationship is getting better and stronger every day—especially after our BIG decision last month."

"What do you mean?" Julia replied.

"Discussing a plan to keep us from getting ourselves into highly-charged romantic situations was the best thing we ever did," said Marcus. "I think it was wise to decide to spend less time alone and more time with other friends and couples. Also, deciding how physically intimate we wanted to be set a standard that didn't entice us to go further!

Not only did we discuss those things, but we are actually doing them, Julia!"

"Amazing, isn't it," said Julia as she chuckled softly, "but following through on our choice and plan has given us the freedom to have more fun. It seems like we feel less pressure to have sex, our communication is getting better, and we're learning to express our love for each other in other ways. I must say it's an effort to keep our physical and emotional feelings under control—or at least it is for me, but I like the way we're helping each other. Keeping our best interests in mind helps in following through on our decision."

Marcus pulled into the parking lot at Julia's apartment and walked Julia to her door. After a warm embrace and a quick kiss, they said good-bye. As Marcus drove away he thought, "Even if Julia and I don't stay together, I'm glad we solved our dilemma this way. I know I would make the same choice again in the future. In fact, I would probably talk about it even sooner than Julia and I did. The best part of all is knowing Julia and I solved this problem together and we are stronger for it."

From Your Perspective

1 How did Marcus and Julia's actions enhance their well-being?

2 Did their actions have the results they anticipated? Why or why not?

3 Were Marcus' actions ethical? Why or why not?

4 What might Marcus and Julia have done differently if they could solve this problem over again?

5 How might this problem-solving experience affect Marcus and Julia's problem solving in the future?

• Pressuring someone about a sexual relationship shows disrespect for the other person. How might a person feel when another tries to pressure her or him into a sexual relationship? What are some successful ways to refuse a sexual relationship and still be respectful to your partner?

When Relationships End

No matter the reasons for breaking up with someone, it can be a painful experience. You may feel sad, angry, hurt, anxious, or relieved. You may feel betrayed and vow that you'll never go out with someone again. On the other hand, you may find a new sense of freedom and security in who you are as a person.

When the Decision to Break Up Is Yours

Deciding to end a relationship often brings about many conflicting feelings. It's normal to wonder if you're doing the right thing. Questions such as "Will I regret this decision?" or "Will I be relieved when it's over?" are common. If you decide to break up a relationship:

- Do your best to treat the other person with respect and dignity. Focus on the differences between the two of you, not on the other's shortcomings.
- Explain why you believe the two of you aren't right for each other.
- Avoid personal attacks, insults, or other negative behavior you may regret later.
- Once your decision has been made, don't give the other person false hopes for starting up the relationship again. Be consistent and firm in refusing to get together once more.

Dealing with Feelings

Getting through a difficult breakup means taking life one day at a time. The following suggestions can help you deal with the feelings and get on with your life:

- **Remember the reasons.** Some people find it helpful to write a list of the reasons why they decided to break up and refer to this list as often as necessary. This helps them avoid a temporary reconciliation that tends to prolong the pain.
- **Seek support.** Ask for support and understanding from friends and family members. Counselors, religious leaders, or peer support groups can also be helpful during this time.
- **Be willing to apologize and forgive.** As part of the healing process, one or both ex-partners may choose to apologize and ask forgiveness for their role in the failure of the relationship. Likewise, individuals may choose to forgive to the other person—as well as themselves.
- **Be realistic.** Accept the fact that each of you will probably find other people to go out with. Your relationship is over, and it's time for you to begin a new phase of your life. After a while, sentimental past memories of the two of you will fade as you take up healthy new interests and activities.
- **Have hope for the future.** People who heal most quickly are those who never lose hope that their lives will continue to get better. They understand that the responsibility for making the situation better is theirs. They give themselves time to get

• Regardless of the reason for breaking up, ending a relationship is generally emotionally painful. **If you were in a situation such as this, what might you do to start the healing process?**

over a broken relationship, being careful not to get involved in other dating relationships before plenty of time for healing has taken place.

Rebuilding Relationships

In some cases, dating relationships can be rebuilt and made stronger than they were before a breakup. Time apart can give couples a chance to step back and gain insight about what went wrong. On the other hand, if a

• Seeking support from friends and family, and learning to forgive and forget are positive actions you can take in dealing with the loss of a relationship. **How might you help a friend through a situation such as this?**

desire to get back together is primarily motivated by loneliness, depression, guilt, jealousy, or financial insecurity, a reconciliation probably won't work.

Some relationships don't actually begin until after partners break up, resolve the issues that led to the separation, and then choose to reconcile. "We never realized how much we liked each other until we broke up. Now we rarely get upset about petty things anymore, " says Janet about her reclaimed relationship with Leon.

In deciding whether to restore a relationship, certain questions need to be answered, such as:

- Do both you and your partner understand the mistakes that were made and the issues that were unresolved when you broke up? Do you both agree on what needs to be resolved so that you can prevent a relapse?
- Have you matured in the areas that made you contribute to the breakup?

At the start of this chapter, we saw that Maria and Keith showed each other warmth, humor, and caring for each other in their possible romance. Going out with others is a wonderful opportunity to learn more about yourself and others.

Understanding Key Concepts

- Today's young adults experience less societal pressure to marry, or to marry at an early age. As a result, their time frame for going out with others has lengthened.

- The same qualities that exist in close friendships tend to be found in successful dating relationships.

- To help make an outing successful, learn as much as you can about the planned activity. If choosing an activity, keep your partner's interests, hobbies, or past-times in mind.

- Respect for yourself and for the other person is necessary for a successful dating relationship.

- Relationships based on *more* than physical intimacy tend to be more long lasting.

- Any instance of rape—whether committed by a stranger, acquaintance, or date—is violence, not seduction.

- Consider the other person's feelings when ending a relationship. Avoid any kind of negative behavior you may regret later.

- Some broken relationships can be rebuilt and made stronger than they were before the break-up.

Checking Your Knowledge

1. What are some places and ways for young adults to meet each other? What safety precautions would you suggest couples take the first time they go out together?

2. Summarize the qualities found in healthy dating relationships.

3. Explain the importance of individuals having similar values in a dating relationship.

4. What steps might you take to plan for a successful evening out?

5. What are some of the characteristics of dating partners in respectful relationships?

6. Summarize positive things you can do to get over a broken relationship.

Making TRANSITIONS

Dealing with Unwanted Workplace Relationships

Good relationships at work can make unpleasant tasks more enjoyable and more difficult tasks easier to handle. Making a point to keep workplace relationships on a professional, rather than personal, level can help avoid unnecessary problems.

Assume one of your coworkers has made a point of showing his or her interest. Although you are not going out with anyone at this time, you prefer not to go out with someone at work.

- What kinds of actions might you take to stop your coworker from pressuring you to go out?
- How might your actions affect your working relationship with other coworkers?

STRENGTHENING *Life* SKILLS

Dealing with Possessive Behavior

Sometimes the desire for closeness can get out of hand. One person in a relationship may become possessive and want the two to spend all of their time together—avoiding contact with other friends and family. When one person is very possessive, the other person becomes a victim. The situation can be very stressful. Possessive behavior suffocates its victim and eventually smothers the love.

Think of a situation in which one person in a relationship has become too possessive of the other. Decide what suggestions you might give to each of the people in this relationship. Then write answers to the following questions:

- How effective do you think each suggestion might be? Explain.
- Have you ever been the victim of a possessive relationship? The possessor in a relationship? How did you feel about your role in the relationship? What did you learn from this experience?

Applying Thinking Skills

1. **Drawing conclusions.** You attend a party with friends in which one young woman seems especially poised and outgoing. What is it about her that most impresses you? What kinds of comments does she make that put people at ease?

2. **Predicting consequences.** If you were to consider setting up your best friend with an acquaintance from work, what's most important to keep in mind before you do this? What would make you decline to do this?

3. **Drawing conclusions.** Think about the platonic relationships you have with the opposite sex. What do you consider the best thing about these kinds of friendships? What's the most valuable lesson you've learned from the relationship?

Practical Applications

1. **Journeying back in time.** Ask your family members, and other adults to describe their social lives when they were young adults. Where did they go to meet people? How did they get to know each other? What similarities are there between their relationships and yours today? Do you think they worried as much about safety?

2. **Listening with the heart.** Make a list of five things you could say or do to help a friend who is experiencing the difficult breakup of a relationship.

3. **Campus research.** Contact a college near you (or the college you plan to attend). Research crime statistics related to safety concerns and sexual violence in particular. Find out what programs the campus sponsors to increase awareness about safety. Also, research to find out if the campus offers dating workshops. Many do. Report to your classmates the most creative ideas you heard regarding dating.

CHAPTER 11

Committing to Marriage and Family

What You Will Learn...

- How to know when you're ready to make a commitment to another person.
- Questions couples should ask each other before marriage.
- Components of successful marriages.
- Factors to consider when you're thinking about having children.
- How various trends affect families.

Terms for Success

commitment
engagement

Antonio and Jana looked down the stairwell. "Do you want to do this?" Antonio asked.

Jana sighed. "About as much as you do." She forced a smile. "What's a girlfriend for?"

Together they descended the steps to salvage what they could from Antonio's flood-ruined cellar. The waters had receded, leaving a layer of mud on the carpet, stacks of soggy cardboard boxes, and the stench of mold in the dank air.

They stared at the devastation. "You do have renter's insurance, right?" Jana asked.

Antonio nodded and gently kicked one box. "Enough to replace anything worth replacing," he muttered. "But it can't replace this!" He picked up a large manila envelope that tore in his hands. Clumps of wet photographs spilled to the floor.

Jana began to pick them up. Her curious frown melted to a smile and delight. "This was our high school graduation . . . and that summer we worked at the camp for sick kids . . ." She held up a photo of a gray-striped cat. "Tilly!"

Antonio still held the tattered envelope. "I guess I took that when I first got my camera. I forgot all about it. Then she died, and you were sad because you didn't have a nice picture of her."

Jana fell silent a long moment. "I think we can save this—maybe all of these."

Antonio shook his head, blinking off a tear of frustration. "That's not it. This was going to be my big buildup. I was going to put these in an album. Then as we looked over all the things we'd done together, everything we'd been through, I was going to ask you to—I was going to say—maybe it's time that we . . ."

Jana looked at the photos again. She busied her hands peeling them apart, feeling a bit flustered by what Antonio was trying to say.

"Let's see if we can dry them out," she suggested quietly. "If not, well, we'll have plenty more where these came from."

What tells you these two might be ready for marriage? What do you know about how these two communicate with each other?

Making a Commitment

You've been introduced to Jana and Antonio at a moment when they've expressed the expectation that they will get married. You can only imagine exactly how they met and what they felt at that first moment. Perhaps one was immediately attracted, the other repulsed. Perhaps they were just friends, and perhaps both were certain from the start that they were meant for each other.

It takes time, maturity, and experience to find the right person. Romantic attraction may develop between two people almost instantly, but it doesn't guarantee a lifetime together.

Like all other couples, Carmen and Marco soon learned that romantic attraction, or infatuation, never lasts. After a while, intense emotions fade, and reality sets in. Even though infatuation was exciting and fun, for Carmen and Marco it was only the beginning of a deepening and more satisfying relationship. Since then, they've made a **commitment** to each other, or pledge to give their relationship high priority. Whether or not their commitment will lead to marriage, they are taking time to see if they're willing to spend a lifetime together.

Are You Ready for Commitment?

The early stages of maturity often involve casual or "semi-commitments." They usually last for a short time and then begin again with someone else. These kinds of relationships are normal and natural. They provide opportunities to meet different individuals and learn what you want in a lifetime partner.

Postponing a serious commitment until later can give people time to mature and accomplish certain goals that are a higher priority at this time in life.

• After dating for a while, some couples feel ready to make a commitment. **What factors could influence your decision to make a commitment to another person?**

How will you know when you're ready to make a lifetime commitment? Start by carefully considering these factors:

- **Maturity.** Successful, lifelong commitments require maturity, patience, and self-awareness. You need to know yourself and what you want out of life.
- **Time.** It simply takes time to get to know the other person well.
- **Education and career goals.** What are your education and career goals? What do you need to do to achieve them? Many young adults find it very difficult to commit to a serious relationship while preparing for a career.
- **Shared interests and values.** Are your views of religion, finances, and lifestyles similar? Do you share similar hobbies and interests? Shared values are essential to a good relationship. Shared interests are helpful as well.
- **Support of family and friends.** How do family members and friends feel about your relationship? Are they supportive of it? Why or why not? Mutual support of family and friends is an important ingredient in most successful marriages.

Take Your Time

Committing to someone for the rest of your life is a significant step. Taking it seriously and learning if and when you're ready can help you avoid making a premature commitment or one that is a mistake.

Take time to observe each other's good points, as well as the faults and flaws. Instead of "falling in love" right away and possibly making unwise decisions, give yourselves time to "grow into love" that will last.

Refresh your Memory

Here are some terms to remember as you think about future marriage relationships:

- **compatibility.** A sense of harmony and agreement.
- **infatuation.** Romantic attraction.
- **trends.** Changes or new developments.

- Many factors enter in to whether or not you are ready to make a commitment to another person. **How will you know when you are ready to make a commitment? Why is it important to think about more than just your feelings of being "in love?"**

Thinking About Marriage

Almost everyone thinks about marriage at some point in life. Unfortunately, some of the reasons aren't likely to guarantee success. People may decide to marry because they are lonely or want to escape a bad situation at home, school, or work. Others may marry because of pregnancy or because they want financial security or recognition from their peers. Without close self-examination, individuals may not understand their own motives. If there are serious doubts, the best time to face them is before marriage and before the possibility of divorce and children.

When you're thinking seriously about marriage, there are a number of important questions for you and your potential mate to consider. Make sure you listen closely to each other's answers and that you answer honestly. Think about the following questions:

- **Values.** What are the things in life you value most? What values guide the way you live? What personal, financial, and professional goals do you have for the next year or two? The next 10 to 15 years?
- **Expectations.** What do you think marriage will be like day to day? How will your parents' relationship or views of marriage be likely to affect your own views?
- **Finances.** How were finances handled in your family? How do you want finances to be handled in your own family?
- **Household responsibilities.** What's the best way to divide the chores? How did you handle household duties while you were growing up?
- **Children.** Do you want children? If so, how many and how often? Starting when? What if having children isn't possible? How might the arrival of children affect marriage?

• In thinking about making a commitment to marriage, the financial situation of each partner is a factor to consider. **Why is it important for a young couple to discuss their financial situation prior to making a commitment to marriage?**

• Expectations about marriage can differ widely even within couples who love each other. **Why should couples share with each other their expectations about marriage, their roles in marriage, and children before making the commitment to marry?**

- **Views on parenting.** How much actual experience with children do you have? What are your views about discipline?
- **Religious beliefs.** How do you think your religious background will most affect marriage? What if your partner's religious background is different from your own?
- **Intimacy.** What are your expectations about affection and sex in marriage? Would you agree to professional counseling if there were problems in this area?
- **Work.** What is the role of work in your life? How secure or stable is your occupation likely to be? What do you want to be doing in five years? In 10 years? How do you feel about each others' career goals?
- **Conflict resolution.** How is conflict handled in your family? How do you expect conflict to be handled when you are married? If a serious conflict develops in your marriage, and you and your spouse have trouble resolving it, would you be willing to accept outside assistance or intervention?

Some or all the answers to the questions above may surprise you. Others may reaffirm what you already know about yourself and your partner. Although no one is perfect and

no relationship is without problems, taking time to learn as much as possible about each other can give you a tremendous advantage in making your marriage a happy one.

Getting Engaged

Why do most people get engaged instead of getting married immediately? What is the significance of an engagement period?

Tim and Lara plan to get married after they finish college next year. They announced their **engagement,** or promise or intention to marry, to their families last weekend. Being engaged will give them time to look seriously at their relationship.

REASON Through Life's Problems

Note the Results of Actions Taken

After taking action on a problem, people need to step back and reflect on how they went about solving the problem and if their solution was successful. Read the situation below and reflect on how Kindra considers her problem-solving skill and the success of her solution.

Kindra stuffed a few more fries into her mouth. She looked at her sister, Jodi, sitting across the table at the fast-food restaurant. Kindra said, "Jodi, I'm not sure I can answer your question about whether I'm glad Vince and I got married. It is not an easy question."

"You do love each other, don't you?" asked Jodi.

"It's not a question of love, Jodi," replied Kindra. "I think it's a question of were we ready to get married—and did we make the right decision for us to get married? We tried to think this through before we got married. Vince and I discussed the pros and cons, and we looked at all the alternatives. However, I'm not sure we were very realistic about what we were thinking."

"What do you mean?" asked Jodi, as she settled in her chair.

"Well, I didn't realize how stressful it would be to take community college courses, plus work in the auto-tech apprenticeship program. I enjoy my work, but combining it with studying, cleaning, cooking, and doing laundry doesn't leave much extra time for Vince. He is going to school to become an ultrasound technician and does help at home. He's had to add more work hours at the restaurant to help us pay the bills. He's also talking about going on to nursing school! Vince and I really love each other and we're committed to staying together, but sometimes I think it would have been easier if we hadn't gotten married so soon."

"So why did you get married?" Jodi questioned.

"Because we love each other and couldn't wait to be out on our own, away from our families, doing what we wanted when we wanted. I just wish we had talked to some married students about combining school, work, and family. Even if we had made the same choice, we would have been more prepared."

"Guess life isn't easy when you're in love," smiled Jodi.

"You're right about that!" Kindra wryly commented as they gathered their things and headed to the door.

▶ From Your Perspective

1 Do you think Kindra would make the same choice about getting married if she had the opportunity to do it over again? Why or why not?

2 What might Kindra do differently in solving a life-changing problem in the future?

3 Was Kindra's and Vince's choice to marry in their best interests? Why or why not?

Unfortunately, many couples see engagement only as a time to plan their wedding ceremony, reception, and honeymoon. Instead, it's best to use the engagement period also as a time to learn more about each other's similarities and differences. If they discover that some of their differences are serious enough to threaten the marriage success, they can use the time to examine and resolve the differences, if possible. Potential trouble spots are far easier to resolve before, rather than after, marriage. This period can be crucial in helping couples build a relationship that will last. If necessary, the relationship can still be ended during the engagement period. Even though breaking an engagement can be a very painful and awkward experience, it is far less traumatic than marriage followed by divorce.

What Makes Marriages Successful?

Allen's parents will celebrate their fortieth wedding anniversary next week. Forty years of talking, sharing, working, and sometimes fighting. They did well at parenting, but fell short of their financial goals for ten straight years because of unexpected health problems or expenses with the kids. However, when they look at each other, they speak volumes with a single glance. They are proud of the life they've made together, and look forward to many more years. Successful marriages such as theirs usually include the following components:

- **Commitment.** Both partners work to make the marriage succeed. They are willing and determined to stay together through both good and bad times.
- **Communication.** Effective communication skills help relationships run smoothly.

Strengthening Marriage

TIPS

When you marry, you'll form a family that, in some ways, is unlike any other family in the world. One way to keep your family special and strong is to establish traditions that you can enjoy throughout the years. Traditions help provide structure to a new family, create shared memories, and strengthen family ties.

Traditions might include the kinds of food you serve at the holidays, how you spend Sunday evenings, or where you go to celebrate your wedding anniversary. Traditions might also include the kinds of gifts you give to your spouse, what you and your children wear on special occasions, or even the kinds of volunteer projects you participate in as an entire family.

Before starting family traditions of your own, consider the following suggestions:

- Begin by thinking about pleasant past experiences that you and your spouse remember. If these experiences seem like something your new family might enjoy, why not give them a try?
- Ask friends and extended family members about traditions they currently enjoy or remember from the past. You'll probably learn about traditions that your new family might enjoy.
- Research family traditions in other cultures or countries. Doing so may give you ideas about interesting traditions for your family.

They encourage understanding and help reduce misunderstanding. Sharing information, thoughts, and feelings with a sense of responsibility and empathy helps make a marriage strong.

- **Acceptance of each other.** Mature couples realize that they can't change each other. People don't become more organized, more considerate, or more patient because of marriage. They are who they are—often unable or unwilling to change. If you don't want to accept the other person as is, it's probably best to let go of the relationship. Entering into a marriage with thoughts of changing the other person is likely to lead to failure.

- **Compatibility.** Compatibility is like a glue that holds a marriage together. It is a sense of shared values, religion, culture, education, and backgrounds. Before you get married, you need to face honestly whether you have enough in common to overcome differences between the two of you.

- **Shared decision making.** Marriages are strengthened when both parties share decision making. This can help avoid hurt, anger, and resentment. Besides, two heads really are better than one in most cases. Also keep in mind that in any relationship compromise is a significant part of shared decisions.

- **Shared responsibilities.** Reach an agreement on who will do what before entering into a lifetime commitment. Otherwise, resentment can build if one person is too heavily loaded with responsibilities. These, in time, may threaten the marriage. Most of today's couples share responsibilities by dividing jobs on the basis of strength, skill, interest, and time available.

- **Conflict resolution.** Conflicts are a normal part of life and can lead to positive changes, new viewpoints, and even greater commitment within a marriage. Couples who are successful at conflict resolution make use of the tools of communication, compromise, and negotiation. In some instances, outside assistance may be necessary.

- Engagement is a time when couples learn more about each other and grow in their commitment before marriage. The engagement period is more than just a time for planning a wedding. **Why is it important to think beyond the wedding day?**

- **Time for each other.** The demands of work, children, and the needs of other family members often compete with time that married couples have alone together. In today's busy world, couples often must make time to be together. They need time to talk about issues, problems, feelings, and ordinary events in their lives.
- **Intimacy.** Intimacy is both a physical and emotional closeness between two people. It comes from meaningful, personal conversations, loving gestures, and respectful displays of affection. It is not the same as sexual contact.

Roles and Responsibilities in Marriage

Callie and Todd are in love. They look forward to a beautiful wedding and a short honeymoon at the beach. Unfortunately, they haven't thought much about the lifetime of roles and responsibilities each of them will have after they say, "I do."

In the past, most men and women had specific roles and responsibilities, primarily based on gender. Over the years, boundaries have shifted, and many roles and responsibilities are no longer clearly divided. For example, today's role of breadwinner is often shared. The same is true for roles such as cook, housekeeper, home repairer, and family accountant.

Marriage also involves many other roles—friend, spouse, daughter- or son-in-law, and parent. As the years go by, your roles and responsibilities will inevitably change and probably even multiply.

At the beginning of marriage, most roles and responsibilities focus on employment, time and money management, and basic housekeeping. The arrival of children presents couples with a more complex set of responsibilities. Many of them during the parenting years are serious and time consuming. Being responsible for the care, guidance, protection, and education of children is made easier with the presence of two mature parents in the family.

- Successful marriages require commitment and working together through good times and times of challenge. Why is it important to think about ways of encouraging success in a marriage prior to getting married?

Resolving Issues About Work and Family

Brian and Nikki are engaged to be married. Brian was raised in a family in which his father managed a store, and his mother was a fulltime homemaker. Nikki was reared by a single, working mother.

Both Brian and Nikki agree that they want to decide before marriage how they will handle their future roles and responsibilities. However, they still haven't come to an agreement on two issues:

- Who will be employed and when?
- If they have children, who will care for them?

Brian feels that Nikki should stay at home whenever they have children. Nikki can't imagine staying at home every day. She believes that she can balance a family and career just as her mother did.

In response to their challenge, Brian and Nikki agreed on the following plan:

- They used the Internet to research estimated costs of housing, children, and other living expenses.
- They went to the library and created a reading list they thought would be helpful during the next few months as they sorted through the issues.
- They made an appointment with a financial planner and a banker to find out the typical kinds of mistakes that newlyweds make (and how they can avoid these).
- They met with a counselor to discuss the impact that financial and parental concerns might have on their marriage—and what they should do to address these issues early.
- They made a point of stating to each other a promise. Each would try to be flexible and committed in the face of those future challenges that are inevitable in marriage, especially those related to children and finances.

Using Your Resources Wisely

1. Why should your values guide your decisions about work and family?

2. What human resources would you seek out in dealing with work and family issues? Why?

Thinking About Children

"I knew I was serious about Susan because when I looked into her eyes, I could see our children. That surprised me. We were married three years before starting our family. I didn't know how much parenthood would change my life. Before, I was a happy-go-lucky guy with hardly any responsibilities. I've grown up a lot since then. I love my son and do my best to be a good father. It takes a lot of work to be a parent," said Jermaine.

• Over the years, household responsibilities have become less dependent on gender and more dependent upon individual skill. **What are your thoughts about household roles and responsibilities in marriage?**

Close-Up

Problems, Conflicts, & Challenges

". . . and they lived happily ever after."

Unfortunately, fairy-tale endings don't accurately describe most real-life relationships. Problems are a fact of life in any family at some time or another. It's important to deal with them as soon as they occur. If not resolved, minor concerns can escalate into arguments or other negative behavior whenever commitment, good communication, trust, and positive self-esteem are lacking.

Some family problems, such as a major illness, accidents, or death come unexpectedly. Others, such as the effects of alcoholism or depression, may build more slowly. What should families do when experiencing problems? Fortunately, many problems can be resolved within the family unit. If everyone responds with commitment, cooperation, and compromise, most misunderstandings and challenges can be addressed if you:

- *Take responsibility for personal actions, rather than blaming someone else.*
- *Respect the rights of others. No one has the right to control or harm another person or to destroy another's property.*
- *Try to accept and tolerate others' differences.*
- *Apologize when you make a mistake. However, do not accept blame for what you did not say or do.*

Think about someone you know who has successfully dealt with family challenges. What seems to make this person successful?

Having a child brings major changes to parents' lives. Some of these changes involve joy and deep satisfaction. Other changes can be difficult when parents aren't prepared for them.

Like marriage, parenting isn't easy. Deciding whether to become a parent is one of the most important decisions you'll ever make. Parenthood is a lifelong commitment. It means having a constant concern for the present and future welfare of another human being. A child's needs for physical care, love, guidance, and financial support often continue well into adulthood.

When thinking about parenthood, you should get as clear a picture of it as possible before making a decision. Also, take a realistic look at yourself and your potential mate. Carefully consider the following factors before deciding whether and when to have children.

- **Emotional maturity.** Age alone is no guarantee of maturity. However, people tend to be more successful parents as they grow older and are able to handle the pressures and responsibilities involved.

- **Desire for parenthood.** Not all reasons for wanting children are mature and unselfish. Important questions such as "Why do I want to be a parent?" and "Why do I want a child now?" need to be answered truthfully. Wanting someone to love and belong to you or take care of you when you grow old are unsound reasons for having a child.

- **Health.** Babies need healthy parents. If either of you has a medical or substance abuse problem, it could affect the health of a baby or your ability to care for the child. The mother's physical maturity is especially important. Being too young at conception and delivery can put the baby at risk and may affect the child's health for a lifetime.

- **Management skills.** How experienced and skilled are you at managing time, energy, and other resources? Being a parent takes good management skills. You need to be able and willing to make sound decisions related to the health and happiness of each member of your family. Once you have become a parent, you can no longer consider only your own wants and needs when making choices and planning for the future.

Sharing Household Tasks

T I P S

Here are some helpful suggestions for sharing household tasks:

- Begin with a written list of tasks to be done.

- Divide the tasks according to each person's likes and dislikes. Keep in mind each other's strength, skills, and time available.

- Reach agreement on how often each task needs to be done and to what standard.

- Avoid criticizing the other person's performance of the tasks.

- Keep the division of chores open for renegotiation. Sharing household tasks is an experiment that may take several adjustments before you find a satisfactory arrangement.

- Children should be included in the division of work. Even young children can help and should be given the chance to do various age-appropriate tasks.

- **Finances.** Having children costs money almost from the moment of conception until each child is grown and self-sustaining. Before making a decision to have children, take a careful look at your finances. You and your mate may have to make changes in your lifestyle and begin a savings plan in preparation for a future family. You also may need to think about other jobs and additional education or training to increase your income.

Pressure to Have Children

Did you or your friends "play house" when you were growing up? Did you pretend that your dolls or pets were babies to be dressed up and cared for? If so, you were like most other children. Many people grow up assuming that they will have children of their own someday.

As years go by, many young married couples are given subtle, or not-so-subtle, hints to have children. Their parents may talk about looking forward to being grandparents. Even casual friends with children may pressure childless couples to join them in parenthood. After a while, it's easy to feel different, or "out of the loop," if you don't have children.

Pressure from others to have children is a very unwise reason to do so. A child should be born because he or she is truly wanted. Both married partners should be mature and ready to accept the responsibilities involved. The decision needs to be theirs alone to make.

Pressure to Not Have Children

In spite of pressure to do otherwise, not everyone chooses to have children. Some couples are involved with careers that take up much of their time and energy. For others, education, travel, or other activities take precedence.

Worldwide issues such as limited resources and threats of nuclear war influence some couples in their decision to have few, if any, children. In other cases, people may simply not enjoy children.

Some people avoid having children because of genetic diseases that can be passed from parent to child. Cystic fibrosis, diabetes, hemophilia, sickle cell anemia, and Tay-Sachs disease are some examples. Because all children may not inherit the disease, genetic testing or counseling can help couples learn about their chances of having a child with the condition.

Many couples lead fulfilling lives after making a decision not to have children. The final decision, however, of whether to be a parent is up to you and your spouse.

• Parenthood is a lifetime commitment which requires maturity and self-sacrifice. Why should young couples think about the factors that influence their decision to become parents?

• Some couples choose to adopt children for any number of reasons. **What are the pros and cons of adopting children?**

Many single adults are serving as adoptive parents.

People decide to adopt for many reasons. Some have difficulty conceiving a baby. Others, while able to have children of their own, decide to adopt one or more children because they:

• Want to help someone who might not otherwise have a home. Many children are hard to place because they are older or have health problems or disabilities.

• Fear passing serious genetic diseases on to their offspring.

Although the majority of couples desire to adopt infants, the demand is greater than the number of babies available. Because of this, the wait for a healthy infant can take a number of years. Some people choose to adopt an older child. Others adopt infants or toddlers with a disability or health problem, or they adopt children from other countries.

Whether it's a healthy infant, an older child, a teen, or a toddler with a disability, adoption can bring satisfaction and great joy to the new parents. Although it is not an easy process, adoption is needed for hundreds of thousands of children who are available and waiting for families to love and care for them.

What About Adoption?

In the past, most nonrelative adoptions involved couples who were infertile. The infants were usually adopted by same-race families who were parenting for the first, or possibly the second, time. Today, the picture of adoption is changing. Families of various incomes, religions, and racial and ethnic backgrounds are urged to consider adoption. So are families without children, as are families who may already be parenting several children.

Trends Affecting Families

Even though change is a fact of life, statistics show that marriage and family are here to stay. For example, about 95 percent of people in the industrialized world marry by age 40. Of the couples who marry, many are in two-career marriages, with smaller families than in the past.

Trends affecting families include these:

- **Couples are marrying later in life than did previous generations.** Young adults with divorced parents are often concerned about committing to marriage before they are ready. Another reason is based on economics. Worries about getting a good-paying job, the costs of housing, and rearing a family play a major role. Also, the desire to finish their education and establish a career often causes people to postpone marriage.

- **Increasing mobility.** Because of frequent moves, families often lack close supportive connections with relatives and friends.

- **Blended families.** Although the trend has decreased in recent years, many marriages end in divorce. A high number of divorced people remarry, producing a growing number of blended families. Also, a growing number of extended families are living together. Adult children, alone or with their own children, often move in with parents. Older relatives may move in with young ones to provide child care or because they need care themselves.

- **Home as work place and school.** One of the most fascinating trends is the number of men and women who are using technology to spend more time at home to be available to their children. Also, in some families, children are being schooled at home.

Identifying trends can help couples better prepare for future changes and challenges. Society needs strong families that can adapt and cope with changes that come their way.

- Increasing mobility is just one trend affecting families today. How could a family rebuild supportive connections after moving away from friends and family?

Understanding Key Concepts

● Marriage is a serious commitment. Waiting until you are ready for this step gives you time to mature and accomplish goals that are important to you.

● Not all reasons people choose to marry are sound and likely to lead to success.

● Breaking an engagement can be painful and awkward. However, it is less hurtful than entering into a marriage that is unlikely to last.

● Successful marriages are based on various components, including commitment, communication, acceptance, compatibility, and intimacy.

● Before marriage, couples should take time to consider seriously whether or not to have children. Their decision should be theirs alone—free of pressure from family members and friends.

● Trends affecting families include marriage at a later age, increased numbers of blended families, more individuals who work out of the home, and increased mobility of family members.

Checking Your Knowledge

1. Explain why some reasons for getting married are unsound and unlikely to lead to a lasting relationship.

2. What questions do you think are most important to ask a potential spouse? Why should both individuals learn as much about each other as possible before deciding to marry?

3. In what ways can good communication skills contribute to the success of a marriage?

4. What suggestions might you give an engaged couple trying to reach agreement on sharing future household responsibilities?

5. How have family roles and responsibilities changed over the years?

6. What factors would you advise a couple to consider when thinking about having children?

7. Which of the trends affecting families are most prevalent in your community or area of the country? Which are least prevalent? Which affect you most?

Making TRANSITIONS

Assessing Your Expectations

In many cases, teens and young adults (and some older adults, too) have unrealistic attitudes and expectations about marriage. They may expect too much from the relationship. They may not realize that choosing the right partner is only the beginning of making a successful, long-term relationship.

Assume you're thinking about what a long-term relationship or marriage might be like. Make a list about your desires for a relationship surrounding the following: traits and values you find desirable in another person; expectations you have for a relationship; and your expectations about the division of household roles. After making your list, answer the following questions:

• What traits, values, or expectations are most important to you?
• Which traits, values, or expectations could you compromise on? Why or why not?
• Would your expectations be different if you were marrying as a teen versus waiting a few years?

STRENGTHENING *Life* SKILLS

Creating Family Traditions

Family traditions offer opportunities to create memories, share love, and build strong bonds between family members. People's happiest memories from childhood often revolve around traditions, or activities that happened with some regularity in their families.

Almost any good idea or activity can be turned into a family tradition. Think about an activity that you would like to develop into a tradition someday. Write a short description of the activity, explaining why you think it would be worthwhile. Then write your answers to the following questions:

- What values would this tradition promote?
- How might this tradition strengthen a close friendship, marriage, or family? In what ways?
- What actions would you need to take to start this tradition?

Applying Thinking Skills

1. **Recognizing assumptions.** What impact does time have on an infatuation? How might assumptions about infatuation lead a couple to rush into a serious commitment?

2. **Predicting consequences.** What consequences might occur for a couple thinking about marriage when they are significantly different in one or more of the following ways: age, maturity levels, education and career goals, or interests?

3. **Comparing and contrasting.** Think about adult friends and family members who are single and have no children and about couples who are married and have one or more children. Compare and contrast the roles and responsibilities they have. What are the similarities? What are the differences?

4. **Drawing conclusions.** What effect might pressure from friends and family to have children have on a newly-married couple? What implications might this pressure have on the success or failure of their marriage?

Practical Applications

1. **Family life in other cultures.** Families of all ages and sizes exist in different cultures around the world. Use library resources to investigate marriage and family customs in another country. Summarize your findings in a brief oral report. Ask your classmates to give reasons why some marriage and parenting styles differ from one part of the world to another. How might learning about families in different countries benefit you in your adult life?

2. **Determining readiness.** "Do I really want to be a parent?" and if so, "When?" are two very important questions couples thinking about marriage need to ask. In a small group, develop a list of questions prospective parents can use in deciding whether they are ready to have children. Share your list with the class.

3. **Writing.** Write a short story about parents' adjusting to life with a new baby. Include typical daily activities in the parents' lives. In a small group, share your story and discuss how realistic it may or may not be.

Unit 3

Enhancing Personal Well-Being

Chapters ▼

CHAPTER 12

Investing in a Healthy Life

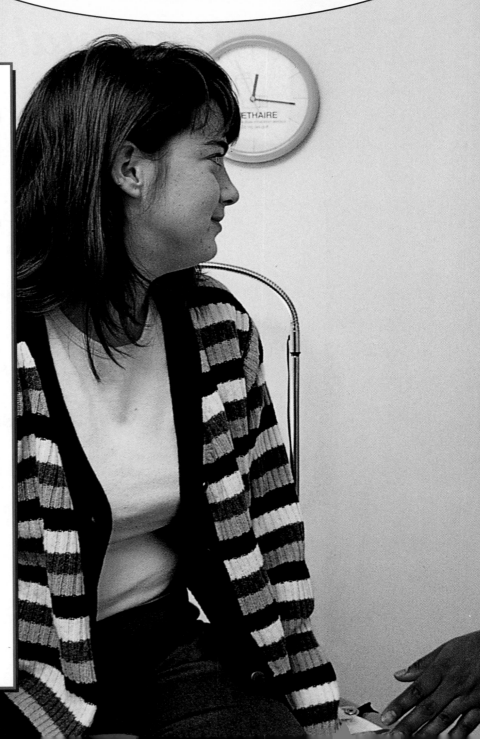

What You Will Learn...

- What you can do to stay healthy.
- How to select your own doctors and medical clinics.
- The difference between traditional health insurance companies and managed care providers.
- The differences between various forms of life insurance
- Ways to prevent communicable diseases.
- The basics of handling medical emergencies.

Terms for Success

acquired immune deficiency syndrome (AIDS)
health maintenance organization (HMO)
human immunodeficiency virus (HIV)
preferred provider organization (PPO)
sexual abstinence
sexually transmitted diseases (STDs)
wellness

Larissa perched tensely on the edge of the exam table, waiting for her first meeting with Dr. Cohn. "Why are you worried?" she asked herself. "You've seen doctors before—but you've never picked your own doctor before."

The exam room door opened. A mature woman, wearing a lab coat, entered. "Larissa? I'm Dr. Cohn. May I call you Larissa, or do you prefer Miss Stevers?"

Dr. Cohn began discussing the information the nurse had gathered. Then she asked Larissa other health questions. "Are you sleeping all right?"

"Usually, I do," Larissa explained, "but I just moved and started a new job. . . ."

"Hmm. How are you handling all these changes?"

Larissa shrugged. "Pretty well, I guess. I like my job. Everyone's really friendly."

"Good." Dr. Cohn sounded pleased. "That'll help you adjust, keep your stress level down. Your regular sleep habits should come back. What's your diet like?"

"Well, it's kind of the same story," Larissa began.

The doctor smiled knowingly. "You haven't unpacked the dishes, so you grab a burger"

Larissa sighed. "I know I shouldn't."

Dr. Cohn laughed gently. "It happens to us all. It's a big adjustment, being out on your own. You have a job, and all the everyday chores and decisions. It's a lot of stress. Eventually, though, you will settle into a routine. Then you'll get your diet, and other things, under control."

Larissa nodded, relieved. She had been expecting a lecture; instead, she was having a conversation. Her other doctors would never have talked to her like this.

"Just find those dishes," Dr. Cohn advised. "especially the salad bowls, the vegetable steamer, the juice glasses . . . and the ice cream scoop." She grinned. "Grown-ups eat ice cream, too."

What kind of medical issues do you expect to face when you are out on your own? What can you do now to prepare for them?

Taking Responsibility for Wellness

Young adulthood is a time for enjoying life and developing confidence in your ability to take control of your life. Some people take risks with poor diet and exercise, by alcohol or drug abuse, or by tobacco use. However, good health is a great personal goal. It's directly linked to personal achievement, problem-solving skills, and longevity.

Wellness can be defined simply as "a state of optimum health." It means that a person has achieved, and generally maintains, his or her highest personal potential for good health. Wellness involves three main components: physical health, mental health, and personal safety. Learning what to do in each of these areas is the first important step. Discipline and motivation will be equally important for a lifetime of dedication to personal wellness.

When Jesse stretched over the apples at the school cafeteria line to reach a piece of chocolate cake, it wasn't because he didn't know which was the healthful choice. To achieve wellness, you must be motivated to put your health knowledge into action.

Routine Medical Care

Having the skills to locate, interview, and select appropriate health care professionals is a necessary part of maintaining good health. When they're feeling sick or needing a medical checkup, most people go to a primary care physician. These are typically either family practitioners or internists.

If your primary care doctor can't provide the care you need, he or she will refer you to an appropriate specialist. For example, when Kent's rash didn't respond to any of the treatments Dr. Haddad had tried, she sent him to Dr. Greco, a dermatologist.

• As you move out on your own, you are responsible for your physical and mental health and your personal safety. What actions can you take to promote wellness?

Choosing Health Care Professionals

As an adult, you will need to identify the health care professionals you want to help you manage your health. The best time to do so is before you need health care. You can find a primary care physician and clinic by:

- Asking people you know for recommendations.
- Checking the yellow pages of the telephone directory.
- Calling local and state medical societies.
- Checking a directory of local health care professionals at your library.
- Contacting the area hospitals for their physician referral services.

- Searching for health care providers on the Internet. Search by the type of professional you need, or the name of your disorder or condition.

When you have a list of possible health care providers, call the office of each person to get the information you want. Physician referral services will also answer many questions about individual doctors. The information on page 206 can help you in making out your list. Although these tips are targeted at choosing physicians, many tips are also appropriate for other health care providers.

• Choosing health care providers to meet your needs takes careful research. **If you were moving to a new community, how might you go about looking for a new doctor or dentist?**

Review these key health care terms:

- **cardiologist:** Heart specialist.
- **dermatologist:** Skin specialist.
- **diagnosis:** The identification of a medical condition or disease.
- **inpatient:** One admitted to a hospital or clinic for treatment or testing that requires at least one overnight stay.
- **internist:** Specialist in internal medicine.
- **outpatient:** A patient in a hospital or clinic whose treatment does not require an overnight stay.
- **paramedic:** Person trained to give advanced emergency medical treatment or assist medical professionals.
- **prognosis:** A professional's prediction of the probable course and outcome of a disease.

Choosing a Physician

Consider these questions when you're choosing a physician.

T I P S

- If not a primary care physician, what is the physician's specialty?
- Where is the office located and how easy is it for you to get to?
- Which hospitals is the physician associated with? Would you be comfortable going to any of these hospitals for treatment?
- What are the physician's office hours? Are they convenient for you?
- What are the average fees?
- What is the physician's philosophy and style? Does he or she consider the patient a partner in making health care decisions? Does he or she emphasize preventive medicine? Does he or she suggest nondrug solutions to medical problems when possible?

Office Visits

Once you have made your selection, schedule a routine health checkup to establish contact. Don't wait until you are sick to make your first visit to a doctor. That first appointment is important. You can prepare for a first visit by recording your medical history, or a record of your medical problems and events.

At your visit, describe any questions or concerns in detail along with your daily lifestyle habits including eating habits, rest, exercise routine, and leisure acitivites. The more information you provide, the easier it is for the professional to help you.

You can evaluate the quality of service you will be receiving by asking yourself these questions:

- Do you feel comfortable trusting this person with your health?
- Do you feel comfortable asking questions and discussing intimate matters?
- Is the professional willing to consult other professionals if your problem is outside his or her area of expertise?
- Does the professional give you his or her full attention and adequate time to discuss your concerns?

If your answer to any of these questions is no, you should consider looking for a different professional.

The most effective professional—patient relationship, is a cooperative one in which both parties respect each other. Some people are unnecessarily intimidated by their health care professionals. Patients should never feel out of control of their health care. The chart on page 207 list patient rights. All patients have these rights, regardless of where they are receiving care.

Selecting Health Care Facilities

When Dion needed knee surgery, he elected to have the procedure done at an outpatient surgery center. Dion went to the center the day before his surgery for presurgery tests. The morning of the surgery, Dion arrived about two hours before the surgery. After the operation, he rested in the recovery area for about an hour and a half before he was released to go home.

Today, outpatient surgery centers are a common alternative to full-service hospitals for some tests and procedures. Many hospitals provide both inpatient and outpatient services. Inpatient services imply the patient will be spending at least one night in the hospital.

Outpatient services imply the patient may spend several hours in the hospital or clinic for a procedure, but will not stay overnight.

General hospitals provide health care for many types of illnesses and injuries. Specialty hospitals provide care for particular health care needs or certain populations. For example, Memorial Sloan-Kettering Cancer Center in New York City specializes in the treatment of cancer, and Children's Memorial Hospital in Chicago specializes in the treatment of children.

If you need medical tests, treatments, or surgery, your physician will tell you with which facilities he or she is associated. Many physicians are associated with more than one facility. If you are given a choice, ask people who have used the facility about their experiences. You may also want to check the fees of each facility and consider the location.

FOCUS ON ...
Your Rights As a Patient

As a patient, you have the right to:

- Open, but confidential, communication with all health care providers.
- Have your symptoms, diagnosis, prognosis, and possible treatments, explained in simple terms.
- Know why you need specific tests or treatments, how much they will cost, what risks are involved, and what your choices are.
- Refuse tests or treatments.
- A second opinion regarding surgery or other treatment.
- Discuss problems with your provider. If you cannot resolve the problem, you can take action. You can contact your local medical society, state licensing board, or Better Business Bureau.
- Change doctors.

• Providing accurate information to your health care provider, makes it easier for the professional to help you. **Think about the types of health care you might need when on your own—medical, dental, eye care, etc. What information might you need to provide to your health care professionals?**

• Selecting health insurance can be an overwhelming responsibility. **What factors should you consider when selecting health insurance?**

Health Insurance

In today's environment of ever-rising health care costs, health insurance, which pays for at least part of most medical care expenses, provides important financial protection for people. Lack of insurance can mean going without needed health care or having to use lower quality care.

Although there are a large number of insurance companies—and each company offers a variety of insurance plans—the basic concept of health insurance is the same: you pay the insurance company a certain amount of money—called a *premium*—each month. If you need medical care that is covered by your policy, the insurance company, will pay all or part of the cost, depending on your policy.

Financial counselors advise people to buy enough insurance to cover the large health care needs that could wipe out their assets and tie up income for years to come.

Conventional Health Plans

Conventional health insurance may be categorized into two major types:

• **Basic coverage:** Sometimes called hospital/surgical coverage, this includes hospital, surgical, and medical benefits. This policy covers payments for only illnesses and conditions that require hospitalization. It does not cover out-of-hospital costs.

• **Comprehensive coverage:** Provides basic coverage and major medical protection. Major medical covers hospital and other medical expenses when basic protection runs out or doesn't apply.

Comprehensive plans offer the broadest protection, but they are more expensive. The cost of monthly insurance premiums is directly tied to the plan you want and to the amount of the deductible you agree to. An insurance *deductible* is the amount of money you must spend on health care out of your own pocket before the insurance company begins to pay anything. As a basic rule-of-thumb, the greater the benefits and the lower the deductible, the higher the cost of the plan.

Managed Care Plans

In recent years, soaring health care costs have caused many people to seek alternative plans to help finance their health care needs. One alternative is a **health maintenance organization (HMO),** or a group of physicians who offer a comprehensive range of health care services for regular monthly fees. HMOs are one option offered by many insurance companies. Members receive all the health care they need at no additional cost or for a small *copayment* at the time of the office visit.

With most HMOs, you must choose a primary care physician who is affiliated with your plan. This physician usually "manages" your health care. If he or she thinks you need to see a specialist, a referral is made to a specialist within your plan's network of physicians. You have fewer physician choices when you're part of an HMO plan. The HMO physicians and administrators decide what care, including preventive care, is needed or not needed. The HMO also decides which hospital or other facilities will be made available to members of the plan.

Another type of managed care is a **preferred provider organization (PPO)**. In a PPO plan, physicians and other health care providers agree to charge less to members of the plan. You have more choices regarding health care providers in a PPO plan, but at a higher cost than other plans.

Dental Insurance

Dental insurance is a relatively new type of insurance offered to many people through their employers. You can also purchase individual dental insurance policies. Dental insurance generally covers preventive dental care, general dental care, and accidental damage caused to teeth. Like other forms of health insurance, dental insurance usually has an annual deductible that you must pay before insurance pays all or part of the remaining cost. If your insurance plan pays only part of the remaining cost, you are generally responsible for the remainder. Some plans have a yearly maximum that you can spend on dental care.

Sources of Insurance

People over 65 years old, injured workers, and those with certain disabilities or who meet certain income requirements may qualify for state or federal government insurance programs. Everyone else who wants insurance must purchase it from private insurance companies.

Sources include private health insurance plans, which may be either individual or group. Group plans are preferred because their cost is usually much lower than individual plans. Your employer may offer group

• As a consumer, you will need to weigh your options about health insurance very carefully. What factors are most important to you in obtaining health insurance?

insurance as a job benefit, and may partially or fully pay the premium. Many professional associations also offer group plans to their members.

You may be able to include your spouse and children on your group plan. If you do not qualify for a group plan, you must purchase an individual program. If you are covered under your own or your spouse's group plan and become separated, divorced, or widowed, federal law (COBRA) requires that the employer continue offering you group rate coverage for 36 months. You must pay the premiums.

Preventing Illness

You can do much to prevent illness from affecting your life. Consider these facts:

- A proper diet combined with exercise helps strengthens your immune system.
- Staying within a weight range appropriate for your height and frame increases longevity and reduces your chances of depression.

- Regular cardiovascular exercise improves the efficiency of your heart and reduces stress.
- Avoiding tobacco use and not abusing alcohol and other drugs can make the difference between good health and poor health.
- Following directions closely when you receive a prescription from your physician can help you recover more quickly.
- Washing your hands frequently with an antibacterial soap during cold and flu season can help prevent you from getting sick.
- Drinking six to eight glasses of water each day and getting a proper amount of sleep each night improves your chances of staying healthy year-round.

Illnesses are often the results of diseases. Most diseases can be classified as either communicable or noncommunicable.

• Although it is a simple thing, thorough hand-washing is one of the most effective ways of preventing communicable disease. **What are some other things that you can do to prevent illness?**

Communicable Diseases

Communicable diseases are passed from one person to another. The common cold, hepatitis, and mononucleosis are examples of communicable diseases. These diseases are caused by tiny organisms called pathogens. Pathogens infect, or invade, your body and attack its cells and tissues. Pathogens are spread by indirect or direct contact with infected people, or by contact with insects and other animals that carry the disease. You can avoid communicable diseases by good hygiene—particularly frequent hand washing.

Vaccinations now immunize people against many communicable diseases that were once deadly including measles, polio, diphtheria, and tetanus. You probably received many vaccinations as a child. Your doctor can tell you what vaccinations you need as an adult.

Noncommunicable Diseases

Noncommunicable diseases are often called lifestyle diseases because personal health habits are important in their development. These diseases can't be passed from person to person. Instead, noncommunicable diseases, such as cardiovascular disease, diabetes, and cancer, develop slowly over time. Many of these diseases can be prevented by good personal health habits. Eating a nutritious diet, getting adequate rest and regular exercise, and avoiding tobacco use, and alcohol and drug abuse will help you lower your risk of these diseases.

Sexually Transmitted Diseases

Sexually transmitted communicable diseases represent a serious threat to your health. **Sexually transmitted diseases (STDs)** are passed from one person to another through sexual contact. Most people become infected by having sexual intercourse with a person who is already infected.

FOCUS ON ...
Cancer's Seven Warning Signs

Early detection of cancer is the most critical factor in treating or curing the disease. You should be alert to these seven warning signs of cancer:

- Change in bowel habit: either loose stools, or constipation.
- A sore that does not heal.
- Unusual bleeding or discharge (as from the uterus, bladder, bowels, or with coughing).
- Thickening or a lump in the breast, or elsewhere (let your doctor decide what the lump means).
- Indigestion or difficulty swallowing.
- Obvious change in a wart or mole.
- Nagging cough or hoarseness.

Other symptoms include fatigue and unexplained weight loss.

The most serious sexually transmitted disease is **acquired immune deficiency syndrome (AIDS)**, which is caused by the **human immunodeficiency virus (HIV)**. There is no cure for AIDS. Medical advances in recent years have done much to deal with the devastation of this disease.

The risks of some STDs are reduced (but not eliminated) if a condom is always used during sexual intercourse. The best medical advice is this: sex is an expression of affection and intimacy that's meant to be shared with someone you want to spend your life with. The only *100 percent effective* method of preventing sexually transmitted diseases is **sexual abstinence**, the decision not to engage in sexual activity.

Sexually Transmitted Diseases*

STD	Symptoms	Treatments
Acquired Immune Deficiency Syndrome (AIDS)	Some people show flulike symptoms in 1-12 weeks after exposure. There may be no symptoms for the next several months or years. The final stage symptoms include a weakened immune system that allows opportunistic infections such as pneumonia to ravage the body.	AIDS can be fatal. However, advanced medical treatments are vastly improving the lives and life expectancy of AIDS victims.
Chlamydia	Males experience pain and burning during urination and an unusual discharge from the penis. For females, symptoms are not always obvious, but they may include unusual vaginal discharge, pain in the pelvic region, and painful urination. This is the most prevalent STD in the United States today. It is a common cause of sterility.	Some antibiotics can cure chlamydia.
Genital warts	Pink or reddish warts with cauliflower-like tops appear 1-3 months after infection. Once infected, a person has the virus for the remainder of life. Genital warts are linked to cervical cancer in women.	Genital warts may be removed by a physician, but may reappear
Genital herpes	Symptoms for both men and women include painful, itching sores in and around the genitals. Sores usually appear 2-20 days after infection and may last as long as 3 weeks. Genital herpes sometimes causes a burning sensation during urination. Herpes sores may spread to other areas of the body and break out periodically, often in response to stress. Linked to cervical cancer in females. Infants born to women who are suffering an outbreak of herpes at the time of birth face serious health risks, including permanent deformity.	Genital herpes is incurable, and there is no sure way to know when the disease is in its contagious stage. Some medications exist to treat symptoms.

(continued)

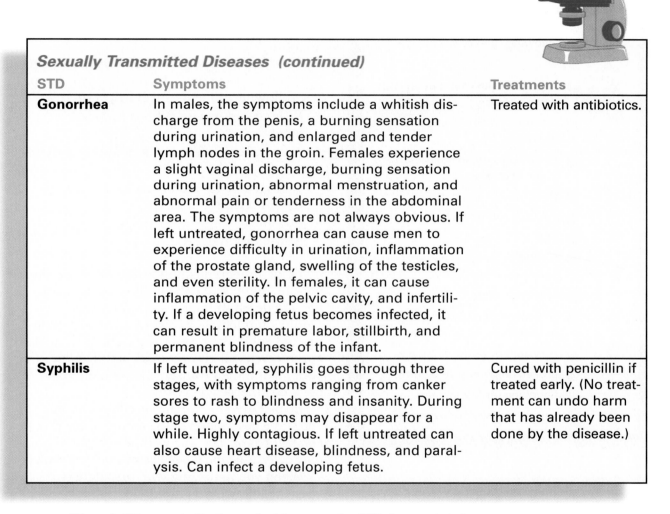

Sexually Transmitted Diseases *(continued)*		
STD	**Symptoms**	**Treatments**
Gonorrhea	In males, the symptoms include a whitish discharge from the penis, a burning sensation during urination, and enlarged and tender lymph nodes in the groin. Females experience a slight vaginal discharge, burning sensation during urination, abnormal menstruation, and abnormal pain or tenderness in the abdominal area. The symptoms are not always obvious. If left untreated, gonorrhea can cause men to experience difficulty in urination, inflammation of the prostate gland, swelling of the testicles, and even sterility. In females, it can cause inflammation of the pelvic cavity, and infertility. If a developing fetus becomes infected, it can result in premature labor, stillbirth, and permanent blindness of the infant.	Treated with antibiotics.
Syphilis	If left untreated, syphilis goes through three stages, with symptoms ranging from canker sores to rash to blindness and insanity. During stage two, symptoms may disappear for a while. Highly contagious. If left untreated can also cause heart disease, blindness, and paralysis. Can infect a developing fetus.	Cured with penicillin if treated early. (No treatment can undo harm that has already been done by the disease.)

*The only 100 percent effective method for preventing STDs is sexual abstinence.

In many cases, early symptoms of STDs are not obvious, and the person does not know that he or she is infected. Left untreated, some STDs can lead to serious illness or, especially in the case of AIDS, death. The chart on pages 212-213 lists the symptoms of some common STDs.

Handling Medical Emergencies

Lila suddenly dropped her tennis racquet, fell to her knees, then slumped to the ground. Anna and Mei rushed to her side. Lila was conscious, but her face was white. Anna immediately tried to help Lila sit up. "No," said Mei gently pulling Lila into a resting position flat on the court. "She's pale; we need to raise her feet." Would you know what to do if someone fainted? Do you know how to stop severe bleeding? What if someone stopped breathing?

You can't always prevent emergencies from happening, but you can be prepared for them. The following guidelines will help you:

- Keep emergency telephone numbers handy.
- Know where safety and first aid equipment is kept.
- Take a basic first aid class sponsored by the American Red Cross.
- Become certified in cardiopulmonary resuscitation (CPR).

Being prepared is important. Your actions literally might make the difference between life and death. If the person's condition requires immediate access to medical personnel and equipment, call the paramedic unit. Paramedics will give first aid, stabilize the patient, and then transport the patient to a hospital emergency room.

Be prepared to give the specific location, and some description of the nature of the problem before you call. The victim's symptoms may determine the type of rescue vehicle sent.

When you're dealing with dispatchers, keep the following in mind:

- If you have to call paramedics, try to stay as focused as possible on giving the most important information. For example, "She's clutching her chest" or "Her left arm is bleeding badly" can be valuable information.
- A good paramedic dispatcher will be able to give you valuable help over the phone. Try to ask, "Is there anything I can do?"

REASON

Through Life's Problems

Recognizing the Primary Problem

Sometimes the hardest part of solving a problem is identifying what the problem really is. See if you can get to the core of Lorenzo's problem in the situation that follows.

"Why am I always so tired?" wondered Lorenzo as he rested his head against the bus window. "Maybe I can catch a few winks before we get to my bus stop."

Lorenzo closed his eyes, but thoughts whirling around his head kept him from resting. "I wonder if there's something seriously wrong with me. I'm too tired to fix much of anything to eat again. I just want to hit the sack when I get home."

Lorenzo had just taken a job in a different city and hadn't made very many friends yet. "It's just as well—I don't feel like doing anything but sleeping anyway," he sighed. "I'm afraid my supervisor notices me yawning all the time, and I'm always too tired to study the project manuals in the evening. All I need is a bad evaluation on my first review."

Once home, Lorenzo stretched out across his bed, wearing his work clothes. "Maybe I should get a checkup, but I don't know where to find a good doctor. I wonder if I have to pick one from a certain list to be covered by insurance. I don't even know what my insurance covers."

As Lorenzo drifted off to sleep, he resolved to do something tomorrow about all of his problems. "Where do I start?" he mumbles to himself.

►From Your Perspective

1 What is Lorenzo's main problem to be solved? What are the related problems? Is there a sequence to the problems?

2 What factors will affect how Lorenzo's problem will be solved?

3 What outcome does Lorenzo hope to achieve?

Average people have been known to deliver babies, successfully perform CPR, and revive choking victims by staying calm, using common sense, and following directions. For less severe emergencies, you can transport the patient in a private car to a hospital emergency room or urgent care center.

When you get to the hospital emergency room or urgent care center, be prepared to give a description of the accident or the patient's symptoms and, if you know it, medical history. If possible also bring the patient's insurance information.

Take Charge

Many professionals can help you achieve and maintain wellness, but the responsibility is yours. You are ultimately responsible for your health and the quality of your health care.

You can also influence those around you—at your workplace, place of worship, or school:

- Consider coordinating a sports team.
- Offer to coordinate a basic first aid, CPR, or STD awareness seminar.

- Organize a weekly lowfat, healthful lunch meal in which everyone prepares a salad, soup or dessert and brings the recipe along.

Be determined to stand as a good example for the people around you. Wellness is a life-long pursuit. Take charge of your own health. Keep up, stay informed, and put your knowledge into action.

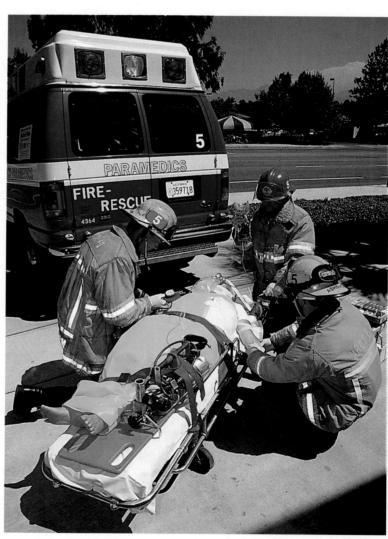

• A paramedic or emergency medical technichian (EMT) is trained to handle emergencies of all kinds. If you come across an accident or medical emergency, call for help. **When do you think that calling an ambulance would be necessary?**

Life Insurance—Do You Need It?

Along with health insurance, many people choose to buy life insurance to protect loved ones from financial hardship in case of the policyholder's death.

Life Insurance Options

Life insurance policies can give you protections for varying lengths of time. There are three basic categories: term, permanent, or combination policies.

- **Term insurance.** These policies provide protection against loss of life for a given period of time. You pay the premiums for coverage for the length of the term designated in the policy.
- **Permanent insurance.** The insured is covered for the duration of his or her life with this coverage. Some view permanent insurance as a type of savings, since part of the premium is put into savings.
- **Combination insurance.** The best features of term and permanent insurance are combined in this option. The most common form of combination insurance is called *universal life*. Policies such as these are basically term insurance with cash value. A portion of the premium is invested and grows interest.

What Are the Costs?

Regardless of the type of policy, all insurance costs money. The cost will be based on your age at the time you purchase the policy and the duration of the policy. Other factors that can affect the cost of a policy include your health, the type of insurance, the company you select, your occupation, your gender, and the basic value of the policy.

On average, the cost of term insurance is very low compared with permanent insurance and combination policies.

Basic Policy Features

Before you purchase any type of insurance, read the policy carefully and understand its contents. Here are some common features in life insurance policies:

- **Premium information.** Your insurance policy will tell you the cost of your premiums and when your premiums are due.
- **Beneficiary information.** When you purchase an insurance policy, you are required to name a beneficiary, a person or group who will receive the benefits of your policy when you die. As your family situation changes, it's important to update your beneficiary list.

Using Your Resources Wisely

1 What factors should you think about in determining your life insurance needs?

2 What values might enter into your decision about life insurance?

3 How would you go about finding specific information regarding life insurance?

Understanding Key Concepts

● To achieve wellness, you must know what behaviors can help you be healthy, and make these behaviors part of your life.

● The best time to choose a health care professional is before you need one.

● Today, outpatient surgery centers are a common alternative to full-service hospitals for some tests and procedures.

● Two major types of conventional health insurance include basic and comprehensive coverage.

● In recent years, many people have turned to HMOs and PPOs instead of traditional insurance companies to finance their health care needs.

● Dental insurance is an option as part of your total health care plan.

● Sexually transmitted diseases (STDs) are diseases that are transmitted by sexual contact. Sexual abstinence is the most effective way to avoid STDs.

● Because medical emergencies can occur any time, anywhere, be prepared.

1. What are the consequences of poor health choices for you? Your family? Your coworkers?

2. What do you need to maintain a healthful lifestyle?

3. Why is health insurance an important part of your wellness plan? How can you use it effectively?

4. What is most important to keep in mind when you choose health care facilities? Health care professionals? Why?

5. Why do you need regular checkups?

6. Why is sexual abstinence the only 100 percent effective method of preventing sexually transmitted diseases?

7. If you or someone you know is at high risk for cardiovascular disease, cancer, or diabetes, what lifestyle changes could you suggest to reduce the risks?

Making TRANSITIONS

Taking Charge of Your Health Care

Use your problem-solving skills to help you plan for and take care of meeting your health care needs. Think about the information you will need to gather and the choices you will need to make.
• What values will guide your choices?
• Develop a plan for meeting your health care needs.

STRENGTHENING *Life* SKILLS

Becoming More Assertive

You're living on your own, and money is really tight. You have a painful sore throat that just won't go away. You've been going to the same doctor for three years but really aren't satisfied with the care you've received. She's always in a hurry and seldom allows you time to ask questions. Also, you find her a little intimidating. You don't really feel comfortable describing your symptoms to her. Think about the following questions. Then discuss your response with a partner in class. Write a brief summary of your discussion.

• What are your options?
• What should you do? Why?

Applying Thinking Skills

1. **Making generalizations.** Analyze some of the reasons people don't make healthy choices. What are the consequences of bad choices?

2. **Predicting consequences.** What physical and emotional consequences can occur when someone engages in sexual activity with multiple partners? How might this affect future relationships and overall wellness?

3. **Drawing conclusions.** Conventional insurance is expensive and is becoming less available to consumers. Managed care plans lower out-of-pocket costs, but choice of physician is limited and people may have to wait for care. With some managed care plans, specialized care may not be available to everyone. Draw conclusions as to whether it is better to have good health care available to everyone at a higher cost, or minimal care for everyone at a lower cost.

Practical Applications

1. **Summarizing articles.** Read two or more current articles concerning the most common health care issues of young adults ages 18 to 25 in the United States. Summarize the issues and discuss with your classmates what can be done about them.

2. **Expressing your opinion.** Many states now require screening for some STDs before granting a marriage license. Write a letter that could be sent to the editor of your local newspaper explaining why you agree or disagree with mandatory screening.

3. **Preparing for emergencies.** Assess your emergency preparedness. What steps will you need to take to improve your ability to respond effectively to emergencies? Write a summary of your plan.

CHAPTER 13

Maintaining Physical Health

What You Will Learn...

- How to achieve physical well-being.
- The importance of making healthy food choices.
- How to develop an exercise program that fits your schedule and holds your interest.

Terms for Success

daily values
eating patterns
nutrient deficiency
physical well-being
repetitive strain injury

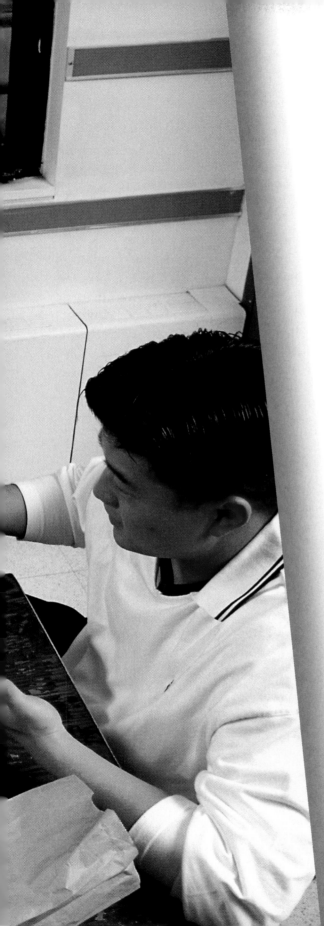

Colin sagged against the counter in the employee lounge, stirring another sugar into his coffee. It was almost 10:30 a.m., and he still felt half-asleep.

His friend Jeff walked briskly into the lounge. Colin blinked and straightened up.

"Hey, Col," Jeff greeted him as he took his lunch sack from the refrigerator. "Haven't forgotten about dinner tonight, have you? Kay and I have discovered a new Chinese recipe. You're going to love it."

"Wouldn't miss it for the world," Colin said.

Jeff paused before his friend. "You're looking a little rough there, pal."

Colin shrugged. "Must be that bug that's going around. I'll be okay."

"Seems like that bug hit you last week, too. I wonder if it has anything to do with only coffee for breakfast and that you are just plain doing too much right now. Colin, did you get enough sleep last night?"

"You're starting again," Colin warned.

"What can I say?" Jeff returned. "I like to take care of my friends." He frowned. "Maybe we should put off tonight. You look like you could use some rest."

"I'll be fine," Colin assured him.

Jeff reached into the lunch sack and set a container of orange juice on the counter in front of Colin. "Here. You need this more than I do."

Colin smiled at the offering. "Now you're on to me," he said. "I only act this way to get free food."

"Then tonight you hit the jackpot," Jeff replied. "We'll send all the leftovers home with you. It'll probably be the only food in your refrigerator."

Colin picked up the plastic glass of juice. Part of him actually did want to stay home tonight. His own words came back to him: "I wouldn't miss it for the world."

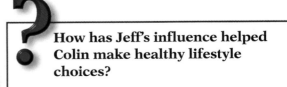

How has Jeff's influence helped Colin make healthy lifestyle choices?

Achieving Physical Well-being

Colin chooses coffee. Jeff chooses orange juice. Colin chooses spray-on cheese. Jeff chooses Chinese vegetables and rice. The decisions you make every day affect your physical well-being. **Physical well-being** refers to your health and to how well you feel. You can avoid many illnesses, disabilities, and premature death if you develop good health habits.

Identifying Lifestyle Factors

People who practice good health habits live longer, healthier lives. The most important habits you can develop to protect your health include these:

- Get 7 to 8 hours of sleep each night.
- Develop healthy eating habits.
- Maintain your recommended weight.
- Participate in a regular exercise program.
- Select and use equipment carefully to avoid risk of physical stress and injury.
- Perform self-examinations regularly.
- Drink six to eight glasses of water each day to flush out toxins and stay hydrated.

Finding Reliable Information

Americans have access to an interesting variety of health, nutrition, and fitness information. You must determine for yourself what is accurate and reliable. Otherwise, you can easily become the victim of health quackery and frauds. Quackery involves promoting a particular food, diet, supplement, or device as a health aid without sound scientific evidence. Falling for health quackery can cause you to waste money. Even more seriously, it can result in injury, illness, or even death.

• The habits that you develop now in your life will influence your physical wellness in later years. In what ways might you improve your physical wellness?

• Making healthful food choices is just part of physical well-being. What are your food choices like during the day? Where do you need to make some improvements?

When you hear or read health information, don't jump to conclusions. Before you follow anyone's health advice, ask yourself whether the source is a reliable one. Make certain the advice will hold true over time.

Choosing Healthy Foods

Food affects everything you do. It affects how you look, feel, and act. It affects how well you function each day. For good health, you will want to observe basic guidelines for making good food choices. You'll need to recognize signs and effects of poor nutrition and any additional nutrition needs you may have.

Choosing a Healthy Diet

A healthful diet should be based on your personal energy needs. The energy your body needs is measured in calories. Calories are a measure of the energy in food and how your body burns this energy. Your body needs energy to carry on basic processes, such as breathing and pumping blood, and to fuel activities, such as walking or running.

How many calories do you need? Your energy needs depend on your rate of growth, body size, sex, age, metabolic rate, and activity level. The U.S. Department of Agriculture makes the following suggestions for calorie intake:

- 1600 calories for inactive women and some older adults.
- 2200 calories for most children, female teens, active women, and many inactive men.
- 2800 calories for male teens, many active men, and some very active women.

If your body uses as many calories as you consume in food, your body weight will stay about the same. However, if the calories do not balance, over time, you will gain or lose weight.

Health experts recommend that you maintain a healthy balance of calories from fat, carbohydrates, and protein. The recommended calorie ratio is 30 percent or less from fat, 55 percent or more from carbohydrates, and 12 to 15 percent from protein.

Scientists have identified more than 40 different nutrients for good health. Nineteen of these are called essential nutrients and should be taken in daily. These nutrients can be found in six main food groups: carbohydrates, fats, proteins, vitamins, minerals, and water. Each has a unique function in the normal growth and functioning of the body.

No one food provides all the nutrients your body needs. The *Dietary Guidelines for Americans* makes the following recommendations to decrease your risk of diet-related health problems:

- Aim for a healthy weight.
- Be physically active each day.
- Let the Pyramid guide your food choices.
- Choose a variety of grains daily, especially whole grains.
- Choose a variety of fruits and vegetables daily.
- Keep food safe to eat.
- Choose a diet that is low in saturated fat and cholesterol and moderate in total fat.
- Choose beverages and foods to moderate your intake of sugars.
- Choose and prepare foods with less salt.

Following the Food Guide Pyramid, a guide provided by the U.S. Food and Drug Administration, helps you meet the recommendations suggested in the Dietary Guidelines. It explains how many servings you should have each day from the six different categories. See page 225 for more information on the Food Guide Pyramid.

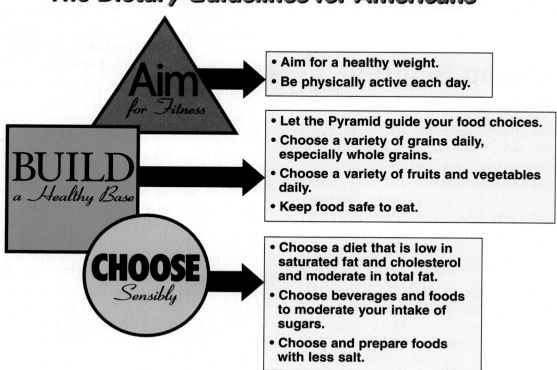

The Dietary Guidelines for Americans

Aim *for Fitness*
- Aim for a healthy weight.
- Be physically active each day.

BUILD *a Healthy Base*
- Let the Pyramid guide your food choices.
- Choose a variety of grains daily, especially whole grains.
- Choose a variety of fruits and vegetables daily.
- Keep food safe to eat.

CHOOSE *Sensibly*
- Choose a diet that is low in saturated fat and cholesterol and moderate in total fat.
- Choose beverages and foods to moderate your intake of sugars.
- Choose and prepare foods with less salt.

• The Dietary Guidelines offer suggestions for meeting your food needs and decreasing your risk of diet related illness. How do the Dietary Guildelines fit with your current eating plan?

In addition to using these two guides, you can also read food product labels to help you make wise food choices. Labels provide a wealth of information. They should indicate the amount of fats, sugars, carbohydrates, proteins, and sodium is in the product. For many of these nutrients, the nutrition label also contains the percent of daily values. **Daily values** are nutrient amounts based on recommendations of health experts. For example, suppose a nutrition label said that a certain food product contained 480 milligrams of sodium and the "percent Daily Value" column on the label tells you that one serving of this food provides 20 percent of the sodium needed per day. Based on this information, how much sodium do you need per day? Remember, the daily values needed of some other nutrients—such as fat, carbohydrate, and fiber—vary from person to person depending upon the amount of calories needed.

Recognizing the Effects of Poor Nutrition

If you make poor food choices, or don't take in enough calories, you probably won't get the right balance of nutrients. You could experience what is called a **nutrient deficiency,** and your health is likely to suffer. You could be more susceptible to illness or infection and other conditions later in life, such as osteoporosis—a common condition in which bones gradually become weak and fragile.

The food choices you make today will affect your health for many years. Poor food choices increase your risk of diseases that can shorten your life or reduce your quality of life. Making wise food choices can increase your chances of staying healthy, strong, and active throughout your life.

Food Guide Pyramid

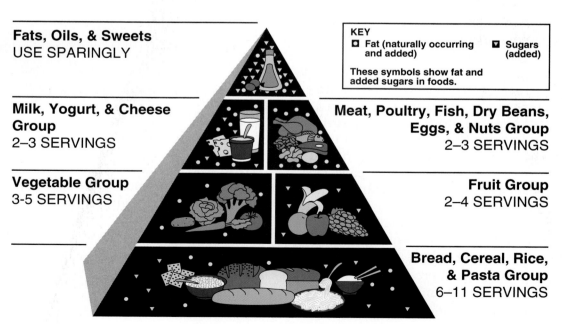

Fats, Oils, & Sweets
USE SPARINGLY

KEY
☐ Fat (naturally occurring and added)   ▼ Sugars (added)
These symbols show fat and added sugars in foods.

Milk, Yogurt, & Cheese Group
2–3 SERVINGS

Meat, Poultry, Fish, Dry Beans, Eggs, & Nuts Group
2–3 SERVINGS

Vegetable Group
3-5 SERVINGS

Fruit Group
2–4 SERVINGS

Bread, Cereal, Rice, & Pasta Group
6–11 SERVINGS

• Using the Food Guide Pyramid as a guide in making your daily food choices helps make sure that you are meeting your body's nutrient needs.

• Pregnancy is a time when good nutrition is especially important to mother and child. Why should good nutrition be a habit before a woman gets pregnant?

Developing Healthy Eating Habits

How are your eating habits when you are rushed or stressed? Sometimes people rush through meals or forget to eat at all. When life gets hectic, it can be difficult to keep up with making wise food choices.

One excellent way to become more aware of your eating habits is to keep a food journal. To do this you simply get a notebook, keep it with you all the time for two or three days. In it, you write down:

• The time you ate.
• Every single thing you ate and the portion size. Even a small piece of candy should be included.
• What you drank and the amount.
• A brief description of where you were, what you were doing, who you were with and what mood you were in.

Keep your food record for three consecutive days, including at least one weekend day. During this time, make your usual food choices.

At the end of the three-day period, review your food choices. For each day, count the number of servings you had from each food group in the Food Guide Pyramid (page 225). Compare your totals with the recommended number of servings.

To gather even more information, you can—by reading labels and looking through a calorie guide—figure out:

• How many grams of protein, fat and carbohydrates you consumed in a day.
• Your total caloric intake for the day.
• What percentage of your diet for that one day was made up of fat.

Once you have identified your eating habits, think about how you might improve them. In what situations did you tend to make poor food choices? Next, think about how to solve the problems you identified.

Making Wise Food Choices

The term **eating patterns** refers to when, what, and how much people eat. Today, eating patterns are becoming more varied. Some people eat three traditional meals each day.

• Keeping track of your food choices for several days will help you identify the strengths and weaknesses of your diet. Although this might seem like a tedious task, how might you benefit from keeping a food record?

inherited physical shape. There are several methods you can use to determine a healthy weight. These include:

- **Height-weight charts.** These offer ranges to stay within. For instance a woman who is five feet four inches tall should weigh somewhere between 115 and 127, according to most fitness experts. One reason for the range is because bodies have different size bone structure. Another reason for the weight range is that muscle weighs slightly more than fat. For example, Jody and Judy are identical twins. Same height. Same bone structure. Jody appears slightly thinner than Judy, but she actually weighs two pounds more. This is because she works out regularly at the gym with a free weight routine than tones her muscles. Toned muscles are thinner but more condensed. They actually weigh slightly more but look smaller.

- **Body fat measurement.** Fitness specialists can determine how much of your entire body is made up of fat. The most common way to measure body fat is by using a set of calipers to measure the thickness of skin folds. Desirable body fat is about 11 to 18 percent for males and 16 to 23 percent for females. A person with an excess of body fat is considered obese. Another important consideration is the location of the fat. Excess abdominal fat increases the chance of heart disease and diabetes more than excess fat located in the hips and thighs.

Others prefer "grazing," or eating several small meals throughout the day. Varied schedules may cause eating patterns to vary from day to day. Whatever your eating pattern, your goal is to make nutritious food choices throughout the day. It's also important to eat regularly.

Nutritious snacks can help you meet your energy and nutrient needs for the day. Healthy snacks include fresh fruits or vegetables, low-fat dairy products, and whole grain breads and cereals. Remember that snacks are part of your total food intake, so choose them wisely.

Maintaining a Healthy Weight

What is a healthy weight? It's a weight that will help you stay healthy throughout your life. It's one that is appropriate for your own

Who Needs Nutrient Supplements?

In addition to changes in diet, people with some health conditions can benefit from nutrient supplements. Some of these health conditions are:

- Pregnant and nursing women have increased nutrient needs.
- Some illnesses affect appetite or nutrient absorption.
- Women may need extra iron to replace iron lost through menstruation.
- Some medications may interfere with nutrient absorption.
- People on special diets may not get enough nutrients from the food they eat.

For most people, however, getting vitamins, minerals, and other nutrients from a balanced diet, rather than from supplements, is the healthiest, safest approach. Nutrient supplements should not be substituted for nutritious food. Never take large amounts of any supplement without checking with your physician.

Using Your Resources Wisely

1 Is taking nutrient supplements a waste of money for most people? Why or why not?

2 Why should you check with your physician before taking nutritional supplements?

No matter what your shape or size, you can benefit from a sound weight-management program. Your goal should be to maintain a healthy weight throughout your life. Studies show that being overweight is a risk factor in heart disease, diabetes, cancer, and high blood pressure.

Once you have reached a healthy weight, your goal should be to maintain it. If you continue to follow good eating and exercise habits, you can maintain a healthy weight.

Achieving Physical Fitness

Physical fitness offers great benefits to almost all other areas of your life. It affects how you sleep and how you learn. If you're fit, you look good, you have energy, and you are likely to feel good about yourself. Staying fit requires a lifelong commitment.

Benefits of Exercise for Fitness

Exercise has many benefits. These benefits include:

- **Increased mobility.** Stretching exercises keep you flexible, relaxed, and improve your coordination.

Close-Up

Risky Weight-Loss Strategies

Many weight-loss plans rely on unsafe methods. Avoid diets based on:

- *800 calories or less. These diets may not provide enough energy or nutrients for good health.*

- *A single food. Your body needs a variety of foods every day.*

- *Fasting for long periods of time. Going without food can be extremely dangerous to your health.*

- *Diet pills. Some contain drugs that can cause serious health problems.*

- *Quick weight loss. Losing more than 2 pounds per week can endanger your health.*

Assume a friend of yours has been using diet pills for an extended time and has lost an excessive amount of weight. What could you do to help your friend to healthfully manage his or her weight?

● Eating a nutritious snack between meals can help you meet your daily food needs. **What are the pros and cons of "grazing?"**

- **Physical strength.** Exercise helps you build a strong body.

- **Better psychological health.** Regular exercise reduces stress and anxiety. As a result, you feel better and tend to have a brighter outlook on life and better self esteem.

- **Better physical health.** It increases your energy level and reduces fatigue. Exercise reduces your risk of osteoporosis, and can also lower blood pressure and blood choles-

terol levels and your risk of heart disease. A strong, toned body resists and recovers from illness faster than a body that is over-weight or in poor condition.

- **Easier weight control.** Exercise can help you lose and keep off excess weight. Your metabolic rate increases during exercise. This causes you to burn more calories than at rest. You continue burning more calories for a short while after you stop exercising.

- **Enjoyment.** Exercise can be fun, especially when you exercise with a friend or in a group. You can probably find several sports and other physical activities you enjoy.

- **Appearance.** When you are fit and healthy, you look fit and healthy.

Weight and Body Mass Index Chart

Height

Weight	5'0"	5'1"	5'2"	5'3"	5'4"	5'5"	5'6"	5'7"	5'8"	5'9"	5'10"	5'11"	6'0"	6'1"	6'2"	6'3"	6'4"
110	21	21	20	19	19	18	18	17	17	16	16	15	15	15	14	14	13
115	22	22	21	20	20	19	19	18	17	17	17	16	16	15	15	14	14
120	23	23	22	21	21	20	19	19	18	18	17	17	16	16	15	15	15
125	24	24	23	22	21	21	20	20	19	18	18	17	17	16	16	16	15
130	25	25	24	23	22	22	21	20	20	19	19	18	18	17	17	16	16
135	26	26	25	24	23	22	22	21	21	20	19	19	18	18	17	17	16
140	27	26	26	25	24	23	23	22	21	21	20	20	19	18	18	17	17
145	28	27	27	26	25	24	23	23	22	21	21	20	20	19	19	18	18
150	29	28	27	27	26	25	24	23	23	22	22	21	20	20	19	19	18
155	30	29	28	27	27	26	25	24	24	23	22	22	21	20	20	19	19
160	31	30	29	28	27	27	26	25	24	24	23	22	22	21	21	20	19
165	32	31	30	29	28	27	27	26	25	24	24	23	22	22	21	21	20
170	33	32	31	30	29	28	27	27	26	25	24	24	23	22	22	21	21
175	34	33	32	31	30	29	28	27	27	26	25	24	24	23	22	22	21
180	35	34	33	32	31	30	29	28	27	27	26	25	24	24	23	22	22
185	36	35	34	33	32	31	30	29	28	27	27	26	25	24	24	23	23
190	37	36	35	34	33	32	31	30	29	28	27	26	26	25	24	24	23
195	38	37	36	35	33	32	31	31	30	29	28	27	26	26	25	24	24
200	39	38	37	35	34	33	32	31	30	30	29	28	27	26	26	25	24
205	40	39	37	36	35	34	33	32	31	30	29	29	28	27	26	26	25
210	41	40	38	37	36	35	34	33	32	31	30	29	28	28	27	26	26
215	42	41	39	38	37	36	35	34	33	32	31	30	29	28	28	27	26
220	43	42	40	39	38	37	36	34	33	32	32	31	30	29	28	27	27
225	44	43	41	40	39	37	36	35	34	33	32	31	31	30	29	28	27
230	45	43	42	41	39	38	37	36	35	34	33	32	31	30	30	29	28
235	46	44	43	42	40	39	38	37	36	35	34	33	32	31	30	29	29
240	47	45	44	43	41	40	39	38	36	35	34	33	33	32	31	30	29
245	48	46	45	43	42	41	40	38	37	36	35	34	33	32	31	31	30
250	49	47	46	44	43	42	40	39	38	37	36	35	34	33	32	31	30

■ Underweight--≤18   ■ Overweight--25-29
■ Acceptable--19-24   ■ Obese--≥30

- Using your body mass index along with a height and weight chart is an effective way to determine if your weight is in a target range. Determine your BMI. Compare it to the chart on this page. How do you rate? What changes might you need to make it in your lifestyle?

Focusing on Fitness

There are three types of exercise. A well-rounded program includes all three.

FLEXIBILITY

Stretching exercises gently stretch your muscles. These exercises will keep your body flexible and can help prevent injury.

ENDURANCE

Endurance, or aerobic, exercises give your heart and lungs a workout. The term "aerobic" means using oxygen. Endurance exercises cause your heart and lungs to work harder. Walking, jogging, stair climbing, bicycling, swimming, and aerobic dance are good examples of endurance exercises.

STRENGTHENING

Strengthening exercises build strong muscles. Having strong muscles aids in everyday activities and helps prevent injury. Strengthening exercises include push-ups and sit-ups.

Another way to strengthen muscles is by lifting weights or using weight machines. Start with lighter weights and gradually increase to heavier ones. Seek advice from a health professional before starting to lift weights. In weight training, do the exercises slowly, taking at least 2 seconds each time you lower a weight. Rest for 1 or 2 minutes between sets.

Do a variety of exercises to strengthen your muscles through the full range of motion. A set consists of 10 to 14 repetitions.

Exercising Safely

Exercise can improve your health, but it can also result in injury if you're not careful. To avoid injury, choose the right type of exercise for you. Learn how to warm up and cool down properly. Check your progress frequently. Use the proper clothing and equipment and follow the correct techniques for each activity. If you feel pain while exercising, stop at once to prevent further injury.

Your exercise program should include three parts:

- **The warm-up.** The first step in warming up is to stretch your large muscles. Stretches should be slow and smooth, not jerky. Stretching helps increase the elasticity of your muscles and tendons. Stretching can help prevent injury during your workout. The second step in warming up is to perform the activity slowly for about 5 minutes. This allows your pulse rate to increase gradually, avoiding unnecessary strain on your heart and blood vessels.

- **The workout.** For your workout, choose an activity that continually uses the large muscle groups. Biking, walking, swimming, running, and aerobics are good choices. You should be performing the exercise at its highest intensity during this part of your exercise program. The appropriate intensity depends on your current fitness level. You should work hard, but not overdo it. Start slowly and build endurance.

- **The cool down.** The purpose of the cool down is to return your body gradually to a less active state. This helps

prevent lightheadedness, even fainting. When you are cooling down, gradually decrease activity by simply slowing down. Slower activity should be done for about 5 minutes, followed by 5 minutes of stretching. You have cooled down adequately when your heart rate is within 20 to 30 beats of your regular heart rate.

You'll want to check your progress regularly. Keeping a journal can help you check your progress. In the journal, list your goals and physical information such as weight, measurements, how you feel, how well you sleep, how long you sleep, and how energetic you feel. Keep track of the frequency, intensity, and duration of your workouts. At the end of six weeks, write down the same information about yourself. Compare the figures. Repeat the process every six weeks. You will be able to see your progress.

• Choosing footwear with a proper fit can help prevent injuries. **Why should proper fit be more important than brand name?**

Dressing properly and choosing the proper equipment can help you avoid injury while exercising. Choose clothing that is appropriate for the activity. Your clothing should be comfortable and allow free movement of your joints. Cotton or other porous materials absorb perspiration and allow air through. Your footwear should have a cushioned heel, good arch support, and ample toe room. Your equipment should be appropriate for you and for the activity. Reading and asking questions will help you determine what is needed.

If you exercise outdoors, take measures to avoid weather-related risks. In hot weather, prevent heat cramps, heat exhaustion, and heat stroke by drinking plenty of fluids before, during, and after you exercise. Restrict your activities on hot, humid days, especially if you are not accustomed to the weather. In cold weather, avoid fatigue and excessive exposure to cold while exercising to prevent frostbite. Dress warmly, covering all exposed skin, especially the head, face, fingers, and toes. If any of these conditions occur, provide appropriate first aid and seek medical advice.

An Ounce of Prevention

Maintaining physical well-being requires continuous effort. Prevention is often the key. In addition to developing good health habits, there are other measures you can take. One is to avoid repetitive strain injuries. Another is to perform regular self-examinations.

Avoiding Repetitive Strain Injury

A **repetitive strain injury** is a painful medical disorder caused by performing a similar activity over and over again. Such injuries may occur in a variety of activities at home, at work, or at play.

• Prevention is the best treatment for repetitive strain injuries. What activities do you participate in that have the potential for repetitive strain injuries? What can you do to avoid injury?

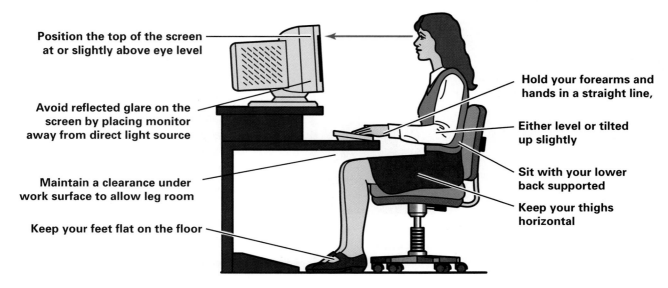

Position the top of the screen at or slightly above eye level

Avoid reflected glare on the screen by placing monitor away from direct light source

Maintain a clearance under work surface to allow leg room

Keep your feet flat on the floor

Hold your forearms and hands in a straight line,

Either level or tilted up slightly

Sit with your lower back supported

Keep your thighs horizontal

Anyone who regularly performs a repetitive task is at risk of developing a repetitive strain injury. Computer users, assembly-line workers, musicians, and tennis players are examples of people who frequently complain of symptoms. *Carpal tunnel syndrome*, a wrist disorder, is the most common repetitive strain injury. Tennis elbow is another. Medical treatment may be necessary in some cases. Surgery may be necessary if other treatments fail.

Prevention is the best treatment. To avoid repetitive strain injuries, pay attention to the organization of your workspace. Select tools and equipment carefully for the task. Learn proper posture and use of tools, equipment, and machines. Learn to maintain a reasonable pace and take rest breaks.

Physical Well-being for a Lifetime

Your quality of life depends largely on your attention to basic health habits. Your quality of life reflects your level of health, your physical fitness, and your satisfaction with your life. Being able to function effectively adds to your enjoyment of life and increases your productivity. Practicing sound decision-making and good health habits can help you maintain a good quality of life now and in the future.

• Adequate sleep and rest helps your body re-energize. **How much sleep do you regularly get? Do you take some time to relax throughout the day?**

Getting Adequate Sleep

TIPS

Part of your overall wellness is getting adequate sleep. Sleep helps your body re-energize and repair itself. Lack of sleep can affect your concentration, slow your reaction time, and lead to depression. Here are some tips to try in getting adequate sleep:

● Exercise at least three hours right before bed. Exercise energizes the body and can keep you awake.

● Avoid eating or drinking beverages with caffeine before going to bed.

● Plan time to unwind before bedtime. For some people, reading a book or taking a hot bath is very relaxing.

● Avoid stress-inducing TV shows and movies right before bed. The added stress or excitement can keep you awake.

REASON

Evaluate Information

Gathering and evaluating information helps create alternatives, and allows you to judge them against reliability factors, as these three friends discover.

Mario, Thad, and Lin are members of their college wresting team. Thad is constantly battling his weight to stay in the proper weight class.

"Some of the guys are using that high fat-high protein-low carbohydrate diet and losing a lot of weight and gaining muscle fast," Thad told Mario and Lin.

"I'm not sure that's such a good idea," said Mario. "It might mean some quick weight loss, but what might it do to your body and health in the long run?"

"I'm not sure. Let's see what we can find on the Internet about these diets," suggested Lin.

The three friends took turns searching Internet sites. They were amazed at the huge number of entries.

"How are we going to decide whom to believe?" Thad wondered out loud. "There seem to be about as many articles saying

these diets really work as there are saying that they are dangerous."

"Well, for one thing, let's check out whom the authors are of each of these sites," Lin said. They found that some of the sites were actually on-line advertisements for weight-loss products, but some of the sites were produced by organizations such as the American Dietetic Association and the American Medical Association.

"Let's ask the coach what he thinks," proposed Mario.

The coach was impressed that the guys were looking at the long-term effects of their diets, and were concerned about the reliability of the information they had found on the Net.

"I have a friend who teaches in the dietetics program. I'll ask her to come over and speak to the whole team after practice next week," the coach offered.

After listening to the dietitian speak, the three friends decided there were just too many risks with the high fat-high protein-low carbohydrate diet. They found out that excess fat and protein can lead to heart disease, cancer, and bone damage through loss of calcium.

"After a few days on a low carbohydrate diet, a person develops ketosis," explained the dietitian. "This is a condition in which the body breaks down stored energy reserves. The reserves may be fats, but they may also be muscle protein and organ tissue. Ketones—the by-product of ketosis—can be damaging to the kidneys."

"I'm glad Coach was able to help us find some reliable information," grinned Mario. "We would have spent the rest of our college careers sorting through all those articles."

▶From Your Perspective

1 Do you think the three friends found a reliable source of information? Why or why not?

2 What other sources of information would you consider reliable for this problem?

3 How might you check out the reliability of information on your own?

Understanding Key Concepts

- The decisions you make every day affect your physical well being both now and in the future.

- It's up to you to determine whether the health, nutrition, and fitness information you encounter is accurate and reliable.

- Health experts recommend that you maintain a healthy balance of calories from fat, carbohydrates, and protein.

- If you make poor food choices, or do not consume enough calories, you may be susceptible to nutrient deficiency and illness.

- Certain situations such as pregnancy, breast-feeding, stress, illness, certain medical conditions, physical disabilities, and food allergies can result in special nutrition needs or challenges.

- Exercise can help you increase mobility, improve both physical and psychological health, make weight control easier, and be fun.

- Exercise should be a regular part of your life. Begin by getting a medical checkup and setting realistic goals.

- Avoiding repetitive strain injury and performing self-examinations help you maintain your physical well-being.

Checking Your Knowledge

1. How can you avoid becoming the victim of health frauds and quacks?

2. What factors affect your calorie needs?

3. What tools can you use in choosing a healthy diet?

4. Describe how to keep a food record. How can studying the results of a food record aid in improving your eating habits?

5. Define the term "eating pattern." Describe two common eating patterns. What role do snacks play in your diet?

6. Describe two methods health professionals use to determine a healthy weight.

7. Describe three benefits of exercise.

8. Using the tips for beginning a successful exercise program, develop a plan for your own exercise program.

9. What can you do to avoid repetitive strain injuries?

Making TRANSITIONS

Workplace Health Issues

Assume that you are an employee in a work setting of your choice. You notice an unsafe or unhealthful condition and need to report it to your employer. With a partner who is taking the role of your employer, role-play a situation for the class in which you carefully describe this hazard to your employer. The employer should describe how he or she is going to deal with this situation. Then answer the following questions:

- What feelings did you have as you were describing this situation to your employer?
- Why is it important to be able to share your concerns in a clear manner?

STRENGTHENING *Life* SKILLS

Getting Rid of Excuses

What keeps you from exercising regularly? Do you ever feel like you can't exercise because you don't have the right shoes, clothing, or equipment? Do you need someone to exercise with you? Is the weather too hot, too cold, or too wet? Is there no activity available that fits your interests?

Whatever your excuses are, they are just that—excuses. They won't help you get fit. They will only distract you from getting started. Exercising can be as simple as putting on casual clothes and going for a walk, a run, or joining a neighborhood group in a basketball game.

- Make a list of creative or clever excuses people make for not exercising.
- Write song lyrics that offer positive alternatives to excuses.

Applying Thinking Skills

1. **Analyzing behavior.** Why do you believe so many people fall victim to health quacks and misinformation?

2. **Determining credibility.** Suppose you are planning to start a weight loss program. Several of your friends are following the plan described in a best-selling diet book. How will you decide whether to follow the plan?

3. **Analyzing behavior.** When Carmen analyzed her food record, she noticed that when she ate at home or alone, she made healthy food choices. However, when she ate with her friends, her choices weren't as healthy. Why might this be true?

Practical Applications

1. **Evaluating advertising.** Have students collect advertisements for products related to health or nutrition. Ask students to evaluate the techniques advertisers used to encourage people to buy the products. What facts are given? How does the ad persuade people to buy?

2. **Computer lab.** If dietary analysis software is available, use it to analyze a sample daily menu. How would you rate the menu's balance of carbohydrates, protein, and fat? How would you rate vitamins and minerals supplied? After making several changes to improve the menu, analyze it again. How do the results differ? Why?

3. **Developing a plan.** In a group, brainstorm ways you can add more physical activity to your daily lives. Choose at least one suggestion you are willing to implement. Keep a log of your physical activity for a week. Then, with your group, discuss the experience and ways to continue to increase your physical activity.

CHAPTER 14 ▷ Taming Your Stress

What You Will Learn...

- How a person's overall health is influenced by how he or she handles stress.
- Common sources of stress during young adulthood.
- How stressors affect people differently.
- The importance of making healthy choices in the face of stress.
- The relationship between stress management and wellness.
- The role of values, goals, and friendships in stress management.

Terms for Success

defense mechanisms
stress management
stressor

"**A**unt Shannon, look what I drew!"

A brown scribble appeared on Shannon's lap, covering the biology text she was trying to read.

"That's nice, Jenna," Shannon commented automatically to the hovering five-year-old.

"It's Dilly. He's my friend Kim's dog . . . " Jenna began.

"Jenna, look, I am really busy," Shannon said, her patience waning. "Can't you show me later?"

Subdued, Jenna took her picture and drifted back to the table scattered with crayons. Shannon checked her watch. "It's after five," she thought. "Where is that sister of mine?"

Shannon scanned the text again. She couldn't remember a thing she'd read in the past 20 minutes. "This is a waste," she fumed. "I can't watch Jenna and study. Meanwhile, my laundry is not getting done, that scholarship application is not getting filled out, and . . . "

"Aunt Shannon? I'm hungry."

Shannon stared at Jenna for a moment, then smiled at the little girl and said, "Give me five minutes. Then I'll make us something to eat."

Jenna smiled and sat down quietly to color another picture.

Shannon quickly wrote down what she HAD to do tonight. She made some quick notes of the most important things she needed to study, then turned to her niece.

"All righty then, what shall it be for dinner?"

"How about pancakes?" Jenna asked.

"Sounds good." Shannon said as she got up from the sofa.

A few minutes later, Shannon was stirring the batter when her sister walked in the door.

? What are the stressors Shannon is facing in this story? What action does she take that's healthy? What are some of the stressors you will face this week, and how do they compare to Shannon's circumstances?

The Impact of Stress on Your Health

The word "stress" is simply everywhere. Building engineers refer to stress as "the forces put on a structure by nature." They ask the question "How do we protect this structure from wind, rain, and even ice storms?"

For Shannon's evening with Jenna, the stress came in the form of constant interruptions from her niece, her upcoming test, and her sister's tardiness, which was putting her behind in her own schedule.

Like wind, rain, snow, and other forces of nature, human stress is part of life. No matter what you do, you can't entirely avoid it. Living in today's world is a fast-paced experience for most people, and it's not likely to slow down.

You really wouldn't want some kinds of stress to disappear from your life. If you managed to live a totally safe, predictable life, one that made absolutely no demands on your mind, your feelings, or your body, you'd be very bored (which is its own form of stress). Being alive means that life is full of demands, and these demands can bring about stress.

Some people seem to handle stress well while others don't cope with it well at all. More often than not, however, every person has certain stressors he or she handles well—and certain stressors that are a struggle. Joan can babysit calmly for six-year-old triplets. Marcia doesn't handle that well, but she's great as a server in a fast-paced restaurant. That's something Joan doesn't handle well.

• Life-changing events, such as joining the armed services, can cause stress. What are some changes that cause you stress?

How people handle stress influences their daily lives and wellness, or overall state of well-being or health. For instance, the way you cope with stress not only affects your physical health but your mental and social health as well. If you are stressed, you may withdraw from others, or you may be impatient with them. If the stress continues over time, your relationships with family members, friends, and coworkers may suffer.

Stress in Your Life

Tremeka's first job evaluation is coming up soon, and she feels stressed about it. She wants to be a veterinarian some day, and her job as a part-time vet assistant is important to her. She needs the work to pay for her college expenses. Without it, and a small scholarship she was awarded, she won't have enough money to go to school.

Like Tremeka, you may be feeling some stress right now. Maybe you wake up in the middle of the night worrying about things that never used to bother you. This is not unusual. Moving from the teen years to adulthood brings about many changes, and many worries about expectations.

Remember what caused you to feel stress when you were younger? Maybe you worried about being one of the group or not having enough friends. Fights with your parents or siblings probably were stressful. Taking tests, doing homework, going on dates, and winning or losing sports games were likely sources of stress.

Mark, a recent high school graduate, has quit worrying as much as he used to about how he looks or whether he'll have a date next weekend. Instead, he's feeling some understandable stress about going away to school and leaving his family and friends.

In high school, Mark experienced stresses common to many teens. Now that he is a young adult, he has other worries, including the desire for independence while still feeling a need for family support and concern. Like Mark, you may continue experiencing some of the stresses common during the teen years, but new ones are certain to be on the horizon.

• Looking for work and supporting yourself can be an added stressor as you transition into your adult life. What stressors seem to be top on your list?

Stress Over Your Future

As you learned earlier, much of the stress felt during early adulthood stems from increased independence and responsibility. When young adults leave the security of their family's home for college, work, or marriage and parenthood, they are likely to experience various degrees of stress. For example, when Ben decided to go to college, he felt some stress while searching for answers to questions such as:

- How much will college cost? How will I pay for it?
- Where will I live: at home, on campus, or in an apartment? Will I need one or more roommates to share the costs?
- How many years will college take? What course of study will I choose?

Growing into adulthood can be both exciting and challenging. As your independence and responsibilities increase, you will have more choices to make and problems to solve. Some of these may be difficult and stressful. For example, being in charge of your money, time, food, housing, and transportation may be exhilarating—but overwhelming. When you add school, work, and relationships with family and friends, calendars can get full, and your stress level may rise.

• Leaving home carries with it a whole different set of stresses. **What concerns you most about moving out on your own?**

Understanding the Effects of Stress

You've probably heard adults say to you or your friends, "Just wait until you get into the real world." This message is a way of saying, "It's work. It's tough. It's stressful, and you don't understand that."

Well . . . there is a very good chance you've already gotten an introduction to the "real world." Many young adults:

- Have experienced the pressures of juggling family life, school, and a part-time job.
- Know an older adult with a drinking problem (and have seen the consequences of this problem).
- Know a teen who is pregnant or already has a child.
- Understand sexual pressures on teens.

All of these are forms of stress. It's possible that you and many of your peers have experienced the positive and negative impacts of stress. The positive impacts are addressed later in this chapter. It is very important to learn the effects of stress so you can keep it from negatively affecting your daily life and level of health.

Physical Signs and Effects

Some physical signs and effects of stress can be easily observed. For example, if you're being chased by an angry dog, your heart may beat wildly and your body may be covered in sweat. If you're giving your first speech in front of a large audience, your mouth may get dry and your face may flush with redness.

Some of your body's responses to stress can be harmful to your physical health. A number of illnesses, including cardiovascular disease, hypertension (high blood pressure), asthma, colitis, and migraine headaches, are thought to be related to stress. Even though it may be difficult to identify stress as the major factor, there is increasing evidence that stressful emotions can cause physical reactions, which, over time, may be damaging to your body.

Some physical signs and effects could be the result of problems other than stress. For instance, there may be some other reason—such as excessive caffeine intake—for an upset stomach, headache, or sleeplessness. However, you may be wise to consider stress as a likely culprit.

FOCUS ON ...
Physical Signs and Effects of Stress

If you notice the following signs, you are probably experiencing the effects of stress:

- Sweating; clammy hands.
- Fast heartbeat.
- Headaches and backaches.
- Tight muscles or pain in the shoulders or neck.
- Upset stomach and diarrhea.
- Dizziness; dry mouth.
- Chronic tiredness or sleeplessness.
- Decreased resistance to infections.
- High blood pressure.

• Short term stress can be positive—helping you focus clearly and act effectively. When stress becomes negative, it wears your body down resulting in symptoms such as severe headaches, irritability, or depression.

When Lou gets stressed, he pulls out a notepad and on one sheet writes *What's Bugging Me*. On the other side he writes *Best Choices in Response*.

If Carl knows he has a pretty stressful week ahead—with two varsity games, two exams and fifteen hours of work at the store—he plans ahead as much as possible. Sometimes he even lays out the clothes he is going to wear each day so he doesn't have to worry about scrambling at the last minute to find something to wear.

Some signs and effects of stress tend to change as people move into adulthood. Eating disorders—serious signs of stress frequently seen in teens—are less prevalent in adults. On the other hand, high blood pressure and cardiovascular diseases are more common signs and effects during the adult years.

Regardless of when they occur, signs of stress are like warning lights. They could be warning you of serious problems. To protect your health, you need to be alert to any or all of the signs and effects, and to practice healthful ways to deal with stress.

Mental and Emotional Signs and Effects

Emotional signs and effects of stress differ from person to person. When Lucia is under too much stress at work, she becomes very critical of herself and her boss. When Troy is stressed, he becomes depressed and withdrawn.

Some people eat more, some eat less. Some talk endlessly; others stop talking completely. Some start drinking alcohol; others go running. Some make good choices; some make mistakes.

FOCUS ON ...
Emotional Signs of Stress

The following signs indicate an emotional response to stress:

- Restlessness.
- Boredom with school or work.
- Irritability and difficulty in getting along with others.
- Anger at self and others; road rage.
- Depression.
- Carelessness or forgetfulness.
- Eating too much or too little (or eating disorders).
- Anxiety; thoughts about suicide.

Taking Charge of Stress

Knowledge of how your body works when confronted with stressful situations is critical to your ability to cope with stress. The more you learn about yourself—what triggers stress in your mind and body and how you deal with the stress—the more resources you will have for facing problems, and joys, that come your way.

Recognizing Stress Triggers

A **stressor,** or stress trigger, is any stimulus that produces a stress response. The stressor can be a person, object, place, or event. Loud noises, heavy traffic, crowds of people, thunderstorms, accidents, illness, perceived danger, and change in one's life are common stressors.

• Stress triggers are different for every person—for some it might be a crowded street, for others it could be a severe storm. **What triggers a stress response in you?**

R E A(S)O N

Through Life's Problems

Select the Best Choice

Making the best choice can depend on many factors. See if you agree with Rhiana's justification for her choice in this situation.

Rhiana didn't even open her eyes as she picked up the phone before it woke her daughter, Star. "Hello," she whispered, propping up on her elbow in bed.

"Rhiana, we need you to come in here as soon as you can. Debra cancelled on us again, and we have to have at least four on the floor today." It was Mrs. Noggin, the personnel manager for the health care agency Rhiana works for.

"I wasn't supposed to come in until 1:00 P.M. today, and I don't know if I can find someone to watch the baby."

"That's your problem, girl. If you want to keep this job, you know you have to be flexible."

Rhiana hung up the phone and felt like crying. She liked her job as a patient care assistant, and the agency she worked for paid more than any other job

she'd ever had. They were always changing her schedule, though, and they expected her to show up on an hour's notice.

She hated calling anyone so early in the morning, but her mom and two sisters were getting used to it.

On her way to work, Rhiana's stomach churned while she thought about her predicament. For her daughter's sake and her own, she needed a better work schedule.

Rhiana had seen an ad in last night's paper for a patient care assistant at a nearby convalescence center. The pay was $2.00 less an hour than Rhiana was making now, but it had specified "day shift." She decided to call about the job when she got home.

Her head throbbing from lack of sleep, Rhiana called about the job.

"This new job looks like a much better choice for Star and me right now," she told her mother. "Even though it's less money per hour to start out, I'd be able to get both of us on a schedule, and could leave Star with you on a regular schedule.

"I wouldn't be able to afford some of the extras for a while, but they said I'd be eligible to get a raise in three months. I'm going to call and schedule an interview tomorrow."

►From Your Perspective

1 What goals do you think Rhiana has for her child's care? Will her choice help meet these goals?

2 What can you learn from how Rhiana responded to her situation?

3 How do you think Rhiana's choice will affect her level of stress?

- Road rage is becoming an increasing phenomena on roads and highways. **What does this tell you about people's ability to cope with everyday stress?**

For weeks after her grandfather's heart attack, Lin choked whenever she heard an ambulance siren. She had been alone with him the night of the attack. Lin had had to call the paramedics, and her response even two months later is understandable.

Yolanda, however, is studying to be an Emergency Medical Services technician. The sight of an ambulance with flashing lights is not stressful to her at all. Instead, it serves as a symbol of the career Yolanda plans to have someday.

Stress triggers can be seen as positive, negative, or neutral. In fact, what is stress for one person may be a source of inspiration, relaxation, or entertainment for another.

Unhealthy Ways of Managing Stress

"My boss chewed me out today for being late for work," says Nicki. He told me if it happens again, I can forget about coming in—ever." It would be easy for Nicki to use some unhealthy ways to deal with the stress she feels. She could get really angry at her boss for being so demanding, or she could give him a list of excuses for being late. She could be impatient with customers, or totally ignore them for awhile—until she had time to calm down. What other unhealthy ways do people use to deal with stress?

Unhealthy ways of dealing with stress can be seen almost everywhere. Inappropriate anger, road rage, communication problems, procrastination, sleeplessness or excessive sleeping, escape or withdrawal, eating disorders, and refusal to accept reality are just some of the many negative ways of coping with stress.

Unhealthy choices include:

- Avoiding dealing with the real problem.
- Leaning on "escape" behavior to excess. Examples are eating, shopping, or sleeping beyond what is appropriate to your needs.
- Overreacting to the stressor.

Some **defense mechanisms**, or strategies to deal with stressful situations, provide only temporary relief. Some strategies create even more stress. Many can negatively affect your well-being; and, in the long run lead to the habit of avoiding day-to-day problems that need your attention.

Dealing with "Mean Streets"

Imagine you're in the middle of rush hour traffic when a severe thunderstorm breaks loose. A driver cuts in front of you, forcing you to slam on the brakes. You grit your teeth, snarl, and hit your horn to show your anger. You're so stressed by the time you get home that you're ready to snarl at anyone.

Unfortunately, discourtesy and anger on the road is on the rise. Unless you learn to cope with impatience, rudeness, and aggressive acts by some drivers, you may unintentionally provoke a confrontation on the road.

Road rage is a societal problem. While hostility is contagious, so is courtesy. Model good driving behavior and feel less stress by:

- *Avoiding competitions with other vehicles. They are weak ways to gain self-esteem. Instead, feel better about yourself by keeping your vehicle clean and filled with music you enjoy.*

- *Don't try to drive from Point A to Point B as fast as possible. If you do, any obstacle will provoke stress or anger simply because it's in the way.*

- *Don't try to block drivers who are racing the clock. If they try to pass or cut in, go ahead and let them. The reason they are rushing has nothing to do with you.*

- *Don't be a vigilante who punishes wrongdoers. You're not going to change their behavior. They will only become defensive and may even retaliate. Instead, just model good driving behavior.*

How have you handled incidents of road rage in the past? How could you handle it in the future?

Healthy Ways to Manage Stress

The supermarket line that you picked turns out to be the slowest one of all. As you stand there, simmering, your sense of irritation is made worse by the fact that the people standing behind you seem perfectly happy—daydreaming, talking with each other, or reading the latest tabloid gossip.

As the previous example illustrates, you may not be able to control some stressors, but **stress management** can help you can control the effect you allow them to have on you. Now is an ideal time to try a variety of healthy ways to manage stress. Some of them include:

- **Rest and relaxation**—to give your mind and body a chance to recharge.
- **Deep breathing exercises and visualization**—to release stress and to picture positive ways of managing it .
- **Physical exercise**—to use and rechannel pent-up energy.
- **Humor**—to release stress that builds up when things go wrong.
- **Singing or playing a musical instrument**— to provide positive outlets for the stress you're feeling.
- **Keeping a journal**—to keep a record of your stressors and analyze your responses to them.
- **Good nutrition**—to provide your body with needed strength to manage stress.
- **Talking with someone you trust, or calling on a support group**—to share your problems and feelings with others.
- **Helping others**—to take your mind off yourself and contribute to others' well-being.
- **Being assertiv**e—to deal with problems directly, in a positive manner.
- **Setting realistic goals that reflect your value**s—to identify what is important and to understand your limits.

- Choosing effective ways to deal with stress benefits you now and in the future. What might be the long term effects of unhealthy ways of managing stress?

- **Managing time effectively**—to be realistic about your plans and expectations and deal better with changes, frustrations, and delays.

Protecting Your Health

While too much stress is harmful, some stress is necessary. It can energize or prod you to get things done. In fact, some people accomplish more in a stressful environment than a calm one. Everyone, however, has a point where enough turns into too much.

Generally, one small stress will not cause a noticeable problem in your life. However, the accumulation of unhealthy stress responses over a period of time can negatively affect your level of wellness. Even though you can't cure stress, you can learn to manage it and be more in charge of your life. Even small changes in how you respond to stress can make a big difference in your overall health and wellness.

Time Management

"I struggled constantly with my schedule until the guidance counselor gave me this material on goal setting," Leah said. "I sat down and thought about my three-, six-, and twelve-month goals for school, my part-time job, and sports. Life became more focused after that."

Once Leah had identified what was most important to her, she was better able to decide how she would spend her time.

"I realized that if I dropped being on the yearbook staff and put this time into studies, I actually had a shot at straight As," she said. "I also realized that I wanted to work full-time this summer while keeping my evenings open to spend time with my family, since I'm moving in the fall. So I made a list of all the places I could work. Next week I'm going to start putting in applications to all of them."

Using Your Resources Wisely

1 What has been the best benefit for Leah in learning how to set goals and plan her time accordingly?

2 What would you identify as your primary personal goals for the next few months in the area of finances, school, family life, church, and health?

3 How might it be helpful to keep a journal to track goal setting and achieving?

Improving Physical, Mental, and Emotional Well-Being

Healthy lifestyle choices include elements that effectively prevent or reduce stress. These focus on balance, which was discussed in Chapter 4. You may want to review that section while going through this material, too.

Regular exercise, a balanced diet and proper sleep are essential in preventing stress and dealing with it when it comes your way.

A good system of support—family, friends, teachers—can make all the difference in your ability to respond effectively to stress. When you're faced with a situation, make a mental list of not only how you will respond but also *whom* you will turn to for help.

It's also important to develop an awareness of behaviors that can cause stress for the people around you. Alcohol and other drug use—along with mismanagement of money and time—can hurt not only you, but the people who love and support you.

• Taking time for leisure activities that you enjoy helps you manage the stress in your life.

Healthy choices in the face of stress include:

- Identifying the real stressor in front of you as it happens.
- Taking a deep breath and deciding what positive actions you can take.
- Being determined not to over-react to the situations and environment.

Stress Management and Health

Regardless of the source of your stress, you are ultimately the one in charge of managing and responding to it. Setting and working toward realistic goals that reflect your values, making the most of your time and energy, and seeking help when necessary are vital components of effective stress management and personal wellness.

Understanding Key Concepts

- Stress is unavoidable; how you handle it influences your daily life and health.
- Stress during the teen years often changes as young adults leave the family home for college, work, or marriage and parenthood.
- Physical, mental, and emotional signs and effects of stress differ among individuals.
- Stressors can be seen as positive, negative, or neutral; the way your body responds to stressors, or stress triggers, depends largely on how you perceive them.
- Unhealthy ways of dealing with stress provide only temporary relief; in time, they can lead to a habit of avoiding, rather than facing, your problems.
- There are many healthy ways to manage stress and enhance your physical, mental, and emotional well-being.

Checking Your Knowledge

1. Describe ways that an individual's physical, mental, and emotional health might be affected by the way he or she handles stress.
2. Give examples of stress faced by teens you know. Give examples of stress faced by young adults as they go out on their own.
3. Describe how a single stressor can result in different perceptions and responses from different individuals.
4. Explain how unhealthy ways of dealing with stress hinder effective stress management in the long run.
5. Give examples of healthy and unhealthy ways of managing stress. How might humor, keeping a journal, and helping others relieve stress?
6. Why is it important to utilize a variety of healthy ways to relieve stress?
7. Give an example showing the role that effective time management can play in stress management.

Making TRANSITIONS

Reducing Stress

Many everyday situations can cause stress. Everything from traffic jams, crowds, noise, waiting in lines, strained relationships, and poor working conditions can cause physical, mental, or emotional tension. Learning how to cope with stress can help you in all areas of your life, including the workplace.

Assume that you are experiencing stress at work because of circumstance that you can't change. Write your responses to the following questions:

- Describe some of your favorite stress relievers, such as running, talking with a friend, or playing a musical instrument.
- What are some stress relievers that you could use at work? Which ones might be helpful before or after work?
- What specific changes can you make in your life right now that would help you respond more effectively to stress?

STRENGTHENING *Life* SKILLS

Looking at Positive Stress

When you experience negative stress, you may feel angry, disappointed, and frustrated. On the other hand, positive stress may make you feel alert and focused. You may also feel excited and challenged.

Working with a partner, think of three situations in which each has experienced positive stress. Next, write your answers to the following questions:

- What happened to your self-confidence when you felt more alert and focused in the face of positive stress?
- How did your friends or family help you with the experiences?
- What advice would you give classmates regarding your own experiences with positive stress?

Applying Thinking Skills

1. **Comparing and contrasting.** Do young men and women react differently to stress? What factors frequently cause stress for young men? Young women?

2. **Clarifying fact or fiction.** "Going to college after high school is less stressful than getting a job and being on your own." Think about young adults you know. Is it true that staying in your hometown and getting a job is always less stressful than going away to college? Explain.

3. **Predicting consequences.** What is the relationship between personal goals and stress? How might unrealistic goals interfere with stress management?

Practical Applications

1. **Seeking support.** Understanding friends give each other support and encouragement during stressful times. How have your friends helped you with stressors in your life?

2. **Exchanging roles.** What are the kinds of stressors your parents face? How are they different from the kinds of stress you face with finances, work, and your parents?

3. **Exchanging stress stories.** "First thing this morning, I had to find where my dog buried my car keys" is a statement that many people can relate to. The experience is both stressful and humorous. Give examples of times when you, your family, or your friends experienced what could be described as "stressful," yet humorous or unusual, events. What can these events teach you about humor and stress?

CHAPTER 15

Considering Safety

What You Will Learn...

- Why you should take responsibility for your safety.
- How to maintain your personal safety.
- Strategies for staying safe whether you are at home or on the road.
- Ways you can contribute to a safe environment.

Terms for Success

safety spots
warning
watch

Matt peered at his watch in the lights of the theater entrance. "That was a great show, but I didn't realize it ran so late," he remarked. "Where did we park?"

Heidi, close beside him, nodded to her right. "In the lot on the next block."

As they crossed a dim alleyway, Matt stopped. "This looks like a shortcut." He took Heidi's hand. "Come on."

Heidi pulled back. "Let's go the way we came. I like to see where I'm going."

Matt tagged after her. "Chicken," he teased.

Heidi smiled serenely. "No, I just enjoy your company so much, I want to take the long way back."

Matt laughed. "I'll bet you're the type who checks the back seat and under the car before you get in."

"Yep," Heidi replied.

"And you told your roommate when to expect us back," Matt went on.

"She's keeping the porch light on for us," Heidi predicted.

Matt shook his head and sighed. "I know you've got to be careful these days, but do you ever take chances? Don't you want to live dangerously sometimes?"

Heidi gave him an even stare. "My cousin is an emergency room nurse. She sees a lot of people who live dangerously—or who died trying."

"I didn't mean it like that," Matt said. "I mean that you have to leave room for adventure. You're only young once, you know . . . " Just then he stumbled over a chunk of concrete on the sidewalk. Staggering headlong, he nearly went to his knees.

Heidi smothered a laugh. "Oh, Matt, just walking down the street with you is an adventure."

How does Heidi balance humor and common sense to keep herself safe in this situation?

Why Think About Safety?

Heidi may hear jokes about her concerns regarding safety, but she knows that a little bit of caution can make a world of difference. Why should you be concerned about your safety? You have much to gain by staying safe—and much to lose if you don't. Taking safety precautions puts you in charge. It protects your health and well-being and even your life. Failing to do so puts you at risk of injury or even death.

You can learn to be safety conscious in all areas of your life. Take charge of your personal safety to avoid becoming a crime victim. Learn to take precautions to prevent accidents wherever you are. Stay informed about the risks posed by pollution and waste in the environment. After all, your safety is your responsibility!

Personal Safety

Your personal safety depends on your ability both to avoid danger and to handle yourself in a variety of situations. If you become a crime victim, you will need to know how to report the crime. The most important information, however, is how to prevent becoming a victim in the first place.

- Over 50 percent of young adults needlessly lose their lives every year because of failure to develop safe habits. Take a moment to think about your safety habits. **What habits might you need to develop?**

FOCUS ON ...

Common Sense Strategies for Self-Protection

The basic strategy for self-protection is common sense:

In Public Places

- Walk with confidence, keeping your wallet or purse out of sight. At night, walk with a companion or a group of friends.
- Choose a route that is well traveled and well lighted. If you get lost, ask directions from a police officer or store clerk.
- Park your car in a well-lighted area and lock it. When you return to your car, have your car keys ready. After getting into your car, lock it.
- Never hitchhike or pick up hitchhikers when you are driving.

At Home

- Install a deadbolt lock on each exterior door. Install special security locks on sliding glass doors or place a thick wooden dowel or broomstick in the door track.
- Keep your doors and windows locked.
- Install a peephole and intercom system, and identify visitors before you open the door. Do not open the door for strangers.
- Never give personal information to strangers over the telephone or over the Internet.
- Install an electronic alarm system.
- Keep parking areas and walkways well lighted and clear of structures and foliage that could conceal someone.
- If you will rent your home, look for security features when you choose a place to live.
- Get to know your neighbors. Form a neighborhood watch group.

Protecting Yourself

Your most valuable self-defense tools are within yourself. Learning to trust your instincts when you sense danger can help you avoid dangerous situations. If you sense risk, get out of an elevator or cross a street rather than take a chance of being attacked.

While jogging near her home, Ginger encountered a gang of adolescent boys who whistled and made suggestive comments. Ginger's self-esteem gave her the confidence to feel secure and avoid being bullied or chosen as an easy target. She used assertive body language—direct eye contact, a strong voice, erect body posture, and a deliberate stride— to send the message that she is in charge of her safety. The boys left her alone.

It's better to be safe than to be a crime victim! Remember that your life and health are more valuable than your property. It is wiser to give up your jewelry, your money, or your car than to be kidnapped, stabbed, or shot.

Avoiding Violence

The best way to avoid violence is to learn to handle conflict effectively. Conflict is a normal part of life. Some conflicts, such as being challenged to a fight, may be dangerous and can have serious consequences. In such cases, how you choose to resolve the conflict may mean the difference between life and death. If you need to review how to handle conflict more effectively, refer to Chapter 7: Dealing with Conflict.

How can you tell if you should avoid a conflict or face it head-on? Each situation must be considered individually. You need to identify what's at stake, what the risks are, and what the possible consequences might be.

- The best way to protect yourself from violence is to avoid unsafe situations. How might you avoid unsafe situations? What would you do?

Reporting a Crime

Despite your best efforts, you may become a crime victim. If this happens, contact the police to report a crime as soon as possible. Whenever you observe suspicious events, report the incident to the police department. Never assume that someone else will make the call:

- **Reporting crime.** To report a crime, you may call either the police department or go directly to the police station. In many locations, you can reach the police emergency number by dialing 911. For nonemergencies, call the police department administrative number listed in your local telephone directory.
- **Calling the police.** When you call, be prepared to calmly provide the police officers with the information he or she requests. He will ask you for details about your location, the incident, the people involved, and any vehicles involved. Be available to assist the officer(s) sent to investigate. Your information can greatly assist the police in the apprehension of criminals.

In some situations, it is wise to avoid a conflict. For example, you should avoid conflict if the issue is unimportant. Jared quickly dashed into a nearby convenience store after encountering an agitated drunk who flashed a knife. Knowing he could be seriously injured, Jared chose to get away quickly.

At other times, it will be better to face a conflict and try to deal with it positively. Marsha stood up to a girl on her basketball team who challenged her abilities. Both girls were willing to listen to the other side and work toward resolution of the conflict. Now they share tips for improving their skills.

Whether you choose to ignore a conflict or to deal with it, your health and safety should come first.

REASON

Through Life's Problems

Outline and Take Action

A good decision doesn't solve your problem if you don't put it into action. In the situation below, Mandy needs to make a plan of action for solving her problem.

Maybe Mom and Dad were not overreacting about the dangers of the big city," mused Mandy as she read the evening newspaper.

"Two apartment break-ins, a drive-by shooting, and a rape—all within a few blocks of here. This is certainly different from my old neighborhood," thought Mandy. She had just transferred from a small community college in her hometown to a large university here in the city.

"It's time that I make sure I protect myself and my property as well as I can," Mandy thought to herself. "I'm going to need to find out what I can do to be as safe as possible."

Mandy started out by going to the Office of Student Life. She found several brochures on campus safety, and skimmed through them quickly. A secretary noticed her reading the brochures, and said, "We're having a free bicycle registration workshop on Tuesday night. We also have an engraver you can use to identify your property. We just required a $25.00 deposit, which is refunded when you return the engraver."

Mandy read that many college students never think about renters insurance. She decided to call the local agency for the insurance company her parents use. Along with his quote, the agent offered to mail her some information on how to protect her property.

Once she had become aware of the need for more information on safety, it seemed Mandy saw helpful hints everywhere. The campus newspaper even had a ten-part series on personal safety. Mandy made a note about the self-defense class being offered.

"I need to make a list of everything I need to do," Mandy decided. "I also need a list of things to buy. I want to get one of those antitheft bars for my steering wheel, and one of those key rings with the ear-piercing alarms on it. I've got to save enough to pay my first three months of my renters insurance premium, too."

Mandy called her family and told them all about her plans.

"I'm going to sleep a lot better tonight knowing you're taking this so seriously," Mandy's mother told her.

""Me, too, Mom. Thanks for caring," Mandy smiled to herself.

▶From Your Perspective

1 What resources did Mandy utilize in making her personal safety plan?

2 What barriers might Mandy encounter in carrying out her plan? How could she overcome them?

3 How might you check out the reliability of information on your own?

- **Giving detailed information.** If you are reporting a crime such as a burglary, robbery, or theft, the police need as much information as possible about the property taken. This means giving a description of the property, its value, and the serial numbers. By providing an accurate and thorough description of his laptop computer, Mark aided the police in its recovery.

Safety Away from Home

Accidents can occur anywhere—at home, at work, or outdoors. To avoid accidents, you will want to be aware of the possible hazards wherever you are. You will want to become safety conscious in all of your activities. Most importantly, you should make a practice of always following basic safety rules.

In Public Places

Even in public places, you can take steps to stay safe and avoid dangerous situations. To avoid danger:

- **Be prepared.** To avoid getting hurt, know the potential risks in different situations. Use safety equipment and observe warning signs.
- **Stay alert.** Get plenty of rest and avoid use of alcohol and other drugs. Pay attention to what is happening around you. Watch for potential hazards to your safety.
- **Resist pressures.** Make your own decisions, especially when it comes to your safety.
- **Stay within your limits.** Be realistic about your physical condition and your skills.

• Providing the police or other emergency personnel with accurate information is important when reporting a crime. **What might you do to develop your observation skills for emergencies?**

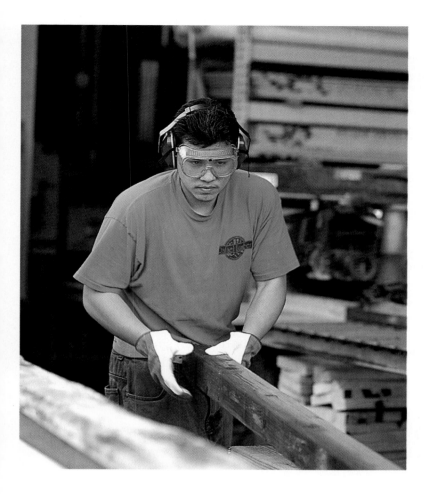

- Employers and employees are responsible for safe working conditions. **As an employee what can you do to make sure your working environment is safe?**

At Work

Preventing accidents at work is everyone's responsibility. Your employer should provide you a safe environment. However, you should report unsafe conditions and practices. You also should follow all safety rules.

The United States Occupational Safety and Health Administration (OSHA) is an agency that enforces safe and healthy conditions in the workplace. OSHA inspectors evaluate worksites to ensure compliance with health and safety standards.

Employers can reduce your risks of injury at work by properly training employees on equipment use, by providing safety equipment, and by rewarding safe practices.

At work, keep these safety guidelines in mind:

- Expect safe work conditions and protection from injury.
- Arrive at work well rested and alert.
- Use machinery only after you have been fully trained to operate it.
- Wear protective equipment, such as goggles, earplugs, or gloves.
- Maintain a safe, steady pace.
- Avoid working for long periods of time without taking a rest break.
- Report unsafe conditions and unsafe practices.

Outdoors

If you participate in sports and recreational activities, you need to be aware of potential hazards. If you do not follow safe practices, your fun can end in an accident, injury, or even death. Preventing outdoor accidents requires planning ahead and taking necessary precautions:

- Learn safety rules for the activity before you participate.
- Know your abilities, skills, and limits and stay within them.
- Avoid getting overly confident, showing off, or trying something you are not ready to do.
- Use the proper equipment and know how to use it properly. Wear protective equipment to reduce the risk of injury.
- Take time to warm up and stretch before you exercise or participate in a strenuous activity.
- Cool down properly after you have exercised or have participated in a strenuous activity.
- Use sun protection and also protect yourself against insects such as deer ticks, which can cause Lyme disease.

Safety on Wheels

Defensive driving is the key to your safety when you drive or cycle. To avoid accidents, follow laws and observe safety precautions.

Auto Safety

You can greatly reduce your risk or injury of death in an auto accident by taking these simple precautions:

- Drive within the legal speed limit.
- Drive defensively. Watch out for other drivers and pedestrians.

- Preventing outdoor accidents requires planning ahead for each situation. **What outdoor activities do you enjoy participating in the most? How might you prepare ahead of time for safety during these activities?**

- Use seat belts. For every 100 young people killed in a motor vehicle accident in the United States, 80 would be alive if they had been wearing a seat belt. Most states have laws requiring their use.

- Never drink and drive. Drinking impairs both judgment and driving skills. You can avoid injury or death by following the law and not driving while you're under the influence of alcohol or other drugs.

Cycle Safety

Motorcyclists and bicyclists are much more likely to be killed in an accident than are people traveling in a car. Cyclists can increase their safety by following traffic rules and by wearing safety helmets and bright, reflective clothing.

Cyclists need to be especially careful on wet surfaces. Darting in and out of traffic can be especially dangerous. John, for example, is sometimes tempted to do this. The most frequent mistake Chrissy makes as a bicyclist is riding on the left side of the road, against the flow of traffic.

TIPS

Gizmos to Protect Your Car

There are many antitheft options available on cars today:

- **gearshift lock:** Locks gearshift in place, which makes the car tough to steal.
- **locking gas cap:** Prevents someone from siphoning gas from tank.
- **tire/wheel locks:** Tool wraps around tire/wheel, immobilizes vehicle.
- **interior hood lock release:** Prevents access to battery and other car components.
- **steering column collar:** Protects entry to ignition through column.
- **electronic alarms:** Activates a siren, horn, or lights—or all three—to frighten away the thief.

• Cycle safety is essential for preventing accidents. **How might you improve your cycle safety on the road?**

Both motorcyclists and bicyclists should follow all laws. In general, cyclists should observe the following guidelines:

- Ride in single file on the right, keeping close to the side of the road.
- Beware of cars and trucks.
- Bicyclists should yield right-of-way to both.
- Watch for cars pulling into traffic and for car doors that open into your path.
- Obey the same rules as other drivers. Signal before you turn. Stop for red lights and stop signs.
- Except when signaling, keep both hands on the handlebars at all times.
- Beware of wet or oil-slick surfaces.

Safety at Home

Your home should provide a place of safety for you, your family, and your possessions. However, homes are not always as safe as they seem. About one-third of all accidental injuries happen at home.

Weather-related emergencies present another danger. Weather poses a threat not just to homes and families but to entire communities. Hurricanes, tornadoes, and other natural disasters can cause widespread injury and death as well as property damage and loss.

Preventing Home Accidents

The most common types of home accidents are falls, electric shock, and burns. Fortunately, most accidents at home can be prevented by using common sense and by taking simple precautions.

Of all possible home accidents, fire is probably the most feared. It can injure or kill people, destroy possessions, and devastate lives. Thousands die each year in accidental fires in the United States. Property losses are in the billions of dollars.

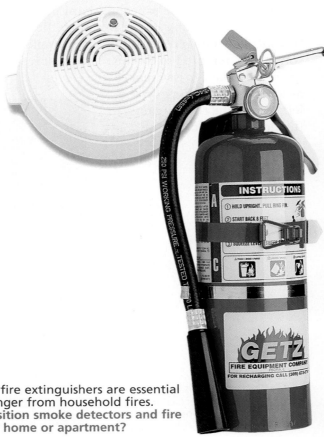

• Smoke detectors and fire extinguishers are essential in minimizing the danger from household fires. **Where might you position smoke detectors and fire extinguishers in your home or apartment?**

Your Fire Escape Plan

When the smoke detector goes off, do you know the safest route out of your home? Knowing can mean the difference between life and death. Here are some ideas that can help you develop a fire escape plan:

- *Plan your escape routes. Determine at least two escape routes from each room or area of your home. In multiunit buildings, ask the manager for a diagram of possible escape route—then be sure to check them all out.*

- *Make sure escape routes are usable. Consider purchasing an escape ladder for upper-story bedrooms. In high-rise buildings, be sure fire escapes work and that fire exits are not locked or blocked.*

- *Designate an outdoor meeting place for all household members. Lives can be lost when someone goes back into a burning building to look for someone who is already outside.*

Periodically practice your escape route so you'll know what to do if an emergency does arise.

Prepare an escape route for your home. Share your plan with your family members and ask for suggestions or improvements.

Smoke alarms and fire extinguishers are essential for a good fire safety plan. Smoke detectors sense poisonous gases in the first stage of a fire and alert residents to danger.

Ideally, you should install a smoke detector in every room except the kitchen and bathroom, where cooking fumes and steam can trigger the alarm. At the very least, there should be one detector on each level of the home.

Keep fire extinguishers on each floor of the homes also, including one in the kitchen. All adult and teen family members should know how to operate the fire extinguisher. If the fire can not be extinguished quickly, leave the building and call the fire department from a safe location.

Preparing for Weather-Related Emergencies

Weather-related emergencies include earthquakes, blizzards, hailstorms, floods, tornadoes, and hurricanes. You should prepare for these that affect the area where you live.

Most communities have emergency warning systems to alert residents of dangerous storms or high winds. When severe weather conditions exist, the National Weather Service issues advisories for blizzards, hailstorms, floods, hurricanes, and tornadoes. These advisories are called "watches" or "warnings." A hurricane or tornado **watch** means that existing atmospheric conditions could develop into these emergencies. A **warning** means one has been sighted. Warnings are often accompanied by instructions:

- **Hurricane.** Preparing for a hurricane usually means securing your home—maybe boarding doors and windows—and then either going to a shelter or evacuating the area. The farther inland you go, the safer you will be.

- **Tornado.** A storm cellar or basement is the safest place to go for protection from a tornado. If neither is available, a hallway, a closet, or a bathtub is the next best choice. If you are caught outside, get into a ditch and lie face down.

- **Earthquake.** If you are inside a building when you begin to feel a tremor, stay in the building. Try to find a **safety spot**. This is an area that provides some measure of safety from falling objects. If you are outdoors when an earthquake hits, stay away from buildings, trees, and power lines.
- **Blizzard.** A blizzard is a snowstorm with winds of 35 miles per hour or greater. The safest place to be during a blizzard is indoors. If you must be outside, wear protective clothing, keep moving, and try to keep your mouth and nose covered.

Protecting Your Environment

Everyone has a responsibility to protect our environment. You can avoid pollutants, reduce waste, and conserve natural resources by being aware of environmental issues. As a consumer, you can make environmentally responsible decisions.

Avoiding Pollutants

In recent years, people have become more aware of the harm pollution causes to the natural environment. To protect your health when pollution levels are high:
- Avoid strenuous outdoor activities.
- Don't smoke.
- If you exercise outdoors, work out early in the morning when the concentration of pollutants in the air is lowest.
- Eat well-balanced meals to make it easier for your body to handle toxic substances.

• Tornadoes and other weather hazards require special safety considerations. **What weather hazards are most common in your area? What might you do to protect yourself from injury during weather emergencies?**

Review these key terms about pollution:

- **carbon monoxide:** A deadly colorless, odorless gas that can be produced by any fireplace or gas burning appliance.
- **radon:** A radioactive gas that occurs naturally in some types of soil and rock.
- **asbestos:** A flame-retardant mineral substance.
- **lead:** A toxic metal that can be found in old paint, water, soil, and air.

• Taking care of our environment is everyone's responsibility. **What are the long-term implications of poor environmental protection?**

Pollution in Your Home

Pollution can also be a problem in your home. Some indoor pollutants may make people feel mildly ill. Other pollutants may have no noticeable effect at first, but can cause serious health problems over time.

- **Carbon monoxide.** This is a deadly, invisible gas that can build up through improperly-vented heating devices. Have your furnace and all other heating units checked regularly to be sure they're working properly. Have a professional make sure they are well vented. Installing a carbon monoxide detector gives you added protection.
- **Radon.** Radon can seep up and into the home through cracks in basement floors and walls. At harmful levels, radon increases your risk of lung cancer. Test kits are available to measure radon levels in your home. If tests show high levels of radon, seek the help of a medical doctor and building contractor to address the problem immediately.

- **Asbestos.** Asbestos is a kind of insulation used in many buildings before 1978. Inhaling tiny fibers of asbestos can cause lung cancer. Only qualified professionals must be hired to remove or seal off asbestos.
- **Lead.** If lead enters the body, it can cause behavioral and developmental problems, particularly in young children. Sources of lead include flaking paint, antique pottery, and lead-glazed pottery imported from other countries, as well as lead pipes and solder found in older homes.

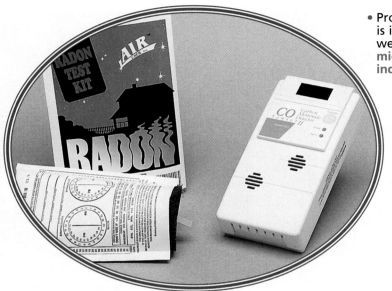

• Protecting yourself from indoor pollutants is important to maintaining health and wellness. **What are some things that you might do to prevent the build-up of indoor pollutants in your home?**

Safety—It's Your Responsibility

Safety can only be achieved through careful planning, common sense, and conscious effort. Safety begins with little things like observing safety rules and extends to more complex projects, such as installing a home security system.

By taking responsibility for your safety, you can avoid many of the consequences of accidents and violent crimes. To do so, you must learn to be safety conscious at all times. In all areas of your life, be aware that your safety is your responsibility.

• Thinking ahead about the products you buy to avoid unnecessary waste helps promote a healthful environment. **How might you improve the choices you make about the products you buy in regard to environmental safety and protection?**

MANAGING YOUR RESOURCES

Conserving Environmental Resources

You make decisions that affect natural resources every day. By not wasting water and energy, by recycling whenever possible, you are saving resources for the future.

You have many opportunities to conserve water and energy at home. Heating and cooling accounts for about 70 percent of the energy used in the home. Water heating uses an additional 20 percent. Lighting, cooking, and small appliances use the remaining 10 percent. There are many ways you can reduce energy used for these purposes.

Precycling

Precycling is a strategy to avoid buying things that need to be recycled or disposed. For several weeks, when Cheryl ran into a convenience store for coffee on her way to work, she bought the coffee in styrofoam cups. One day her boyfriend Jarod went with her and surprised her with a refillable mug.

You can make a difference by observing these guidelines for precycling:

- Buy bulk and unpackaged goods.
- Choose products with packaging that can be reused, refilled, or recycled.
- Choose products packaged in recyclable materials like paper, glass, aluminum, or cardboard.
- Avoid buying disposable products, such as cups, plates, napkins, razors, and diapers, which add to already overflowing landfills.
- Avoid single-serving containers for items such as juice or raisins.
- Say, "No bag, please," for small purchases.

Recycling

Recycling means less need for incineration and landfills. More than four out of five items of household waste can be recycled. These include aluminum, cardboard, glass, oil, paper, and plastics. Biodegradable household wastes include, clothing and household items, such as food scraps and newspaper. Grass clippings and other yard wastes and nonanimal food wastes can be composted. Composting refers to the biological decomposition of organic waste material under controlled conditions. Compost can be used as a soil conditioner, mulch, or plant cover.

Using Your Resources Wisely

1. Approximately 10 percent of all recyclable household waste products are actually recycled. What reasons can you give for this low percentage?

2. How can you do your part in conserving environmental resources? Develop a plan of action you can take now and in the future.

Understanding Key Concepts

- Being safety-conscious in all areas of your life can protect your health and well-being and even your life.
- Your personal safety depends on your ability to avoid danger and handle yourself in a variety of situations.
- If you become a crime victim or if you witness a crime, report it immediately to the police.
- To avoid danger in public places be prepared, stay alert, resist pressures, and stay within your limits.
- Preventing outdoor accidents requires planning ahead and taking necessary precautions.
- Defensive driving is the key to your safety when you drive or cycle.

Checking Your Knowledge

1. How can common sense help you avoid becoming a crime victim? Give five examples.
2. How can you decide when to avoid a conflict and when to face it head-on?
3. Summarize the information you would need to report a crime.
4. What steps can you take in public places to stay safe and avoid dangerous situations?
5. Develop safety guidelines for a specific outdoor activity you enjoy.
6. Compare and contrast the behavior of safe and unsafe drivers.
7. Explain five things you can do to prevent home accidents.
8. Describe how you would prepare for weather-related emergencies in your area.

Making TRANSITIONS

Workplace Safety

Workplace safety is a common concern among workers in all walks of life. Office workers may be concerned about ergonomic work stations. Factory workers could be concerned about chemical spills or equipment that operates correctly and safely.

With a partner, choose and develop a role play situation in which a worker reports an unsafe or unhealthy condition to an employer. Identify the work situation and the hazard in detail. Show the employer's reaction and how he or she plans to resolve the problem. Present your role play to the class.

STRENGTHENING *Life* SKILLS

Becoming More Safety Conscious

Identify an area of your life in which you need to become more safety conscious. To do so, consider your behavior in public places, at work, outdoors, when driving or cycling, and at home.

For a week, keep a diary describing your safety consciousness in this area of your life each day. What guidelines did you observe? What did you ignore?

At the end of the week, write a summary of this activity based on the questions that follow:

- In what ways were you more safety conscious by the end of the week?
- How can this experience help you become more safety conscious in other areas of your life?

Applying Thinking Skills

1. **Recognizing assumptions.** If common sense and simple precautions can help people avoid becoming crime and accident victims, why are so many people victimized, injured, and killed each year? What assumptions do people make about the risks they face each day?

2. **Drawing conclusions.** Why must police rely on citizens to report crimes and suspicious events? What would happen if most citizens refused to accept this responsibility?

3. **Drawing conclusions.** You are visiting friends in a city you've never been to before. You are in your car and driving to meet them in a part of town that is intimidating to you. What precautions can you take to keep yourself safe?

Practical Applications

1. **Developing a fire escape plan.** Determine at least two escape routes from each room or area of your home. Make sure each escape route is usable. Select an outdoor meeting place. Post the plan where it can be easily seen. Have your family practice using the fire escape plan. Revise if necessary.

2. **Waste reduction plan.** Survey your home to identify ways your family can reduce waste. Develop a plan to precycle and recycle materials your family now wastes.

3. **Emergency safety kit.** List five things you can stow in the trunk of your car to keep yourself safe when you travel.

Unit 4
Using Your Consumer Skills

BASIL
99 EA

CHAPTER 16 ▷ Improving Consumer Skills

What You Will Learn...

- How to analyze methods to balance your needs and wants.
- Ways to get informed about goods and services before buying them.
- How to analyze advertising and marketing techniques.
- How to shop for value when buying goods and services.
- The rights and responsibilities of consumers.
- How to effectively resolve consumer disputes.

Terms for Success

advocates
garnishee
marketing

"**D**ave," Ravi called, "look at this."

Dave raised his eyes from the sports magazine. He smothered a laugh. His roommate stood across the living room with arms extended. The left shirtsleeve fit snugly at the wrist; the right sleeve hung in folds from his shoulder and lapped over his knuckles.

"It looks like they sewed together two different shirt sizes," Ravi complained.

"You didn't notice that when you tried it on?" Dave asked.

"Well, I didn't exactly try it on," Ravi admitted. "I tried on a shirt just like it, and it fit fine. Then I decided I needed two shirts, but there wasn't time to try on the second one, so I grabbed this one. Is it asking too much that two shirts, the same style and size from the same maker, should fit the same way?"

"I wouldn't think so," Dave replied, "but that's what dressing rooms are for. Can you return it?"

Ravi sighed. "No. I bought it at a little shop when I was home last week. I'm not going back home until spring break. Besides, I need a shirt now." He frowned and contemplated his mismatched sleeves. "You know," he mused, bunching the extra material on the right side, "if it could be taken in along here, and shortened, it might fit. Maybe a student in one of our classes could handle that, don't you think?"

"It's worth a shot," Dave agreed.

"Maybe we could work something out," Ravi said hopefully. "Someone could fix this shirt, and I could format his or her term paper on my computer."

> **Why should you carefully check merchandise before you buy it? Why is keeping purchase receipts and knowing a store's return policy important?**

Making Purchasing Decisions

Ravi needed to buy a couple of shirts. He thought he could buy them on a quick shopping trip while he was home from school. Would Ravi have had the same problem if he had taken more time to make his purchase?

It's possible to get good quality products and services at fair prices almost anyplace in the world. However, successful results don't always happen automatically, so it usually pays to do some marketplace homework. Start by becoming familiar with available products, prices, and standards of quality. Find out which features to choose or avoid in the products and services you plan to buy.

Balancing Your Needs and Wants

How successful are you at balancing your needs and wants? Do you spend more on what you want—at the expense of what you need or owe? Do the totals in your checkbook indicate that you should keep your wants and needs in better balance?

If your wants often overpower your needs, take a look at what influences your desires. For example, magazine and TV ads tend to make you want things you don't even know about until you see them advertised. Peer pressure can also put your pocketbook in peril. You may want items just because friends or coworkers have them. You may feel that you would be more attractive or popular if you bought certain pieces of clothing, jewelry, or the latest CDs.

Wise consumers put themselves—rather than others—in charge of balancing their needs and wants. They identify what they really need and avoid purchasing things that bring temporary pleasure but cause their budgets to become seriously unbalanced.

• When making purchases, you need to find the balance in buying the things you need versus the things you want. **How disciplined are you in putting off purchases of things you want so that you have the money to buy the things you need?**

Impulse buying can quickly cause wants to overpower your needs. To control impulse buying, you must be able to identify your needs and wants. Before making any purchase, determine whether it fits into the needs and wants you've outlined. You can learn more about impulse buying on page 290.

With creativity and planning, people often can buy goods and services they need and still have money or other resources to spend or barter for something fun or frivolous. Sewing skills can be used to make garments that you want—but can't afford at the store. Mechanical skills come in handy when you find a car or bike that needs repair but is for sale at a price you can afford. With thought and planning, you may choose to borrow, swap, rent, repair, or make items that you want but can't afford to buy. By doing so, you can get more of what you need and want.

Planning Purchases

Just as a calendar can help people schedule the use of their time, a long-range buying plan can help you schedule the use of your money. A well-thought-out plan can assist you in paying less for many things you need and want. To carry out a plan, you need to save some money each payday for items you'll buy in the future. Then you can purchase each one at the best possible buying time—when prices are lowest.

- The first step in making a buying plan is to inventory, or list, the items you have now. Note the condition of each item, checking to see how long it may last and when it might need to be replaced.

- Impulse buying has been known to get many consumers into trouble by spending more money than they have. **What do you do when you are tempted to buy something that you really don't need and can't afford?**

- The second step is to determine what you'll need to buy during the upcoming year. For example, after doing a clothing inventory, think about your needs for work, school, sports, and dress clothes—as well as clothing for different seasons. If the clothes you have on hand won't meet these needs, you can plan to buy the clothes you'll need.

By using this two-step buying plan, you can avoid purchasing a necessity when it's selling at a higher price.

- Planning ahead for things you need helps you maintain control over your money. **How well do you plan your purchases?**

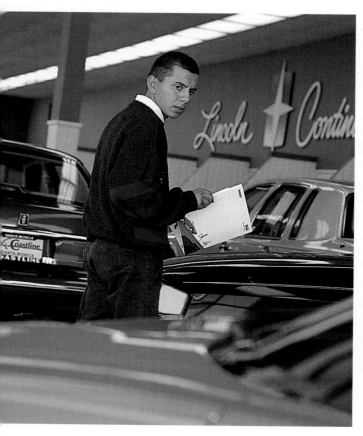

Getting Informed Before Buying

You can make your money go further by learning as much as possible about what you plan to buy. Ask the opinions of people you know who own products or use services you are considering purchasing.

Comparison shopping is another way to get facts about goods and services that you plan to buy. Visit various stores or call providers of services you're interested in. Also, read labels, booklets, and other information from manufacturers and companies to get helpful technical information. You can use it to compare features of various brands before choosing which one to purchase. Magazines such as *Consumer Reports* and *Consumers Research* are helpful for comparing products. These publications test and rate different brands for quality, safety, and price.

Other sources of consumer information include local libraries, cooperative extension offices, the U.S. Consumer Information Center, and the Better Business Bureau. Also, newspapers, magazines, radio, TV, and various Internet sites, bulletin boards, and forums provide consumer information.

While getting informed about products and services you wish to buy, keep in mind the reliability of the information you receive. Ask yourself questions such as:

- How objective and reliable is the source?
- What does the source have to gain (if anything) from the sale?
- How current is the information?

Advertising and You

You can learn about new or improved products and services through advertising. You also can compare everyday prices of various items as well as learn about current or future sales. Shopping this way can save you time and money.

REASON

Through Life's Problems

Note the Results of Actions Taken

Unfortunately, problem solving isn't an exact science. Even when problem solving is used, not all solutions will be satisfactory. Step back and take the cause and effect test. What effects did your actions cause? Why wasn't the outcome satisfactory? It may be necessary to begin the entire problem solving process again. In the situation below Jody is not satisfied with the way she chose to handle a faulty purchase.

"I wish I could just pick up this refrigerator and throw it out with the trash!" Jody stormed as she mopped up a puddle on the floor.

Jody had purchased the refrigerator more than a year ago. The refrigerator had started leaking soon after she had brought it home. She had a friend work on it several times, but it still leaked. Now when Jody had finally called a technician to come and fix it, he told her there would have been no charge for the repair if it had been done two months ago, before the warranty ran out.

"Isn't there any way to change the dates, so that it will still be under warranty?" Jody winced as she started writing out the check for the repairs.

"Absolutely not," answered the technician. "Why didn't you have it repaired sooner?"

Jody felt foolish and embarrassed. She wished she hadn't asked the question. Jody was really upset at herself for not keeping track of her paperwork and for not being familiar with the one-year warranty.

This was an expensive way to learn a lesson," muttered Jody to herself. "Where did I go wrong?"

Jody reflected on the refrigerator purchase. She came up with several reasons how the problem had gone from bad to worse.

"I should never have listened to the salesman who said the store would provide any service I needed. The store was out of business in six months. This was not a reliable source of information.

"I should have read the warranty more closely, and have known exactly what was covered and for how long," she continued. "I could have marked the date I bought the refrigerator right on the warranty.

"Come to think of it, I don't think I ever really looked at any other refrigerators. I found that refrigerator on sale for what seemed like a good price, but I never really compared price or service with those of any other stores. I might have even been better off buying a used refrigerator" Jody thought.

"Well, I won't make these mistakes again," she resolved. "Next time I'll really shop around for the best deal and make sure that I buy from a reputable retailer that will still be in business when I have a problem. I'm going to make a file for each of my major purchases and put the warranty in there, with the receipt stapled to it. I need to make sure I return all these product registration cards to the manufacturer, too. I'll never have a friend repair something that's under warranty. I won't have to—I'll know how to get it serviced for free!"

►From Your Perspective

1 How has Jody's experience affected her future problem solving?

2 What do you think Jody has learned through this experience?

3 Were Jody's actions ethical? Why or why not?

- Consumer publications can help consumers make wise use of their resources. Which consumer resources have you found to be most helpful?

However, advertising can also cost you money. In order to pay for their advertising, most companies have to raise the prices of their products. You may be tempted to make purchases you don't need—or didn't plan to make. Carefully planned messages urging you to buy are all around you: on TV, radio, and in newspapers and magazines—even in sky-writing messages carried by planes and blimps.

Marketing Techniques

Activities such as packaging, shipping, advertising, and selling all go together to make up **marketing,** the process of getting goods and services to consumers who want them. It's an important function of the free enterprise system.

Marketing techniques can be simple or very sophisticated. Manufacturers and other companies pay billions of dollars studying human behavior and employing talented writers, artists, and salespeople to market various products and services. These companies frequently use persuasive techniques that are clever and indirect. Often you may not even realize you're being influenced to buy something.

Other marketing techniques are more direct:
- Seasonal sales at various times of the year.
- Coupons.
- Product sampling, sent through the mail or given out at stores.
- Contests.
- Rebates.
- Attention-grabbing merchandise displays.

- Product presentation, including pleasing aromas, music, and attractive color combinations.
- Product positioning of higher-priced goods at eye level and less expensive ones on higher or lower shelves.
- Impulse items displayed at eye level or at the checkout counter.

Shopping for Value

Getting good value for your money takes effort and objectivity on your part. Peer pressure, advertising and other marketing techniques, and impulse buying can influence or take charge of your purchasing decisions.

However, if you want to get good value for your money when you're buying goods and services, you have to decide where your money will go.

Whether you are shopping for goods—a pair of jeans, backpack, or a sofa—or for services—auto repair, dental care, or dry cleaning—you have to ask and answer different questions before you buy.

To get the best value when shopping for goods, consider:

- **Amount of use.** Will you use the item occasionally, seasonally, or often?
- **Care.** Will it need to be dry-cleaned or laundered? If machinery, how should it be maintained?
- **Purpose.** Is it a decorative object or one that will be used regularly?

• Marketing techniques are especially designed to capture your attention and get you to spend money. What advertising and marketing techniques affect you the most?

- **Product life span.** Do you expect to have it for a short or long time?
- **Construction.** How and from what materials has the item been made?

When shopping for services, assume nothing and ask about:

- **Limits.** What services does the price include and exclude? For example, will the carpet cleaners move the furniture?
- **Extras.** Will you have to pay more for extras like replacing buttons in addition to the dry cleaning cost?
- **Equipment.** Is the service being provided using modern, high-tech equipment like painless dentistry, for example?
- **Warranty.** Does a warranty accompany the service in case something should break or go wrong within a certain time?

- **Options.** Are different levels of service available for corresponding costs? For example, could you spend a little more and receive a better warranty?

Goods and services of better quality usually cost more than those of lesser quality. However, sometimes a less expensive item or service is just as good as one that costs much more. Several circumstances can cause products of the same quality to have different prices:

- **Supply and demand.** If a certain item or service is the focus of an intensive advertising campaign, consumer demand may cause the price to go much higher than that of a similar item that's not being advertised. Any item or service in demand—but in short supply—will usually cost more, regardless of quality.

- Getting the best price on good quality services can be a challenge. What could you do to find out which service providers offer excellent service for the fee charged?

- **Quantity buying discount.** Large companies buy in large amounts, enabling them to buy at a lower price than a small company purchasing smaller amounts. Consequently, the small company usually charges its customers more for the same item.
- **Brand names.** Many people think well-known brands are of better quality. However, this isn't always true. Many products sold under store, or house, brands are identical or very similar to higher-priced, nationally known brands. For example, household appliances made by a large company are often sold to smaller companies, who then put their own brand names on the appliances. This is also true for food canning companies. Different labels are wrapped around cans with identical contents.

When shopping for value, you often can get the same high-quality items much more cheaply under less familiar or less advertised names.

Consumer Rights and Responsibilities

As a consumer, you have certain rights and responsibilities. These rights and responsibilities go hand in hand and are very important both to the buyer and the seller.

President John F. Kennedy introduced the Consumer Bill of Rights in 1962. Presidents Nixon and Ford later expanded the bill, which now includes six specific rights.

• When goods or services fail to measure up, one of your consumer responsibilities is to take action as outlined in the warranty. **Why is it wrong for consumers to expect replacement of goods when a product has knowingly been used in the wrong way or for the wrong purpose?**

Debit Cards: Pros and Cons

You can use the statement to track your spending.

With a debit card, purchase amounts are automatically deducted from your checking account and are shown on your monthly checking account statement.

Also, it is important to know what your daily limit is and to keep track of daily card activity so you know how much money is available for additional purchases or withdrawals that day.

Banks emphasize the convenience and speed of debit cards at the counter—rather than writing checks. It is important to protect debit cards from misuse and theft.

FOCUS ON ...

Consumer Bill of Rights

Every consumer is guaranteed the following protection rights by law:

- **The right to safety.** Consumers have the right to products that are safe. Laws may ban some goods that are hazardous to health or life. In other cases, labels provide warnings that the product can be dangerous. Specific directions are given for the safest possible use.

- **The right to be informed.** Various federal agencies work to make sure that companies provide accurate information about products, both in advertising and in labeling. Consumers have the right to ask for all the facts needed to make good choices.

- **The right to be heard.** Consumers can speak out when they're not satisfied. They should receive a full hearing and fair treatment. They have a voice in making consumer laws by presenting their views to congresspersons and government agencies.

- **The right to choose.** Consumers have the right to choose from a variety of goods. Having options helps keep prices competitive.

- **The right to redress.** This is the right to have problems quickly and fairly corrected.

- **The right to consumer education.** All consumers are entitled to information about consumer issues.

Your Responsibilities as a Consumer

Besides knowing your rights as a consumer, it's important to know—and accept—your responsibilities. For example, a driver's license gives you the right to drive a car, but with it comes the responsibility to follow the rules of the road. As a fair and honest consumer, you have a responsibility to:

- **Use products safely.** Manufacturers include with their products recommended guidelines explaining care and usage of the items.

- **Use information.** Libraries and the Internet are good sources for information to compare and evaluate different products. Government agencies, such as the Food and Drug Administration, work to develop quality standards.

- **Choose carefully.** By buying from companies that are ethical and produce safe products, consumers make good use of their buying power.

- **Speak up.** Notify public officials of your opinions on consumer issues.

- **Seek redress.** Hold businesses accountable when their goods or services don't measure up to standards. Seek legal action if necessary.

- **Learn.** Educated consumers will get the most value for their money. Know the laws that protect consumers and the recommendations from government consumer agencies, such as the Consumer Product Safety Commission.

Returns, Refunds, and Replacements

Returning merchandise is a privilege, not a right. Unless a store has sold you something fraudulently or with deception—or the product is defective—the store is not legally compelled to accept the return of any item you have purchased. Discount and warehouse stores often have "final sale" or "no return" policies. The same is true for "going out of business sales." Most businesses, however, have a policy allowing goods to be returned in the same condition as at the time of purchase and within a specified period.

If there's a possibility you might need to return an item, it's important to inquire about the store's return policy—*before making the purchase*. Most state laws require that a store's policy be posted in a prominent place on the premises. If the store accepts returns, carefully read its policy, making sure you understand all the conditions. Keep sales receipts in one location, so you can find them easily if you have to return an item.

If you need to return a purchase, the first step is to go to the store's returns department or to the person who sold you the product. Going in person with both product and sales receipt is usually the most successful way to make a return or resolve a problem. Politely state your situation or problem and how you think it should be resolved:

- Replacement of identical item.
- Exchange for different item.
- Refund of purchase price.
- Store credit for future purchase.

If you are not satisfied with the initial response, the next step is to talk with the store manager or supervisor. Again, politely repeat your situation. Most problems are resolved at this level. However, if you are not satisfied with the response, don't give up.

If the company is a national one, or the product is a national brand, find out if there's a toll-free number for its consumer relations or customer service department. Telephone or write to the head of this department or to the company's president. You may need to get names and the company address from the local library or the Internet. In a businesslike manner, restate the problem and your preferred resolution. Include your daytime telephone number and times you may be reached. Enclose copies (not originals) of your receipts and any other information supporting your case. Be sure to keep a copy of your letter along with the original receipts.

If things work out well, your letter will get results. If the company doesn't respond, or if you get a noncommittal reply, you may wish to take your case to an outside source for assistance.

• Before you purchase an item, be sure to check out the return policy for defective merchandise at the store. Why shouldn't you assume that all stores have similar return policies?

Store Policies are as follows:

• No refunds given

• Purchases of non-sale items may be exchanged within two weeks for store credit only

• All exchanges must be accompanied by the original sales slip

• Sales of reduced merchandise are final sales

• Holiday gifts may be exchanged for store credit by January 10th

Resolving Disputes

Most companies depend on satisfied customers to stay in business. Honest firms attempt to resolve problems quickly and fairly—if consumers bring these problems to the company's attention. However, in the case of legitimate complaints that a business has been unwilling or unable to resolve, consumers may seek help from a number of sources outside the company. These sources vary in the services they offer, the approaches they take, and the types of complaints that are handled. These sources include:

- **The Better Business Bureau.** The BBB is a nonprofit organization sponsored by private businesses. It accepts only written complaints and will contact a local business on your behalf. A complaint is resolved when the customer receives satisfaction or a reasonable adjustment, or the company provides proof that the complaint is unreasonable or not factual.

- **Occupational and professional licensing boards.** If you have a problem with professional or occupational services, such as a physician, dentist, physical therapist, hair-

dresser, or property manager, you may be able to get some help from a state licensing or regulatory board. The state licensing board may do an investigation while seeking a satisfactory solution to your problem.

- **Media programs.** Some newspapers and radio and TV stations offer "consumer hot line" services for people needing assistance. These sources often get successful results, because unfavorable publicity is a persuasive way to convince a company to resolve a consumer complaint.

New Marketplace, Familiar Challenge

In today's marketplace, you have more opportunities to buy than ever. Along with traditional options, such as malls and catalogs, you can shop using your television or computer. These new technologies are convenient and fun to use. However, can their razzle-dazzle lead to spending too much because of impulse buying?

Enticing Options

Television shopping networks, infomercials, and CD-ROM advertising capture your interest through product demonstrations and testimonials. By making your wants and desires seem like *real* needs, the advertisers entice you to buy.

Shopping on the World Wide Web offers even more temptation. On some websites, shopping can seem like playing a computer game as you click on products and put them into your "virtual" shopping cart. The problem is that you are spending *real* dollars.

What can you do to limit the temptation to impulse buy? Plenty!

Outsmarting the Marketplace

As you learn to manage your resources more effectively, there's a lot you can do to curb impulse buying. These tried-and-true tips really work!

- **Plan ahead.** Make your list according to your needs. Prioritize your list according to what's most important. Keep your list handy as a reminder of your needs whenever opportunities to shop come up.
- **Watch the temptation to browse.** Whether shopping on the Web or at the mall, browsing can easily lead to impulse buying.
- **Resist pressure tactics.** Phrases such as "only 5 minutes left to call" or "supply limited—call now" are pressure tactics used by advertisers to get you to buy their products. Resisting these tactics allows you to make wise choices.
- **Take time to consider choices.** Suppose you see something on the Web you hadn't planned to buy but suddenly "just can't live without." Make a note of it and promise yourself you'll think about it for at least a few days. If it still seems important later, shop around for the best buy.
- **Calculate the cost.** Before giving in to an impulse, figure the cost of that "good buy." Will you have enough money left to meet your needs? If not, skip the purchase.

Using Your Resources Wisely

1. Do you often give in to impulse spending? If you do, what tempts you most? If you don't, how do you protect yourself against impulse spending?

2. Which of the new marketplace shopping options do you think is most tempting to consumers? Why?

- **Private consumer groups.** These groups exist in every state and are called **advocates**, *individuals who speak out for consumer interests*. Some consumer groups help individual consumers with complaints. Others focus on the needs of special populations, such as the elderly, women, minorities, and low-income people. For information about consumer groups in your area, contact your local or state government consumer affairs office.

- **Governmental consumer affairs offices.** If you're not satisfied with a company or individual's response to your complaint about a product or service, your local or state consumer affairs office may be of help. Keep all receipts and other related information to use when you're contacting the agency.

- **Mediation and arbitration services.** Some communities provide free or low-cost services to help resolve financial disputes. Either party can request the use of a mediator—an impartial third party who will listen and make suggestions regarding the dispute. However, neither side is legally bound to abide by the mediator's suggestions.

  If informal mediation fails, an arbitrator can be brought in to reach a decision. An arbitrator is a trained impartial third party, who will listen to both sides and make a fair and equitable decision. The parties involved must agree beforehand to abide by the arbitrator's decision—

which is legally binding on both the consumer and the business.

- **Legal last resorts.** Claims usually ranging from $100 to $3,000 can be resolved relatively easily in small claims court. Court fees are charged, and lawyers usually are not needed and, in some states, are not permitted. If you win, court fees are refunded. Depending on local laws, some courts are allowed to order the losing party's employer to **garnishee** or *deduct money from his or her paycheck and give it to the winner of the lawsuit*.

  If the amount in dispute is larger than the maximum your state allows in a small claims court, you may need the help of an attorney. The cost of legal assistance often is substantial. Before consulting a lawyer, ask for references as well as information about legal fees.

• There are many consumer services that will assist consumers with legitimate consumer complaints. **What consumer services are available in your area?**

16 Review and Activities

Understanding Key Concepts

● Several ways exist to control impulse buying and balance your spending.

● You can pay less for many of the things you need and want by carefully planning your purchases.

● Advertising can be a helpful source of consumer information.

● A variety of marketing techniques are used to influence consumers to buy goods and services.

● Shopping for value can help you get quality goods and services at fair prices.

● All consumers have certain rights and responsibilities in the marketplace.

● Returning merchandise is a privilege, not a right.

● When a problem occurs with a product or a service, it's important to notify the company or store.

● A number of sources are available to help you resolve a legitimate complaint about a product or service that a business has been unwilling or unable to resolve.

Checking Your Knowledge

1. Give examples of how peer pressure influences people to purchase goods and services they don't need or can't afford.

2. Explain how controlling impulse buying can help consumers keep their wants and needs in balance.

3. Explain how bartering, renting, or repairing items can help consumers balance their wants and needs.

4. Why is an inventory, or list, important in making a buying plan?

5. In what ways is advertising helpful to consumers?

6. What marketing techniques are directed most often toward consumers your age? Which ones do you think are the most successful in influencing your purchases? Why?

7. Summarize the rights and responsibilities of consumers.

8. What steps should someone follow who is planning on returning a never-used item to the store where it was purchased?

9. Summarize sources of help for consumers trying to resolve a dispute.

Making TRANSITIONS

Shoplifting Solutions

Imagine you're an assistant in a department store. Part of your job is to reduce shoplifting and to write progress reports on store losses. As one of your first tasks, create an eye-catching poster designed to persuade individuals not to shoplift. Before beginning your design, write out your answers to these questions:

- Who will be your target audience? Why?
- Would a positive or negative message be more effective? Why?
- Where might be the most effective places in the store to display copies of your poster?
- What notices about shoplifting have you seen in stores? Do you think they have any effect on shoplifters? Why or why not?

STRENGTHENING *Life* SKILLS

Determining What's Important

Unfortunately, many people believe that it's important to always wear the latest styles or particular brands of clothing. Sometimes the more money a person has to spend, the more likely he or she is to buy expensive or luxury items. These "status symbols" are not necessarily of higher quality but are simply signs of financial success.

Make a list of what's "in" and what's "out" in fashion. Make a second list of status symbols in clothing, vehicles, food, sporting goods, and appliances.

- Do you own clothing that is in good condition but is no longer in style? Do you choose not to wear it? Why? What could you do with this clothing?
- Do you own any of the items on your status symbol list?

What influenced you to buy them? Are they of good quality? Do you think you received good value for the prices you paid?

- How does the advertising for status symbol items seek to influence the consumer to buy? Compare this advertising with that for comparable, but lower-priced items? Who is the target market for status symbol items?

Applying Thinking Skills

1. **Clarifying fact or fiction.** Some people think they have to buy brand name, rather than "no-name," items to display their status or importance. How would you respond to this position?

2. **Predicting consequences.** What positive and negative consequences might result in a new marriage when one partner frequently buys on impulse and the other carefully plans his or her own purchases? What suggestions would you give to help the couple deal with their differences in spending and help them balance their needs and wants?

3. **Thinking about change.** Have you ever been in a situation in which you were tempted to buy something but you didn't have money? What did you do? Would you handle the situation and your response to it differently now? Explain your answer.

Practical Applications

1. **Journeying back in time.** Advertising and marketing techniques have changed over the years. Ask your parents or guardians, or other adults to describe advertisements and commercials they remember during their childhood and adolescence. Use library resources to find examples of earlier advertisements. Which techniques—past or present—appear to have more influence on consumer spending? Why do you think this is so?

2. **Evaluating value.** Learning to shop for value takes time, study, and practice. With a partner, prepare a quality comparison demonstration. For each item, have at least two samples—one representing the high end of the quality scale, the other representing a lower quality. Take turns contrasting the various features that influence the quality of each item. If possible, include the prices of the items, and discuss the relationship between price and quality.

CHAPTER 17

Making Food Choices

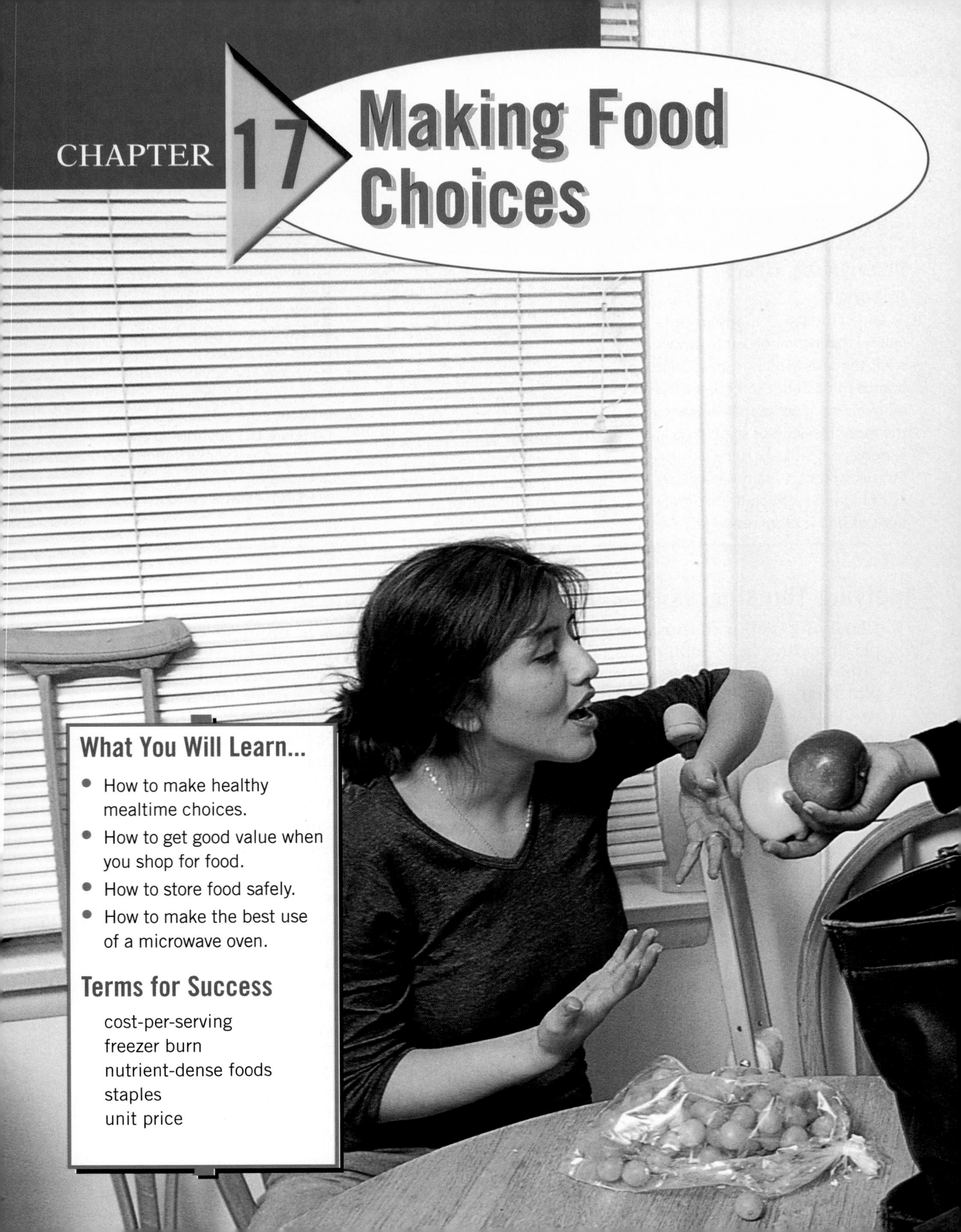

What You Will Learn...

- How to make healthy mealtime choices.
- How to get good value when you shop for food.
- How to store food safely.
- How to make the best use of a microwave oven.

Terms for Success

cost-per-serving
freezer burn
nutrient-dense foods
staples
unit price

Lucinda tilted forward on one crutch and peered into the canvas bag her friend had set on the floor. "Thanks for doing my shopping, Carol, but these things weren't on the list."

"Oh, that's my stuff," Carol explained, swinging two more bags onto the table. "I've never been to a farmers market before. I couldn't believe all the stuff they've got. I guess I went a little nuts."

"A little," Lucinda agreed. She held up a plastic bag of firm, round, reddish-purple fruit.

"Plums," Carol said. "I tried one. They're great. You could eat them for dessert. Take a few for yourself." She dug out a tub of cottage cheese from another sack. "I know this isn't the brand you asked for," she said, setting the container in the refrigerator, "but it was on sale. A lady who was buying it said it was really good, and I checked the labels. The vitamins and calcium are the same as your brand, so—why not?"

Lucinda gave her friend an amused smile. "I didn't know you were so serious about groceries."

"I haven't been," Carol said. "In fact, lately I think my motto has been Fast Food Today. I'll try eating better tomorrow."

"So the farmers market was fun," Lucinda said.

"Well, when I do go there, I usually buy what I've always bought, or whatever I feel like eating," Carol said. "But your list was so detailed, it got me thinking about all the choices there are. You know, I eat the same kinds of cereal I ate when I was a kid. Why not try something else?"

Lucinda grinned. "It looks like breaking my leg was the best thing that ever happened to your eating habits."

Carol nodded thoughtfully. "You should have done it a long time ago."

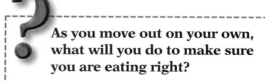

As you move out on your own, what will you do to make sure you are eating right?

Making Mealtime Choices

As you move out on your own, few decisions you make will impact your health as much as the decisions you make about what you eat. Yet this can be overlooked by many young adults.

"Time is limited. Fast foods are convenient. I'll try to eat better tomorrow," Carol would say.

Whether you eat in your own apartment, a cafeteria at your worksite or technical college, or in a university dining hall, the best advice is to try to select foods with the most nutrition per dollar.

Where Will You Eat?

Dining at home requires you to plan ahead, shop for groceries, and develop basic food preparation skills. A basic cookbook will provide you with a set of standardized recipes for a variety of foods. Once you have a basic cookbook, you can expand your recipe collection in a variety of ways. Recipe sources include your family and friends, magazines, newspapers, and the labels on many foods.

Mark files his recipes by categories like meat, vegetables, and desserts. Jasmine puts hers together by meals—breakfast, lunch, dinner, and snacks. Some recipes they got from their parents. Others came from cookbooks and magazines. These can also give you tips for creating a well-organized kitchen, a pleasant dining area, and a nutritious meal plan.

Eating Out

If you are a typical American, you will eat more than one-fifth of your meals away from home. These meals may be eaten at restaurants, purchased from vending machines or convenience stores, or taken with you.

• Having nutritious food available for meals once you are out on your own doesn't happen automatically. It takes time, a little thought, and a few basic food preparation skills. Why is it worth your while to learn how to prepare simple, nutritious meals?

Meal Planning

Planning a meal involves making important decisions about what foods to include and how they will be prepared. You will want to consider your daily eating pattern, your nutrition, others eating the meal, and your resources. Like those of many other Americans, your daily eating pattern may include three meals a day plus snacks.

Tawnie explained to her grandmother her frustration over coordinating a special weekend dinner for her family.

"It just seems like the details—the planning, the shopping, the cooking—are overwhelming. I've got so much to learn. What's the best way to do all this?"

• With careful choices, you can get the most nutrition for your money when eating out. Why is regularly eating out instead of preparing meals at home not always the best option for meeting your nutritional needs?

When selecting a restaurant, you will want to consider selection, price, and how quickly you want to be served. As with at-home meals, wise choices can help you get the most nutrition for your money when you eat out.

Blair works in a factory and decided to start packing his lunch because he could eat better food for less money than if he purchased food from the vending machines every day. Sometimes it's leftovers like turkey, barbecued chicken, or cold pizza. Sometimes it's soup in a thermos, fresh fruit, and rolls.

"That's what you have a lifetime to learn," said her grandmother. "I'll help you with the meal. In fact, I'll show you how my mother would have put this one together."

When planning what you'll eat, arm yourself with a copy of the Food Guide Pyramid, a personal budget, and your schedule. To plan nutritious meals, select nutrient-dense foods from the five basic food groups in the pyramid. **Nutrient-dense foods** are foods that are low or moderate in calories and rich in important nutrients. Use the Food Guide Pyramid and the Dietary Guidelines described in Chapter 13 as planning tools.

From there it's a matter of common sense: stay within your budgets of time and money.

Prepare a meal that is nutritious and meets the dietary needs of the people who will eat it. Be as creative as possible.

There are many resources that can help you throughout your life in meal planning:

- Take a class in basic nutrition at your university or community college.
- A hospital in your area may offer courses on balancing the components of nutrition, stress, time, and exercise.
- Explore the topic at your public library or check the Internet.
- Call your county's extension agent. Many areas—including urban areas—have agents who teach classes on food preparation and nutrition.

As you plan each meal, consider your options for purchasing and preparing the foods you include. You may have the choice of purchasing a food already prepared (packaged, frozen, or canned), partially prepared such as a cake mix or pre-cut salad greens, or making the food entirely from scratch. These options may vary in cost, preparation time, and nutrition. Beware of convenience foods that are high in fat, sodium, or sugar.

• Planning simple, nutritious meals takes a little planning upfront but can save you time and money in the long run.

R(E)A S O N
Through Life's Problems

Evaluate Information

Finding reliable information is an important step in solving practical problems. Read the following scenario and note how Jeff gathers the information he needs and evaluates its reliability.

"Oh no! Another two pounds," Jeff groaned as he stepped off the scale. "That makes seven pounds I've gained since I started school. If I keep going at this rate, I'll weigh a ton by the time I graduate!"

Jeff had just started college two months ago. He lived in a dorm, and had purchased the meal plan for the commons, but didn't care for the food it served. He was constantly tempted by the wide array of fast-food eateries surrounding the campus.

Jeff's stomach was growling. Deciding it was time to start eating more healthfully, he grabbed his meal ticket and headed to the commons. After he had selected the grilled chicken breast and rice, he made a list of how he could get nutritional information.

His roommate suggested the Internet, and together they went online.

"But how will I know I'm finding reliable information?" Jeff questioned as he started the computer. "Anybody can put a Web page on the Internet."

"You'll have to check out the sources pretty carefully. Look at these entries: they are just advertisements for weight loss products and exercise centers," his roommate pointed out. "However, here's a site by the American Dietetic Association. This would be a reliable source of information. I think the U.S. Department of Agriculture and the American Dairy Association have a lot of nutritional information, too."

"There is a wealth of information right here at my fingertips," Jeff said as he scanned through Web pages. "There's even cost-per-serving information for a lot of foods."

The next day when Jeff was at the college book store, he noticed a pocket guide to the fat content of foods. He checked to make sure it included many of the foods served in the commons. "I'm sure this can't be perfectly accurate, because the foods might not be prepared the same way, but at least it gives me an estimate to base my decision on," he thought.

Jeff stopped by at several of his favorite fast-food restaurants while he was out, not to buy food, but to pick up their nutritional information. Back in his room, Jeff looked over all the information he had gathered. He sat down and figured the cost per meal at the commons, and compared that to what he spent on fast food. Then he compared the fat content of his typical fast-food meal and an average meal in the commons.

"It looks like it would definitely cost fewer calories and less money to eat in the commons," he concluded. "However, I'm not sure I'm ready to give up all those burgers and tacos. I need to come up with a plan that will save me money while I eat healthier and still enjoy it. Maybe I can come up with a compromise—eat some meals out, but choose the lower fat items. I'll do some more figuring on it after lunch—in the commons, of course!"

► From Your Perspective

1 What values are involved in Jeff's situation?

2 Does Jeff have enough information to make a decision? Why or why not?

3 Could anyone else be affected by Jeff's decision? Who and how?

FOCUS ON ...

"Grazing"

Yolanda grew up in a family that emphasized three square meals each day. Paige, however, grew up in a family that emphasized smaller meals four or fives times a day. This is called "grazing," the same term given to *cattle grazing* in a pasture throughout the day.

Despite the association with lumbering cows, grazing is often recommended by physicians for patients wanting to lose weight and for those with certain types of medical conditions. Smaller meals throughout the day are burned more efficiently by the body.

If you graze, try to divide servings evenly. Keep in mind that the day's total servings should meet your nutrient and calorie needs, just as if you were eating three traditional meals.

Meal planning may seem time consuming at first, but becomes easier with practice. After you've developed several week's worth of meal plans, rotating the plans will give the variety you need and save you time. Planning meals ahead of time can also simplify food preparation and save actual time spent in preparing food.

Scheduling

Actually scheduling time to prepare meals is simple, but takes a little practice. A smart strategy for meal preparation involves several steps. Try these out as you begin your meal preparation adventure:

1. Make a list of tasks that you'll need to do as you prepare your meal. These tasks could include washing salad greens, chopping vegetables, or cooking ground beef.

2. Decide how to organize the tasks that need to be completed. See page 301 for more information on sequencing your tasks.

3. Estimate how much time it might take you to complete each task. The first few times you do these tasks you might want to allow a bit more time than you think you'll need. To find your total preparation time, add up all of the times needed for all of your tasks.

4. Determine your meal preparation start time. To do this, subtract your total preparation time from the time you want your meal to be ready. For example, imagine that your total preparation time for a meal is one hour and thirty minutes. If you want to eat your meal at 6:00 p.m., you need to start your meal preparation by 4:30 p.m. Then follow the sequence of tasks you determined earlier.

Once you have a little experience with scheduling and preparing meals, you'll likely find it to be second nature. In time, you may not need a written time schedule unless you're preparing a special meal.

Food Preparation Tasks

When determining the sequence, look for ways to save time and effort. You can save time by following these tips:

T I P S

- **Group similar tasks.** Grouping tasks like measuring or cutting saves time and makes better use of equipment.

- **Dovetail tasks.** Overlapping tasks saves time and makes it easier to have all the foods in the meal ready at the same time.

- **Prepare some foods ahead of time.** Including foods that can be prepared earlier in the day or even the day before they are to be served helps when time is limited.

Shopping for Food

Wise food shopping can save you time and money. Before you shop, you will want to make a list of the foods you plan to buy and decide where to shop. In addition, you will need to learn how to judge quality and how to get good value for your food dollar.

Making a Shopping List

A shopping list can help you manage your money as well as your time. A shopping list speeds your shopping and eliminates special trips to the store for forgotten items. A list also helps prevent buying items you did not plan on and don't need.

After you have planned your meals for the week, check your menus and recipes to see what foods and ingredients you need. If you don't have these items on hand, write them on your shopping list. Include the amount needed for each item.

• Keeping things simple allows you to make the best use of your resources. Which one of your personal resources might be the most limited when it comes to meal preparation? How might you overcome that limitation?

Also check your supply of staples. **Staples** are the basic items you use on a regular basis, such as flour, sugar, rice, pasta, and nonfat dry milk. Check your supply of "quick-to-fix" foods, such as frozen dinners and canned soups. Also check nonfood items, such as cleaning supplies and paper products.

You may find it helpful to keep a reminder list handy in the kitchen. Whenever you notice that items are running low, write them on the list.

To save time shopping, organize your shopping list logically. Group together items that are found in the same area of the store, such as produce, dairy foods, meats, and frozen foods.

Using a Microwave

TIPS

A microwave long ago proved itself to be a great time-saving piece of equipment. To make the best use of a microwave, consider the following tips:

- Arrange foods carefully inside the microwave. Keep in mind that the microwave cooks food from the outer edges to the center. Put thicker parts of food toward the outside of the dish and thinner parts toward the center.

- Cover foods to retain heat, keep foods moist, and help the food cook evenly. Covering foods also keeps the microwave clean, especially when heating sauces, which can splatter and even explode in the microwave.

- Stir or rotate foods to cook evenly.

- Don't forget the standing time. When food is cooked in a microwave, it continues to cook even after you have taken it out of the oven.

- Remove odors from the microwave by boiling a mixture of 1/2 cup lemon juice and 1 cup water for several minutes. Leave in the microwave oven for at least 5 minutes after boiling.

• A shopping list and knowing what you are looking for can help use your time efficiently at the supermarket. **How might shopping without a list impact your resources?**

Deciding Where to Shop

Once you've decided what to buy, decide where you will shop. You can buy food from several kinds of food stores: supermarkets, warehouse stores, convenience stores, or specialty stores. Prices, quality, and services may vary widely. Your choices will depend on your preferences and which stores are closest.

Consider what you want in a place to shop for food. Which are more important to you: a variety of services or lower prices; shopping around for bargains or shopping at one store?

Consider how far the store is from your home, the kinds of food the store sells, and its cleanliness. Look for a store where the food appears to be in good condition and is stored at safe temperatures. Note the special promotions the store uses to attract customers. Will these promotions actually save you money?

Judging Quality

As you select food items, you will want to judge their quality. Food labels, appearance, seals, and grades all provide clues to quality.

Food labels are valuable tools for making food choices. Food labels give information about the contents and nutritional value of a food product.

The information label tells you:

- The type of food.
- The amount of food by weight or by volume.
- The name and place of business of the manufacturer, packer, or distributor.
- The ingredients in the food, in order by weight from largest amount to smallest.

• Nutrition labels are valuable tools in making healthful food choices.

The nutrition label provides information that can help you make more healthful food choices. It provides the following nutrition facts:

- **Serving information.** Serving size and number of servings per container.
- **Calorie information.** Number of calories per serving and number of calories per serving from fat.
- **Nutrition information.** The amount of each nutrient, given in grams or milligrams.
- **Daily value. Daily values** are reference amounts based on Food and Drug Administration recommendations. They are designed to help you understand the relationship of the nutrients provided by the food to your total diet. Nutrient amounts are also listed as a percentage of the daily value.

Watch for other important clues to food quality. Watch for these signs when you shop:

- Buy fruits and vegetables that are mature, firm, typical in shape and color, and medium in size. Avoid ones with bruises and breaks in the skin.
- Choose whole grain products whenever possible, or be sure the product is enriched. Look for products low in fat, sugar, and sodium.
- Look for inspection and grading stamps on meat, poultry, and eggs.
- Buy fish from a reliable source. Judge the quality of fresh fish by appearance and aroma. If it smells fishy, it's not fresh.

The Nutrition Label

Serving size: At the top of the label, you will find the number of servings and the serving sizes. The serving sizes indicate the amount of food generally eaten at one time. The FDA has specified standard amounts for different varieties of food.

Key nutrients: The nutrition label provides information about key nutrients that are important to most consumers. This list is standard on all food products.

Nutrition Facts

Serving Size 1/2 cup (114 g)
Servings Per Container 4

Amount Per Serving

Calories 90	Calories from Fat 30

	% Daily Value*
Total Fat 3 g	5%
Saturated Fat 0 g	0%
Cholesterol 0 mg	0%
Sodium 300 mg	13%
Total Carbohydrate 13 g	4%
Dietary Fiber 3 g	12%
Sugars 3 g	
Protein 3 g	

Vitamin A	80%	•	Vitamin C	60%
Calcium	4%	•	Iron	4%

* Percent Daily Values are based on a 2,000 calorie diet. Your daily values may be higher or lower depending on your calorie needs:

		Calories	2,000	2,500
Total Fat	Less than		65 g	80 g
Sat Fat	Less than		20 g	25g
Cholesterol	Less than		300 mg	300 mg
Sodium	Less than		2,400 mg	2,400 mg
Total Carbohydrate			300 g	375 g
Fiber			25 g	30 g

Calories per gram:
Fat 9 • Carbohydrates 4 • Protein 4

Calorie information: The label provides you with the total calories, the total calories from fat, and the total calories from saturated fat. These figures help consumers keep track of, and limit, the amount of fat consumed.

Percent of Daily Values: These percentages are based on recommendations by health experts. These figures help consumers determine how a serving of a certain food fits into an overall daily food plan. These percentages are based on an average 2000 calorie diet.

Irradiated Food

Food irradiation has been the subject of more research than any other food process in history. Still, the public knows little about the process. So how safe is it?

- **What is irradiation?** Irradiation is the process of exposing food to gamma rays to increase its shelf life and kill harmful microorganisms.

- **Will irradiation make food radioactive?** No.

- **What happens to food when it's irradiated?** Irradiation can cause minor changes in flavor and texture and slight vitamin loss.

- **How could irradiation improve food safety?** It could reduce food-borne illness and eliminate the need for dangerous pesticides.

- **Has consumer demand for irradiated foods increased?** No. This may be due to a lack of advertising by food processors or to people's negative associations with the word "radiation."

- **What concerns do critics of irradiation have?** Critics claim that irradiation produces harmful by-products that can cause cancer and birth defects. They also fear that the radioactive chemicals used in irradiation plants pose a danger to workers and to the community.

- **Does irradiation of foods have FDA approval?** Yes. The FDA (Food and Drug Administration) approved use of irradiation for spices years ago. It has also approved the process for fruits, vegetables, beef, poultry, and seafood.

- **How can I tell if a food has been irradiated?** It is almost impossible to tell by flavor or appearance whether foods have been irradiated. However, foods that have gone through the irradiation process bear the irradiation symbol:

Voicing Your Opinion

1. *If you were to choose between a food product that had been irradiated and one that had not, which would you choose and why?*

2. *Debate the benefits and risks posed by irradiating foods.*

- Avoid cans and packages that are dirty, bulging, dented, rusty, leaking, or damaged in any way. Packages that have been opened may have been tampered with.

- When buying frozen foods, avoid packages that are stained, irregular in shape, or covered with ice. The ice means the package may have been thawed and then refrozen.

Getting Good Value

Once he had his own apartment, John learned quickly the value of a dollar at the grocery warehouse. For some things like his breakfast cereal or spaghetti sauce, he prefers to stick with name-brand or national-brand items. These are products sold across the country. They are advertised in the national media, which increases their prices.

For other things, like canned soup, John discovered he likes store brands (also called private labels). These are specially produced for the store selling them. They are generally less expensive than name brands because stores do not spend as much in advertising as food manufacturers do.

At times he also buys generic items. These have plain labels and are usually less expensive than either name brands or store brands.

Comparing Prices

To find the best food buys, do some comparison shopping. You can use unit prices or cost-per-serving to determine the best buy. The **unit price** is the price per ounce, quart, pound, or other unit. In many stores, the unit price is shown on the price label on the shelf edge below the item. If the unit price is not shown, you can calculate it by dividing the total cost by the number of units.

• The nutritional value among national brands, and generic items is generally equal. You might find differences in quality, however. **In what instance might you choose a national brand over a generic label product?**

Sometimes cost-per-serving is a better way to compare prices. To find the **cost–per–serving,** first determine how many servings a given amount will yield. Then divide the price by the number of servings. The result is the price for one serving.

Here are some additional suggestions for saving money on food:

- Be flexible when using your shopping list. Look for unadvertised specials that you could substitute for items on your list.
- Buy fresh foods in season when they are most plentiful.
- Compare prices for different forms of food (fresh, frozen, canned, or dried).
- When using coupons, compare prices to make sure you are really getting the best buy.
- At the checkout line, pay attention as your purchases are rung up. Watch the display as each item is entered or scanned. The clerk could make a mistake or the incorrect price might be stored in the store's computer. If you think an error has been made, politely ask the clerk to check the price.

Storing Food

Channon thought it was the flu, but her roommate Debbie discovered the truth when she opened the refrigerator and saw the leftovers from what Channon had for lunch.

"I thought your symptoms seemed to hit you pretty fast, Channon," Debbie said. "You have food poisoning."

Proper storage of food supplies and leftovers is essential for your health.

When you get your food home, store it carefully to retain its quality. Each food has a shelf life, or length of time it can be safely stored. The length of time a food retains its quality depends on the type of food, its packaging, its storage temperature, and how the food is handled.

• When frozen foods are stored properly, foods retain their nutritional value and flavor. **What is the benefit of rewrapping foods like fresh meat before freezing?**

Basic Storage Principles

To retain the quality of the food you buy, observe these basic storage principles:

- Buy only what you need and can use before it spoils.
- Follow the principle of first in, first out. Store new purchases behind food already on hand.
- Use Sell By or Use By dates on food containers as guides for food use or write the purchase date on the container before you store. Use canned foods within a year.

Cold Storage

Perishable foods spoil quickly at room temperature. Perishable foods are usually stored in the freezer or refrigerator.

Freezer Storage

Freezing permits long-term storage of many foods. At freezer temperatures of 0°F (-18°C) or below, foods keep from one month to a year. How long they keep depends on the type of food and its packaging.

Foods purchased frozen should be stored promptly to prevent thawing. Many other foods can be frozen to increase their shelf life. You may freeze fresh meats, poultry, fish, and baked goods such as breads and rolls. Many leftovers can be frozen for future use.

Foods purchased frozen can be stored in their original packaging. Foods frozen at home must be packaged to avoid freezer burn. **Freezer burn** results from improper packaging or lengthy food storage. Improperly packaged food dries out and loses flavor and texture.

To retain the quality of foods you freeze at home, packaging materials must be vapor and moisture-resistant. Choose plastic containers with tight-fitting covers, heavy-duty plastic freezer bags, heavy-duty foil, or freezer wrap.

For best results, label all packages and containers with contents, amount, date frozen, and any special instructions. Freeze food quickly by spreading packages out. Leave enough space between packages for air to circulate. When the food is frozen, stack like items together.

• Properly storing refrigerated foods leads to less waste and better use of your resources. **Which foods are properly stored? Why or why not?**

- The "first in, first out" rule of thumb can help you keep foods from getting "lost" in the cupboard. **Develop a system that you would use to keep track of foods in your cupboard and in your freezer.**

Refrigerator Storage

After storing frozen foods, store foods that must be refrigerated. These include foods that were refrigerated in the store, most fresh fruits and vegetables, whole grain products, and baked goods with fruit or cream fillings. Your refrigerator should be kept at 40°F (4°C).

Observe the following guidelines when you're storing food in the refrigerator:

- **Avoid overloading the refrigerator.** Refrigerated foods require constant circulation of cold air to prevent spoilage.
- **Store refrigerated foods tightly covered.** This keeps them from drying out. It also prevents transfer of odors from one food to another.
- **Store meat, poultry, and fish in their original wraps.** If one is damaged, or leaking, put the package into a plastic bag or place something under it. Leaking liquids can contaminate foods stored below.

Room Temperature Storage

Many foods will keep well at room temperatures. At 85°F (29°C) or below, these foods will last for weeks or even months. Foods that require room temperature storage include most canned foods, dried beans and peas, oils and shortening, and many grain products (except whole grains). Some perishables, such as potatoes and onions, are best stored in a cool, dry place.

Watch for these signs of spoilage in canned and bottled foods: bulging cans, liquids that spurt when you open the container, or liquids that are cloudy when they should be clear. If you see these signs, do not taste the food. Wrap it and discard it where no person or animal can get to it. Use the garbage disposal if you have one.

Making the Most of Your Food Dollars

Making wise food choices will help you make the most of your food dollars. Whether you dine in or eat out, planning is important. By planning ahead, you can enjoy nutritious and appetizing meals that make the most of your resources.

Review and Activities

Understanding Key Concepts

● Dining at home requires you to plan ahead, shop for groceries, and develop basic food preparation skills.

● A basic cookbook will provide you with a set of standardized recipes for a variety of foods.

● When planning meals, you need to balance costs, nutrition, and preparation time.

● A well-organized shopping list helps you manage your money as well as your time.

● Choose a grocery store based on quality, services, distance, and competitive prices.

● Food labels provide important information about the foods you eat.

● Storing food properly is essential to your health.

Checking Your Knowledge

1. How could you benefit by starting a recipe collection now?

2. Explain how you can get the most nutrition for your money when you eat out.

3. Develop a chart showing nutrient-dense and nonnutrient-dense foods. How do foods in these categories differ?

4. Describe the advantages and disadvantages of shopping at supermarkets, warehouse stores, convenience stores, and specialty stores.

5. Explain how you can judge quality when shopping for food.

6. Compare the advantages and disadvantages of buying name brands, store brands, and generic food products.

7. How can unit prices and cost-per-serving help you determine the best food buys? Give an example using one of your favorite foods.

8. Develop a list of three tips each for freezer storage, refrigerator storage, and room temperature storage of food.

Making TRANSITIONS

Sharing Mealtime Responsibilities

Antonio, Terry, and Devin share an apartment near their college campus. They have limited budgets and food preparation skills. They have only basic cooking equipment. Their schedules vary, so it's not always possible to eat meals together. However, they are all tired of frozen dinners and take-out food and would like to consider other options.

Develop a plan describing which of the three roommates will be responsible for different food preparation tasks such as planning, shopping, cooking, and cleaning up. Will tasks be rotated or assigned permanently? How will they plan meals they will all enjoy? How will they budget for food? How can they fit meal preparation into their busy schedules? What equipment can save time and energy in the kitchen?

Choose five recipes that might work for them. Consider one-dish meals, microwave meals, and recipes that can be doubled and frozen for future use. Look for versatile recipes that can be used in a number of different ways.

STRENGTHENING *Life* SKILLS

Planning Meals on Your Own

Imagine that you are living on your own. Plan your meals for a week. First, describe your lifestyle and identify the resources you'll need to consider in making meal choices.

Next, decide which meals will be eaten out and which will be eaten at home. Include at least two packed lunches. Plan for dinner at a restaurant on Friday night. Include one meal for three friends on Saturday. Consider how these choices help meet your nutrition needs each day.

Plan menus for meals to be eaten at home. Be sure to include snacks in your plans. Locate recipes for the foods to be prepared at home. Then develop a shopping list for the meals to be prepared at home. Group food items logically. (You may assume that you have staples such as flour and sugar on hand.)

- Did your mealtime choices meet your nutrition needs each day?
- How did your resources affect your decisions?
- What problems did you encounter in planning your meals for the week?

Applying Thinking Skills

1. **Predicting consequences.** Imagine you have a friend who has eaten out every single meal for the past week. What are the consequences regarding costs? Time? Nutrition?

2. **Developing criteria.** Given your current lifestyle, explain what staples would be essential for your very own pantry. What staples could you add to improve nutrition?

3. **Drawing conclusions.** Which of the food preparation resources described in this chapter are likely to have the greatest impact on how you plan your meals? Why?

4. **Analyzing advertising claims.** What misconceptions could people have about foods that are labeled fat free or low fat? How might these misconceptions affect people's eating habits?

Practical Applications

1. **Making menu choices.** Analyze the menus of three different fast-food restaurants. Identify the most nutritious lunch possible from each menu. Write a short paper explaining your findings.

2. **Considering alternatives.** Plan nutritious menus for a day for a person who prefers grazing instead of following a traditional meal pattern.

3. **Developing a shopping list.** Create a shopping list for food and nonfood items that might be purchased in a supermarket. Categorize items into logical groups. Compare your shopping list with those of classmates. What features make a shopping list useful?

CHAPTER 18

Clothing for an Active Life

What You Will Learn...

- How to look your best.
- How to plan a wardrobe that meets your needs.
- Ways to get the most for your money.
- Procedures for caring for clothes.

Terms for Success

comparison shopping
cost-per-wearing
multipurpose garments
pretreatment

Devlin browsed through a stack of knit shirts, looking for his size. Carrie, standing beside him, commented, "These stripes are nice. Very bold."

"Uh-huh," Devlin agreed. "but I need something for work. Everyone dresses kind of formal. I think solid colors are more professional."

"In that case, how about a dress shirt?" Carrie suggested. "They look very . . . serious."

"That's an idea." Devlin found a rack of sleek, neatly pressed, long-sleeve shirts. He inspected a white one. "This is what I need."

Carrie turned the price tag for Devlin to read. He grimaced and hung up the shirt. "How can you dress for success if you go broke paying for it?"

Carrie frowned thoughtfully. "Do you remember that blue-striped tie you wore to your brother's wedding? That looked very classy, even with a short-sleeve shirt. Maybe you should invest in a few nice ties."

Devlin tried to visualize the effect. "That might do it. I could get a couple of plain cotton shirts; it'd be just the right look."

"Get one yellow shirt," Carrie advised. "It would look great with your gray slacks."

"Yes." A look of realization spread across Devlin's face. "You pay a lot of attention to what I wear."

Carrie smiled and glanced away casually. "I always have. I wouldn't even have noticed you that first time, except you were wearing that white parka, with those big white mittens and white earmuffs. You looked like a giant bunny rabbit."

"Well, it worked, didn't it?" Devlin defended himself. "It made you look."

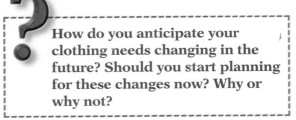

How do you anticipate your clothing needs changing in the future? Should you start planning for these changes now? Why or why not?

Looking Your Best

The first impression others form of you is based on how you look and act. The first step in making a good first impression is looking your best. To do so, you'll need to know how your appearance affects others. Then you can take the steps necessary to make sure the impression you make is a good one.

Making a Clothing Statement

Every time you get dressed, you are making a statement about yourself. By observing what you wear, others can learn something about who you are and what groups you are a part of. Your clothing choices provide clues about what type of person you are. What does your clothing tell others about your values, your cultural heritage, your personality, your self-image, and even your mood?

Before you've even been introduced, the other person has already formed a first impression based on your appearance. When you go for a job interview, what does an employer see first when you walk through the door? It's not your personality or your list of accomplishments; it's your clothes. Be sure the statement your clothes make about you is a positive one.

However, it is also important to recognize that impressions based on what others wear are often inaccurate. Using clothing as the basis for judging someone without really knowing them is unfair.

Planning Your Wardrobe

Planning your wardrobe takes time. You will want to consider the influences on your clothing choices, identify your clothing needs, and take stock of what you have before you plan new additions to your wardrobe.

• The types of clothing people wear often tells a lot about their values, their work, and their personality. What do your clothing choices say about you?

- It's inevitable. The types of clothing you'll need as you move into your adult life will change from what you currently need. **What types of clothing do you anticipate needing in the future?**

What Will You Need?

As you become more independent, your lifestyle and clothing requirements will change. You may need to rethink your wardrobe when you go to college, start a new job, or marry. Each of these events can mean new activities. Some of your clothes and accessories will probably work well. However, you will probably need some new items better suited to your new lifestyle.

The apparel you will need for work will depend on your job. You may be required to wear a uniform, or you may be expected to observe a company dress code. Written dress codes are usually described in employee handbooks. Otherwise, you will need to watch what other employees are wearing, and choose similar apparel.

The same principle applies if you will be a student. Notice what other students on campus are wearing. Then choose clothing that is appropriate at the school you attend.

As you move into adulthood, you'll make new friends and will get involved in new leisure activities. The apparel you choose for leisure should be attractive, practical, and durable. While special items have been designed for many activities, you'll need fewer leisure clothes if you choose items that can be worn for several. From time to time, you'll need clothing appropriate for special occasions.

Your resources—both financial and personal—influence your clothing choices. How much can you afford to spend on clothes? Do you have skills you can use in building your wardrobe? Perhaps you have a knack for shopping, the skills for sewing, altering, or redesigning clothing, or a flare for choosing or creating accessories. How much time can you spend shopping or sewing? Can you use your creativity to accessorize garments?

Taking Stock

The best way to plan your wardrobe is to make an inventory of what you already own. Your inventory can help you determine which clothes best fit your lifestyle and what wardrobe additions you'll need.

• Taking a clothing inventory is the first step in identifying what your future clothing needs might be. **What articles of clothing do you own now that will not meet your future needs?**

Begin your inventory by sorting your clothes into three groups:

- **Clothes you plan to keep.** These clothes fit well, are in good condition, and are ones you like to wear.
- **Clothes that need repair.** These are clothes you like and can wear, but they need repair.
- **Clothes you don't wear.** These clothes are ones you don't like, no longer fit, or are beyond repair.

Make a list of the clothes in each group. Note the type of clothing, the color, and the fabric of each item.

Studying each group will help you develop your wardrobe plan. The clothes you like will help you define your clothing preferences in terms of style, color, and fabric. The clothes that need attention can make you a better judge of quality when you shop for clothes and can improve your clothing care skills. The clothes you don't wear will help you evaluate your purchasing habits. Were some of these clothes impulse buys? Were any of them things someone else talked you into buying? Are there garments that match nothing else you own? Were some items fads that are now out of date?

Finally, study your remaining wardrobe to determine whether it fits all of your activities. What items do you need to replace? Do you have too many clothes for some activities and not enough for others? Make a list of the additions you plan to make.

Wardrobe Make-Over

Of course, the easiest way to add to your wardrobe is to buy new items. When you purchase new clothes, however, think about how you can meet your needs with a minimum of expense. You'll feel that you have more clothes if you learn to choose multipurpose garments and mix-and-match garments, use color effectively, and make wise clothing investments.

Stretching Your Clothing Dollars

If your clothing budget is limited, take a look at ways to stretch your resources. Your clothing resources include money, shopping and sewing skills, time, creativity, and other people. By using these resources wisely, you can meet your needs without overspending.

- **Money.** If you don't have enough money for all the clothes in your wardrobe plan, first rethink your plan. Can you do without some of the things on your list or delay purchasing them? Would multipurpose garments meet several needs? Can you find new uses for garments by mixing and matching? Next, rethink your budget. Can you adjust other areas of your budget? Can you increase your income?

- **Skills.** You can make your money go further by developing good shopping skills. Do you look for items on sale or at discount stores? Do you know when you can expect to find items on sale? Can you spot a bargain? Have you considered buying previously owned clothes at resale stores, thrift shops, antique stores, flea markets, and garage sales? You can also save by learning to sew. Do you know how to make simple repairs and fitting adjustments? Can you update garments that you no longer wear? Can you complete an easy-to-sew project, like a T-shirt or shorts? Can you handle a more complex project, such as a shirt or jacket?

- **Time.** If you have plenty of time, you can spend it shopping for bargains, sewing, or being creative. If your time is limited, a well-thought-out wardrobe plan is essential. Before you shop, decide what you need and where you will be most likely to find it. Don't waste your limited time "just looking."

- **Creativity.** You can use your creativity to meet your clothing needs. Mix-and-match garments to create new combinations. Decorate garments with fabric paint or trims. Add interesting accessories to create new looks. Make some of your own accessories.

- **Other people.** Sometimes you can share or trade clothes with a family member or friend. This is a good alternative instead of investing in a new outfit for a special occasion. Renting is another option for special occasion clothing. Uniforms and costumes can also be rented.

Using Your Resources Wisely

1. What are the advantages and disadvantages of each of these options? When would each be a good choice? Why?

2. Where can you find previously owned clothing in your community? What types of clothing can you rent locally?

Multipurpose Garments

You will need fewer clothes if you choose multipurpose garments. **Multipurpose garments** can be worn for more than one activity or season. A carefully chosen tweed jacket can be paired with dress slacks for a polished look or with jeans for dress-down occasions. Twill pants in a medium weight can be worn all year, while wool tweed pants may be appropriate only during late fall and winter.

Your goal is to have a versatile wardrobe. A shirt that can be paired with several pairs of pants is a good choice. Remember this when you shop for clothing.

Mix-and-Match Garments

One way to expand your wardrobe is to choose garments that can be combined in a variety of ways. You may find that you can mix and match the clothes you already have in new ways. Look for new ways you can mix individual pieces, colors, and fabrics.

One way to encourage new pairings is to group garments in your closet by type—tops, sweaters, jackets, pants, and so on. By separating garments you usually wear together, you may see new possibilities.

As you shop for new additions to your wardrobe, look for garments you can mix and match with items you already own

Using Color

When selecting colors for your wardrobe, consider your personal coloring and your body shape. Do you look your best in bright, bold colors, or softer, more subdued colors? What colors highlight your best features, such as your eyes, hair, or skin tone? How do colors affect your apparent size and height? If you have trouble deciding what colors are right for you, ask someone you trust for advice.

Plan most of your wardrobe around a few neutral or basic colors. Choose versatile colors for garments like a coat, suit, jacket, or basic dress. Neutrals such as black, navy, or brown are a good choice for skirts, pants, and shoes. Reserve less versatile colors for shirts, blouses, fun clothes, and accents.

- Multipurpose garments can be mixed and matched for a variety of occasions during most seasons of the year. **What multipurpose garments do you currently own? How might these garments meet your future needs?**

REASON

Through Life's Problems

Recognizing the Primary Problem

Practical problems are complex, and focusing on exactly what is the problem to be solved can be confusing. Read the situation below and study how Shawna identifies her primary problem.

"I'm so excited!" Shawna practically screamed at her roommate, Abigail. "Ben asked me to the winter formal! It will be my first really big dance!"

"Oh, that will be fun!" Abigail squealed. "What are you going to wear?"

Shawna groaned. "I don't have anything that will do. Since I lost all that weight, nothing that I have fits. In fact, I gave all the dresses away."

"Can you afford to buy something new?" Abigail asked.

"Not with school fees due in two weeks. Too bad those thrift stores have gone out of business. I used to find dresses with the tags still on them for just a couple of dollars. Why aren't any of these stores around here anymore?" Shawna said.

"Maybe they are, and we just haven't found them and don't have a way to get there," Abigail answered. "Let's go to the mall this afternoon and see if we can find any good deals on the clearance racks."

The two girls scoured every store at the mall, looking for a formal Shawna could afford. They found nothing in her price range. As they were leaving the last store, feeling very dejected, Shawna spotted a beautiful gown on a mannequin.

"I wish I could buy that dress," she murmured. "It's even my favorite color. That would really turn Ben's head!"

"Let's try it on, just for the fun of it," Abigail suggested.

The dress looked beautiful on Shawna. It fit perfectly, and the color made her blue eyes sparkle.

"Why don't you buy the dress and return it after the dance," Abigail advised. "Then you would have the dress you really want, and could have the money back in time to pay for your fees."

"This doesn't seem very honest to me. What about the poor person who buys it after I have returned it? They would be paying full price for a used dress? What if I spill something on it? What in the world would I do with all these tags on it?"

"I'll help you pin them inside. I've done it dozens of times—everybody does. What do you think? Let's go pay for it!"

"I'm not sure," Shawna said as she looked longingly at the dress. "There's got to be a better way to get a dress."

▶ From Your Perspective

1 What is the primary problem Shawna needs to solve?

2 What contextual factors will affect Shawna's decision?

3 What would you suggest Shawna do to get a dress without "weekend stealing"?

Using Accessories

A change of accessories can often transform the appearance of a garment. A new belt, scarf, tie, hat, buttons, or jewelry can create a new look for an old outfit. Fashion magazines are a good source of ideas. They will help you identify the newest trends in colors and accessories.

Clothing Investments

You'll want to invest your clothing dollars wisely. Good clothing investments fit your lifestyle and have the potential of becoming frequently-worn favorites in your wardrobe. Such clothing investments are especially important for expensive garments, such as a coat you will wear for several years. Investment garments are also a good way to build a "work" wardrobe. If a potential purchase meets the standards that follow, your money will be well spent:

- Quality in design, fabric, and construction.
- Classic design.
- Flexibility.
- Durability.
- Comfort and fit.

Shopping for Clothes

Once you have identified your clothing needs, you are ready to shop for clothes. Before you shop, however, you will need to be prepared.

Getting Ready to Shop

Prepare for buying new clothes by gathering information and determining your size range. Your efforts will help you find just the right additions to your wardrobe and get more for your money.

Gather information and ideas from a variety of sources—magazines, newspapers, radio and television, catalogs, computer services, and billboards and posters. Labels and hangtags are another important source of product information.

• A few well-chosen clothing accessories can transform the appearance of many garments, helping you expand the usefulness of clothing currently in your wardrobe. **What accessories might be most beneficial for your wardrobe?**

Getting the Most for Your Money

Comparison shopping means looking at design, quality, price, and warranties to compare value before you buy. As you shop, you will be able to compare your selections with the information you have gathered.

Advertising, however, doesn't provide all the information you need to know about a product. Other information comes from the labels and hangtags that are attached to the garments. These will give you information about fabric content and care requirements. Additional information may include sizes, trademarks or brand names, warranties or guarantees, and union labels.

When a garment catches your eye, ask yourself these questions:

- Does it fit into my wardrobe plan?
- Will it go with anything else in my wardrobe?
- Can it be worn for more than one occasion or activity?
- Will I need to buy special accessories to go with the garment?
- What type of care does it require?
- Do I really need this item?

To find out if a garment fits properly, you will need to try it on. When you are in the dressing room, look at yourself in a full-length mirror. Check both the front view and back view. Are there any wrinkles, bulges, sags, gaps, or pulls, which indicate a poor fit? Stand up, bend over, reach up, move around, and sit down to check comfort. Is it uncomfortable to do any of these things? If so, the garment doesn't fit properly. See this page for some basic fitting guidelines.

To check the quality of a garment, inspect the fabric and construction carefully. Make sure the fabric is suited to your intended use of the garment. Check how the garment is made to determine the quality of workmanship.

FOCUS ON ...
Basic Fitting Guidelines

Proper fit is important for both appearance and comfort. When you try on clothes, observe these basic fitting guidelines:

- Straight grain of fabric should hang vertically for most designs.
- Ease should be appropriate for comfort, the type of garment, and the style.
- Waistband or waistline should feel comfortable without pulling or binding.
- Collar or neckline should fit close to the neck without gaping or binding.
- Fasteners should not pull or gap as you move and should open and close easily.
- Sleeves should allow free movement and not get in the way. Long sleeves should cover the wrist bone when the arm is bent.
- Armhole seams should lie at the edge of the shoulder unless designed otherwise. Shoulders should feel comfortable and not be so snug that they restrict arm movement.
- Chest and back should fit smoothly and allow room for movement. Fabric should not pull; closings should not gap.
- Hip area should fit smoothly without pulling or forming folds. Wearer should be able to bend and sit comfortably.
- Hemline should be parallel to the floor, meet evenly at openings, and be the right length for body proportions and current fashion. Pants should break at the top of your shoes or feet.

FOCUS ON ...

Cost-Per-Wearing

One way to evaluate the cost of a garment is to estimate its **cost-per-wearing.** This is the total purchase price plus the cost of cleaning divided by the number of times you expect to wear the garment. For example, if you purchase a wool sweater for $25.00, anticipate wearing it 16 times and having it cleaned 4 times for a total of $16.00, its cost-per-wearing would be $2.56. On the other hand, suppose you spend the $25.00 for a pair of cotton twill pants you can wear 64 times in 2 years and can launder for about a $1.00 a year. The pants would cost only 42¢ per wearing.

The type of care a garment requires can be an important consideration in your buying decision. How often will the garment need to be cleaned? This will depend on how easily it shows soil and whether the fabric is resistant to stains and spots. What care does the garment require? Extra time is needed for hand washing and for air drying. Dry cleaning costs are usually much higher than laundry costs. Does the garment wrinkle easily? If so, you will have to iron the garment every time it is washed. You may even have to press it before every wearing.

Finally, consider the overall cost of a garment before making the decision to buy it. Ask yourself:

* Is the price within my budget?
* How long will I wear this garment?
* How long can I expect it to last?
* Can I buy something similar for less?
* Can I buy it for less somewhere else?
* Can I save money by waiting for it to go on sale?
* Could I make the item for less?

• By comparison shopping, you can get the most out of your clothing dollars. What questions do you ask yourself before you buy an article of clothing?

Caring for Clothes

If you take care of your clothes, they will last longer and look better. Your clothes will be ready to wear when you need them. In the long run, taking care of your clothes saves you money. You will want to develop clothing care routines to keep your clothes clean and in good repair.

Spend a few minutes each day caring for your clothes. If they can be worn again, take time to air clothes out before putting them away. Brush off lint. Check for soil, spots, and stains. Check each garment to see if it needs repairs. Get into the habit of putting your clothes away in a closet, into a drawer, or onto a shelf. This will help prevent wrinkling and may save you from pressing your clothes before you wear them again. Set aside dirty clothes that need to be laundered or dry-cleaned.

Keeping Clothes Clean

To choose the correct method for cleaning a garment, check the care label inside. Care labels tell you what cleaning method to use, what water temperature and dryer setting to use, and whether the clothing can be machine dried. The label may indicate whether the fabric can be bleached and what type of bleach is safe to use. Labels may also provide specific warnings, such as *Do Not Dry-Clean* or *Do Not Bleach*.

Before you clean garments, stains should be pretreated. **Pretreatment** means applying stain-removal techniques before cleaning a garment. Regular cleaning methods can then more easily clean it. For washable garments, treat stains by using a commercial prewash or presoak product. Before using any pretreatment product, read the label carefully. For nonwashables, take the garment for dry-cleaning as soon as possible. Point out stains to the dry cleaner so they can be treated before the garment is cleaned.

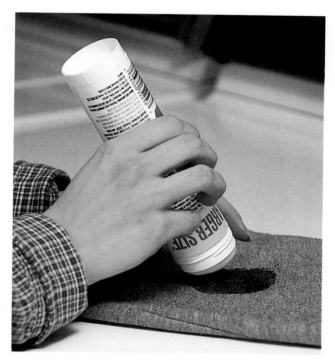

• Pretreating a stain increases the likelihood of getting the stain out of the garment during laundering. **What has been your experience with stains that have not been pretreated?**

Sorting

The first step in cleaning clothes is sorting. The basic rule is to sort clothes by cleaning method, color, fabric, and amount of soil. Refer to care labels for recommended procedures.

• First, group together clothes that can be machine-washed at the same temperature setting. Set aside clothes that must be hand-washed or dry-cleaned.

keep them from getting tangled with smaller items. Group heavily soiled clothes together, because they need a longer wash cycle and can dull other fabrics.

Washing and Drying

After you have sorted your laundry, you are ready to put the first load into the washing machine. You'll generally find the instructions for using the washer on the inside cover of the machine. The directions for loading it will tell you whether to add the detergent or soap first or the clothing first. Never fill the machine more than three-quarters full with laundry. If you do, items will not move freely for good cleaning action. Overloading also causes wrinkling. For top-load models, distribute items evenly around the agitator.

- Next, separate the clothes by color. Dark colors should be washed together to prevent any bleeding of colors onto lighter clothes. White fabrics may become dull and gray after repeated washings, so wash them separately.

- Finally, consider the type of fabric and amount of soil. Create separate groups for knits and delicate fabrics that require a short cycle and can be damaged by heavier items. Avoid washing fabrics that create lint, such as terrycloth towels and fuzzy sweatshirts, with fabrics that might attract lint, such as corduroy, velveteen, and fabrics with durable press finishes. Wash sheets and other large items together to

- Sorting your clothes carefully before laundering helps your clothes maintain their new appearance longer. **What might happen to your clothes if they are improperly sorted?**

Hand Washing Clothes

TIPS

Hand washing is recommended for woolens, silks, and other delicate fabrics. It can also be used for single items that need to be washed separately. When hand-washing:

- Use a mild detergent and gently squeeze the water through the garment to clean.

- Rinse the garment in cool or cold water until the water is clear.

- Roll the garment in an absorbent towel to remove as much water as possible.

- Lay flat to dry or use a portable garment drying rack.

• Choose the proper water temperature and wash cycle for each load of clothing to help fabrics retain their new look. **What might happen if you choose the wrong water temperature or wash cycle?**

Clothing care labels provide instructions on drying. Clothes may be machine-dried, line-dried, or dried flat. For machine drying, select the proper fabric and temperature settings for the load. Cotton or linen can be dried at higher temperatures than manufactured fibers. The durable press cycle has a cool-down period at the end of the cycle to reduce wrinkling. The air cycle can be used for rubber and plastic items.

For best results, do not overload the dryer. Do not dry lint-producing fabrics with lint attracting fabrics. Always clean the lint filter after each load. Remove clothes promptly when dry. Fold or hang clothes immediately to prevent wrinkling.

Dry-cleaning

Dry cleaning uses special liquid-containing solvents rather than soap or detergent and water to clean clothes. Clothing is placed into a machine where the solvent is released and agitated with the clothing to remove soil. Then the solvent is spun away, and the clothing is tumbled or air-dried to remove the solvent. Steam pressing removes wrinkles and restores creases and pleats.

Professional dry cleaners do all the work for you. They receive and tag your soiled clothing. They inspect garments and pretreat stains before cleaning the garments. Some cleaners also make minor repairs and alterations. Then they dry-clean and press the garments.

Coin-operated dry cleaning machines are available at some laundromats. These machines are faster and cost less than professional dry cleaning. However, you must do the spot removal and pressing yourself.

Some home dry cleaning products are now available on the market. These products don't entirely replace professional dry cleaning, but are effective at removing mild soil. The manufacturer's directions must be followed carefully when you're using these products.

Pressing and Ironing

To remove wrinkles from fabrics, you must use heat, moisture, and pressure. Ironing and pressing are two methods of smoothing wrinkles in fabric. *Ironing* is sliding the iron back and forth across the fabric. Move the iron in the lengthwise or crosswise direction of the fabric to prevent stretching. In *pressing*, lower the iron to the place to be pressed, then raise and lower it again at the next spot. Knits and wools are pressed to prevent flattening or stretching the fibers. Iron or press small garment parts, such as collars, cuffs, and sleeves before large flat areas, such as the front and back of a shirt or skirt.

Set the iron at the appropriate temperature for the fabric. Most irons have several heat settings that are labeled with fiber names such as Linen, Cotton, Wool, and Rayon. Cottons and linens require higher temperatures to remove wrinkles. Manufactured fibers are sensitive to heat and should be ironed at lower temperatures. For fabric blends, such as polyester and cotton, choose the lowest suggested setting. An iron that is too hot can damage the fabric.

• Professional dry cleaners do all the work for you—pretreatment, cleaning, and pressing. **What are the pros and cons of having clothing dry cleaned?**

Making Simple Repairs

Occasionally, you will need to make some clothing repairs. By making them as needed, you can keep your clothes attractive and wearable longer. Some examples of simple repairs you can make are shown on pages 328-329.

Storing Clothing

Organizing your storage space keeps your clothes neat and easy to find. Decide which garments to store on hangers, on shelves, and in drawers. Store out-of-season clothing where it stays clean and dry.

In your closet, group similar clothing together: tops, jackets, pants, skirts, and dresses. Store the same type of items, such as socks or underwear, together in drawers or on shelves.

• Storing clothes effectively helps keep them looking their best. Imagine that you're starting you first full-time job after high school. How might you benefit from having your clothing effectively stored?

Simple Garment Repairs

- **Replacing fasteners** You may need to re-stitch or replace buttons, snaps, or hooks and eyes. You may want to add a snap or hook and eye for increased security or better appearance. You need to repair fabric under the fastener as well.

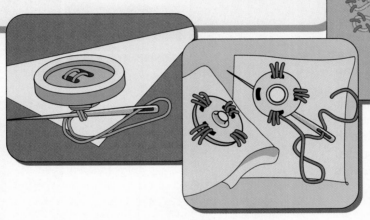

- **Re-stitching seams and hems.** You can repair stitches with machine or hand stitching. Be sure that your stitching does not show outside. Overlap stitching for added strength. If an area like the crotch receives extra stress, use a double row of stitching $1/8$ inch (3 mm) apart.

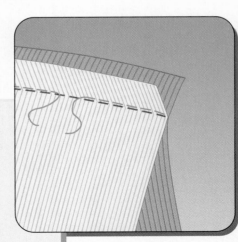

• **Repairing snags.** Knitted or loosely woven fabrics may get unattractive snags, or loops of yarn on the surface. Insert a small crochet hook, snag fixer, or needle threader through the fabric and pull the snag through to the underside of the garment. Smooth out any puckers by gently stretching the fabric in the direction of the pulled thread.

• **Mending a tear.** A straight tear can be mended by stitching back and forth across the tear to hold the edges together.

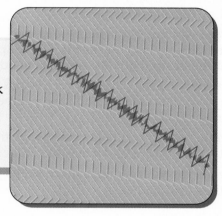

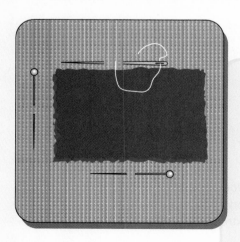

• **Patching a hole.** A patch can be applied by hand stitching, machine stitching, or fusing. First, trim away any frayed threads from around the hole. To make your own patch, cut a piece of fabric, slightly larger than the hole. Pin the patch to the inside of the garment. Fold in the edges of the patch and stitch in place using hand or machine stitching. On the outside, turn under the edges of the hole and stitch to the patch. For fusible or iron-on patches or mending tape, follow the package directions.

Understanding Key Concepts

● People often evaluate others on appearance, so it pays to look your best.

● Your clothing choices are influenced by many factors including your lifestyle, your resources, and current styles.

● In planning your wardrobe, take an inventory of what you already own.

● A successful way to stretch your clothing dollar is to build a wardrobe of classics and mix-and-match garments.

● Before you buy a garment, consider whether it meets your needs, fits properly, is of the desired quality, and is a good buy.

● By simply taking care of your clothes, you can keep them longer and save yourself money.

● Simple repairs can help you keep your clothes attractive and wearable longer.

● Organizing your storage space keeps your clothes neat and easy to find.

Checking Your Knowledge

1. What does the outfit you're wearing right now tell others about you?

2. Which items do you consider most important when you shop for clothes: price, fit, style, or practicality? Why?

3. If you were building a basic wardrobe of ten classic garments that could be mixed and matched, what would you include? Why?

4. Differentiate between image ads and information ads.

5. Describe how you would comparison shop for a new winter coat.

6. How can a clothing care label inside a garment aid you in choosing the correct method for cleaning it?

7. Summarize procedures for washing and drying clothes.

8. How can organizing your storage space aid in caring for your clothes?

Making TRANSITIONS

Dress for Success

When you go to an employment interview, you will want to look as though you really want the job! Uncertainty about what to wear to an interview is a common feeling among many people. Dressing too casually or wearing extreme fashions can ruin your chances for getting a job.

Imagine you are interviewing for work in a career of your choice. Describe in detail how you would dress for the interview.

STRENGTHENING *Life* SKILLS

Selecting Your Best Colors

The colors that look best on you depend on your personal coloring and your body shape. Your personal coloring refers to the color of your skin, hair, and eyes. A good color for you will make your eyes and hair seem to sparkle. Your complexion will look healthy and glowing.

Colors can create illusions about your body shape. They can make you look taller or shorter, larger or smaller. If you want to look larger, choose light colors, warm colors, and bright colors. Dark shades, cool colors, and dull or soft colors, in contrast, can minimize your size. Wearing one color or colors that are close in value and intensity from head to toe will help to make you look taller. Wearing sharply contrasting colors, either in hue or in value, on top and bottom will make you look shorter.

Color can be used to draw attention, too. Wearing a collar in a contrasting color attracts attention to your face. A belt in a bright, contrasting color draws attention to a slim waistline. A narrow belt in the same color as your outfit hides a thick waistline. Answer the following questions:

- How can you use color to highlight your skin, hair, and eyes?
- How can you use color to create color illusions that flatter your body shape?

Applying Thinking Skills

1. **Drawing conclusions**. What factors influence your clothing choices? Which factors are the most important? Why?
2. **Prioritizing.** You have just landed a full-time job in an office. What are your immediate and long-range clothing needs? What factors will influence your needs and priorities?
3. **Decision making.** You have two similar rayon garments. The clothing care label on one says it should be dry-cleaned, the other indicates that it may be hand-washed in cold water. How would you decide which cleaning method to use for each?

Practical Applications

1. **Gathering information.** Assume you've just been hired for a job you've really wanted. The job requires a certain level of professional dress. You've been given a $300 clothing allowance to help improve your wardrobe. Using current clothing catalogs, plan as many outfits as you can, using mix-and-match classics. Put together an attractive display and share your selections with the class.
2. **Creativity.** List five garments in your wardrobe. Describe two or three new ways to wear each one.
3. **Smart shopping.** List all consignment clothing stores in your area. Visit one and compare the quality and price of the clothing there to your favorite retail clothing store. Based on what you've discovered, list the pros and cons of consignment shopping.

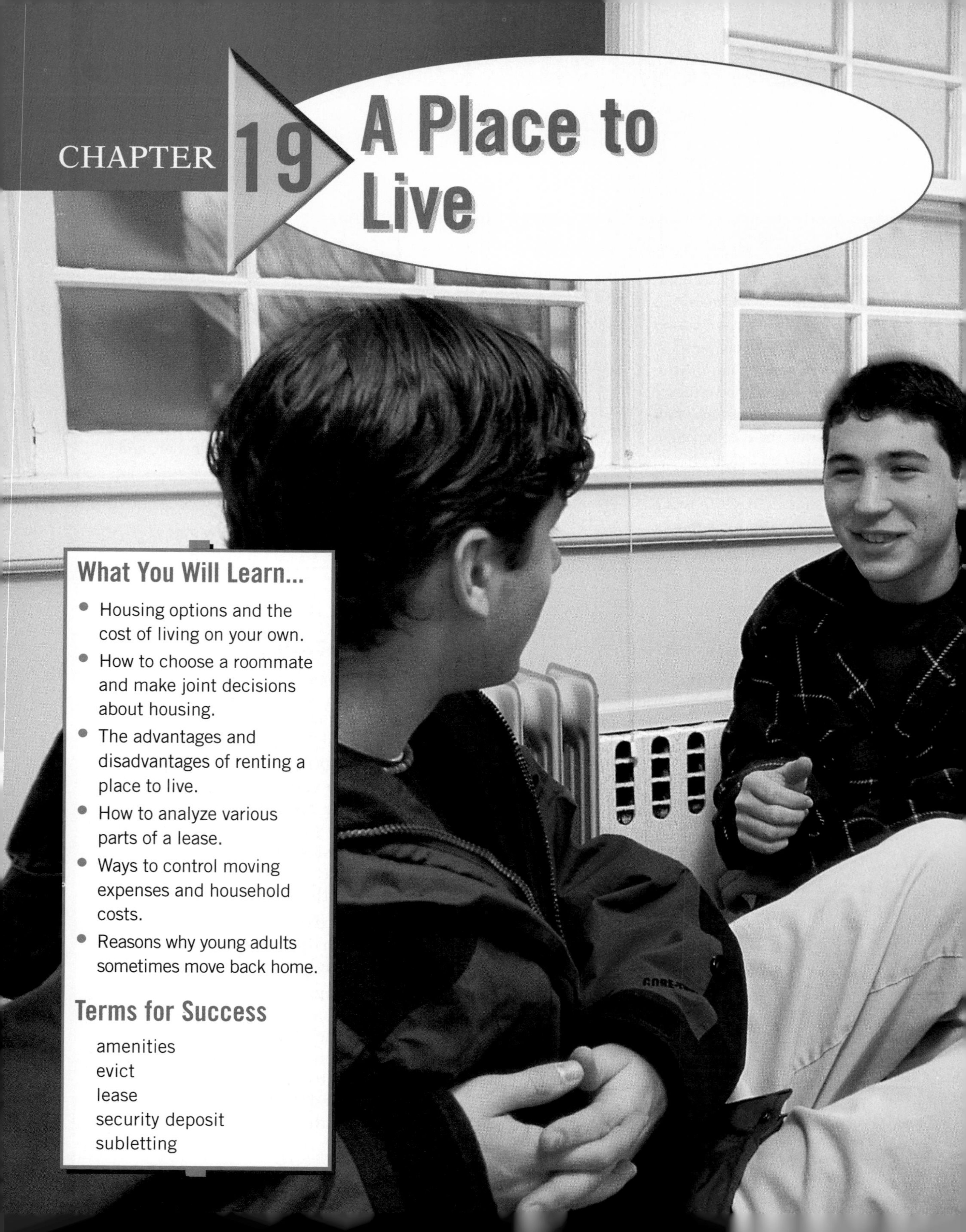

CHAPTER 19

A Place to Live

What You Will Learn...

- Housing options and the cost of living on your own.
- How to choose a roommate and make joint decisions about housing.
- The advantages and disadvantages of renting a place to live.
- How to analyze various parts of a lease.
- Ways to control moving expenses and household costs.
- Reasons why young adults sometimes move back home.

Terms for Success

amenities
evict
lease
security deposit
subletting

"Thirty-six steps to this place," Carlos announced, mounting the last one, "not counting the ones outside."

Robbie unlocked the door of his new apartment. "It'll keep me in shape for basketball." He led his younger brother into a large, empty room. Their voices and footsteps echoed against the walls and hardwood floor.

"This is the living room," Robbie said, "and the bedroom, and the dining room. . . "

Carlos peered behind the counter that separated a sink, range, and refrigerator from the rest of the room. "This is the kitchen? Big enough to heat a can of soup, I guess."

Robbie turned on the light in a room next to the kitchen. "This is the bathroom."

Carlos poked his head inside the door. "No tub? Just a shower? You finally get your own bathroom, and you can't even take a hot bath."

Robbie shrugged. "I wouldn't have time anyway. Between school and work and student government, I don't plan on spending much time here. Besides, it's only a half mile from school, so I can save gas money. Also there's a laundromat a few blocks away."

Carlos looked about the room again. "I suppose it's what you need," he agreed. "I thought your first place would be better than this."

"So did I," Robbie said, "until I saw what they're asking for the better places. Compared to some of the other places, this is a palace."

Carlos wrinkled his nose. "Hmm. What's that smell?"

Robbie smiled. "There's a bakery on the corner. If you go in after 6:00 in the evening, you get everything half-price."

Carlos grinned. "So that's why you picked this place! The way you chow down the cinnamon rolls, you're going to need those 36 steps—a couple of times a day."

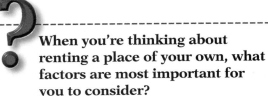

When you're thinking about renting a place of your own, what factors are most important for you to consider?

Analyzing Your Housing Situation

Robbie had to change his expectations of what it would be like to live on his own. He made a list of priorities based on the cost of having his own place and what he could afford. He was glad to be independent, but he would have to start small and expand later.

An increasing number of today's young adults are leaving home later than in the past, waiting until they're financially self-supporting and ready to handle the responsibilities of adult living. Also, many young adults wait longer to marry, staying in the "family nest" a while longer. Most, however, leave when they have completed high school, enter college or technical school, or get a job. Others leave to get married or join the armed services.

When you have finished school, do you plan to stay at home or move into your own place? If you have a choice, you might want to consider the advantages of living at home, at least for a while. Since usually it's less expensive than renting or buying your own place, you could probably save more money if you lived at home temporarily. Also, rather than living alone or with someone you don't know well, you may prefer the companionship of your parents and siblings. Sharing household tasks with family members, rather than living alone and doing them all by yourself, may be important, too.

Some young adults have little choice but to move out of the family home—whether they want to or not. Others look forward to being on their own, experiencing independence for the first time in their lives. Whatever the circumstances, moving out is a major change that requires major decisions.

• Everyone makes housing decisions at some time in life. **What are your ultimate goals in regard to housing?**

What Are Your Housing Options?

Have you thought about what it would be like to move away from home? Where would you like to live? Would you prefer to live alone or have one—or more—roommates? How much will you be able to afford for rent and other expenses? Answers to these and the following questions can help guide your thinking about options available to you:

- Are you likely to stay in your hometown or move to another location? What type of housing is available where you might live?

- Do you prefer an apartment, duplex, house, mobile home, and so on?

- Would you like to room with someone? If so, with whom? If you prefer to live alone, will you be able to afford it?

- Will you need a place that is furnished, or will you be able to provide furnishings?

Finding a Place to Live

Before you look for a place to live, you need to determine how much you can afford to pay for housing each month. By knowing what's within your budget, you can eliminate what you can't afford and concentrate on actual possibilities.

Be realistic in the size of a place you want. Size costs money. The least expensive choice may be a room in a private home—where you may share a bathroom and may or may not have use of the kitchen. An efficiency or studio apartment has one room with minimal kitchen and bath facilities. Larger, more expensive apartments have one or more bedrooms. Usually, renting a single-family home is the most expensive option.

Here are some terms to remember about housing:

- **contract:** A legally binding agreement.

- **duplex:** A building containing two separate living units.

- **efficiency apartment:** A unit with one main room, a small kitchen area, and a bathroom.

- **floor plan:** A diagram of a home or other structure that shows the arrangement of rooms.

- **landlord:** A person who owns a property and rents it to someone else.

- **renters insurance:** An insurance policy that covers a renter's personal property against loss due to theft, fire, or other stated hazards.

- **tenant:** A person who pays rent to occupy property owned by someone else.

Many financial advisers recommend that your monthly cost of housing be no more than one week's take-home pay. Others suggest that one-third of your monthly income is more realistic. When deciding what you can afford, consider all of your other expenses. If you have a car payment, for example, you may not be able to pay as much rent.

REASON

Solving a Problem

Practical problems usually don't have one right solution. The solution might vary from person to person, depending on their values, feelings, and needs. In the scenario below, each alternative meets Justin's basic needs, but note how he seeks the solution that's best for him.

Justin, a third-year engineering student, has accepted an internship with a company in a neighboring state. One Friday, he met with his supervisor concerning his internship responsibilities. His supervisor, Kate, also discussed the salary with him.

"Oh," Justin thought to himself when he saw the salary. He had hoped it would be higher. It'd be difficult on this salary to make payments on his schooling, car, and car insurance, plus have enough left over for housing and food. However, the opportunity to learn the newest technology in the field, and the hope of future employment with the company made Justin willing to work for less.

Over lunch, Justin asked Kate and other employees where he might look for an apartment.

"There are some new apartments around the corner from here," one employee suggested. "I've heard they're expensive."

"The cheapest apartments are over on the west side, but they're less secure," another employee commented.

On the way out of the restaurant, Justin picked up a free apartment guide that he had spotted by the newspaper stand.

"I have another option for you to consider," Kate offered. "My mother has an efficiency apartment over her garage. I believe it's empty now. Would you like for me to ask her if she wants to rent it?"

"That'd be great," Justin responded.

On Saturday morning Justin drove around town, looking at several apartments he'd circled in the apartment guide. Dismayed at the rental prices, he returned to his motel room to find a message asking him to call Kate. She told him that her mother was very interested in renting her apartment. Kate offered to pick him up to go meet her mom.

The apartment above Mrs. Lennon's garage was spacious and bright. It had its own entrance, an adjacent bathroom, and even a tiny kitchenette.

"I like the apartment very much," Justin told Mrs. Lennon. "How much rent do you charge?"

"I charge $450 a month," Mrs. Lennon answered.

Justin was visibly disappointed. "It's just what I've been looking for, but more than I can afford," he said. "Is there any work around here that I could do for you in place of part of the rent?"

"This sounds like a good idea, Mom," Kate interjected. "You know there's a lot of yard work for you to keep up with now that Dad's died."

"Yes, you're right," Mrs. Lennon shook her head sadly. "There's maintenance work that I would have to pay someone to do. Let's both think about this, and I'll call you tonight or tomorrow, Justin," Mrs. Lennon suggested.

Back at the motel, Justin outlined his options. All options would work for him, but each had positive and negative consequences. "I really don't want to borrow money from Mom and Dad, yet I want a safe, pleasant place to live." The phone rang. He was relieved to hear Mrs. Lennon's voice.

"Justin, I'd like to offer the apartment to you. I'm very impressed with your enthusiasm and willingness to work. I'm willing to cut the rent in half in exchange for your doing all the yard work and five hours of other maintenance work per week," she offered.

"That sounds like a great deal to me," Justin answered

Through Life's Problems

enthusiastically. "Mrs. Lennon, I was sitting here trying to figure out my best option. With your offer to reduce the rent, I can afford to live in your rental unit, feel safe, and save money for school. I've always enjoyed working outside, and I'm handy at fixing things, too."

Three weeks later, Justin was settled in his new apartment and excited about his internship. He enjoyed Mrs. Lennon, who gave him plenty of privacy. She seemed to appreciate all the yard work and maintenance that Justin did.

"I did well in finding a place to live," Justin thought to himself. "I'm paying less for a whole lot more than any of those other apartments I looked at. I can take advantage of the renters credit on my state income tax, and I'm even able to put some money into savings! It's a good feeling to know that I'm helping Mrs. Lennon out, too."

ALTERNATIVES	CONSEQUENCES FOR SELF AND OTHERS
Rent an apartment nearby.	**I:** Would live in a nice place; low transportation costs to work; feel secure with quality security system; would not have enough money to pay bills and save for school; have to borrow money from parents for next year's tuition and current bills. **Others:** Parents would be financially strapped in helping brother and me with next year's tuition.
Rent an apartment on the west side.	**I:** Could afford to pay bills and save a little money for next year's tuition; would not feel safe in a higher crime area than in other parts of town; would need to spend a lot of time cleaning the apartment; would need to have several things fixed; would be disturbed by the noise level in the building and neighborhood. **Others:** Parents might not need to help pay next year's tuition.
Rent Mrs. Lennon's efficiency apartment.	**I:** Would enjoy a pleasant, spacious, quiet place to live; could meet current bills with little financial strain; have difficulty in saving for next year's tuition; would need to be careful regarding not getting in the middle of Kate's and her mom's relationship. **Others:** Parents might not need to help pay next year's tuition.

▶ From Your Perspective

1 What's the primary problem Justin needs to solve? What situational factors are affecting his decision?

2 Where did Justin obtain the information he needed? Do you think these were reliable sources? Why or why not?

3 What alternatives did Justin identify? What're the long-term and short-term consequences of each alternative? Are any other people affected by his choice?

4 Do you think Justin would make the same choice if he were starting permanent employment with the company? If he were being paid more? Why or why not?

The Cost of Living on Your Own

Moving into a place usually involves some major expenses. In many larger complexes, payment of the first and last month's rent in advance is standard. You may also have to put down money as a **security deposit**, money that a landlord holds as a guarantee against damages. All or part of the deposit may be refunded when you move out if you haven't damaged the rental unit. An additional cleaning fee is common in some locations. Seldom refundable, it covers the cost of cleaning the unit after you have left.

• Living on your own generally involves some major expenses. **Estimate how much it could cost you to move out on your own in your community.**

6th & Butler Incredible corner apt. with wide-open views of river and city! 2BR, 2 baths, sep DR, big kit, hrdwd flrs, gar, utils pd.

Riverside Rented by owner, 1BR, 1 bath, furn, immed occ. Nr. bus. W/D in basement. $500/mo + util.

Silverdale Immed occ.! 2BR, 1 bath, grt vw, no lse. LR w/fpl. EIK, pvt entr. Call soon to find your great new home!

Capitol Park 3BR apt, xtra lg MB, hardwd flrs, c/a, refs req'd. Incl h/hw. Great location. Appt only.

E. 13th & Main Studio apt. Grt vw! Cpts & drps, grt clst spc, BB heat. No pets! New WWC. Nr bus dist. Avail Nov 1.

22nd & Birch Cozy efficiency w/grt vw and gar. D/W, ldry in bldg, c/a. Conven all trans. No lse, $400/mo, utils pd.

7th & Park Spacious new 2 BR, 1 1/2 bath. This garden apt has hrdwd flrs, W/D, LR w/fpl, and cpts & drps. BB heat and c/a. Appl include. Immed occ, call now! No lse.

KEY	
appl incl	appliances included
appt only	by appointment only
avail Nov 1	available November 1
BB heat	baseboard heat
BR	bedroom
c/a	central air conditioning
conven all trans	convenient to all transportation
cpts & drps	carpets and drapes
D/W	dishwasher
EIK	eat-in kitchen
furn	furnished
gar	garage
grt clst spc	great closet space
grt vw	great view
hrdwd flrs	hardwood floors
immed occ	immediate occupancy
include h/hw	includes heat and hot water
kit	kitchen
ldry	laundry
LR w/fpl	living room with fireplace
new WWC	new wall-to-wall carpeting
no lse	no lease
nr bus	near bus
nr bus dist	near business district
pvt entr	private entry
refs req'd	references required
sep DR	separate dining room
utils pd	utilities paid
W/D	washer and dryer
xtra lg MBR	extra large master bedroom
$500/mo	rent is $500 a month
+util	utilities paid by tenant

Hook-up charges and deposits for utilities, such as gas, electricity, and telephone, vary depending on the company providing the service in your area. Some companies may refund the deposit at the end of a year if all payments have been made on time. Your rent payment may include the cost of water and heat. Whatever the arrangement, be sure you can afford all the monthly payments, including any options, such as cable TV and extra telephone services.

Other expenses you need to plan for are furnishings—if the unit is unfurnished—and housewares. Window coverings may also be needed. Your landlord will probably have insurance on the building itself. However, this insurance will not pay to replace your personal belongings in case of burglary, fire, or other calamities. Liability coverage, which protects you in the event someone is hurt in your apartment or outside your unit, is also your responsibility. If you have a number of valuable personal possessions, you may wish to purchase renters insurance. A small monthly premium—when compared to the cost of replacing everything—is likely to be a bargain.

Renters Checklist

Living Area
- [ ] Living and dining area
- [ ] Number of bedrooms
- [ ] Number of bathrooms
- [ ] Clean, well-maintained
- [ ] Fresh paint, new/clean carpeting
- [ ] Strong doors and locks
- [ ] Windows have screens, shades, and locks
- [ ] Appliances in good working order
- [ ] Adequate lighting
- [ ] Plumbing in working order
- [ ] Wall receptacles in good condition
- [ ] Air conditioning, optional

Facilities and Services
- [ ] Location is convenient
- [ ] Building and grounds well-maintained
- [ ] Effective security
- [ ] Well-lighted entrances, hallways, and stairs
- [ ] Smoke detectors and sprinkler system
- [ ] Fire exits, clearly marked
- [ ] Laundry facilities
- [ ] Convenient parking
- [ ] Extra storage areas
- [ ] Trash disposal area
- [ ] Recreational facilities

Monthly Costs
- _____ Rent
- _____ Gas
- _____ Water
- _____ Electricity
- _____ Telephone
- _____ Security deposit
- _____ Maintenance fees
- _____ Other

Additional Features
- [ ] Pets allowed
- [ ] Children allowed
- [ ] Decorating allowed

• Using a checklist is a helpful tool when investigating places to live. **Which checklist qualities are most important to you?**

The Search Begins

After analyzing your financial situation, you may be ready to look for a place to live. Start by asking family members, friends, and coworkers if they have a place for rent or know of housing that's a good value. Also, look at rentals in the classified ads in the newspaper and on the Internet. To save time, energy, and transportation costs, call to get additional information before traveling to places that may not meet your needs.

Signs informing people about available housing often are posted at apartment buildings. Some communities have apartment locator companies and real estate agencies that can help you find housing. These businesses usually charge a locator fee, so find out whether you—or the landlord—must pay the fee.

Before you decide on either a furnished or unfurnished place, compare the rent for each one. If the rent is quite a bit less for unfurnished units, buying and borrowing basic pieces of furniture may save you money. In many cases, a refrigerator and a range are included in the rent, even for unfurnished places.

Selecting a Roommate

Most first experiences at independent living involve one or more roommates. Some people move into group housing, such as a college dormitory or barracks at a military base. Others move into an apartment complex to live with a roommate or two.

By sharing housing, roommates split expenses and live in places they could not otherwise afford. These expenses include rent, utilities, and often, food. Some roommates may provide certain pieces of furniture, an appliance, or TV to make up for what the other person doesn't have on hand.

Besides providing help with expenses, roommates often offer companionship and a

FOCUS ON ...
Renters Insurance

In addition to protecting your personal belongings from loss or damage due to fire or theft and providing personal liability protection if someone is injured in your home, the following may also be covered in renters insurance:

- Personal belongings temporarily located at another location.
- Loss of the use of your home, including additional living expenses if damage makes all or part of your living quarters unusable.
- If you sublet part of your home to others, fair rental value if damage makes your home uninhabitable.
- Legal defense against personal lawsuits, including judgments and out-of-court settlements against you.
- Medical expenses of other people who are accidentally injured in your home or because of your leisure-time activities.
- Damage to others' property if you borrow an item.
- Credit card loss due to theft, forgery, and counterfeit money.

measure of security. While most roommate experiences work out well, some friendships have ended because of conflicts that occurred from sharing housing. Before you decide to share a place with someone, ask yourself the following questions:

- Can I get along with this person? Will I want to spend a good deal of time with him or her?

- Are our lifestyles compatible? Will this person interfere with my activities with other people? Will I interfere with their activities? Will a roommate prevent me from doing the things I need or want to do?
- Is this person willing and able to share the expenses and household tasks?
- What rules will we follow regarding guests, privacy, housekeeping, and personal possessions?
- What will happen if we don't get along? What if my roommate loses his or her job and has to move out? Will I be able to afford all the expenses until I get another roommate?
- If we buy items jointly for the apartment, who will get them if one of us moves out?

Take time to get answers to these questions before deciding to share a place to live and choosing a specific individual. The success of a roommate experience will depend on how carefully you choose someone. You can save a great deal of pain by learning about each other ahead of time.

Compatibility Issues

Carlotta and May have recently moved into an apartment together. Before deciding to be roommates, they discussed their lifestyles, work hours, social life, and privacy needs.

Gregg and Bob, on the other hand, didn't spend any time getting to know each other before moving into the same apartment. They met during a party and discovered that Bob's rent had gone up, and Gregg's previous roommate had moved out.

Unfortunately, Bob and Gregg's experience at sharing housing didn't turn out well. Bob liked order, but clutter didn't bother Gregg. Bob got up early each morning and turned the TV up loud. Greg liked to sleep late and was bothered by the TV volume. He also had frequent guests who stayed up late and slept overnight on the living room sofa. Not surprisingly, it wasn't long before these two roommates decided to part company.

• Sharing housing with a roommate lessens the load of expenses while offering companionship. **What issues are most important to you in selecting a roommate?**

Basic Housing Requirements

A number of factors should be considered before you make your final selection of where to live. These basic requirements can help you evaluate various places and arrive at a decision that is likely to be successful. They include:

INTERIOR CONDITION.

- Clean and in good repair.
- Any specific things to fix before you move in, such as loose carpet or plumbing leaks.
- Good condition of doors, windows, screens, and locks.
- Signs of pest or insect infestation.
- Functional kitchen and bathroom fixtures and plumbing.
- Sufficient water pressure and hot water.

FLOOR PLAN.

- Easy access to all rooms.
- Convenient placement of bedrooms with adequate privacy.
- Sufficient space for personal belongings, such as books, stereo equipment, lamps.
- Ample space for furnishings.

SAFETY AND SECURITY.

- Relatively low-crime area.
- Secure locks on doors and windows.
- Rekeyed locks so previous tenants can not use their keys to enter.
- Front door peephole to see who's at the door without opening it.
- Adequate exits in case of fire, especially on upper floors.
- Conveniently located, locked mailbox.
- Well-lighted entrance and parking area.

STORAGE SPACE.

- Sufficient size closets, as well as drawers and cabinets in kitchen and bathroom.

LOCATION.

- Comfortable and safe neighborhood, including surrounding buildings, vacant lots, and parks.
- Convenient to work, school, shopping, recreation facilities, and public transportation.
- Reasonable traveling distance from friends and family members.
- Quiet, free from excessive traffic, airport, and other noise.

AMENITIES.

- Any **amenities**, or special features, included in the rent, such as swimming pool, tennis court, or clubhouse.
- Secure garages or covered parking spaces.
- Parking fee included in rent or extra.
- Convenient and safe laundry room with functional machines.

EXTERIOR CONDITION.

- Clean and well–maintained outside grounds and structure.
- Yard or recreation area.
- Safe and convenient place to park.

Besides not knowing anything about each other, Bob and Gregg lacked mutual respect—a key ingredient in making roommate relationships work. Roommates need to respect each other's schedules, privacy, and personal possessions. Also, roommates need to establish ground rules for household standards, routines, and shared expenses.

As in any other relationship, there will be ups and downs whenever you room with someone. Remember that no one is right all the time. Most problems can be solved when people take time to talk things through.

Mutual Decisions

One of the first decisions that roommates need to make is how to divide expenses. For paying the rent and regular monthly utility bills, the easiest method is to divide the expenses equally among the people living in the unit. One exception might be the telephone bill, with each roommate paying for his or her long distance calls. Another might be the cable TV charge, especially if one of the roommates seldom or never watches television.

Some roommates contribute to a common fund that's used for buying groceries and household supplies. Others buy needed items and split the bills later. To help ensure harmony, rules about food and drink need to be clear among all concerned. Important questions to ask each other at the beginning are: Is food to be shared equally? Will each have his or her own food supplies that the other will not use? What kind of system can we follow to keep track of food and household supplies to buy? What if *your* guests eat *my* food?

When deciding on household responsibilities, many roommates make a list of duties and divide the jobs fairly between each other. This can be done in several ways. Roommates might each have certain jobs they enjoy or do consistently, such as one roommate who shops for food and cooks, and another who cleans and takes out the trash. Another possibility is to take turns doing tasks. Roommates should come to a mutual agreement about household responsibilities based on what works best for them.

• Thinking about the type of housing that will meet your needs ahead of time will make it easier once you begin your search. **What considerations are most important to you in regard to cost, convenience, and amenities?**

Renting a Place to Live

When most people first move out on their own, they join the millions of people who rent—or pay money to live in places owned by someone else. Buying a place to live isn't for everyone, and for some, isn't right at certain stages of their lives. Instead, many individuals and families choose renting for one or more of the following reasons:

- **Convenience.** They may have no time for, or no interest in, home maintenance. Lawn care, painting, and household repairs usually are the obligation of the landlord. However, some owners may charge less rent if you agree to paint or make minor repairs yourself. If you rent a single-family dwelling, you may be responsible for lawn care and basic home maintenance.

- **Fixed costs.** With the possible exception of utility payments, tenants know the exact amount they must pay each month when they sign a rental agreement. Unlike homeowners, renters do not have extra costs for maintenance and repairs.

- **Flexibility.** Some people choose not to commit to the long-term responsibilities of home ownership. They may move often because of their jobs or be unsure about the type of housing they prefer. Perhaps they may not know if their incomes will remain steady for a long period. Unlike homeowners, renters don't have to sell their home—which can be a long and costly process—when it's time to move.

Disadvantages of Renting

Just as renting has its advantages, it also has its disadvantages. For example, some people dislike having a landlord or apartment manager. They may object to signing a lease or other agreement with specific rules and

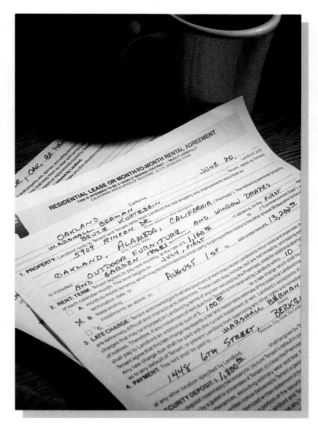

- Before you sign a lease, make sure that you understand all of the details in regard to the rules, rights, and restrictions specified in the lease.

guidelines. Renters may miss a feeling of permanence and stability where they live. In some situations, renters aren't free to decorate or remodel their units to meet their personal needs and tastes. Also, money paid for rent goes to the landlord, not toward property ownership. Rental payments, unlike what you would pay to buy a place of your own, cannot be deducted from federal income taxes.

• When you are ready to sign a lease, be sure you go over all all of the details with the landlord. **What could be the negative consequences of failing to go over all the details in the rental agrement?**

Rental Agreements

Written, rather than verbal, rental agreements, are required by most landlords. Although verbal housing agreements sometimes take place—usually between relatives or friends—they will not hold up in most courts of law. If either a tenant or a landlord breaks his or her promise in a verbal agreement, the courts cannot make the person fulfill the promise. For this reason, it's smarter to put an agreement in writing—and to examine it carefully before signing it.

One common type of rental agreement is a **lease,** or written contract between a landlord and a renter, stating the responsibilities of both parties. The majority of leases are binding for one year, although you may be able to negotiate the period. Some landlords require a lease; others don't. Once you have signed a lease, you are obligated to pay the rent for the specified time whether you live in the place or not.

If you aren't sure how long you want to rent, a more expensive unit that requires a written agreement, rather than a lease, may be more economical than a less expensive one with a lease. A written agreement is similar to a lease except it allows tenants to rent for an indefinite period, such as on a month-to-month basis. The arrangement is a good alternative for renters who move frequently. However, with some written agreements, landlords can force tenants to move out at any time. Most landlords prefer leases since they guarantee a longer occupancy of their units.

Read Before You Sign

In most states, anyone 18 years or older who signs a contract is legally responsible for fulfilling it. For that reason, don't sign any contract, including a lease, until you have read and have understood it. If necessary, take it home to read without pressure from anyone. If you don't understand parts of it, take the contract to someone knowledgeable about rental agreements, such as your parents or a family friend. In some cases, renters pay an attorney to review the contract before signing it.

Whenever you are ready to sign a lease, make sure it addresses each of the following points:

- The address and number of the rental unit and the specific date you are to move in.
- The length of time the lease is valid and procedures for renewing or ending the lease.
- The amount of the rent; when it's due; when it's considered late; the amount of a late fee, if there is one; and action the landlord may take if you fail to pay the rent, including the right to **evict,** or force you to move out.

- What utilities, if any, are included in the rent, and whether there are additional fees for services such as garbage collection or parking.
- The amount of the security deposit and conditions for refund.
- Restrictions, including landlord entry into unit, pet ownership, window treatments, wall decorations, and painting.
- Length of time required for you to give notice to move out and whether the unit may be sublet. **Subletting** is the process of letting someone take over the dwelling temporarily and pay the rent—usually with the landlord's approval.
- A written inventory of all items in the unit and their condition. Have the landlord note in the lease any damages found in the unit *before* you move in. Otherwise, you may be held responsible for these damages when you move out. If the landlord promises to make repairs, they should be stated in writing, along with the promised completion date, and signed by the owner.

If you and the landlord agree to change part of the lease, both of you should initial the change. Any changes should be written in ink. Never sign a contract until all the blanks have been filled in. Also, never sign a lease for a unit that's under construction or hasn't yet been built. Otherwise, you may end up paying rent on a dwelling that's not available or doesn't exist.

Whenever you sign a lease, file a copy of it in a safe place where you can find it. Make a second copy to keep with a family member or friend.

Rights and Responsibilities

T I P S

Consider the following renter's and landlord's rights and responsibilities:

Renter's rights:
- Property use as stated in the lease.
- Clean and safe unit.
- Privacy.

Renter's responsibilities:
- Property maintenance.
- Damage repairs.
- Timely rent payments.
- Respect for other tenants' rights.
- Give notice of moving.

Landlord's rights:
- Timely rent payments.
- Property maintenance.
- Dwelling changes, such as reassignment of parking spaces.

Landlord's responsibilities:
- Clean and safe property.

• Moving to a place of your own can be costly. What are the pros and cons of renting a vehicle to move yourself or hiring professional movers?

Moving to a Place of Your Own

Sooner or later, the day will come when you move into your own place. As with everything else, moving will go much easier if you plan it carefully and make thoughtful decisions. A well-planned move can save time, energy, and money; reduce the chance of lost or damaged furnishings; and give you a good start to independent living.

Begin ahead of time by getting rid of items you rarely or never use. Some things you may wish to donate to other family members, friends, or local charities. Also, decide if you want to move only what you'll really use—or everything you own. Chances are the storage in your new place will be limited.

In most cases, the best method for moving depends on how much furniture you have. It also depends on the distance you'll be moving and what you can afford to spend on the move.

If you'll be moving large, heavy furnishings, especially to an upstairs apartment, you may want to hire a professional mover. This is the most expensive option. If you'll be moving only dishes, bedding, clothing, and small furnishings, you can probably handle the move yourself. An in-between alternative is to rent a trailer, van, or truck and ask friends and family members to help.

If you decide to hire a professional mover, you'll be asked to sign a contract. The contract should detail the date of the move, the cost, and the mover's responsibility for damage. You can save money by packing dishes and clothing yourself, since movers charge extra for packing items.

If your new place needs cleaning, do it before you move in. You can do it better—and faster—if the dwelling is empty. Also, set up accounts and arrange for the utilities—gas or fuel oil, electricity, water, and telephone—to be turned on. Check to see if you need to be present when this is done. Notify your bank, employer or school officials, family members, friends, and the post office of your new address. The post office will forward your mail to your new address for a period of several months, thus helping prevent lost or delayed mail. Finally, when you move, make sure you leave your part of the home clean and orderly. This will say a great deal about your readiness for independence and responsibility.

Setting Up Housekeeping

Choosing a place to live is only the first step in getting ready to move into your own residence. The next step involves setting up housekeeping. This consists of accumulating items needed in the home to conduct your daily life.

Very few young adults have all the furnishings, equipment, and supplies they would like when they move out on their own. It takes time, energy, and money to get these things. Many of the items you'll select will depend on your budget, as well as your values, needs, wants, and personal taste. Someone who wants to make a place into a cozy, comfortable retreat will have far different ideas of what's needed from someone who only wants a place for sleeping and an occasional meal. Nevertheless, a number of furnishings, equipment, and supplies can provide basic comfort levels in any housing situation.

Cleanliness and Safety

Setting up housekeeping involves basic cleanliness and safety. Most people develop their own systems for keeping a place clean, depending on their time schedule and standard of cleanliness. You may find it worthwhile to spend a few minutes each day quickly putting everything in order. Picking up newspapers and magazines, straightening sofa cushions, hanging up clothes, and making the bed don't take long. If you share a place, it helps to agree that each person will share equally in keeping personal belongings put away. Also, it's helpful to set up a regular schedule for sweeping, vacuuming, dusting, and cleaning the bathroom and refrigerator. Since these tasks require little concentration, you may enjoy doing something fun at the same time, such as listening to music or watching a favorite TV program.

• Keeping your home clean and safe is important for your personal well-being. **How can having a cleaning routine be a benefit?**

Technology in Today's Apartments

Competition among many large apartment complexes has resulted in the installation of various advanced technologies. These features can make life easier—and safer—for both tenants and landlords. For example, units are wired to accommodate multiple phone lines, computers, modems, and fax machines. Some are furnished with "smart" appliances, such as refrigerators that alert you if freezer doors have been left ajar or if maintenance is needed, or dishwashers that can sense how dirty the dishes are and provide the appropriate cleaning level. Satellite dishes may be provided, offering more TV channels and better reception. Special light bulbs that can last as long as 15 years are often installed on top of poles in parking lots or in stairwells where they're difficult to reach. Common areas may have smoke sensors that sound an alarm, light a safe exit path, turn off unneeded electricity, and call for help during a fire.

For additional safety, some apartment complexes provide electronic door locks that allow doors to be locked or unlocked with the push of a button. Locks can even be hooked up to a timer for automatic locking at night, or they can be activated from a remote location. Closed-circuit television is used in some complexes to view hallways, pool areas, and other sites that tenants and owners want to keep secure.

Voicing Your Opinion

1. *What advanced features are available in rental housing units in your community? Which ones would you like to have where you live now? Why?*

2. *What new technologies would you like to see developed in the next few years for use in apartments and other dwellings?*

A clean and well-maintained home usually is safe and secure. On the other hand, when basic cleanliness and maintenance are neglected—or when items aren't used properly—accidents and even illnesses can occur. For example, items on the floor can cause someone to fall. Electrical equipment that isn't used safely can become a fire hazard or can cause electrical shock.

Controlling Household Costs

As a tenant, there's little you can do to control the cost of your monthly rental payment. However, you can help reduce the cost of some of your other household expenses. For example, turn down the heat and turn off the lights when you leave for the day. Don't leave water—or other utilities—running unnecessarily.

When you select telephone service, sign up for only those options you really need. Also, compare the costs and services of the various long-distance providers. Keep your budget in mind when you're calling long distance.

Think before signing up for expensive cable TV options you may never use. If you seldom watch TV, you may choose to forgo cable TV altogether and use the money you will save for things you really need or want.

Putting Down New Roots

Moving out on your own is an exciting time of life, but it can be lonely living away from familiar relationships and surroundings. You'll have to take the initiative to meet and make friends with neighbors in your apartment building or neighborhood.

Planning and participating in activities with coworkers or fellow students can provide social balance to your life. Take advantage of opportunities to volunteer your services in the community. The benefits of volunteerism are discussed in chapter 5.

Being open to new friendships and getting involved in the community are wonderful ways to put down roots and feel a part of where you live. Potential friends often can be found next door, across the street, in a nearby place of worship, at a recreation center, or in a neighborhood store. Taking the first step to meet people in your community is a skill you can develop and can put to use throughout the rest of your life.

• Taking the time to build friendships with other tenants helps you put down roots. **What are some other benefits of developing relationships with other tenants?**

Understanding Key Concepts

- Most young adults move to a place of their own when they have finished school.
- Information about available housing options in a community can be obtained from a variety of sources.
- A tenant may have to pay several major expenses before moving into a rental unit.
- Renting a place to live has advantages as well as disadvantages, and specific factors should be considered.
- A successful roommate relationship is based on predetermined compatibility, mutual respect, and prearranged household and financial responsibilities.
- It's important to read and understand all parts of a rental agreement before signing it.
- You can take steps to make the moving process more efficient and less expensive and to control household costs.

Checking Your Knowledge

1. Give examples of housing options available to young adults in your community.
2. Summarize initial costs renters may have to pay before they move into a unit.
3. Explain why the purchase of renters insurance may be a wise investment for tenants.
4. What sources of information about rental housing are available in your community?
5. Summarize the factors to consider when you're choosing a place to live. Which of the factors do you think would be most important to you? Why?
6. Explain why it is important to ask specific questions before selecting a roommate.
7. What is the difference between a written agreement and a lease? Why is it important to read and understand all parts of a rental agreement?
8. What suggestions would you give someone to make the moving process more efficient and less expensive?
9. Why is it important to put down new roots when you're moving to a place of your own?

Making TRANSITIONS

Selecting a Roommate

"How do I go about finding a roommate?" may be a question you're asking yourself. In some cases, potential roommates have known each other through school, work, or just growing up in the same neighborhood. In other instances, prospective roommates are total strangers.

Imagine that you're looking for a roommate to share an apartment with you. Write an attention-getting announcement to post on an employee bulletin board that'll persuade someone with similar interests, values, and standards to call you. In the announcement, describe yourself, the apartment, and the type of person you want as a roommate.

STRENGTHENING *Life* SKILLS

Rules for Roommates

Success in sharing any kind of housing requires mutual respect, financial responsibility, and a spirit of cooperation. Working with two others in your class, imagine that the three of you are making plans to move into a furnished apartment next month. Think of some guidelines, or household rules, that are important to each of you. Write down the rules for future reference. Then answer the following questions:

- How would you respond if one or more roommates failed to pay their share of rent or assume their share of household duties?

- What suggestions might you have for sharing a single telephone, television, or computer? A single living area? Kitchen and dining area?
- How might household rules help you avoid or resolve potential conflicts with each other?

Applying Thinking Skills

1. **Identifying relevant information.** What questions do you think are the most important to ask a prospective roommate? Why? How would you answer the same questions if a prospective roommate asked them of you?

2. **Predicting consequences.** What positive and negative consequences might result when one roommate attends college and works part time while the other has difficulty keeping a job and hangs around the apartment most of the time? What suggestions would you give to help them deal with their different lifestyles and manage finances and housekeeping tasks fairly?

3. **Recognizing values.** What advice would you give a young adult who's thinking about staying with his or her family for another year before moving to another place? Explain your answer.

Practical Applications

1. **Evaluating value.** Analyze classified advertisements of furnished one-bedroom rental units, making note of ads that appear to represent good value. Next, analyze ads for one-bedroom units that are unfurnished, and contrast the differences in cost of the rent. Which of the units might be the best value for you? Why?

2. **Researching security systems.** Use classroom and library resources to research the latest advances in security alarm products and systems. Check magazine and newspaper articles and advertisements to get information about them. Write a summary.

3. **Taking inventory.** In preparation for living on your own, make a list of your valuable personal property. Write a brief description each item, when it was purchased, and the purchase price or value. In the case of family heirlooms, you may need to have them appraised by a professional to determine their value.

CHAPTER 20

Transportation Options

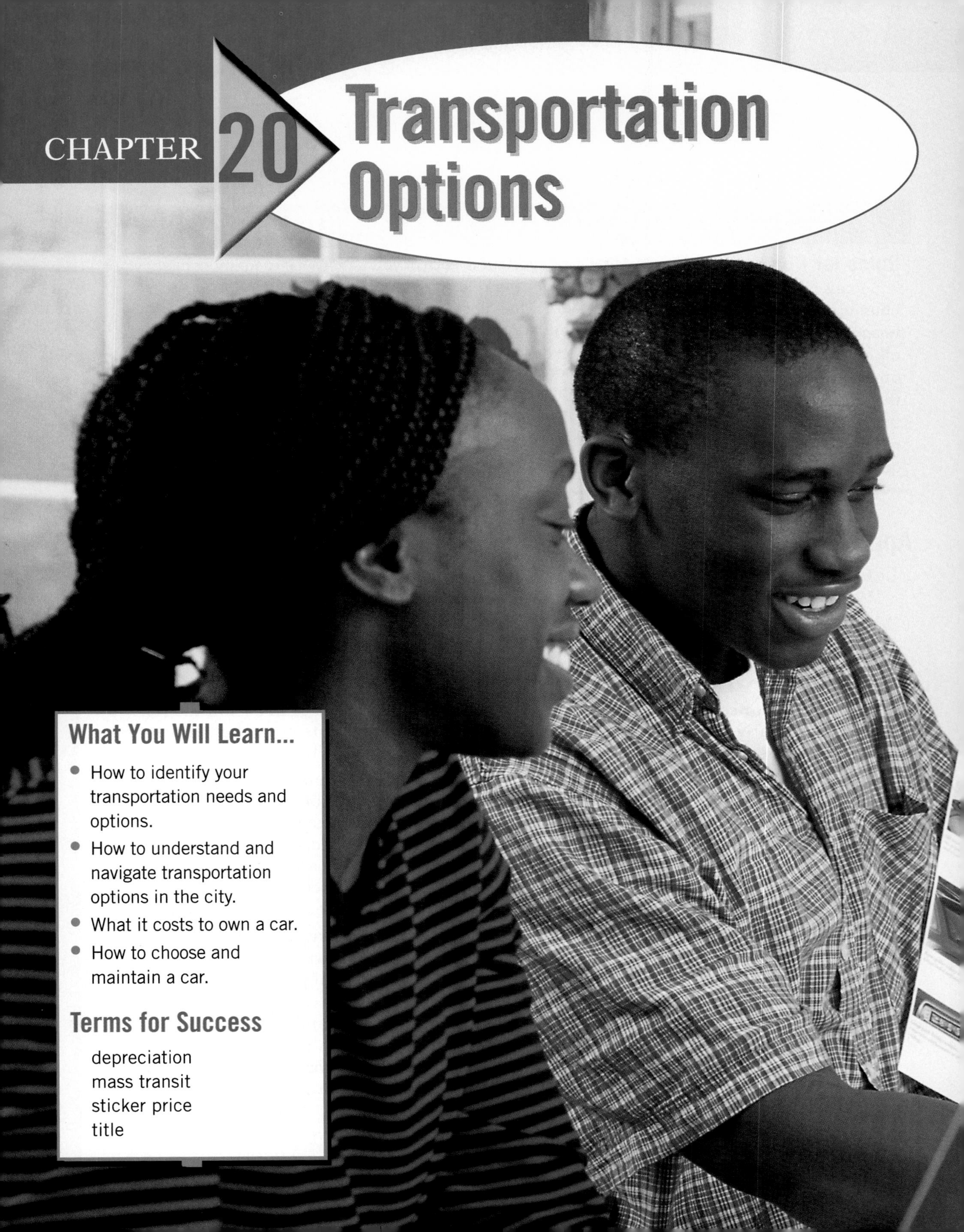

What You Will Learn...

- How to identify your transportation needs and options.
- How to understand and navigate transportation options in the city.
- What it costs to own a car.
- How to choose and maintain a car.

Terms for Success

depreciation
mass transit
sticker price
title

Kris glanced at the new car brochures that her friend Aaron had strewn across the kitchen table. "Are you shopping for my birthday present already?" she teased.

Aaron smiled wearily and handed her a glossy photo of a gleaming blue sports car. "Happy birthday. That's as close as I'll get to buying one."

Kris dropped into the chair beside him. "I take it the great mass transit experiment is over."

"I tried," Aaron sighed. "I know, you're big on taking the bus and riding a bike, and I do this more often now. Even so, I run around so much for work, I really need my own wheels. Also, I don't trust the old station wagon to get me out to see my sister and her family next month." He pushed aside the brochure he'd been reading. "Anyway, these are way out of my range. I'll have to buy used."

"Don't knock it," Kris warned. "In my family, used cars are a tradition."

"Do you think your dad would go around with me to some of the dealers," Aaron asked, "and tell me what I'm looking at?"

"Sure," Kris replied, "but Mom is the bargainer. She'll tell you a few things about getting a good deal. Any idea of what you want?"

Aaron scanned the spread of brochures. "I had a list . . . somewhere," he said. "Honest. I'd figured a price range, and features, and miles per gallon." He gave up the search. "How does anyone keep track of all this stuff? It takes all the fun out of buying a car!"

Kris gazed at the impressive-looking photo still in her hands. "Yes," she said softly, "but isn't it nice to have these tough decisions to make?"

Aaron knew this tone of voice. "Yes, it is." He pounded the table in good-humored resolution. "A thousand used cars in this city, and one of them has my name on it. I won't rest until I find it."

Think about your transportation needs now and in the future. What factors enter into your choices about transportation?

Transportation: An Important Issue

Americans are a people on the go. As an active young adult, you will no doubt spend a lot of time, energy and money getting to and from work or school. You will also spend resources traveling to visit family and friends, doing errands, and taking part in a variety of recreational activities. The fact is that the choices you'll make about transportation can have a large impact on your time, energy, wallet, and, most important, your quality of life.

Maybe you've always dreamed of riding to your first real job in a red convertible, but your bank account is finally forcing you to do a reality check. Maybe it's more realistic that you consider buying a used car or not getting a car at all but instead riding the subway or bus. Perhaps you were once dedicated to the idea of cycling to work to save money and keep yourself fit; Now you realize that the distance you have to travel to night school is just too far. Besides, you don't feel safe riding your bike in the dark. Whatever your transportation needs will be in the next few years, one thing is certain: there will be many factors to consider in choosing how you will get to where you'll need to go.

Identifying Your Needs and Wants

Considering both your needs and your wants is the way to start when you're thinking about the issue of transportation in your increasingly independent life. As with many other areas of your life these days, learning to tell the difference between what you need and what you want is critical. When it is finally time for you to assess your transportation needs, start by asking yourself the following questions:

- How far do I have to travel on a regular basis?
- How much time do I have to get to my usual destinations?

• There are many means and modes of transportation from which to choose? Which transportation options could be most important to you as you move out on your own?

- Do I need to combine travel time with other necessary activities, such as studying or doing paper work?
- What considerations, such as availability of service or special physical needs, must I take into account?
- What are my safety needs?
- How much money will I have and will need to pay for my transportation?

Next, ask yourself the following questions about what you want from the kinds of transportation you'll eventually choose to use:

- Do I want to travel alone, or with others?
- Do I like to travel only with people I know, or am I willing to travel with strangers?
- If I travel with others, do I want to share the driving and expenses in a particular way?
- If I travel with others, can I be certain the other driver(s) will not smoke, speed, or otherwise drive unsafely?
- Do I consider independence from others' schedules a priority so that I can come and go as I please?
- Do I like to take the most efficient or the most scenic route to work or school?
- Do I have any particular psychological or physical likes or dislikes when it comes to travel? For example, do I avoid tunnels at all costs or am I allergic to bus fumes?

Considering Others

As in all other areas of decision making, the choices you make about transportation can affect the well-being of others as well as yourself. For example, if you choose to buy an unsafe car because it is cheap, you may put yourself or others on the road at the risk of being injured or killed. If you are committed not to adding to pollutants dumped into the atmosphere by commuters every day, you

• Public transit can give you access to a wonderful smorgasbord of people. What are some other benefits of public transportation?

might choose an electric rail service over a gas-guzzling car. Perhaps you decide to drive your aunt to work each morning, since she has a car and you don't, but you have a license and she can no longer drive. Your transportation choices can make a difference not only to you but to others in your life. In fact, these choices can have a true impact on some of your relationships.

In considering the kinds of transportation you will eventually choose, consider not only your own needs and wants but the well-being of others by asking yourself these questions:

- How will my choice affect the safety of others?
- How will my choice affect the health of the environment?
- How will my choice improve the quality of life not just for me but for others?

Weighing Your Transportation Options

There are many transportation alternatives, and each has its advantages and disadvantages. By taking the time to "travel through" each of these transportation options, you'll be able to make a well-informed decision. Your choice may also be affected by whether you live in a rural, suburban, or urban setting, where your daily destination is, and whether you need to travel short or long distances.

FOCUS ON ...
Revving Up Your RV

Let's say you've already considered your transportation needs and wants, but you still find yourself idling, or stuck in place, when it comes to making transportation choices. That's when it may be time for "revving up your RV" and turning to the formula below.

Usually, the initials RV stand for "recreational vehicle." Right now, however, as you face important transportation decisions, think of the letter *R* as standing for all of your *Resources* (money, time, physical fitness, and so on) and *V* as standing for your *Values* (your principles based on ideas of what is right or good both for yourself and for others). Then complete the equation below to help you narrow your transportation choices.

R + V = Your Transportation Options

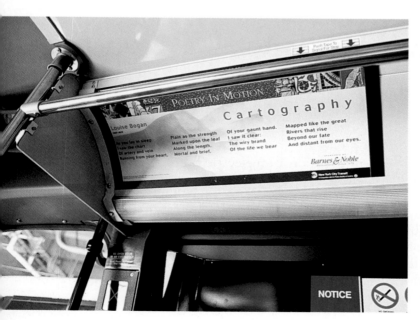

- Programs like "Poetry in Motion" on city buses in New York City can make mass transit an added learning experience.

• Some people use in-line skates to get around the city, although rollerblading in traffic can be risky. **What might be some of the benefits of "foot" transportation?**

Public Transportation

Mass transit, or public transportation, is often less expensive than owning a car. Riders of public transportation do not have to worry about finding parking spaces or paying parking fees. People who ride buses avoid rush hour traffic, and special bus lanes may allow them to reach their destinations sooner than people who drive cars. Also, bus and train passengers can relax and read while en route, while drivers have to pay close attention to their driving.

When people use mass transit, the community also benefits. Less fuel, a nonrenewable resource, is consumed. When fewer cars are driven, exhaust emissions are reduced, and air quality improves. Public transportation requires less space than automobiles, resulting in less traffic congestion in a city's downtown area.

However, there are some disadvantages. Equipment and facilities are not always well–maintained. Schedules are sometimes missed. Waiting in the rain or cold for your ride can also be a negative experience. Fear of crime is another reason some people avoid some public transportation.

In recent years, however, many mass transit systems have been upgraded, and incentives have been provided to increase the number of riders.

By Foot, Bike, and More

Several other options may meet part or all of your transportation needs. If you don't live very far from work or school, walking can be a healthful, revitalizing option. It is not only cheap (with wear and tear on the shoes only), but you can enjoy the sights along the way. Riding bicycles and motorcycles is less expensive than cars, but, like walking, it may not be desirable in certain kinds of weather or climates. Safety is also a factor.

Many cities are now working on "traffic calming," or making it more difficult for vehicles to travel fast where there are pedestrians and bicyclists. Many city planners are also working to improve cityscapes, landscaping to make walking and biking not only safer but quieter and more attractive.

By Car

The United States is very much a "car culture," and automobile driving is often necessary. However, before you automatically decide a car is the way to go, you should consider both the pluses and minuses of traveling this way.

Driving a car to work or school can give you a greater sense of freedom and allow you to change plans or do errands on the way home from work. Carpooling may also save money and reduce traffic congestion, though it probably won't meet all of your transportation needs and may be inconvenient.

The Mix-and-Match Approach

Some commuters find the "mix-and-match" approach to transportation the most useful. This involves using several different types of transportation to fit particular needs. For example, you may wish to walk to work on a sunny day but take the bus on a rainy one. You might drive to a cheap parking area, then take the trolley the rest of the way into work. Differences in weather, schedules, or the need for variety might dictate changes in your travel "menu" for a particular day, week, or month.

Travel in the City

If you decide to live or work in a city, you may need additional information about the many means and modes of urban transportation available. As with transportation issues in other kinds of settings, city travelers need to consider speed, capacity, rush hours, reliability, and costs. Typical peak rush hour crowding and delays may be of special importance, if you need to get to work or school on time.

The most common form of public transportation is the bus. Many city buses still use polluting diesel fuel, though other types of less-polluting fuels are sometimes now used. Bus travel is above ground and can show you the sights on the way to work or school, but buses can also be crowded and noisy, and they can suffer frequent and frustrating delays.

FOCUS ON ...

From Tokens to Tickets: Many Ways to Pay

When you first start to ride on public transit systems, it can be confusing to know how much to pay for service and how to gain entry to the system. Finding out in advance from a station attendant can make all the difference between an easy first commute and a frustrating one. Here are some ways you might pay for service:

- **Cash.** Many mass transit systems, such as city buses, use coins, but you must have exact change. Go prepared.

- **Tokens.** Tokens can be purchased at a ticket booth from a station attendant. Place the token into the slot by the turnstile to gain access to the subway platform. Some city buses also take tokens.

- **Fare cards.** Fare cards have a magnetic strip. They are generally sold for a week or month at a time. Swipe your card through an electronic reader which allows you to pass through a turnstile.

- **Passes.** These are prepaid cards that are used in place of cash, single-ride tickets, or tokens. Passes are often bought on a monthly, weekly, or daily basis.

- **Tickets.** These may be purchased at some bus or train stations and less commonly on board the bus or train.

- **Transfers.** A transfer is a paper receipt indicating that you have already paid for a ride on a previous bus or train. When you need to ride more than one bus or train to complete your trip, ask the operator to give you a transfer.

• Using a bicycle for short-distance commuting is made easier in some communities because there are bike paths or bike lanes.

In addition to city buses, many large cities also have subway systems, or fast underground rail lines, which stop at high-platform stations. The subway, also known in different places by the terms "rapid transit", "the metro", or "the elevated train," is an electric rail system that draws electricity from a third rail or overhead wire. Entrance to the subway may require a token. (See page 360.) Subway trains can be local and stop at each station along the route, or express, stopping only at certain stations and thus making the trip faster. Subways can be fast and convenient and may run 24 hours a day. Subway systems don't add to air pollution, but they do vary greatly in noise levels.

Cities also offer taxis, or cabs, single cars that you pay for according to the fare totals accumulated on a ticking meter. Generally, you pay a fixed amount for the first small amount of time or distance and an additional amount for each additional time or distance of travel. Taxis can be very expensive, so make sure you're prepared to pay the cost.

In many cities, there are special transportation services available to people with disabilities and to senior citizens. For example, paratransit systems may have wheelchair-lift-equipped buses or vans or special shuttle services. Sometimes these are on-call services that you'll need to arrange for the day before the service. In some cities, to get such services, photo ID cards may be required. Many transit systems also have timetables and routes available in Braille.

Buying a Car

Even though many people rely on some form of mass transit, more than 84 percent of the households in the United States own at least one car, according to the U.S. Bureau of the census. Buying a car is the second largest purchase most people make. (Buying a home ranks first.) It is often the first big purchase a young adult makes. Since buying a car is a major purchase, you should give careful thought and planning to every detail.

Costs of Owning

Owning a car involves more than its initial cost. It includes the costs of financing, depreciation, maintenance, insurance, gasoline, and more:

• **Cost of vehicle.** The **sticker price** refers to the price information affixed to the vehicle window. On a new car, the sticker lists the manufacturer's suggested retail price for the car and the factory-installed options,

• Some commuters spend the equivalent of at least a whole work week each year sitting in traffic. What are the negative consequences of such gridlock?

transportation or destination charge for shipping the car to the dealership, and EPA fuel-economy estimates. A used car provides warranty information on a "buyer's guide" sticker. You may pay less than the sticker price.

- **Financing.** Unless you can pay cash when you purchase a car, you will make a down payment and finance the balance through monthly payments. The larger the down payment, the less money you will need to borrow. The longer the period, the smaller the monthly payment, but the more you will pay in finance charges. New car loan rates are usually lower than used car loan rates. Until your loan has been paid in full, the bank or other lender will keep your title, which is a legal paper that shows who owns the automobile.

- **Depreciation.** Cars depreciate, or lose value, at different rates. One car may lose 40 percent of its value the first year, another only 15 to 20 percent. In three years the average car loses about two-thirds of its value. After that, depreciation continues at a slower rate.

- **Maintenance costs.** Maintenance is an ongoing cost of owning a car. Generally, the older the car, the more maintenance it will require. To keep your car in good repair, follow the maintenance schedule in the owner's manual. Failure to do routine maintenance will increase your cost of owning the car.

- **Insurance costs.** You must buy insurance to protect your car and yourself against loss if you damage someone else's property or injure someone in an accident. The exact coverage and the amount of coverage will be specified in your automobile insurance policy. If you buy a new car, you'll need more insurance coverage than if you purchase an older model.

- **Gasoline.** Gasoline is a continuing cost of owning a car. To save money, select a car with good fuel economy, maintain it well, and develop efficient driving habits.
- **Other costs.** Other costs of car ownership include your operator's license, annual automobile registration, and license plate renewal. If you live in a city, toll fees and parking charges may be additional costs.

Choosing a Car

Automobiles are classified according to size and type. From smallest to largest, cars may be classified as subcompacts, compacts, mid-size, full-size, or luxury cars. Other choices include vans, sport or utility vehicles, and pickup trucks. Each is available with a wide range of features, such as air bags and CD players. Standard equipment features are included in the basic price of an automobile. Vehicles may be purchased new or used. If you buy a new car, you have the advantage of being its first owner. You don't have to worry about how the car was driven or maintained. You will have the full factory warranty.

However, a used or "pre-owned" car is well worth considering. Many used cars are only a year or two old and in good shape. If purchased from a dealer, a used car may include a warranty. By buying a used car, you can avoid the high depreciation a new car has the first few years. Since a used car costs less, you may also save money by paying cash and avoiding finance costs. In addition, insurance on a used car is cheaper.

You can get information on new and used vehicles from a variety of sources. Consumer magazines and websites compare performance and price of new cars.

For used cars, you can learn the book value, the suggested retail price of the make and model you're considering, from consumer price guides. The annual *Consumer Reports Buying Guide* also provides useful information on prices, frequency of repairs, and desirable and undesirable used cars.

FOCUS ON ...
Transportation Info on the Web

In many cities and communities, you can get vital and up-to-date transportation information on the Web. By searching under headings such as Mass Transit or Transportation, Routes and Schedules, followed by the city, town, and state for which you need the information, you can be led easily to a wide array of helpful information, including:

- Bus and rail timetables and schedules, fares, or prices.
- Station and stop locations.
- Special assistance for people with disabilities.
- Customer assistance.
- Lost and found.
- Bike rack locations.
- Park-and-ride locations.
- Subway and other on-site maps.
- Sales locations. You may even be able to purchase your tickets on-line.
- Information about special passes, such as those for students or seniors.

REASON
Through Life's Problems

Select the Best Choice

Practical problems don't have one right answer. Different people will choose different alternatives because of the unique situational factors and differing values. However, everyone should be able to justify a choice. Read the following scenario and judge if Damon's decision is ethical, workable, and relevant.

"I can't believe I got the job!" Damon told his brother, Tyrone.

"That's great, Damon, but how are you going to get there? You don't have a vehicle since you totaled your truck in that accident," Tyrone reminded him.

"I know it seems impossible. I've got to have a job to get a vehicle, but I can't get to the job until I get something to drive!

"I've been thinking about ways I can get to work until I'm able to buy another truck. Want to see what I've come up with?" Damon asked. "Here's a chart outlining my alternatives."

"So what have you decided?" asked Tyrone.

"I'm going to take the bus for now. It's not my favorite way to travel, but I don't want to have to depend on Mom. I ought to be able to get myself to work. "

"What about Grandma's car? You're so good at fixing stuff," Tyrone asked.

"I don't want to spend all that money fixing her car and still not have the vehicle I want."

"It sounds like you've really thought this out," Tyrone said. "When do you start?"

"I start tomorrow."

ALTERNATIVES	CONSEQUENCES FOR ME AND OTHERS	
Ride with Mom to work	Me:	No expense; will not work if Mom's shift changes; won't have a way to work if Mom is sick. Mom drops me off at front door.
	Mom:	Will have to leave earlier in order to be to work on time; more money spent for gas; will feel like she has to take me even if she has the day off.
Repair Grandma's car	Me:	May not be able to fix it myself; no money to buy the parts it needs; it's an old car that's going to have more things wrong with it; I'll have my own car.
	Others:	Grandma would be pleased I'm fixing and using it.
Ride the bus	Me:	Don't like riding the bus; will take longer than riding with Mom; I will have to walk from the bus stop; it costs money; more independent, not having to depend on Mom.
	Mom:	Won't have to get up earlier, won't have added gas expense; won't have to worry about how I will get to work if she has the day off.

▶ From Your Perspective

1 Who are the other people affected by Damon's choice? Did he consider the effect his decision would have on them? How?

2 What values were important in Damon's decision?

3 What factors might change Damon's decision?

• The cost of owning a car is an on-going cost factor.

Getting a Good Deal

After considering your needs and budget, you can probably narrow your car choice down to a few specific makes and models. Find out the frequency of repair for the ones you are considering. Talk to your insurance agent. Insuring some kinds of cars, sports cars, for example, can be very expensive. Eliminate those with added costs beyond your budget. Now you're ready to take the necessary steps to get a good deal.

Choosing a Dealer

How can you find a dealer who will treat you fairly? Look for dealers who have been in business for several years. Talk to relatives and friends about their experiences with various dealers. Call local consumer protection agencies.

For used cars, you have a wide choice of sellers. Major sources include new car dealers, used car dealers, and private parties. New car dealers often sell "almost new" cars with special warranties. Used car dealers specialize in selling used cars. Used car superstores have hundreds of vehicles and feature no-haggle pricing and on-site financing. Independent used car dealers are likely to have lower prices, but quality may be lower, too. Private individuals often use classified ads or signs to offer their vehicles for sale.

Finding the Right Car

When you go to the dealership, introduce yourself, explain what you're looking for, and give a price range for what you plan to spend. Don't reveal anything about how you plan to pay or whether you plan to trade in your car.

If you are interested in a particular car, get a general impression of its quality. On the exterior examine the fit of parts and trim, the finish, and the paint. Inside, check the workmanship. Evaluate your comfort getting in, the headroom and legroom, the seat support and comfort, the ease of access to controls, visibility, and trunk space.

If you're still interested, test-drive the car or one that is very similar to it. Plan your test route in advance to ensure that you drive in different kinds of traffic, at different speeds, and in different conditions (such as city and highway). During the test drive, evaluate the riding and handling by checking acceleration, passing ability, hill climbing, cornering, steering response, road feel (bumps), and braking. Listen for interior noise, rattles, and squeaks. Be sure you can operate the air conditioner without overheating the engine.

When examining a used automobile, check carefully for defects caused by wear. (See the illustration on pp.368-369) To make sure you don't miss any defects, arrange for a reliable mechanic or a diagnostic center to conduct a thorough check of the vehicle. If the mechanic finds problems, ask for a written repair estimate. In your negotiations, you can ask the seller to make the needed repairs or adjust the asking price accordingly. If the car needs (or will soon need) extensive repairs, reject it.

• Choosing a dealer carefully is an important factor in buying any car—new or used? **What questions might you ask a dealer to check out quality of service and integrity?**

Settling Purchase Terms

If you are still interested in the car at this point, you are ready to negotiate the terms of the deal. This involves agreeing on a price for the new or used car you're buying and on a price for your trade-in, if any. Don't discuss a trade-in or financing until you have agreed on a price for the car you're considering.

Don't be afraid to negotiate. Here is a simple and effective approach. Using your research as a guide, ask for the lowest price the dealership will accept. Explain that you plan to shop around, and the dealership with the best deal will get your business. Resist any pressure to buy the car immediately.

After you think you've agreed on a purchase price, the salesperson or the business manager may try to sell you dealer extras, such as rustproofing, paint sealant, fabric protection, or an extended-service contract. These extras are generally overpriced.

The price does not include the sales tax. Depending on the tax rate in your state, this tax can add a sizable amount to the purchase price. Remember to include the sales tax when you decide how much you can afford to pay for a car.

Once you've agreed on the price of the new car, you can discuss the trade-in separately with the dealer. If you have a car that's in good condition, you may get more by selling it yourself.

When you reach an agreement, the salesperson will write up the purchase agreement. Once the purchase agreement has been written up and approved, the salesperson will ask you to sign it. Before you sign, read the contract carefully. Check whether all points agreed upon verbally are included in writing. Don't sign the contract until all blanks have been filled in.

If the car has a warranty, you will receive a written copy. Make sure you understand all warranty provisions. A new car comes with a

manufacturer's warranty that specifically states what it covers and the length of time or miles to which it applies. An adjustment warranty may be provided by the dealer to cover smaller problems, such as rattles, leaks, alignment, noise, and other problems that develop within the first 60 to 90 days. Most used cars come as is or with a 30- to 90-day warranty. Some used cars may still be covered by the manufacturer's original warranty.

Choosing a Mechanic

TIPS

If you don't know a mechanic you trust, ask for recommendations from friends, family, and other people. Also consider the following tips:

- Call several repair shops to compare prices and warranty policies.

- Look for certificates or window decals showing that the repair shop is licensed or certified by an organization such as the American Automobile Association (AAA).

- Check the shop's record of complaints with your state attorney general's office or local consumer protection agency.

- Choose a shop that looks clean and well maintained, has up-to-date electronic diagnostic equipment, and has employees who are polite, and ask detailed questions about your problems.

INSPECTING A Used Car

UNDER THE HOOD

Look for signs of wear on the engine. Watch for frayed hoses. After warming up the car, check levels of coolant, oil, and transmission fluid (on cars with automatic transmissions) and for signs of leaks. If the engine is too clean for its age, be a little suspicious.

ON THE ROAD

Note whether the gears shift smoothly and quietly. As you drive and brake, notice if the car seems to drift or pull to one side. Check to see if the wheel vibrates or shimmies at highway speeds. Notice unusual engine noises, signs of overheating, or blue exhaust smoke. Check out the cruise control. Try turning everything on at once to see how well the car handles the load. Stop on a steep slope and try the parking brake. After driving the car, try restarting the engine.

OUTSIDE

Check the finish and underneath fenders and doors for signs of accident damage or rust. Watch for misalignment of doors, exterior trim, and panels. Look under the car for leaking oil, coolant, or transmission fluid. Check for worn shock absorbers. Be sure the exhaust system is well secured to the car and in good condition. Examine the depth of tire tread and any signs of uneven wear on all four wheels.

INSIDE

Check the mileage shown on the odometer. Ask to see the mileage statement from the previous owner and the maintenance books. Check roof and doors for signs of leaks. Check pedals and upholstery for signs of excessive wear. Check the comfort of each seat. Note cleanliness and odors. Check out everything that turns on or moves. Inspect the trunk to be sure the spare tire and tire tools are there and for signs of rust underneath the carpet.

When you take delivery of the car, inspect it carefully. Make sure the vehicle identification number and odometer number match the numbers on the **title** (a legal document indicating owenership), the mileage statement, and the financial contract. If repairs or maintenance were to be performed, ask for proof that it was done as agreed. When you take delivery, you should receive the owner's manual and maintenance record books and two sets of keys.

• Carefully examining the purchase agreement and warranty before signing any agreement is essential.

Taking Time to Make a Decision

Still confused by all your transportation options? Don't worry. Just pull off the "reading road" for a minute to weigh your transportation needs and choices. In fact, whenever you are faced with an important transportation decision, just take the simple Triple A approach by considering these three factors:

- **Availability.** Does the transportation option exist where I live and work?
- **Affordability.** Do I have the money to pay for it?
- **Acceptability.** Is this option in keeping with my values?

Above all, don't panic. If you discover that one means or plan of transportation doesn't work for you, there are many other routes to go. You'll find your way.

Making Transportation and Travel Plans

Travel plans involve choosing a destination, arranging transportation, and deciding on lodging and food.

- **Destination.** The destination you choose for your vacation should give you a change of scenery and reflect your personal preferences. The possibilities are endless. You can obtain information about possible destinations from your local Chambers of Commerce, state department of parks and tourism, and from travel books and magazines. Hotel and motel chains supply folders describing their facilities. Send to franchised campgrounds for colorful booklets listing camp locations and facilities. Travel agents are another source of information.

- **Transportation.** A number of transportation alternatives are available for your vacation. Your schedule and destinations can be more flexible if you travel by car or motorcycle. However, the availability and cost of gasoline may be concerns. Buses, trains, and airplanes are other options. Modern buses are comfortable and spacious, and fares are usually reasonable. Most modern trains, which can travel at speeds up to 125 miles per hour, are comfortable, may offer meal or snack bar service, and may have sleeping cars available. For greater distances or when speed is important, you may prefer to travel by air. Service usually surpasses that offered on buses and trains. Food, music, and films may be provided on some flights. Discount prices are often offered.

- **Lodging.** Comfortable rooms are available at hotels and motels throughout the United States at various rates. Bed and breakfast lodgings are another alternative. Luxury resorts frequently offer saunas, pools, golf and tennis facilities, and gourmet meals. For many young people, youth hostels are another lodging alternative. Hostels generally have dormitory sleeping accommodations, recreation rooms, and equipped kitchens. Tents and recreational vehicles are other lodging options. Families especially find these low-cost ways to travel.

Using Your Resources Wisely

1. Which vacation options seem most desirable to you? Why?

2. Compare and contrast motel accommodations to those of hostels. What are the benefits of each? Which would you prefer and why?

Understanding Key Concepts

● Identifying your needs, wants, and available transportation will help you decide which transportation option is best for you.

● In cities, many transportation options other than owning a car exist to meet your needs.

● The cost of owning a car includes the costs of financing, depreciation, maintenance, insurance, and gasoline in addition to the vehicle's initial cost.

● When choosing a car, you will need to make decisions regarding size and type of vehicle that will best meet your needs and whether to buy a new or used vehicle.

● Choose a dealer who will treat you fairly.

● When you have found a car that meets your needs and is within your price range, examine it carefully and test-drive the car or one that is very similar to it.

● If you are still interested in the car, negotiate the terms of the deal, which include the price for the car you're buying and the price for your trade-in, if any.

● Read the contracts carefully, and make sure you understand all warranty provisions.

● When you take delivery of the car, inspect the car carefully.

Checking Your Knowledge

1. How can you determine your transportation needs and wants?
2. What are the advantages of using mass transit instead of owning a car?
3. How do you know how much you can afford to pay for a car?
4. What are the costs of owning a car?
5. What are the advantages of buying a used car?
6. Where can you get information on buying a car?
7. What is the main thing you want from a car dealer?
8. Why is it important to examine a car carefully and test-drive it before making a decision to buy?
9. How can a mechanic or diagnostic center aid you in deciding whether to buy a used car?
10. What steps are involved in settling the purchase terms?

Making TRANSITIONS

Driving and the Workplace

Some jobs involve driving company vehicles. Most companies hire only workers with good driving records.

Assume that you are applying for a job that involves driving a company car to make deliveries. As part of the application process, write a one-page summary of your driving experience, moving violations, and accidents. Summarize what you would do to maintain a safe driving record in a company vehicle.

STRENGTHENING *Life* SKILLS

Considering the Costs of Public Transportation

Research the public transportation system in a city in your state. Find out how the system is financed, how much it costs, what subsidies or support are provided, and what fares are charged.

Obtain information on the system's safety and efficiency records. Find out who uses the system and what officials do to attract riders.

Write a position paper supporting or opposing government expenditures for public transportation. In your paper, consider the following:

- Should mass transit be self-sufficient?
- Should people who do not use public transportation have to pay for it?
- What would make public transportation more appealing?

Applying Thinking Skills

1. **Recognizing values.** Think about the types of transportation that appeal to you most and write down at least two options. What values influenced your choices? Why? What factors might cause you to choose another transportation option other than those you originally chose?

2. **Drawing conclusions.** Assume that you make car payments of $120 per month, pay $525 annually in insurance premiums, average $495 a year in operating costs, and pay $100 a year for taxes and license. If you have a net income of $18,000 a year, are you paying more or less than 13 percent of your income for your car? What other options could you have for transportation other than owning a car?

3. **Compare and contrast.** Some people say that electric vehicles are the answer to the pollution problem caused by gas-powered vehicles. Research the benefits of electrically powered vehicles. How do they compare in cost, availability, and pollution savings to gas-powered vehicles?

Practical Applications

1. **Gathering information.** Assume you are looking for a used car. Using consumer publications, obtain information on three comparable used vehicles. Analyze the information and write a one-page report describing your findings. Based on your findings, which vehicle would you buy? Why?

2. **Planning a test drive.** Choose a local car dealership you feel is reliable. Then, using a city map, plan the route you would take when test-driving a car. Label the road features that would aid in testing the car. How can planning your route ahead of time benefit your decision making?

3. **Calculating the cost.** On a $12,000 auto loan, assume that your monthly payments (which include interest) would be $398.57 on a 36-month loan or $316.00 on a 48-month loan. How much would you save by paying for the car in three years instead of in four?

Unit 5

Developing Your Financial Skills

Chapters ▼

CHAPTER 21

Using Money Effectively

What You Will Learn...

- How you will use your financial resources.
- How to develop a budget.
- How to keep financial records.
- How to avoid financial problems.

Terms for Success

average annual
  expenditure
dividends
fringe benefits
gross earnings

Lisa held the pair of midnight blue shoes admiringly, then turned them over to check the price.

"Hey, you'd look good in those," gushed Reggie.

With a sigh, Lisa set the shoes back on the shelf. "Not this month," she remarked.

"Why not?" Reggie laughed. "Are blue shoes out of style in April?"

"No." Lisa nudged him along the mall walkway. "But I spent my clothing allowance for the month—that new blouse for my cousin's wedding."

"Oh. Maybe you could buy the shoes and cut out something else for a while, and make up for it," Reggie suggested.

Lisa smiled. "Let's see. These shoes cost about the same as . . . four boxes of cereal, one gallon of milk, and three bags of mixed vegetables. I'll just give up eating next month."

"Okay, maybe that wasn't my best idea," Reggie admitted.

"Or my electric bill," Lisa went on. "I'll just light my place with candles. Except if my insurance company found out, they'd probably raise my renters insurance premium."

"I get the picture!" Reggie exclaimed as Lisa began laughing. "This wouldn't be a clever way of asking for a loan, would it?"

"No," Lisa said seriously. "I want to prove to myself that I can stick to this budget. I don't want to get into the habit of borrowing or giving up stuff I need. It's called Ôliving within your means.' Anyway, thanks for offering."

"Of course," Reggie pointed out as they walked on, "you could buy a lot of new things if you worked more. But then you wouldn't get to spend as much time with me."

What does "living within your means" mean to you? What happens when people don't live within their means?

How Will You Spend Your Money?

Lisa might have been tempted to buy the shoes she had seen in the mall, but she was determined to live within her budget. As a young adult, you will be fine-tuning your skills in how to use your financial resources to reach your goals. To do so, you will need to understand the factors that affect resource use. You will need to identify your financial resources, set financial goals, and plan for saving.

Factors That Affect Finances

The way you use your financial resources is determined by some very personal factors—your values, goals, needs, wants, stage in life, lifestyle, and resources. Your attitude toward money will also influence how you use it. You may be cautious about spending and find that saving is easy for you, or you may tend to spend freely and save little.

Identifying Financial Resources

Your financial resources are what you use to get the goods and services you need or want. Your most important financial resource is money. Your primary source of money will probably be your earnings from a job. You may also receive money in the form of interest or dividends from savings and investments. **Dividends** are a part of the profit from a fund or an organization. You might receive money as a gift or inheritance.

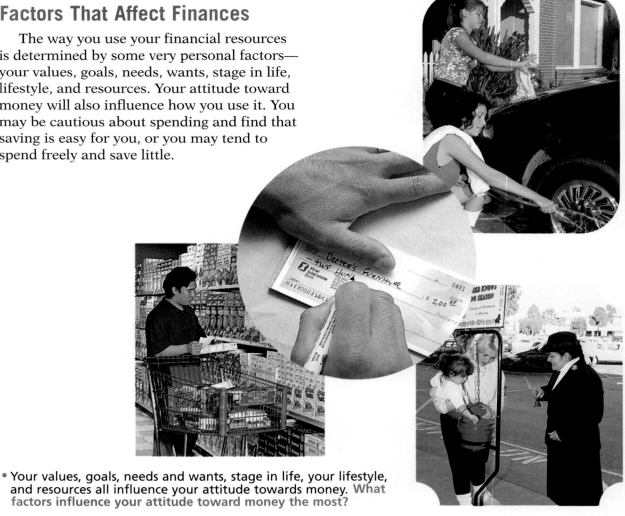

• Your values, goals, needs and wants, stage in life, your lifestyle, and resources all influence your attitude towards money. What factors influence your attitude toward money the most?

Resources and Expenses

- **human resources:** Personal resources (such as knowledge, skills, time, and energy) and people (including family and friends).

- **material resources:** Money and possessions that a person can use to accomplish goals.

- **community resources:** People, facilities, goods, and services that are available for use at minimal or no cost to local citizens.

- **natural resources:** Useful things that are found in nature, such as air, water, soil, plants, animals, minerals, and sources of mechanical energy.

- **fixed expenses:** Expenses that have been agreed to be paid by a certain date.

- **flexible expenses:** Expenses that can be adjusted or come due irregularly.

Human, material, community, and even natural resources can influence your financial resources. These can help you make the most of your money.

How much money will you have to spend or save each month? A large part of the answer will likely depend on your wages. You will need to know where your money comes from and what deductions are taken from your paycheck.

Your employer will determine the method by which you are paid. Employers pay employees several ways:

- **Hourly wages.** Nonsalaried workers are paid only for the number of hours they work. If you work more than 40 hours a week, you will receive overtime pay. However, avoid counting on overtime when you figure your income.

- **Salary.** Salaried employees are paid over a certain period, usually a month or a year. They receive the same amount of money regardless of the number of hours worked.

• Depending on the type of career you choose, you may get paid in any number of ways. This young woman receives a commission as her source of income. **What are the advantages and disadvantages of different types of wages?**

REASON

Analyze Alternatives and Consequences

Sometimes the hardest part of solving a problem is deciding between two alternatives that seem to be equally good. Read the scenario below and see how Tika analyzes the alternatives chosen.

Tika is a high school senior who is trying to complete her plans for college next year. Tika and her parents have met with her guidance counselor, Mrs. Williams, several times to discuss Tika's choice of college and financial aid. Her parents have been very uncomfortable about disclosing their financial information on the financial aid application.

"I don't see why all this personal information is needed just to get into college," Tika's father complained.

"It's really not necessary for college admission, but supplying information is the only way to access much of the financial aid available," answered Mrs. Williams.

Tika has received the preliminary financial aid packages from three colleges. Northern University, about two hours away from her home, is a small,

privately funded college and is the only private college to offer the pre-vet major. Its tuition is about $6,000 more per year than the state university's, but Tika will qualify for almost $5,000 in grants.

State University is about an hour away from Tika's home—too far to commute on a daily basis. The tuition is $6,000 less than Northern University's, but Tika has qualified for only $1,000 in grants. However, she would qualify for a student loan at a very low rate.

The branch campus of the state university is only 20 miles away from Tika's home so it would be possible to commute every day. Tika qualifies for the same financial aid as that of the main campus, but she would avoid the expense of room and board. She could complete the first two years of general courses there and then transfer to the

main campus for her junior and senior years.

Tika evaluated her personal finances. She has $5,000 in certificates of deposit, which will mature during the summer and first few months of college. She also has $250 in a savings account and a Rotary Club academic scholarship for $500 per year.

"Let's sit down and look at my alternatives," Tika suggested one afternoon. She charted the three possibilities on a big piece of paper:

After charting and discussing the three alternatives, Tika's father asked, "Well, what is your decision?"

Tika studied her chart. "I'm going to have to think about this before I make a choice. I'd better get busy on my homework right now, or I won't have to worry about going to college anywhere—I'll be back in high school next year!"

▶ From Your Perspective

1 Does Tika consider all the possible alternatives or are there other possibilities that would meet her goals?

2 What are the short- and long-term consequences for each of her alternatives?

3 How would each alternative affect other family members?

Through Life's Problems

ALTERNATIVES	CONSEQUENCES
Northern University	Tuition is more More grant money Two hours away More time, travel expense to come home Will have room and board expense Has pre-vet major Will need to take out student loan Mom and dad will need to provide more financial information for loans Will probably need to work part-time Independence——out on my own!
State university	Tuition less Less grant money Close enough to come home often, less travel expense than Northern Will have room and board expense Has pre-vet major Will need to take out student loan Mom and Dad will need to provide more info for loan applications Will probably need to work part-time Independence—out on my own!!!
Branch campus	Least cash outlay——no expense for room and board Will not have to take out student loan right away Mom and Dad won't have to fill out any more loan applications for awhile Could work part-time to save for when I go to main campus Doesn't have pre-vet major, but can take general courses which will all transfer to main campus Not as much independence Not as much adjustment for me or Mom and Dad

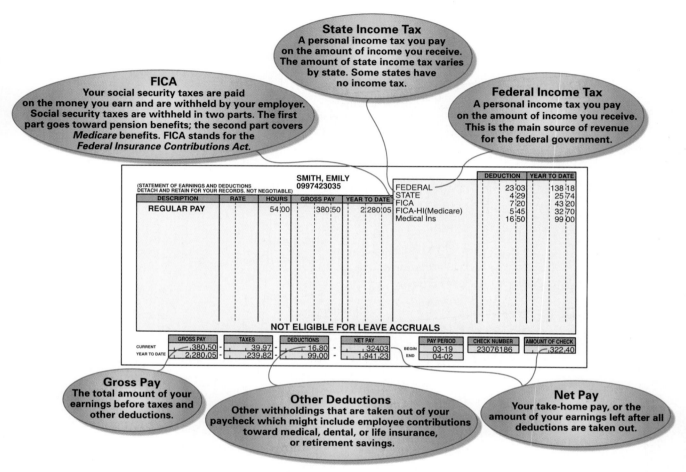

FICA
Your social security taxes are paid on the money you earn and are withheld by your employer. Social security taxes are withheld in two parts. The first part goes toward pension benefits; the second part covers *Medicare* benefits. FICA stands for the *Federal Insurance Contributions Act.*

State Income Tax
A personal income tax you pay on the amount of income you receive. The amount of state income tax varies by state. Some states have no income tax.

Federal Income Tax
A personal income tax you pay on the amount of income you receive. This is the main source of revenue for the federal government.

Gross Pay
The total amount of your earnings before taxes and other deductions.

Other Deductions
Other withholdings that are taken out of your paycheck which might include employee contributions toward medical, dental, or life insurance, or retirement savings.

Net Pay
Your take-home pay, or the amount of your earnings left after all deductions are taken out.

(STATEMENT OF EARNINGS AND DEDUCTIONS DETACH AND RETAIN FOR YOUR RECORDS. NOT NEGOTIABLE)			SMITH, EMILY 0997423035			DEDUCTION	YEAR TO DATE
DESCRIPTION	RATE	HOURS	GROSS PAY	YEAR TO DATE	FEDERAL	23 03	138 18
REGULAR PAY		54 00	380 50	2 280 05	STATE	4 29	25 74
					FICA	7 20	43 20
					FICA-HI(Medicare)	5 45	32 70
					Medical Ins	16 50	99 00

NOT ELIGIBLE FOR LEAVE ACCRUALS

	GROSS PAY	TAXES	DEDUCTIONS	NET PAY	PAY PERIOD	CHECK NUMBER	AMOUNT OF CHECK
CURRENT	380,50	39,97	16,80	32403	BEGIN 03-19	23076186	322,40
YEAR TO DATE	2,280,05	239,82	99,00	1,941,23	END 04-02		

• Your paycheck stub provides useful information for planning your budget. Should you use your gross pay or net pay in planning your budget? Why?

• **Commissions.** Salespeople earn wages based on a percentage of the total amount they sell. During a training period, some salespeople earn hourly wages or a salary. Commission earnings will vary.

• **Fringe benefits.** This is less obvious income such as from sick leave, savings plans, retirement funds, or health and life insurance plans. The value of fringe **benefits** is important to consider when you're evaluating job offers.

As an employee, you'll probably receive a paycheck every week, every two weeks, or every month. The amount of your paycheck will be the amount of your **gross earnings,** or the total wages you earned for that period, less deductions. You can learn what deductions were subtracted from your earnings by studying your paycheck stub. It also shows your earnings and deductions for the year. Your employer may withhold money for other purposes, such as savings or charitable contributions, from your paycheck as a service if you request it.

Setting Financial Goals

Your financial goals will help you determine how to use your financial resources. Consider what objectives you want to achieve and write them down. You are more likely to work toward them if they are important enough to write down.

Financial goals can be long term or short term. Your long-term goals might include going to college, purchasing a car, buying a house, paying for a wedding, saving for retirement, or other objectives that involve large amounts of money. Your short-term goals might include buying a computer, purchasing a new coat, buying a bicycle, or other more immediate ends that involve smaller amounts of money.

Your long-term and short-term goals are interrelated. Kaleb and Julia's children are growing fast and their car needs repair, so they must delay adding to their savings for a house. Demetria is willing to put off buying new clothes until she graduates from business school.

Review your goals at least once a year to see what you've accomplished. Decide whether your goals still reflect where you want to go.

• Planning for saving takes careful examination of your values and goals. What are some ways that you can save money?

Planning for Saving

Saving money is important whether you are single or married. As an adult, you will have many reasons for saving. You may want to save for emergencies, expensive purchases, recurring expenses, retirement, or special goals.

To develop an effective savings plan, you will need to view saving as an important activity. You will be more likely to save money if you resolve to set aside part of your income *first*, then live on what is left.

How much you save will depend on your income, your financial responsibilities, and your goals. One guideline for saving is to save part of every paycheck. A reasonable goal would be to save at least eight to ten percent of your net income, or take-home pay. If you have few responsibilities and expenses, you can save more. If you have many responsibilities and expenses, or a very low income, you may only be able to save five percent of your income regularly.

FOCUS ON ...

The trick to saving is to make saving a habit. If you start by saving small amounts now, you will develop the discipline to do so regularly. Later, saving will become an automatic part of your financial planning. Consider using these techniques to help you save systematically:

- **Self-discipline.** When you plan your budget, decide how much of your paycheck to save. You may want to set aside a percentage of your income. When you get your paycheck, place the set amount in your savings account immediately so you won't be tempted to spend it.
- **Payroll deductions.** Your employer may encourage saving by permitting payroll deductions. If so, you can authorize the transfer of a specific amount from each paycheck to a savings fund.
- **Automatic deductions from checking accounts.** Your bank may allow you to automatically transfer money from your checking account to your savings account. If so, you can specify that a certain amount of money be transferred to savings at the same time each month. You will need to subtract that amount from your checking account balance.

For most people, saving money is necessary to reach their goals. Even if your income is small, you can find ways to save. By taking your lunch from home, finding inexpensive sources of entertainment, adjusting your buying habits, and using your credit cards less frequently, you can find money to save. Even small amounts add up over time. If you save just $5 each day, in a year you will have nearly $2,000. Would you have guessed you could save that much in a year?

Developing a Budget

Have you ever heard someone say that she ran out of money before she ran out of month? If so, you may have been talking to someone who lacks a plan for spending and saving based on an estimate of income and expenses—a *budget*. To meet your needs, your budget should be based on your own values, goals, and personal situation.

• Living within your means requires using a budget to plan for spending and saving. How might living on a budget be less restrictive in the long run than not living on a budget?

The main purpose of a budget is to help you live within your means. However, the budget process has other benefits as well. Budgeting puts you in control of your money. Budgeting can help you reach important goals. It highlights your spending patterns, and enables you to identify problems and make changes. Budgeting can also provide the financial records you need for tax, investment, and other purposes. Most important, it gives you a clear picture of your financial health.

The budgeting process is the same for either an individual or a family. Most spending and savings plans are set up on a yearly basis. This allows you to plan for expenses that occur only periodically such as quarterly insurance payments, summer vacation, or gift giving.

The plan is often broken into regular monthly periods. This is useful because many expenses such as rent, car payments, and utilities are paid by the month. It may also be necessary to plan for weekly expenses such as personal allowances, laundry costs, and lunches.

The budgeting process involves four stages: estimating income, estimating expenses, planning for saving, and developing a trial budget.

Financial Rules of Thumb

Managing finances can be a challenge for many people. In order to prevent overspending and large debt, keep the following rules in mind:

- **The debt rule:** Your total debt (not including your mortgage) should be less than 20 percent of your annual take-home pay.
- **The housing rule:** Spend no more than 30 percent of your monthly take-home pay on rent or mortgage payments.
- **The savings rule:** Save at least 10 percent of your take-home pay each month.

Estimate Income

The first step in planning a budget is to estimate how much money you have to spend during your planning period. For budget purposes, your income includes all the money that you receive regardless of the source.

Base your monthly budget on the least amount of money you expect to receive. Avoid counting anticipated income, such as overtime pay, bonuses, or gifts of money when figuring your budget. Your income amount should be your income for one month. If you are paid every week or every two weeks, you will need to do some math to figure out your monthly income. If your earnings are irregular, planning will be more difficult.

Estimate Expenses

After you have figured out how much money you have available, you can plan how you will spend it. There are several ways to figure your expenses.

- Estimate your expenses based on previous spending experiences.
- Use your financial records to identify your spending patterns.
- Keep an expense record for at least one month.
- Estimate amounts based on the **average annual expenditure,** or the normal amount of money spent each year by other consumers.

- Taking the time to estimate your expenses is the first step in developing your financial management plan. What expenses do you have now? How will they change in the future?

Plan for Saving

The cornerstone of your financial plan should be saving. Set the amounts you must save to reach your goals when you plan your budget.

Every budget should include an emergency fund. This is money you put aside to help meet unexpected expenses or replace lost income. For example, you may need to buy a new car battery or may lose income due to a layoff. You will need to add money to your emergency fund each planning period until it equals two or three months' income. As you acquire more financial responsibilities, you will want to build your emergency fund to a six-month cushion.

You will also need to save for irregular expenses such as dental visits, vacations, or gift giving. Because these expenses occur irregularly, you will need to put the money for them into a savings account until it is needed.

Develop a Trial Budget

After studying your expected income and expenses, you are ready to develop a trial budget, usually for one month. Your budget should include several key figures—income, fixed and flexible expenses, and savings.

The categories you use should reflect your personal situation and spending habits.

Your spending plan should ensure that you live within your means. Compare your expected income with your total anticipated expenses and savings. If your income is larger than your total expenses and savings, you can increase the amount in one or more categories. If your expenses and savings total more than your income, you have three choices. You can cut your spending, reduce your savings, or increase your income.

Once you have made any necessary adjustments, you are ready to use your trial budget. Stick to your budget unless there is good reason to make a change. Keep a record of your actual income, expenses, and savings. Compare this record with your budget at the end of the month. Note any problems you encounter. If your budget needs revision, you'll have the information you need to make appropriate changes.

Keeping Financial Records

The key to successful budgeting is keeping accurate records of your income and expenses. Income records include paycheck stubs, interest or dividend statements, and records of tips, gifts, or bonuses. Expense records include canceled checks, receipts, and credit card statements.

An organized system for filing and maintaining your records is essential. Keeping a file folder for each type of income or expense is the first step in organizing your records. Use an accordion folder, a filing cart, or a small filing cabinet to store your file folders. Store important documents, such as insurance papers, in a safety deposit box at a bank.

Choosing a Recordkeeping System

The recordkeeping system you use is a matter of personal preference. Here are four common recordkeeping methods:

- **Envelope system.** This system works for Julian because his income is small. He simply divides his weekly pay into categories and places it in separate envelopes for each budget purpose. He keeps his expenditure records on slips of paper inside each envelope.
- **Record sheet system.** As Omar's income and expenditures increased, he needed a more formal record system. He uses ruled paper marked into columns. He might have chosen a budget book or a computer financial management software program.
- **Checking account system.** Cynthia uses her checking account as a recordkeeping device for all of her expenditures. By comparing the amounts on her checkbook stubs with her budget estimates, Cynthia can see how well her spending plan is working.
- **Combination system.** You can combine two or more methods to create your own system. Marcus combines the checking account and envelope systems, for example. He deposits money for fixed monthly payments into his checking account. He adds money for savings and emergencies to his savings account. He keeps money for daily expenses at home in envelopes.

In Your Safety Deposit Box

TIPS

- Birth certificates.
- Adoption papers.
- Citizenship papers.
- Marriage certificate.
- Divorce decree.
- Death certificates.
- Passports.
- Military discharge.
- Veterans Administration papers.
- Stock certificates.
- Bonds.
- Automobile title.
- Real estate deeds.
- Contracts.
- Household inventory (with photographs).

• The recordkeeping system you choose to use is your personal preference. The important thing is that you use one. **What are the consequences of not using a recordkeeping system?**

Following Your Budget

Budgeting is a simple process, but the key to successfully managing your money is self-control. Most people have a limited income and must make choices. The key is to manage your spending so your expenses are less than your income. This means using self-discipline not to spend money when doing so will hinder your financial success.

Budgeting is more likely to work if you make it a habit. This will be easier if you make the process as easy as possible.

Adjusting Your Budget

At the end of each budget period, check to see if your income and expenses balance. If you had money left over, what are you going to do with it? If you ran short of money, what expenses can you reduce next month?

If you experience a shortage of money, you can adjust your budget by increasing your income or by reducing your expenditures. George considered getting a second job or switching to a different job that pays more. He found several areas where he could reduce his spending. When Sue's layoff caused long-term budget problems, she found a less expensive place to live, traded an expensive car for one that cost less, and transferred her outstanding credit card debt to a card with lower interest rates.

Making Your Budget Work

TIPS

Here are some tips to make budgeting easier:

- Keep your budgeting materials where they are handy.
- Choose a regular time to work on your budget.
- Use a pocket calculator or financial planning software to make calculations easier.
- Round off figures to the nearest dollar.
- Reward yourself for the progress you make in using a budget.

FOCUS ON ...
Budget Bonanzas

Here are some tips to help you make budget adjustments.

- **Review budget categories in which you spend the most money.** You should be able to trim five to ten percent from these categories. Likely categories to trim are food, clothing, and entertainment.

- **Check spending details.** How much do you spend on recreation? What do you spend eating out each month? What do you spend on candy bars and fast food? The answers may surprise you.

- **Keep track of your cash.** If you find that cash slips through your fingers, keep a piece of paper in your wallet for recording cash expenditures. Every time you spend cash, write down the amount you spent and what you bought. This will help you find budget leaks that can be plugged without drastically affecting your lifestyle.

- **Review your spending habits.** Could you save gasoline by grouping errands? Do you pay more for items purchased at the corner grocery instead of at the supermarket? Do you really watch all the cable channels to which you subscribe? Do you really need call-waiting, caller-ID, or other telephone services? Could you take advantage of less expensive long distance rates? Could you earn extra money by recycling cans and bottles?

Avoiding Financial Problems

You can avoid financial problems by following these guidelines:

T I P S

- Be realistic in estimating your expenses.
- Be specific in setting up budget categories.
- Plan for predictable expenses that occur irregularly.
- Don't let your spending get out of hand.
- Use credit with care.
- Pay your bills on time.
- Consult an attorney before making a major legal financial commitment.
- Cut back on your goals or take longer to reach them, if necessary.

As changes occur in your life, you will need to adjust your budget. Having a child resulted in reduced income when Alena decided to stay at home. A transfer to another city meant a raise in pay for Daniel, but it also resulted in a higher cost of living. Your budget should be adjusted to reflect such changes.

• Adjusting your budget to reduce your expenses is sometimes needed to live within your means. **What things do you spend money on that could easily be eliminated to reduce your expenses?**

Getting Financial Help

Ray and Lynn never thought they would ever be completely destitute, but they are. Lynn quit her job when the new baby was born two months ago. Since then, the baby has had several medical problems. To make matters worse, bad weather has kept Ray's construction business at a standstill for weeks. The final blow came when the family's mobile home caught fire while the family was visiting neighbors across the street. With almost no money left, Ray and Lynn need help right away.

Where should they seek assistance? Someone suggested they call the local welfare office. Some programs may be available to provide immediate assistance. Others can provide funds for medical costs, heating fuel, food, and shelter in emergencies. Federal, state, and local assistance organizations have offices in most communities.

Information about community services is usually available at the nearest courthouse and is often listed in the local telephone directory. Ray and Lynn may also be able to get help through charitable organizations such as the Red Cross, Salvation Army, United Way, or local churches. Neighbors at the mobile home park may also be able to help.

Using Your Resources Wisely

1. What should be Ray and Lynn's priorities at this time of financial crisis?

2. What long-term concerns might they have?

3. What resources are available in your community to help a family with similar financial problems?

Avoiding Financial Problems

Money problems can be caused by emergencies, such as job layoff or loss, accidents, illness, or disasters. Money problems often result from poor planning, overspending, abuse of credit, or failure to save for emergencies.

You can solve many money problems yourself. Consider the effects of any changes in your personal situation. Reevaluate your financial goals. Study your budget carefully to identify problems. If you can't resolve the problem yourself, consult a professional financial planner or credit counselor.

Understanding Key Concepts

● Before making a financial plan, you will need to identify your financial resources, factors that affect your finances, and your spending and saving goals.

● Your net income depends on the type of earnings you receive and the deductions from your gross earnings.

● Developing a budget plan involves estimating your income and expenses, planning for savings, and creating a trial budget.

● When using a budget, you will need to select a recordkeeping system.

● Effective use of a budget plan requires adjusting your budget as needed and taking steps to avoid financial problems.

Checking Your Knowledge

1. Give an example illustrating how human, material, community, or natural resources might help you make the most of your money.

2. Identify one advantage and one disadvantage of each method by which you might be paid.

3. Identify two short-term and two long-term goals you want to accomplish as a young adult. How are these goals interrelated?

4. Identify three guidelines for saving.

5. Identify three purposes of budgeting.

6. Describe the four stages in the budgeting process.

7. Why is it important to have an emergency fund?

8. Why is it important to differentiate between fixed and flexible expenses?

9. Describe the four common recordkeeping methods. Which would you prefer to use? Why?

10. List five specific reasons you might need to adjust your budget.

11. Give five guidelines for avoiding financial problems.

Making TRANSITIONS

Values, Conflicts, and Money

Assume you have been single for several years. You have never made a budget, but have had no trouble managing your money. You have even managed to save enough to fund a three-month emergency fund. You are planning to marry soon. You have noticed that your fiancé has trouble saving anything and spends money freely. He frequently borrows money from you just to make it through the month. Will you assume that things will work out after you marry, or will you act now to prevent future problems? Explain what you would do and why.

STRENGTHENING *Life* SKILLS

Planning for Transportation

Whether or not you own a car or use buses and taxicabs, you will need to budget for transportation. Create two columns, one for car ownership and one for public transportation. Estimate the costs involved for each. Under car ownership, list items like car loan, insurance, maintenance, and repair. Under public transportation, include trips to and from work, school, shopping, recreation, and worship. Is it more expensive to own a car or take public transportation? Which is more convenient?

Applying Thinking Skills

1. **Analyzing results.** Do you think people need money to be happy? Why or why not?

2. **Predicting consequences.** Consider how a person's past experiences (and those of other family members) affect attitudes toward money.

3. **Forming opinions.** Would you prefer receiving hourly wages, a regular salary, or being paid on a commission basis? Give reasons for your answer.

4. **Defending your position.** Give your opinion on each of the following budgeting points of view. Then defend your position.

   - "I know how much I earn and how much I spend. Why should I keep a written record?"

   - "I keep a record of major expenses only. There's no point in bothering with nickel-and-dime items."

   - "I have a complete record of every cent I've spent for the past 10 years."

Practical Applications

1. **Comparing decisions.** Make a list of 20 items you could spend money on as a young adult. Include both necessities and luxuries. On a separate piece of paper, identify each of your items as a need or a want and tell why. Exchange lists with another student. Identify the items on the other student's list as needs and wants. Compare your decisions on both lists, and draw conclusions about how different people view needs and wants.

2. **Creating a form.** Create a chart, form, or worksheet that could be used to record a monthly budget or financial record. If possible, use a computer to do your work. Share your form with the class.

3. **Analyzing expenses.** Make a list of your expenses for recreation and other non-essentials during the past week. Identify ways to reduce these expenses by substituting activities that are more economical or by reducing or eliminating some expenses.

CHAPTER **22**

Using Financial Services

What You Will Learn...

- How financial services can help you manage your money.
- Various financial services and how each can meet financial goals.
- How to select financial services that will help you manage your money and reach financial goals.

Terms for Success

asset
commission
diversify
inflation
maturity date
statement reconciliation

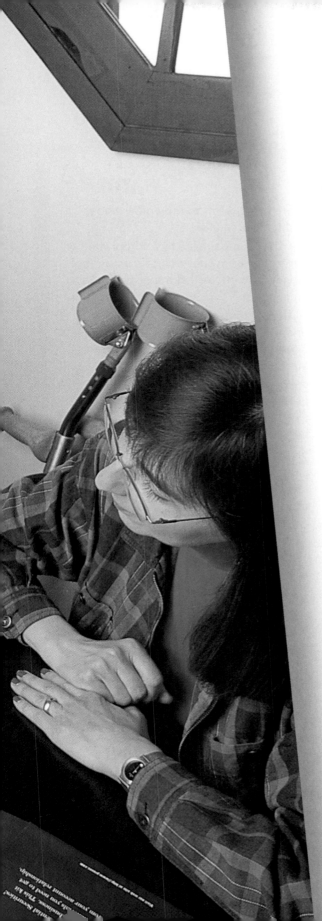

Mrs. Guidry smiled at her son's hunched figure as he pored over the brokerage firm's earnings statement. She announced solemnly, "Aaron Guidry—financial wizard."

Aaron grinned and shook his head. "Not quite. I'd be happy just to understand all these numbers. Do you know what they mean?"

"Most of them," Mrs. Guidry replied. "I know enough to tell whether our stocks are earning or losing money, and by how much."

Aaron turned the pages over and back. "Which stocks do you own? I don't see any listed."

"It's a mutual fund," his mother explained. "The management group picks stocks in a lot of different companies. We get a full listing at the end of the year. It runs about six pages."

Aaron looked impressed. "Wow. That must make you feel rich, owning parts of all those companies."

Mrs. Guidry chuckled. "Not exactly rich . . . but responsible. For instance, one of the reasons we picked a mutual fund was that it spreads out the risk, but still gives a decent return on our money. That's important when you've got a family. Also, this fund picks only socially responsible companies that have good records on things like worker relations and the environment. That's important to us, too."

"I think I might like to try something like this," Aaron mused, "when I've got the money to invest."

"It never hurts to start looking at your options," Mrs. Guidry agreed. "Maybe you can talk to someone at the bank about getting a CD."

Aaron assumed a confused look that hid a sly smile. "Why should I go to the bank for a CD? I always get mine from Riley's Music World."

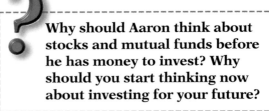

Why should Aaron think about stocks and mutual funds before he has money to invest? Why should you start thinking now about investing for your future?

How Should You Handle Your Money?

Imagine that your money is like a flowing river. If you put your hand into a river, water flows through your fingers, just as money flows into and out of your possession. Sometimes dams are built on rivers to control the flow of water for recreation or to generate electricity. Financial services, in a similar way, can help you control the flow of your money. These services are tools you can use as you manage your funds to reach the financial goals you've set.

Financial businesses provide ways to pay bills easily, earn money on your money, and help with recordkeeping. Using financial services can help you be an effective money manager.

Keep It Safe

One ongoing challenge in money management is to keep your money safe. Cash can be lost, stolen, or spent. Having large amounts of cash means you always have the risk of loss.

Refresh your Memory

Here are some terms to remember about using financial services:

- **bond:** A promise made by a corporation or government to repay a certain amount of money, plus interest, at a specific future time.
- **certificate of deposit (CD):** A receipt from a financial business that guarantees to repay a certain amount of money, plus interest, after a specific length of time.
- **dividend:** A share of an organization's profits paid to an owner in proportion to the shares of ownership.
- **interest:** Payment for the use of borrowed money.
- **mutual fund:** A pool of money from many investors used to buy stocks, bonds, or other financial assets.
- **stock:** An ownership share in a company.

Hometown Bank Earns Record Profits for Year

Andrew P. Salavar, President of Hometown Bank, announced today that the bank has earned a record-breaking $4 million dollars in profits this year. Profits were based on increased volume of business and higher interest rates on loans and mortgages.

• Financial services businesses must earn profits to stay in business. How could it benefit you to keep track of the earnings of various financial service businesses before deciding to use one or more of these services?

Financial businesses are designed to keep your funds safe. They have security to physically protect the money they have on hand. In addition, their recordkeeping systems are designed to keep track of who owns the cash they take in.

Some businesses, like banks, credit unions, and savings and loans, are insured up to certain limits by the government against loss of customers' funds. If you know what kind of protection a business provides for your money, you can make a better choice about whether or not you want to use it.

Understand the "Money" Business

Most businesses that provide financial services have goals of making profits. While they provide important services to help you manage your money, they make money from your accounts.

Most financial institutions loan the money customers have in their accounts to other customers. They make a profit by being able to loan the money you have in your account to someone else at a higher interest rate than they are paying you. For example, if you have money in a bank account that's paying you five percent interest, and the bank can loan your money to someone who pays eight percent to borrow it, the bank makes a profit. Paying lower interest rates or charging higher rates than competitors can increase profits.

Another way financial businesses make profits is to charge fees. Some checking accounts have monthly service charges. If you buy stocks through a brokerage firm, you pay a commission. A **commission** is a fee paid to someone for a service, in this case the service of buying the stock.

As a consumer of financial services, you must be able to figure out how much a service is going to cost and how you'll be charged for it. This information is important in deciding the type of account you want and which business you want to use. You should comparison-shop for financial services, just as you do for other products you buy.

• Financial institutions offer a variety of services to their customers. As you move in to your adult life, which services seem most important?

Financial Services

Financial services can be categorized and described in different ways. One way is to consider whether you can withdraw your money at any time without penalty. A *demand* account is one in which the business must return your funds at your request. Checking and passbook savings accounts are examples.

In contrast, *time* accounts involve leaving your money for a certain period before you can withdraw it without penalty. Examples include certificates of deposit (CDs) and bonds. Andrea says, "I put my savings into a two-year CD because the CD earned a lot more interest than my savings account. Then I needed my savings to move to a new apartment. I was furious about the amount of the penalty. I hadn't understood that if I didn't leave the money in the CD for the full two years, I'd make more money putting it into my savings account."

Another way to look at financial services is to consider whether you are lending your money or buying something.

- **Lending.** You lend your money when you put it into a checking or savings account or buy a CD or a bond. As long as you meet any time deposit requirements, you'll get your original amount back and earn interest on the money loaned.
- **Buying.** You can use money to buy an **asset,** which is an item of value that a person owns. Assets include real estate, stocks, or other property. Some assets earn money and you may receive a dividend. You can only get your money back if you sell what you own.

A variety of institutions want to provide financial services to you. Laws control the services each type of business provides. It's useful to know exactly what services each business provides so you can choose one that best serves your financial needs.

FOCUS ON ...

Types of Financial Businesses

Choose a financial business that provides the services you need for reasonable fees and is located conveniently.

- **Bank:** A financial institution that receives, loans, and protects money for individuals and businesses.
- **Savings and loan association:** An institution, that offers a full line of services, but specializes in providing loans to home buyers.
- **Credit union:** Offers similar services to a bank but is owned by its depositors, or members. Membership is often connected to an employer or organization. Credit unions often have different names for their services. For example, checks are called *share drafts*, because depositors are selling ownership shares when they write checks.
- **Brokerage company:** A business that buys, sells, and holds stocks, bonds, and other assets for customers.
- **Mutual fund company:** A business that pools customers' funds to buy stocks, bonds, and other financial assets.

Checking Accounts

As you move into adulthood, you'll become responsible for more and more of your own expenses. It's usually inconvenient and unsafe to keep enough cash on hand to pay all your bills. A checking account is one tool to manage your cash.

Checking accounts are available at banks, savings and loans, credit unions, and some brokerage firms. Costs for checking accounts vary widely. Several kinds of checking accounts are available:

- *Regular checking accounts* usually have monthly fees but don't require a minimum balance. They may have other types of charges and fees as well.
- *Negotiable Orders of Withdrawal* (NOW) and *money market* deposit accounts earn interest and usually have no fees. Sometimes the number and amount of checks that can be written are restricted. A minimum deposit amount is required.

Danny says, "I would love to have a NOW account and earn interest instead of paying fees, but I don't have the $500 minimum deposit, so I have a regular checking account."

Checks Make It Easy

When you open a checking account, you deposit funds into the account and buy checks. You must sign a signature card so the business knows who is authorized to write checks on the account. A *check* is a legal document that guarantees payment of a specific amount of money to the named person or business, or *payee*. With a checking account, you can deposit and withdraw money and you can write checks to pay for purchases.

When you fill out a check, you are authorizing the business where you have your checking account to pay the amount of money indicated on the check. It'll be paid to the payee's name you've written on the "Pay to the order of" line.

• Because a check is a legal document, it is important to fill it out completely and accurately. **What consequences could result from failing to pay attention to these details?**

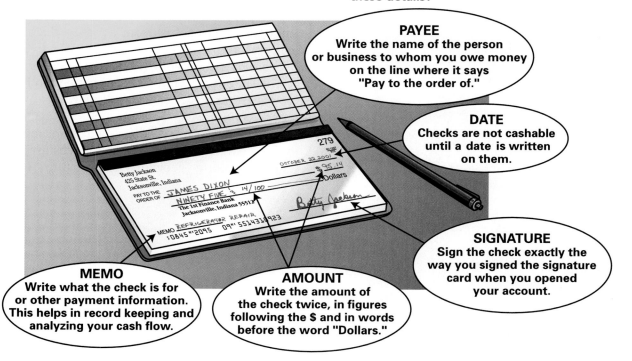

PAYEE
Write the name of the person or business to whom you owe money on the line where it says "Pay to the order of."

DATE
Checks are not cashable until a date is written on them.

SIGNATURE
Sign the check exactly the way you signed the signature card when you opened your account.

MEMO
Write what the check is for or other payment information. This helps in record keeping and analyzing your cash flow.

AMOUNT
Write the amount of the check twice, in figures following the $ and in words before the word "Dollars."

You must be sure that you have enough money in your account to cover the amount of the check. If you do not, your account will be *overdrawn*. Your check will be returned for insufficient funds, you'll be charged fees, and you can be prosecuted.

You can deposit cash or checks into your account. If you receive a check, you must sign, or *endorse*, it on the back. Three types of endorsements are common:

- A *simple endorsement* consists of only your signature. Once you have endorsed a check, anyone can cash it. It's best to wait to endorse a check until you're at the financial business.

- A *special endorsement* means that you limit payment to someone else. On the first line on the back of the check, you could write "Pay to the order of Luke Thompkins," then sign your name on the second line. This means that the money can be paid to Luke only after he has also endorsed the check.

- A *restrictive endorsement*, which is used when depositing checks, limits the use of the check. When you write "For Deposit Only" above your signature, the check can be put only into your account.

Moving Your Money Electronically

Many checking accounts allow you to move your money electronically. Some employers offer *direct deposit*: you can arrange to have your paycheck deposited into your account automatically. You can also have bills paid electronically.

Automated teller machines (ATMs) are a convenient way to deposit into and withdraw from your account. You receive a plastic card and a personal identification number (PIN) that you use to access your account electronically. Memorize and guard your PIN carefully. Never write it on your ATM card or carry it in your wallet with your card. Anyone who has your card and PIN can withdraw funds from your account.

Fees may be charged for each transaction at an ATM. If you know what the fees are, you can make better decisions about using ATMs.

• Using automated teller machines is easy and convenient, but does have some drawbacks. **What should you do to protect yourself when using any electronic financial service?**

While convenient, ATMs also have drawbacks. Errors made when using an ATM are often harder to correct than human errors. Don't deposit cash into an ATM because the ATM receipt isn't legal evidence of a deposit if there is a dispute. If you use an isolated ATM late at night, you may be a target for a thief. Most ATM crime takes place between 7 P.M. and midnight.

Debit cards are an electronic way to pay for purchases directly from your checking account. Using a debit card is like using an electronic check. Money is immediately withdrawn from your checking account. While convenient, debit cards increase your risk of loss. Anyone with your card can pay for purchases with money from your checking account.

Keeping the Record Straight

A checking account requires accurate recordkeeping to help you manage your money and to keep from being overdrawn. Recordkeeping is especially important for electronic transactions because they affect your account instantly. If you've used your debit card to buy flowers in the morning, the money is immediately taken from your account and deposited into the florist's account. If you want to withdraw cash from an ATM in the afternoon, you must first subtract the amount you spent on flowers to see how much money is left in your account.

A check register or ledger is used to record information about deposits made, checks written, and electronic transactions. You should write details of each transaction, including the date, payee, and amount. A column is provided to keep track of the current balance in your account.

When bill payments are automatically deducted, you must make sure that there's enough money in your account on the payment date so that the payments can be made.

Every month, the business where you have your checking account will send you a *statement* of your account. This is a record of all the deposits and payments made on your account. Your account statements are important records and should be kept in a safe place.

When you receive a statement, your job is to do a **statement reconciliation.** This is the process of bringing your account records into agreement with the statement. One way to reconcile a statement is shown on pages 402-403.

CHECK NO	DATE	CHECK ISSUED TO	AMOUNT OF CHECK	√	DATE OF DEP	AMOUNT OF DEPOSIT	BALANCE
							524 50
267	3-14	SALLY'S GROC. (CAKE FOR PARTY)	14 70				509 80
X	3-15	ATM CASH WITHDRAWAL	20 00				489 80
X		DEPOSIT			3-20	465 73	955 53
268	3-21	GENERAL TELEPHONE	89 62				865 91

• Keeping accurate records in your check register is necessary for keeping your account in balance. **What consequences can there be from keeping poor financial records?**

STEPS IN RECONCILING YOUR CHECKING ACCOUNT

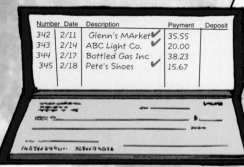

Step 1

Gather supplies you will need: check register, bank statement, calculator, paper, and pen or pencil.

Step 2

In your register, make check marks beside all the checks that are listed as paid on your statement.

Number	Date	Description	Payment	Deposit
342	2/11	Glenn's MArket ✓	35.55	
343	2/14	ABC Light Co. ✓	20.00	
344	2/17	Bottled Gas Inc ✓	38.23	
345	2/18	Pete's Shoes ✓	15.67	

Step 3

Make a list of the checks you've written that haven't been paid. Total this list.

Outstanding Checks

#344 $38.23
#367 135.00
#369 $28.23

Step 4

In your register, make check marks beside all deposits that are shown as deposited in your account.

Number	Date	Description	Payment	Deposit
353	2/21	Shoe Place	25.99	
	2/24	deposit		✓ 75.00
354	2/24	Bottled Gas Inc	28.23	
355	2/24	Bob Martin (rent)	325.00	

Step 5

Make a list of deposits you've listed in your register that aren't shown on the statement.

Step 6

Draw a line down the middle of a sheet of paper. At the top of one side of the paper, write "Bank Statement." On the other write "Checkbook".

BANK STATEMENT	CHECKBOOK

Step 7

Under the words "Bank Statement," write the ending balance that's shown on the statement. Under the word "Checkbook," write your checkbook ending balance.

BANK STATEMENT		CHECKBOOK	
Statement Balance	$144.54	Register Balance	$191.52

Step 8

On the statement side, add the total of the deposits that are listed in your check register, but that the statement doesn't list. On the checkbook side, add deposits the statement has recorded that you may not have, such as interest.

BANK STATEMENT		CHECKBOOK	
Statement Balance	$144.54	Register Balance	$191.52
add; Deposits		add; Unrecorded	
in transit	$286.44	Deposits	$45.00
	$430.98		$236.52

Step 9

On the statement side of your sheet, subtract the total of outstanding checks that you've written but that aren't listed as paid on the statement. From the checkbook side, subtract any bank charges that you may not have entered.

BANK STATEMENT		CHECKBOOK	
Statement Balance	$144.54	Register Balance	$191.52
add; Deposits		add; Unrecorded	
in transit	$286.44	Deposits	$45.00
	$430.98		$236.52
Subtract;			
Outstanding Checks			
#344 $38.23		Subtract;	
#367 135.00		service charge	$7.00
#369 $28.23	$201.46	Adjusted balance	$229.52
	$229.52		

Step 10

After you have done the math, the two sides should match.

Step 11

If they don't match, look for math errors, fees charged that you haven't entered in your register, withdrawals or deposits you forgot or entered incorrectly, automatic payments, or withdrawals you didn't enter, or transposed numbers (writing $15.43 rather than $15.34).

Step 12

If you can't find the error, you may want to take your materials and talk to a customer service representative at the business where you have your account. These representatives are experienced in solving checking account problems.

Most checking account statements have a worksheet on the back that will help you reconcile your account. The steps shown here are one way to complete this process.

Reconciling a statement is a frustrating process for many people, especially if they have not kept accurate records of deposits and withdrawals. If you don't reconcile, however, you won't know exactly how much money is in your account and therefore available to you.

Saving Your Money

When people refer to savings accounts, they are generally talking about accounts in which the business holding the money is loaning it to someone. Most of these types of accounts earn a set amount of interest. You'll learn what that rate of interest is when you open the account. If the interest rate and the amount can be changed, you'll learn how that change is calculated when you open the account.

"I got one of the new three-year CDs my bank is offering," explains Jenny. "My interest rate can go up or down every six months. I got a brochure that explains how they figure these rates when I deposited my money."

With these types of accounts, you'll receive back the money you put in. At the end of three years, Jenny will receive all the money she put into the CD, plus the interest she earned.

An interest-earning demand savings account is where you want to keep your emergency fund. It's considered a safe way to save because you get your money back with interest, and most of these accounts are insured. When you need money in a hurry, you won't have to pay a penalty for early withdrawal.

The main drawback to this type of account occurs when national economic conditions are changing. If there's **inflation**, a period of time when prices of goods and services rise sharply, money buys less. Your purchasing power has been decreased. In a period of inflation, $100 in a savings account will buy less a year from now than it buys now.

FOCUS ON ...
▶Retirement . . . That's Years Away!

Retirement probably seems very far away to you. Saving for retirement may seem unimportant when there are so many things you need and want now.

Special retirement accounts offer tax advantages to encourage you to begin saving early for retirement. These accounts also restrict access to your money so that you'll leave it in your account until you retire. Usually, you cannot withdraw funds without paying a penalty until you are 59½ years old. Two common types of retirement accounts are:

- **Individual retirement account (IRA):** This is an account you set up and manage. Laws governing IRAs change, but the amount you can contribute each year is limited. You may get a deduction on your income taxes for the amount contributed.
- **401K plans:** These are retirement savings accounts offered by employers. You can contribute up to a certain percentage of your wages. Money that goes into a 401K plan is not taxed. Some companies match all or part of your contribution.

IRA money can be put into most types of savings or investment accounts. You might have a CD, bond, or mutual fund in your IRA. The types of savings or investments for 401K plans are limited to what is offered by your employer. Usually, four to six choices are given, such as stock or bond mutual funds or a guaranteed interest account.

Money invested in retirement accounts grows over the years. Your interest and dividends are not taxed until you withdraw them from the account.

When you are ready to save money, compare types of accounts and various businesses. Which type of savings account and which financial firm will safely earn the most interest for you? Use your consumer skills to comparison shop and get the best account.

Investing for the Future

There are generally two major differences between saving and investing. First, saving more often refers to short-term goals and results while investing usually means a long-term outlook. Your focus on saving may be a few months or a year or two. You may plan investments that bring results five or ten years in the future. Second, saving generally means loaning money, while investing refers to buying assets, such as real estate, stocks, or mutual funds.

One trait of most types of investment is uncertainty. You could make money or lose money. When you buy an asset, there's no guarantee that you'll be able to sell it for the amount you paid. There's no assurance that your property will pay dividends. "For graduation, my granddad gave me 10 shares of stock in the company he worked for," says Courtney. "The shares cost him $60 each. Now they are worth only $36 each. If he'd put the money into a savings account, I'd have all the money plus interest. He says I'm too impatient—my stock will eventually be worth more than any savings account."

Owning assets may bring you a better return than loaning your money through a savings account. There is, however, the risk that you'll lose money—maybe all your money. The more potential reward an investment has, the more risky it is.

Financial planners stress that people should have adequate savings before they begin investing. They shouldn't invest money that they'll need soon or can't afford to lose.

• Investing in stock is often a long-term investment. What could happen to an investor who goes into buying stock for the short term?

Taking Stock

Owning stock means you own part of a company. Selecting what stock to buy can be a very confusing experience. Thousands of companies sell their stocks to the public.

Stocks are bought and sold through brokerage companies. Full-service brokers offer advice and information about the stocks you own and potential stock purchases. You're charged a commission when you buy and sell stocks from these brokers. Discount brokerages, simply buy and sell stocks that you select. Internet trading services function like discount brokerages.

The price of a stock can change every day. Stock tables are published in most daily newspapers. Current prices are also available on cable television stations and on the Internet.

Those who are successful in selecting stocks spend hours analyzing financial and management information about companies before making choices. In addition, they **diversify,** which means putting their money into a variety of investments, so they reduce their risk of loss in any one stock or industry.

Because beginning investors usually do not have the money to diversify, most financial planners suggest that they purchase stock mutual funds. When you buy a mutual fund, you're hiring professionals to select stocks for you. You also own shares in many companies, so if one company does poorly, another doing well can make up for it. The initial amount of money it takes to buy a mutual fund is often less than it takes to buy shares of individual stocks.

Selecting a good stock mutual fund takes research and work. Many funds focus primarily on one type of stock. For example, a fund may specialize in large companies that pay dividends to stockholders. Another fund may own only small, fast growing companies that pay no dividends. A sector fund may buy only stocks from one industry, such as health care.

Bonds—An Interesting Mixture

Bonds are financial assets that have mixed characteristics. Because they are often held for long periods, they are thought of as "an investment." On the other hand, a bond involves loaning money to others, which is usually considered "savings." United States savings bonds are financial assets offered by the government.

While U.S. Savings Bonds can be purchased at banks, other types of bonds are usually sold through brokerage firms. Businesses or government units at the local, state, and federal levels can issue bonds. For example, your school district probably issues bonds when it needs funds to build a new school.

Bonds have a **maturity date,** a date when the person loaning the money will receive the original amount back. Short-term bonds mature sooner than long-term bonds, which often are issued for 20 to 30 years. Long-term bonds generally earn more interest, because of the uncertainty of economic conditions over a long time. Interest is usually paid periodically during the life of the bond, although some bonds pay only when they mature.

Bonds make the most sense when you plan to hold them to maturity. You'll then get back the money you put in plus the guaranteed interest. If you must sell a bond before the maturity date, you'll pay commissions and you're not guaranteed to get the full amount of the bond back.

Bonds, like savings accounts, lose value in times of inflation. Because the interest rate is set, you don't have the chance to make a larger return, as you do when buying an asset. On the other hand, you reduce your risk of losing your investment with a bond.

Bond mutual funds offer the opportunity to buy bonds with a small amount of money. You can select funds that specialize in long-, intermediate-, or short-term bonds. You can choose a fund that buys federal government bonds, municipal (local or state government) bonds, or corporate bonds. Owning a bond mutual fund reduces your risk because you're diversified, owning a small part of many bonds.

• Municipalities often use money from the sales of bonds to create parks, schools, and other community amenities. **From your perspective, what are the pros and cons of buying bonds?**

Other Services

Financial institutions may offer a variety of other services besides checking, savings, and investing opportunities. Three of these are described below:

- Safety deposit boxes are storage compartments in special fireproof vaults where you can store important papers. Elizabeth keeps her birth certificate and a CD in her safety deposit box.
- Traveler's checks are issued by travel or credit card companies. They can be used in place of cash where a personal check might not be accepted.
- Special checks that a bank guarantees will be paid include certified checks, cashier's checks, or money orders. J. T. used a cashier's check for the down payment on his truck.

A fee is usually charged for special services. If you'll use these services often, you should carefully compare fees at different firms.

The Choice Is Yours

The financial services business is very complex. There are dozens of options and alternatives for every dollar of your money. It can be hard to know what type of financial institution to choose.

The first step is to identify your specific financial needs. What are your goals and what services do you need to reach them?

The basic services you'll probably need now are checking and savings accounts.

Whatever type of business you're considering, ask yourself a few basic questions:

- Can this business help me reach my financial goals by providing services I need?
- How does this business make its money? What fees and costs will I have to pay?
- How much risk will I take using this company's services? What return will I get?
- How convenient and safe will using this company's financial services be?

- Valuable papers, such as birth certificates and savings bonds, can be kept in a safety deposit box at the bank. **What additional papers should you consider keeping in a safety deposit box?**

REASON

Through Life's Problems

Outline and Take Action

After selecting the best alternative, it's important to come up with a plan of action. Deciding step-by-step what needs to be done will help you get the results you're looking for. In the example below, note how Shane develops a plan of action for keeping his checking account balanced.

"I can't believe this mess!" Shane grumbled at himself. "Another bounced check! These insufficient funds charges are costing me a bundle. I've decided to keep my checkbook balanced monthly to avoid these charges. It's time to come up with a plan to stay on top of this."

Shane had been out on his own for six months, working full-time as a carpenter and making good money. However, he opened a checking account without much thought as to how he would manage the necessary bookkeeping.

Shane headed to his desk with a pile of unopened checking account statements. "For one thing, I do a horrible job of recording the monthly service charges. I've got to get in the habit of opening these statements as soon as I get them instead of letting them pile up like this. Then I'll remember to record the monthly fees."

Knowing that he also did not always record the check he wrote, Shane resolved to get duplicate checks. "That way, every time I write a check, I will have a record of it. I will also quit tearing out checks and carrying them around in my wallet. I'll keep the whole checkbook with me."

As Shane worked through his statements, he discovered that he had made several errors in addition and subtraction on his checkbook register. "I'm going to do all my adding and subtracting in pencil, and then check it with a calculator.

"Finally!" Shane exclaimed as he reached the same balance as his last statement. "Now I'm all up-to-date and know exactly how much money I need to transfer into this account until payday. Plus I know how I'm going to keep it that way!"

From Your Perspective

1 What resources does Shane need to solve his problem?

2 Do you think Shane's plan is workable? Why or why not?

Investigate Your Options

Most people use financial services that are conveniently located in their communities. What are the available options in your area? Get brochures or call for information from those that seem promising to you.

Talk to people you know who use financial services. What services do they use? Who provides them? How happy are they with their choices?

There are advantages to using local services. You may know people who work in the business you select. Local checks are usually more readily accepted for purchases. It's often easier to resolve problems in person rather than over the telephone or by letter.

Opening Your Account

Once you have selected a financial institution, the next step is to open your account(s). You'll need to provide certain facts about yourself, including your Social Security number. A customer service representative will help you get set up.

Once you are established, you'll need to monitor how well your accounts work for you. Are they convenient to use? How helpful are personnel when you have a problem? Are the fees in line with what you expected?

Reevaluate Your Situation

When your circumstances change or if a business does not live up to what you expected, you may decide to change companies, add an account, or close one.

As an adult, you are responsible for your own money. Your values and goals will directly affect your money management decisions, including what financial services you need and use.

Financial services firms are like other businesses. They advertise, try to sell you their services, and work to keep you as a customer. In the end, however, you are in charge of your finances. You must decide what you value and need in financial services firms. Your financial success depends on choosing those businesses that will work for you.

• Once you've chosen a financial institution, meet with a representative to open your accounts. **Why should you carefully choose your financial institutions?**

Which Is the Best Way to Save?

Rebecca has a good kind of problem to solve. She just got a $2,000 check! "It is scholarship money for my first year of college. I have some money saved for the fall semester, so I won't need this money until spring. I was going to put the check into my savings account at the bank. Mom said I should look at a money market deposit account at the bank instead. Then Jarod told me he had a money market mutual fund that earns more than anything a bank would. I'd like to earn as much interest as possible, but I've never had a mutual fund before. Besides, the money market fund is in another state."

- **Money market deposit account.** This is a type of checking account offered by banks and savings and loans. Usually you need a large minimum balance to open and keep the account, and you may be limited in the number of checks you can write. You earn a changing rate of interest that is usually higher than that earned on regular savings or checking accounts.
- **Money market mutual fund.** This is a special type of mutual fund. You own a share of the money market fund and receive dividends, just as with other mutual funds. While the value of most

mutual funds varies, the value of a money market fund share is set at $1. When you redeem your money market fund, therefore, you receive back your original investment plus dividends. In contrast, owners of other mutual funds may receive more or less than their original investment because the shares can change in value.

Money market mutual funds are demand accounts—money can be withdrawn at any time. They typically earn more than savings or money market deposit accounts. These characteristics make them an attractive alternative. Most of them, however, do not have government insurance against loss.

Using Your Resources Wisely

1 Compare the differences of traditional savings accounts, money market deposit accounts, and money market mutual funds.

2 How important are location and safety in choosing a financial business for saving money?

3 What type of account would you choose for your scholarship check?

Understanding Key Concepts

- Financial services can keep your funds safe, let you earn money on your money, make paying bills easier, and help you keep accurate financial records.
- Financial institutions make a profit providing services to customers.
- Comparison shopping is as important in choosing financial services as in buying other products and services.
- Checking, savings, and investment accounts vary; select those that will help you meet your financial goals.
- ATMs and debit cards are convenient electronic ways to access checking accounts, but require careful use and accurate recordkeeping.
- Savings are generally short term and involve loaning money; investments are longer term and usually mean buying assets.
- Using mutual funds as a way to own stocks and bonds provides professional stock selection, management, and diversification.
- When selecting financial services, evaluate convenience, cost, risk, return, and safety before making your choices.

Checking Your Knowledge

1. Explain why the customers of banks, credit unions, and savings and loans will get their money back if the businesses fail.
2. Why is it important to know the cost of the financial services you use?
3. What are the similarities and differences in demand and time accounts?
4. What are the advantages of a NOW or money market deposit account? What are the advantages of a regular checking account?
5. Why are debit cards more risky to use than checks?
6. Explain why accurate recordkeeping is important with a checking account. Why is this especially true for electronic transactions?
7. What types of accounts are most suitable for short-term or emergency fund savings? Why?
8. Explain the effect inflation has on savings. Does it have the same effect on investments? Explain your answer.
9. Why are mutual funds recommended for those just beginning a stock investment program?
10. Describe the possible consequences of redeeming a bond before it matures.

Making TRANSITIONS

Moving and Financial Services

Young adults tend to move frequently. They may move to a college dorm, into an apartment, then home again. Each of these moves can impact the financial services they need and use.

Assume that you are going to attend college in a town about 200 miles away from your home. You currently have a checking account and a passbook savings account at a local bank. The bank doesn't do business in your college town. Make a plan that lists the financial services you'll need while you're living at college, how you'll select the businesses to provide them, and what you anticipate they'll cost.

STRENGTHENING *Life* SKILLS

Evaluating Risks

Taking risks is a part of everyday life. You take risks every time you get into a car—but you can reduce that risk if you wear a seatbelt. With a partner, discuss five risks you might face as a student and suggest at least one way to reduce each risk. Next, identify five risks you might face when you use financial services. Suggest and discuss at least one way to reduce each risk.

Write a paragraph summarizing your conclusions and answering the following questions:

- What financial risks are you willing to take? Not willing to take?

- Do you have the same attitude about financial risks as about other kinds of risk taking? Why or why not?
- How can you evaluate when a potential financial risk is worth taking to try to gain a larger reward?

Applying Thinking Skills

1. **Recognizing assumptions.** A humorous quotation says "Among the books with unhappy endings are checkbooks." If this statement is true, what assumption must be made? Explain your answer.

2. **Drawing conclusions.** Consider the following: Two friends are going shopping. One says he doesn't know how much money is in his checking account, so he needs to call the bank so he'll know how much he can spend. The other laughs and tells him this won't do any good—the bank doesn't know how much money he really has. Who is right? Explain your answer.

3. **Comparing and contrasting.** Compare and contrast the characteristics of a passbook savings account, a CD, and a bond.

4. **Predicting consequences.** What consequences might occur if an investor used all of his or her savings to buy stock in a company that has developed a new drug it says will cure cancer.

Practical Applications

1. **Intergenerational survey.** Talk to a teen, a young adult, a middle-aged adult, and an older adult to find out what financial services each uses. Compare your results with those of your classmates. Which age used the fewest services? The most? Explain why the need for and use of financial services varies over time.

2. **Investigating fees.** Find out the amount, if any, that is typically charged in your community for: ATM fees, overdrawn account fees, money order fees, debit card fees, duplicate statement fees, per check fees, and balance inquiry fees. Why is it important to be aware of these fees?

3. **Tracking stock prices.** Select a local company and track the price of its stock for two weeks. Make a bar graph showing the stock price each day.

CHAPTER 23

Understanding Credit

What You Will Learn...

- Opportunities and problems that exist in using credit.
- How to identify and compare various forms of credit.
- The role credit will play in helping you reach your financial goals.

Terms for Success

collateral
credit bureau
credit report
garnishment
grace period

"**Y**ou're the math major. Tell me what I'm doing wrong!"

Olivia raised her eyes from her magazine and picked up the sheets of paper and calculator that had just landed beside her on the bed. "What's this?"

"My credit card statements for the last three months." Jill, her roommate, sounded agitated. "I've been paying $40 each month, but that's not what they take off my bill. Look, I owed $190, then I paid $40, but the next statement says I still owe $165. I may be new to using credit cards, but I've been subtracting since second grade. Even at 15 percent interest, that's not right."

Olivia scanned the rows of figures. Holding back a smile, she asked, "How long have you been multiplying fractions?"

"What?"

"You forgot to compound the interest." Olivia handed back the statements. "They're charging you 15 percent interest on the balance plus the interest that's been building up. It's like a savings account, only in reverse."

Jill stared at the papers in dismay. "I'm paying interest on my interest! No wonder people get into trouble with these things. You can pay off a big chunk of your bills, but as long as there's a balance, you're building up your debt without buying anything else."

"Well, I'm paying off this whole thing now, even if I have to empty my checking account. Then I'm cutting up my credit cards."

Olivia smiled. "No, you aren't. You just need to be a little careful. Credit cards can be really useful. Like last month, I saw this beautiful glass unicorn that I knew a friend would love for her birthday, but I didn't have enough cash on hand. Fortunately, I had my credit card."

Jill grinned at the glass figurine sitting on her dresser. "I hope I get out of this mess before your birthday," she remarked. "Otherwise, your present may be delayed a few months."

? **What factors do you think influence the misuse of credit? How can credit cards help meet financial goals?**

The Seduction of Credit

Jill *thought* that she understood how her credit cards worked. Credit seems simple on the surface, but it can be complicated.

Using credit may seem like the most natural thing in the world to you. You may be convinced that you can have whatever you want—whether or not you have the cash to buy it. Consumers are seduced into using credit because it's available, easy to use, and provides instant gratification.

In every way possible, businesses present credit use as an alluring way to get what you want immediately. You may receive pre-approved credit card applications in the mail. Eye-catching advertising says "No one turned down." Credit is so widespread in today's society that its use seems normal and desirable.

Credit is actually rented money. You rent a certain amount of money (*the principal*) for a certain length of time (*the term*) by paying a rental fee (*interest or finance charges*). Renting funds to others is very big business. Huge amounts of money are spent on advertising to convince consumers that they have a right to what they want now—and that credit is the best way to get it.

Credit, in reality, is a tool for reaching your financial goals. Just as you wouldn't use a hammer to paint a wall, credit shouldn't be used in every financial situation. Tools are most effective when they're used on a job for which they were designed. The same is true of various types of credit.

Credit—A Way to Make Life Better

There's no doubt that there are many advantages to using credit. It allows you to make immediate purchases. Many people couldn't afford large items, such as homes,

Refresh your Memory

Here are some helpful terms to remember about credit:

- **principal:** The amount of money borrowed.
- **interest rate:** The percentage of the principal that is the annual fee for borrowing.
- **term:** The length of time that money is borrowed.
- **simple interest:** Interest calculated on principal only. Figured with the formula: principal x interest rate x time (in years) = interest owed.
- **compound interest:** Interest calculated on a total that includes principal plus interest owed.
- **finance charges:** The costs for borrowing money. Sometimes refers only to interest but usually includes interest plus other fees.

cars, appliances, or furniture if they had to pay the cost in cash. "I rode the bus to work for about a year," says Muhammad. "It took more than an hour to get there, and I had to transfer three times. When I had saved enough money for a down payment, I was able to finance a car. The trip to work is an easy 20 minutes now."

Credit is convenient to use. If you use credit cards, you don't have to carry cash and you can pay for many purchases with one monthly check. You have funds available in emergencies, whether for purchases or cash advances.

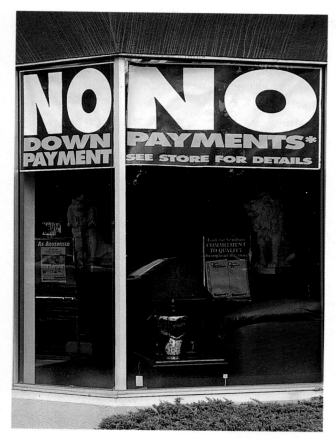

• Advertising by lenders makes credit use seem simple and easy.

Credit cards allow you to order tickets or make reservations over the telephone. You may not be able to rent a car without a credit card. Using a credit card is one way to establish a record of your credit use.

Credit—A Way to Make Life Miserable

With the advantages of using credit and the barrage of media encouraging credit use, why would anyone not want to use credit? There are several very good reasons.

Items bought on credit cost more than those purchased for cash. The rental fees you pay for the money you borrow increase the cost of every purchase you make. What seems like a bargain in the store may not be when you pay the bill. Hal says, "I used my credit card to buy a new guitar when it was on sale. It took a couple of months to pay for it, so I had to pay interest. I figured out later that by adding the interest to the price, I didn't save any money even though the guitar had been on sale."

Credit is easy to use on impulse, and makes impulse purchases easy. Credit, like other items, is better purchased after thoughtful decision making. Like most impulse purchases, impulsive credit use may be a mistake. You aren't likely to get the most for your money when you use credit on impulse.

One of the main drawbacks of credit is the potential for overuse. While you might enjoy a serving of cake and ice cream for dessert, you'd probably be miserable if you'd eat an entire cake and a half-gallon of ice cream. In the same way, sensibly used credit brings pleasure and enjoyment. Overindulging in credit use can bring pain and misery.

Credit Problems

Purchases made on credit have to be paid for sometime. If you have charged too much, you may not be able to make your payments when they come due. The consequences of not being able to pay your bills are severe, unpleasant, and costly.

The simple fact is, if you borrow money that you cannot repay, you have stolen that money. There will be legal consequences, just as though merchandise was stolen.

Some of the consequences of failure to pay include:

- A bad credit report that makes it impossible to obtain more credit. A credit report is a record of your performance in paying bills.

- Your wages may be subjected to **garnishment**, a legal procedure in which your employer is required to withhold part of your wages. The withheld money is sent to the court for payment to your creditors.

- Lenders will take back and resell collateral. **Collateral** is property you pledge in exchange for borrowed money. It is also called "security."

- You could be sued and face large legal fees.

• Most individuals and families can not afford big purchases like a house (or car) without using credit.

Any time you use credit, you should have in mind how you are going to pay the bill. Failure to plan for repayment has serious consequences.

Can You Get Credit?

Businesses loan money to people based on four general factors, sometimes known as the four Cs. These are:

- **Character.** This relates to your ability and willingness to pay back the borrowed money. Are you a responsible person who'll live up to your obligations when you borrow money?

- **Capacity.** This is your ability to pay back borrowed money. Guidelines for debt say that your debt repayments (excluding housing) shouldn't be more than 15 percent of after-tax income. For example, Nikki's take-home pay is about $1,000 a month. To fall within the guidelines, her car and furniture loan payments and credit card bills should be no more than $150 a month.

- **Collateral.** The more collateral you have to offer a lender, the more likely you are to be offered credit. If you don't repay the borrowed money, the lender can take the collateral. For example, when Dana didn't make the payments on her CD player, it was repossessed.

- **Credit report.** A **credit report** is a list of your credit use and repayment history. When you are between 18 and 25 years old, you will set the pattern for your credit report for years to come.

• Sticking to your budget and planning expenditures can help you avoid a financial crisis.

How a prospective lender assesses you on the four Cs will affect whether you get credit. Jonathan, who had no credit report, got credit on his character and capacity to repay a loan. A loan may be made to someone with no or poor credit record if enough collateral is offered. Chelsea's parents provided a certificate of deposit as collateral for her car loan. A good credit report may mean that no collateral will be required.

• Employers who receive a garnishment order from the court must withhold money from employees' pay checks.

Credit Reporting Services

Collecting and distributing information about people's credit histories is a billion dollar business. A company that does this work is called a **credit bureau**. Several national credit bureaus may have local offices in your community. Many areas also have local credit bureaus.

- **Information only.** Credit bureaus do not make decisions on whether or not people can get credit. Instead, they provide information on prior credit use and repayment histories. They have information on who has issued you credit, your repayment history, and whether you have been subject to legal actions involving credit. They do not collect information on your checking, savings, or investment accounts.

- **Credit rating.** The actual business that loans the money uses the information supplied by the credit bureau to decide whether to extend credit to an individual.

A credit score or a credit rating is prepared from your credit report. A computer using a specific formula often does these. Because credit is widely used and such an important part of daily life, a good credit report is very important.

- **Availability.** Your credit report is available to many businesses for use in deciding whether to extend credit to you. The report can be used not only to determine whether you can get a credit card or a loan, but it may also be used by landlords, telephone or insurance companies, utilities, or prospective employers. Because Mike's credit rating was poor, he had to put down a large security deposit to get a telephone in his new apartment.

- **Access.** You have a legal right to know what's in your credit report. You must send a written request for your history to the credit bureau, enclosing a payment if it's required. You will need to provide your social security number, present and past addresses, date of birth, and other names you've used.

- **Clarity.** Credit reports can be puzzling to read. If you don't understand your report, find someone to help you. It's important that you understand the information about you that's being distributed.
- **Accuracy.** You can challenge any inaccurate information in your report. Federal laws force the credit bureaus to look into your challenge, but the bureaus aren't required to change a report on your say-so. You, however, have the right to include a 100-word statement in your record to give your side of the issue.

Types of Credit

The three main types of credit in today's economy are credit cards, loans, and charge accounts. While all involve borrowed money, each type of credit has unique characteristics.

Credit Cards

Credit cards generally are one of three types. The differences among them are based on who issues the cards. They are all used in the same way, although not all merchants accept all cards.

- **Bankcards.** These are issued by various financial institutions and processed through the VISA®, Mastercard®, or Novus® (Discover) networks. A special bankcard for people with poor or no credit history is called a "secured card." Money in the amount of the credit card limit is kept on deposit as collateral. If the customer does not pay the credit card bill, the bank cancels the card and keeps the collateral.
- **Travel and entertainment cards.** Companies such as American Express® or Diner's Club® issue these cards.
- **Single company cards.** These cards are issued by—and can be used only at—one business, such as one brand of gasoline retailer, one department store, one telephone company, or one catalog.

Many credit cards can be used to gain cash advances. Depending on the card, cash advances may be obtained from an ATM or with special checks.

• Credit reporting agencies can give you a report on your credit status over the Internet with encrypted messages.

Guilty Until Proven Innocent

Credit reports frequently contain inaccurate information, sometimes enough to affect whether credit is granted. You want your credit report to accurately reflect your credit history.

Your record may simply be incomplete. Problems that are more serious can occur, however. Human error in the millions of data entries made by credit bureaus may affect your report. Another person's bad history can get into your file. Your on-time payments may be credited to someone else. Recently, reports of *identity theft* have increased. This involves someone stealing your credit record, charging merchandise, not paying, and leaving you with a disastrous credit report.

If the credit bureau has made an error in your report, it's up to you to see that it gets corrected. In other words, you are guilty until you prove yourself innocent. Correcting your records is often not as easy as it sounds.

If you think there may be a problem, contact the credit bureau immediately. Find out the best way to proceed. Follow up your phone call with a letter addressed specifically to the person to whom you talked. Keep a copy of your letter. Send copies (not the originals) of bills and receipts to support your claims.

You may have to be assertive and persistent to get the matter resolved. Credit bureaus earn their money from moneylenders, not credit users. Correcting individual records may not be a high priority.

Request a copy of your report again a month or two after a problem has supposedly been fixed. This will assure you that the credit record being distributed is accurate.

Voicing Your Opinion

1. *Should credit bureaus be required to correct errors in their reports? If so, how might this be accomplished? What proof of error should be required?*

2. *Is it a violation of privacy for credit bureaus to get and keep so much detailed personal information about consumers? Why or why not?*

Credit cards are advertised nationally, but are also available through local financial service businesses. If you don't have a solid credit record, you may find it easier to get approval for a local credit card. On the other hand, locally issued cards may not compare well in terms of costs and credit conditions.

Andrew explains how he got his first card "I got a credit card when I was in high school, because people at the bank knew my family. The interest rate was high, so later when I had a good payment record, I got a card with a lower rate from a national bank."

Each month you'll get a statement from the credit card company. It'll list your payments and credits and your charges and interest. A minimum payment amount will be indicated. It's important to check every statement when you receive it. You need to compare it to the receipts you have saved and make sure that all the charges are legitimate. If there's an error on your bill, you must follow specific procedures. These are described in the information you received when you got your card.

If you lose a credit card, report the loss to the company right away. This will limit your financial losses if someone else uses your card. Keep a copy of your card numbers and the issuers' toll-free telephone numbers in a safe place, so you'll have them if you need them.

• The availability of credit cards is one more factor in promoting the widespread use of credit.

Loans

Loans can be used for a variety of purposes. Most people borrow money for large purchases, such as a home or car. Personal loans can be used to buy furniture or pay for a vacation. Educational or student loans are for college costs.

Although the costs and conditions of loans vary, the basics are the same. You borrow a lump sum for a specific length of time, and you pay interest on the money you have borrowed until the loan has been repaid.

Loans often require collateral or security. If you have financed a home, car, and refrigerator, the items are probably collateral for your loan. If you don't pay, the lender becomes the owner of the property. If you have an unsecured loan, no collateral is required—just your promise to repay.

Loans can be provided from a variety of sources. Generally, credit unions and banks provide the lowest cost loans. Loan or sales financing companies tend to have the highest costs.

In considering a loan, you will want to make the amount of the loan as small as possible and the term as short as possible. This will minimize the interest you have to pay. The lower your monthly payments and the longer the payback time, the more interest you will pay.

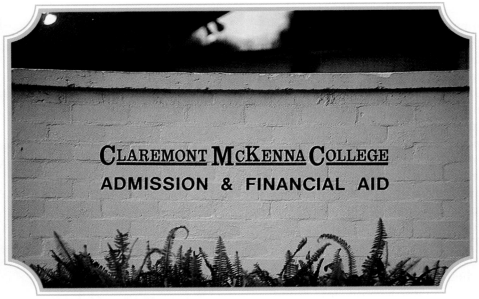

• Student or educational loans are often arranged through the college financial aid office.

Charge Accounts

Individual stores or businesses may have charge accounts available. These firms will extend you credit for merchandise from their businesses. Charge accounts are not as common as they once were. Rather than offering charge accounts, many department stores offer their own credit cards.

While stores may offer credit for purchases, frequently they do not operate their own charge accounts. Instead, their credit business is handled by an outside finance company. Brad says, "I bought a new bed on credit at a mattress store. I thought I'd be making payments to the mattress store, but instead I make them to a finance company."

Layaway accounts are a type of charge account. You make a down payment, and the store holds the merchandise for you. After making regular payments to complete the purchase, you receive the merchandise. If you do not complete the payments, the store keeps the merchandise and, typically, the payments you have made.

Comparing Credit

Buying credit is just like any other consumer purchase. You need to comparison shop, compare costs, and compare products.

Costs

When you understand the costs of credit, you can make better choices about its use. Moneylenders make their profit in two general ways: through interest payments and through fees.

Types of Costs

Credit card issuers make money when you pay interest or finance charges on your balance. There also may be fees for late payments, exceeding your credit limit, or replacement cards. Some cards have an annual fee or a membership fee. In addition, every time you use a credit card, the store where you bought merchandise pays a percentage of your total purchase to the credit card issuer. All of these payments and fees are part of the cost of using credit cards.

When a loan is made, there are often fees in addition to the interest charged on the loan. Examples include origination fees, application fees, credit search fees, attorney's fees, and late fees. Fees and interest rates are often higher on loans with no collateral.

Loans can have one interest rate for the term of the loan. This is called a *fixed rate*. An *adjustable rate* means the interest rate may change, usually every six months or year. Fixed rates usually begin higher than adjustable rates. Over the term of the loan, adjustable rates may increase to become more than the fixed rate. "I took a fixed rate loan for my truck," says Madison. "I like the thought of my payments going down, but not up! This way I know exactly how much I have to pay each month until my truck is paid for."

In a similar fashion, charge accounts also have interest and may have fees. The cost of a charge account varies by the type of account and who issues the credit.

Given a choice, lenders would prefer that customers get their credit through credit cards. In most cases, credit card debt earns the lender more interest than loans or charge accounts.

Interest Rates

Interest rates can be calculated in a variety of ways. Federal laws require businesses to calculate an Annual Percentage Rate (APR) in a standard way. This allows you to compare rates from one business to another.

The APR is critical information in understanding credit. When there are other fees involved, however, the APR is not actually the true cost of the credit. A lower APR may mean the lender charges more or higher fees.

With credit cards, there is another factor for you to consider in looking at interest rates. Although two cards may advertise the same APR, the amount of interest you pay may be significantly different because of the way your balance is calculated. Be sure you understand when interest will be charged on your purchases.

• Purchases made on layaway involve making regular payments for merchandise that the store holds for you.

Conditions of Credit

In addition to the costs of using credit, it is important to compare the conditions of the credit. Conditions are the restrictions and procedures that govern the credit. They're spelled out in the truth-in-lending statement the lender is required to provide. Be sure to read and understand this statement. If you don't understand the terms of your credit, you can lose your money as well as the merchandise you have purchased on credit.

It is also important to know whether the conditions of your credit can change. Credit card agreements usually allow the credit card company to change the conditions on short notice. This may mean your interest rate could be changed, your credit limit lowered, or fees added. The conditions for loans usually are more constant, but can be changed under certain circumstances. Be sure you understand when and how changes can occur.

Maintaining Good Credit

TIPS

Try these tips for maintaining good credit:

- Read it all! Understand every word of the information you have before you sign a credit application or other credit document.
- Pay every time and on time.
- Guard your cards. Even if you don't lose credit or debit cards, someone else can use your account numbers. These fraudulent uses will affect your credit record.
- Check your credit report. Take steps to correct any errors.

• Reading and understanding the information provided by a lender is important so that you understand what your obligations are.

Every type of credit and every lender has different conditions. For example, bank credit cards and travel and entertainment cards usually have different conditions regarding fees and repayment. Your skill in understanding the requirements of the credit and asking questions when you don't understand are important. Only then can you accurately assess whether the costs of the credit are worth the opportunities it brings.

Repayment Plans

Credit can be repaid in installments, in one lump sum, or through a revolving credit plan. Each of these three repayment plans has different kinds of conditions.

- **Installment payments.** Regularly scheduled payments are made until the credit is repaid. Payments usually include interest as well as repayment of principal. This is how a home mortgage is repaid. In the beginning, most of the payments go to interest costs. The proportion changes over the life of the loan until the payments at the end are mostly principal.

- **Lump sum payment.** If repayment is to be made in one lump sum, interest payments may be required before the principal is repaid. Lump sum repayments usually are more common with business loans than with consumer credit.

- **Revolving credit plans.** Revolving credit is the same as open-ended credit. You make monthly payments, but you don't have to pay the entire amount. There's no plan or time limit for repaying your total balance. You are free to charge again up to your credit limit. Of course, interest is charged on the unpaid balance. Bank credit cards and charge accounts are usually revolving credit plans. There's lots of flexibility and potential for abuse in revolving credit. People pay a minimal amount, but the total they owe increases even with no further charges, because the interest is compounding.

• The credit reporting agencies in your community will be listed in the telephone yellow pages.

- Lenders have "sales" on credit to encourage consumers to borrow money. What should you think about *before* taking advantage of such sales?

Missing a Payment

Another important condition to check is what happens if you miss a payment. The minimum penalty is usually a late fee. With some revolving credit accounts, however, a missed payment may mean that the entire balance is due. If you don't pay, all the merchandise you have charged will be taken back. Matt says, "I was making payments to a finance company for a computer, a VCR, and a CD player. I missed a payment for the computer and the total for all three things was due right then. I couldn't possibly pay that much. I only had one payment left on my VCR, but it didn't matter. They took that back, too."

Grace Periods

When comparing credit cards, look at how interest is charged. Does the company assess interest from the day the merchandise is charged or is there a grace period? A **grace period** is a period of time when interest is not charged if the balance is paid in full by the end of the time. Some credit cards have a 25-day grace period. Credit card cash advances usually have no grace period. In addition, getting a cash advance may start interest expense on any charges you've made that month. Check your card's policy statement to find out the specifics.

Advertised Specials

You will often see credit "sales," because credit is such a competitive business. These are designed to encourage you to use credit just as a clothes sale encourages you to buy new jeans or shoes. As with any other sales item, you must analyze and use your consumer skills to see if the advertised credit sale really is a good deal for you.

Low interest rates are advertised to appeal to bargain hunters. Sale rates are attractive, but it's the rate over the life of the credit that's important. Bethany says, "I got a credit card with a rate of 6 percent for six months. I transferred a $300 student loan to the credit card, since I was paying 10 percent on the loan. I ended up charging too much, so now I'm paying 18 percent on my student loan as well as on what I charged."

If a company advertises "No payments until next year" or "90 days same as cash" you need to know the conditions of the credit. When is interest being charged? How much will putting off paying until next year cost you? Melody says, "I got a "90-day same as cash" deal on a refrigerator for my apartment. I thought that meant that no interest was charged for those 90 days. I was lucky—my friend told me that it meant no interest is charged if you pay within those 90 days. Once that 91st day arrives, you pay interest on the whole time."

Credit card companies may advertise "skip a payment" plans. Before you accept their offer, find out how this will affect the interest that you pay. You may be allowed to skip your payment, but that may mean interest is charged from the date that every purchase was made.

Managing Without Credit

Here are some tips for getting by without using credit:

TIPS

- Pay cash or go without.
- Be smart—use prepaid (smart) cards where available.
- Save, save, save. Pay yourself first, then use your savings instead of credit.
- Have no interest. Calculate the interest "saved" when you pay cash. Reward yourself when you've "saved" a specific amount of money.
- Look into the future. In a week, will you still want what you are thinking of charging today?

FOCUS ON ...
Help for Credit Problems

One of the challenges in using credit is to avoid credit problems or to solve small problems before they become large ones. If you begin to have a credit problem, you should consider getting help before the problem gets overwhelming. The faster you tackle the problem, the easier and more quickly it can be solved.

The *National Foundation for Consumer Credit* is a nonprofit organization that helps clients work out ways to manage debts. Credit counselors may be available through non-profit or government agencies, such as the Cooperative Extension Service, or a financial service business, such as a bank. Look for a counselor who can be impartial and objective.

Be alert to the possibility that someone may want to solve your credit problems by selling you more credit. In many cases, refinancing or consolidating debt is a good solution to a problem. It may be, however, that the "solution" you are learning about is just another sales pitch. You need to evaluate the options presented to you and decide whether or not you will accept the advice.

The more you know about credit, the fewer credit problems you are likely to have. Information about credit is available in books, magazines, pamphlets, and on the Internet. Most financial service businesses and lenders have informational materials that can help you learn about credit. They may have customer services representatives who will talk with you about credit options. Taking advantage of the services and information available can help you prevent or solve credit problems.

Using Credit Wisely

In using credit wisely, it's important to think about your financial goals and whether credit is the right tool for the current situation. Each time you consider using credit, ask yourself these questions:

- Is the reason I'm borrowing money important enough to go into debt?
- What source of credit is best for me?
- Is the interest rate on the credit as low as possible for this purpose?
- Are there conditions to this debt that could cause problems later?

When you make the choice to use credit, be sure you're aware of the consequences of your decision. You have legal obligations when you accept credit. Can you meet these obligations?

One of the most important actions you can take in using credit wisely is to know your limits. Your personal financial and credit limits are based on your values and goals, spending patterns, income, earning power, and financial self-discipline. It's only when you take into account your personal approach to money and credit that you can use it most wisely.

You weren't born knowing how to use credit wisely. You can learn, however, by trial and error and from others. Your knowledge of credit is a powerful tool to help you reach your financial goals.

- Debt counselors advise that the best way to reduce credit temptation is to get rid of your credit cards. **Do you agree or disagree with this advice?**

R E A S O N

Through Life's Problems

Note the Results of Actions Taken

An important step of the problem-solving process is to evaluate the result of your decision. In the scenario below, Jake notes the results of his first experience with a major credit purchase.

His arms full of groceries, Jake could barely get the door of his apartment unlocked. He struggled to get the bags untwisted off his arms and onto his new kitchen table.

"Boy, it sure is nice to have a table in here now," he thought as he started to unpack the groceries and put them away. Jake had really worried about whether or not to start buying some new furniture. He was tired of getting along with family members' castoffs or doing without. He grinned as he thought about using the sofa cushions as floor pillows after the frame had broken beyond repair. His friends sometimes teased him about his eclectic furnishings, but he was determined not to get himself into the same kind of trouble with credit that his sister had. Sure, Suzy had a beautifully furnished apartment for a while, until the store repossessed all her luxurious leather furniture for lack of payment. It

was going to be a long time before any store would approve her for a credit purchase again.

"What if everyone went bad on their creditors like she did," Jake pondered. "It's no wonder the furniture store was so careful to check out my credit history. I'm glad I've had that gasoline credit card for a while, and paid it off each month when it was due."

Unlike his sister, Jake had carefully planned a budget and knew how much he could afford to spend on a monthly payment for furniture. He was still hesitant to buy on credit, but he wanted to establish a good credit history so that he could buy a house someday.

Jake had shopped carefully for almost two months before he had found the deal he was convinced was the best: no interest, no payments for a year. Although he was tempted to spend that money on something else, he knew he had the self-

discipline to make his 12 payments and avoid paying any interest. If he didn't have the whole principal paid off in 12 months, he would have to pay interest figured on each of these months. He was determined to avoid paying that interest!

"I'm really glad to have a few pieces of some quality furniture that will last for years. I think it was time to class up my place. I've got some money in savings, and I can keep it there since I'm buying this furniture over time. It's not costing me any more, as long as I pay it off in one year."

Stretching out in his new recliner, Jake smiled contentedly to himself. "It makes me feel good to know I'm handling my finances responsibly, and that I will be able to get more credit when I need it. Not to mention how good it feels not to be sitting on the floor anymore!"

▶From Your Perspective

1 What could change Jake's ability to make his payments on time? Do you think he has considered this?

2 Have you shown self-discipline in managing your finances? Give an example.

Understanding Key Concepts

● Credit is a tool that, if used wisely, can help you reach your financial goals.

● Credit is seductive because it is widely available, easy to use, and offers instant gratification.

● Credit involves paying a fee to use someone else's money for a period.

● Using credit costs more than paying with cash, contributes to impulse buying, and can lead to financial problems.

● Lenders use character, capacity to repay, collateral, and credit reports to decide whether to lend money to a consumer.

● Credit cards, loans, and charge accounts are the three main types of consumer credit available.

● It is important to compare costs and conditions when evaluating credit so that you can find the best option for your situation.

Checking Your Knowledge

1. Explain why the use of credit is seen as normal and desirable in today's society.

2. Identify two advantages and two disadvantages of using credit.

3. Identify at least three consequences of misusing credit.

4. Summarize the four Cs used in determining whether or not to loan money.

5. Explain the role credit bureaus play in the credit business.

6. Why is it important to understand the information in your credit report?

7. List the three major types of credit cards and explain the differences among them.

8. What determines whether collateral is needed for a loan?

9. What are the two main ways lenders make money from loaning money?

10. Explain a fixed interest rate and an adjustable interest rate. How are they similar? Different?

Making TRANSITIONS

Comparing Credit

Imagine that you need to borrow $2,000 to pay for tuition for your final semester at the community college. You expect to be able to repay the money within a year after graduation. You can get a student loan at 10 percent interest through financial aid that accrues no interest until you graduate. Your grandmother has offered to let you put the tuition on her credit card. She says you must be responsible for all payments and interest, which is 18 percent You have an account at the college credit union, which will loan you the money at 7 percent interest to begin compounding immediately.

• What are the advantages and disadvantages of each option?
• Which would you choose? Why?

STRENGTHENING *Life* SKILLS

Applying for Credit

To apply for credit, various personal and financial information is needed. You will be asked for your employment and banking history. Depending on the type of credit involved and the lender, you may be asked to provide your W-2 forms, federal income tax returns, current paycheck stubs, account numbers for credit cards, and bank statements. The larger the loan, the more information a lender may require.

Prepare a packet of personal financial information that you could use in applying for credit. Consider how you could document your ability to fulfill the four Cs of borrowing. When you have finished collecting the information, answer the following questions:

- When applying for credit, what would be the advantages of finding out what is needed and organizing your materials in advance?
- Do you think a lender would evaluate your information favorably and lend you money? Explain your answer.
- What could you do to strengthen your qualifications for credit?

Applying Thinking Skills

1. **Predicting consequences.** Imagine that you have decided to apply for a loan to buy a television. You comparison shop for the loan at your credit union, a finance company, and the store where you will buy the TV. You decide to take the loan that offers the smallest monthly repayment. What impact could this choice have on the total cost of the television? The length of time you have to pay?

2. **Drawing conclusions.** Which credit card would be better for a consumer—one that has a 15 percent interest rate with a 25-day grace period or one that has no grace period but offers a 10 percent interest rate? What information about the consumer do you need to answer this question? Which credit card would you choose? Why?

3. **Identifying factors.** What factors should a consumer consider before taking advantage of a credit "sale"? Why is each factor important in making a decision?

Practical Applications

1. **Get a credit report.** Find out what information and fees are required to get a copy of your credit report from a credit reporting service. Write a letter requesting your credit report. If appropriate, send your letter and any necessary fee.

2. **Analyzing credit advertisements.** Find at least one advertisement for credit. Show the ad to your classmates, identifying the type of credit offered, whether the credit is "on sale" or not, what the cost and conditions of the advertised credit are, and why the ad makes using credit appealing.

3. **Credit planning.** Make a list of the major items and services you expect to want or need over the next three to five years. Place a C beside each item on the list that you think you will need to use credit to purchase. What type of credit could be used to pay for each? What can you do now to make sure that you will have access to credit in the future?

Unit 6
Shaping Your Career

Chapters ▽

CHAPTER 24

Looking Ahead

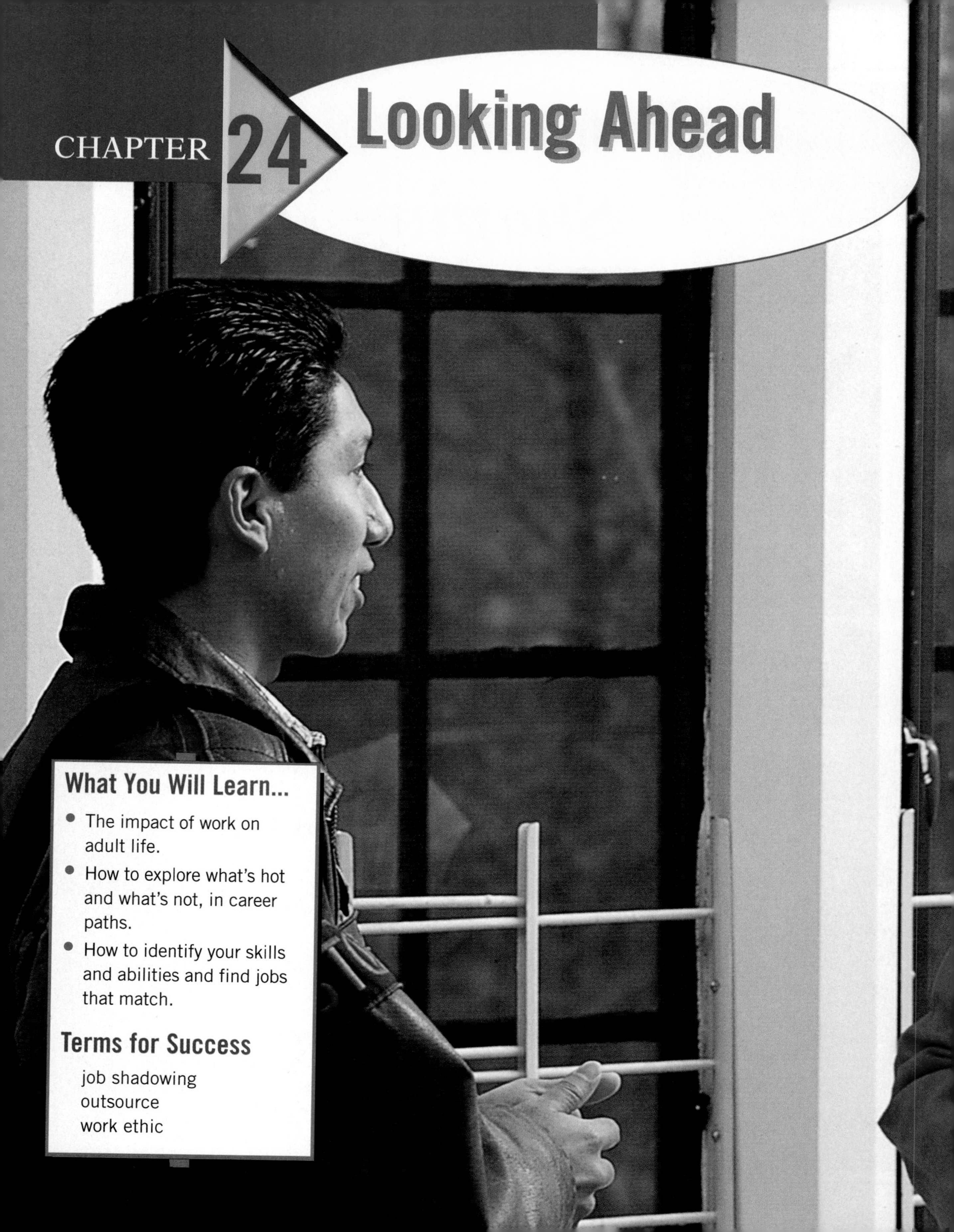

What You Will Learn...

- The impact of work on adult life.
- How to explore what's hot and what's not, in career paths.
- How to identify your skills and abilities and find jobs that match.

Terms for Success

job shadowing
outsource
work ethic

Breathless, Vin dashed into the chemistry lab, "Sorry I'm late, Mrs. Baker," he told his instructor. "I was helping Mr. Eads plant marigolds around the flagpole."

Mrs. Baker sighed patiently. "I'm glad to give you extra help, Vin, but try to be on time."

"Sorry," Vin repeated. "I guess I have more fun in a garden than I do in chem lab."

Mrs. Baker smiled in surprise. "You like to garden? A garden *is* a chemistry lab."

Now Vin looked surprised. "It is?"

"Sure," Mrs. Baker replied. "Making food from sunlight, drawing nutrients from soil—these are chemical processes."

"I guess so," Vin agreed. "I know that plant sprays have chemicals, but I never thought about a chemist in a lab actually making them. I always thought of gardening as 'low-tech.'"

"Not at all," Mrs. Baker said. "Those marigolds you planted? Scientists probably developed them. Have you been to Neptune's, that giant nursery west of town? They use a CAD program—computer-assisted design—to help customers plan their landscaping. Of course, farmers need every advantage modern technology can give."

Vin looked impressed. "I've always wanted to work with growing plants, but I figured it would be as a gardener or groundskeeper. I didn't know that there were so many jobs connected to gardening. How do you know so much about it?"

Mrs. Baker smiled. "I've planted a petunia or two. Speaking of which, let's get started. I have to get home to cover my roses. We might get a frost tonight."

"You know, they've made a frost-resistant strain of tomato," Vin said. "Maybe someday I'll help develop a frostproof strain of rose."

Mrs. Baker smiled. "For now, let's just get you through chemistry."

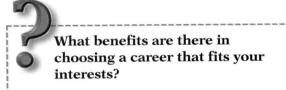

What benefits are there in choosing a career that fits your interests?

The Challenge of a Lifetime

Vin views digging in a garden more like fun than work. When he's unable to get his hands into the soil, he's reading about recent developments in plants. What subject fascinates you? What activity would you choose whether or not you were paid for it?

Those who anticipate going to work each day have chosen a career that matches their natural interests and abilities. One of your challenges as an adult is to find work that brings out your positive qualities and provides a comfortable living.

Choosing work for a lifetime may seem an overwhelming task. When you are making work decisions, however, keep in mind that you'll have chances to change your mind. The job choices you make at any point are rarely set in stone. You are less likely to want to change, however, if you make thoughtful decisions.

The Impact of Work

If you are like most other teens, your life revolves around school. You get up in the morning to be there when classes start. You generally work, play, and spend time with others when school isn't in session.

In the same way, work is the structure or framework that organizes the lives of most adults. The type of work you do will affect where you live, the hours you sleep, and the time and money you have for leisure activities. Earning minimum wage, Angie stocks shelves at a supermarket on the night shift. How does this job affect the structure of her life?

From a practical standpoint, work is important because it provides money for people's needs and wants. Without income from work, most people struggle financially.

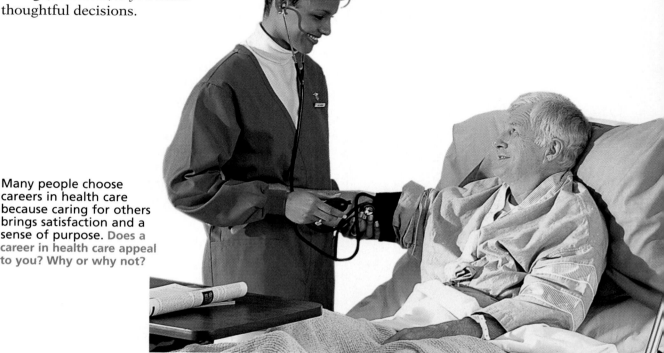

• Many people choose careers in health care because caring for others brings satisfaction and a sense of purpose. **Does a career in health care appeal to you? Why or why not?**

Refresh your Memory

Take note of these career related terms:

- **career:** A series of related jobs.
- **job:** Work people do for pay.
- **entrepreneur:** A person who creates and develops his or her own business.
- **work ethic:** Holding work as an important value in life.

Beyond the income you earn, there are psychological benefits of work:

- **Work provides opportunities for people to be with others.** Humans are social beings, needing contact with others to be happy.
- **Work brings feelings of accomplishment.** Doing a job well leads to fulfillment and satisfaction.
- **Work allows people to contribute to society.** Every job is important and inter-related to other jobs. One industry depends on another. Countries rely on their workers' productivity.

Because work is such a central part of adult life, your attitude toward it will influence your success. Your **work ethic** means your choices whether or not to work hard, do the job right, and give it your best. Someone who does just enough to get by and pick up a paycheck has a poor work ethic. An employee who brings commitment and dedication to the job has a good work ethic.

- Work and its demands create a structure for the lives of most adults. **How does work structure your life as a teen?**

• Typewriters have been replaced by computers in most offices as word processing technology has advanced and improved. **What other careers can you think of in which technology has played a major role?**

detour in his work life when he was in a serious car accident and couldn't work for more than a year. Whatever happens, on the job or on a trip, you'll have decisions and choices to make.

The average thirty-year-old American has already had seven jobs. Because the workplace is constantly changing, a job you choose today may not exist tomorrow. New jobs are created, primarily because of advances in technology. The job of Web master did not exist until the Internet evolved. You may have to make new choices about your career several times in your lifetime, primarily because the job market changes. Michaela's first job out of high school was keypunching computer cards. Today, she designs Internet websites for businesses—a job that didn't exist until a few years ago.

To cope with the changes you will face in your work life, you'll need to be flexible and willing to learn new skills. This will become easier if you have a good educational foundation. With a solid background in courses like math, science, English, and social studies, it will be easier for you to be flexible in making career choices.

Expect Choices and Changes

Think about the similarities between a trip and things that could happen in your work life. You might be driving on a dead-end road and have to turn around and retrace your path. In work, you may take a job that turns out to be wrong, or a dead end, for you. You may opt for work you enjoy rather than maximize the amount of money you make, just as you could choose to enjoy scenery over maximizing speed on a trip. There may be detours due to road construction. Zach had to take a

Decisions Make A Difference

Your goals and values are the foundation for your life. The amount and kind of resources you have to build on this foundation are usually directly related to the kind of work that you do. The decisions that you make about your work life will impact all aspects of your adulthood.

Personal Well-Being

The work you do will have a powerful effect on your health and well-being. Doing something that you enjoy and that brings you satisfaction promotes emotional health. You'll be more apt to maintain good physical health if you have safe working conditions and a manageable workload.

What job traits help workers feel good about themselves and their work? Research has found that:

- Satisfied workers have some autonomy and control over their work.
- Workers prefer to do a variety of tasks.
- Good relationships at work are related to job satisfaction.
- Workers seek recognition for their work. They expect someone to notice a good job and hard work.
- Most workers want to take more responsibility and earn more money.

When you think about spending up to 50 years of your life in the workforce, it makes sense to choose a work path that you'll enjoy. Make your choices based on work that will promote your occupational and personal well-being.

A Ripple Effect

Very few people can completely separate their work and nonwork lives. In choosing a job or career, think about how your choices will impact others who are important to you.

When you feel good about work, you'll usually have a feeling of well–being off the job. Your frame of mind affects your family members and friends. Sarah says, "My friend Tyler is in construction, but he hates it. I avoid being with him right after he gets off work, because he's a big grouch until he can unwind. I wouldn't want a job that affected me like that!"

- One fact of military life is that it involves living away from family and friends? From your perspective, what are the pros and cons of military life?

The location of your work affects your relationships. If you enlist in the military after you graduate, you're obviously going to be separated from your family and friends. When you form your own family, they will probably live wherever your job is. A job that requires traveling may mean you will be away from your family and friends for days or weeks at a time.

The amount of money you earn at work affects the kinds of activities you can afford with your friends and family. Your salary will affect what possessions you and your family can afford to buy.

What Are Your Options?

As you consider the possibilities, think about what options you have. How can you best take advantage of your opportunities? How can you discover what job or career areas will suit you and will provide the kind of adult life you want?

Just the Facts

Learning what career field or job is right for you requires the investigative skills of a detective. You probably can easily identify jobs and career areas found in your neighborhood. There are many more, however, with which you may not be familiar. How can you learn more about the various opportunities you have?

- The *Internet and World Wide Web* contain vast amounts of information about jobs. Using the computer, you can explore various facets of the world of work, specific jobs and careers, their locations, and the educational requirements. You can find lists of available jobs and apply for them on line. In the future, using the Internet may be the primary way people look for work.

• The results of the interest inventory will help this teen focus on career areas that are related to his/her interests and aptitudes. What are your interests and aptitudes?

- Your *school or community library* can be a source for learning about specific jobs. U.S. Department of Labor materials, business magazines, and audio- and videotapes about businesses are all valuable resources found in libraries.
- Contact *people* who work in areas in which you are interested and ask them to talk about their jobs. Holly talked with Mr. Wong, an engineer who worked for a manufacturing company. The interview helped her decide to major in chemical engineering at college.
- *Spending time on the job* with someone is called **job shadowing**. This will give you an idea of the types of activities and choices the worker faces.
- *Volunteer work* is another way to explore various possibilities. Review the section on service learning in Chapter 5. Whatever your interest, there is a group that could use your talents and skills.
- *Public and private job services or agencies* are available to help you find information about work. Experienced job counselors usually staff these agencies. There may be fees associated with their services.
- *Part-time work or work-based learning programs* promote understanding of specific jobs or businesses. They can help you identify career areas that you might or might not want. Keely wanted to be a pharmacist, so she got a part-time job in a drug store. She soon learned pharmacy was not for her.
- Your *school counseling office* is a first-line resource for information. Most have books or brochures about specific jobs, the job outlook, trends in employment, and other work-related topics.

Finding Your Niche

TIPS

Here are some tips to help find a career that's right for you:

- **Ride your "hobby" horse to a job.** What kinds of jobs are related to your hobbies and interests?
- **Pay your dues.** School and community clubs and organizations are a good way to meet people, learn about different career areas, and have a good time.
- **Explore the real world.** Find a business or organization that interests you. Apply for a job there. Research and observe to learn more.
- **Volunteer your services.** Who can resist an offer of help? You learn while you contribute!
- **Practice writing, speaking, thinking, and problem solving.** Work on knowledge and skills that could be used in many jobs or careers.
- **Don't panic!** You have time to choose and prepare. Sometimes the only advantage to an early decision about what you want to do is that you'll be among the first to see your mistake.

The more you learn now, the better prepared you'll be for the future. Your investigative skills can help you learn what you need to know so you can make informed choices.

• Computer repair and computer network management are two areas where job growth is expected to continue in the future. **Do you find computer work appealing? Why or why not?**

The Job Market Puzzle

The job market is huge, complex, and confusing. It's like a gigantic jigsaw puzzle. When you begin to put the pieces together, then the "picture" becomes clear.

The U.S. Department of Education has grouped jobs and careers into 15 clusters based on similar job characteristics. These clusters are shown on pages 446 to 447. In each cluster, jobs range from unskilled to skilled. There are many opportunities in each cluster, depending on your education, skills, and interests.

Think about which cluster appeals to you. If more than one cluster has appeal, you may be able to find a job that includes both. Susan was educated as a teacher, but now trains workers at a large company how to use the latest computer software.

In each career cluster, there are opportunities to work in various types of organizations.

There are large businesses with thousands of employees and small shops that may have only two or three workers. Would you prefer a for-profit business or would you like to work for a nonprofit group, such as a charity or religious group? Government work includes working at schools, libraries, parks, or prisons, as well as in city, county, state, or federal government.

Some people want to work for themselves. Entrepreneurs may work for others from their homes or start companies of their own. To be successful, an entrepreneur must choose a business needed in today's world.

The workplace today is global in scope. Although you may never work in another country, what happens there can impact your career. The job market worldwide is the frame of reference. Joyce worked for an appliance manufacturer. She lost her job when the company decided to build its appliances in Thailand.

It's a Trend

Just as trends and fashions in clothing constantly change, the workplace also continually evolves and changes. Therefore, it's important to look at job and career trends when you're making choices. What industries are growing? Which ones are declining? Observing trends in the jobs that are being created or cut will help you see the options that are most promising. Here are some trends of interest:

- **Growth in technology.** More and more tasks are being performed with computers or machines containing computerized parts. Methods of communication are changing and becoming faster. No matter what job or career you choose, you'll be involved in technology in some way. There are increasing opportunities for those who can install and repair technological equipment.

- **Demand for services.** The increased demand for services means there are likely to be service jobs available, including retail work. The drawback is that service jobs tend to be low paying.

- **Changing business methods.** The way companies do business is changing, as are their relationships with employees.

- **Growth in temporary or part-time workers.** When business picks up, companies are likely to use temporary or part-time workers. While these workers may earn as much per hour as permanent employees, they don't often receive benefits. Companies save money because benefits can be worth up to one-third of an employee's wages. In addition, it's easier to release these workers in the next business downturn.

• This teen enjoys working as a salesperson for a florist. **What careers related to sales would you consider?**

So...what will it be?

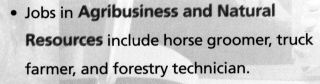

- Jobs in **Agribusiness and Natural Resources** include horse groomer, truck farmer, and forestry technician.
- Jobs in **Business and Office** include receptionist, bookkeeper, computer servicer, and claims examiner.
- Jobs in **Communications and Media** include cable television technician, book editor, computer artist, and technical writer.
- Jobs in **Construction** include electrician, roofer, surveyor, and building inspector.
- Jobs in **Family and Consumer Sciences** include child-care worker, floral designer, and jeweler.

- Jobs in **Environment** include hazardous waste management technician, sanitary engineer, and pollution-control technician.
- Jobs in **Fine Arts and Humanities** include actor, cartoonist, musician, and dancer.
- Jobs in **Health Care** include dental hygienist, nurse's aide, home health aide, and operating room technician.
- Jobs in **Hospitality and Recreation** include cruise director, fitness instructor, park ranger, baker, and pastry chef.
- Jobs in **Manufacturing** include tool maker, production supervisor, and industrial laser machine operator.
- Jobs in **Marine Science** include diver, marine engineer, and ocean technician.
- Jobs in **Marketing and Distribution** include insurance agent, auto sales worker, retail buyer, and real estate agent.

- Jobs in **Personal Service** include barber and hairstylist, cosmetologist, and bridal consultant.
- Jobs in **Public Service** include teacher, firefighter, paralegal aide, and member of armed services.
- Jobs in **Transportation** include airline pilot, automotive mechanic, and airline reservations agent.

ACTIVITY

Choose one or more career clusters that interest you. Investigate at least two careers for each cluster of your choice.

- **Increased outsourcing.** Many businesses **outsource,** that is, they pay other companies or individuals to do certain tasks, rather than hire employees of their own to do them. While this means fewer full-time employees, outsourcing creates jobs for entrepreneurs and other businesses.

- **New job creation.** At the same time that companies are laying off workers, there are also jobs being created. These jobs, however, are usually in different locations and job areas from those that were lost. For example, a laid-off factory worker might not be qualified for the computer repair job that was created.

The Spotlight's on You

In considering all the options open to you in the world of work, it's important to look at yourself. What are you like? What skills do you have? What do you enjoy doing? The more information you have about yourself, the more likely you'll be to find a job and career that's right for you.

What's Your Pleasure?

Do your favorite activities involve working with *things,* such as tools or machinery, *people,* or *information,* including ideas, facts, symbols, figures, and statistics? Which of these three areas fits your personality and interests best? You'll often be most satisfied in a job that is related to your interests.

● Many people have hands-on abilities. In what careers would a mechanical aptitude be useful?

The Office Is... at Home

More people will be working in home offices. They are freelance workers or entrepreneurs who run businesses from their homes. In addition, some people are telecommuters. They work for companies, yet do part of their job at home through electronic means. Most telecommuters spend at least two days at their firms.

Those who work at home need equipment to service their customers or access their companies' computer network. A computer with a modem is standard, and a dedicated phone line is preferred. Home offices often are small. Therefore, a multifunction business machine is a good idea. Some models combine a fax, printer, scanner, copier, telephone, and answering machine.

Voicing Your Opinion

1. *Should a telecommuter be required to purchase equipment for a home office, or should the company provide it? Explain your answer.*

2. *What would be the advantages of working at home? The disadvantages?*

3. *Would you enjoy working at home? Why or why not?*

Aptitudes and Abilities

Think about how you could use your aptitudes and abilities in various jobs and careers. An *aptitude* is potential for learning certain skills. Esther's aptitude for music makes learning to play musical instruments easy for her. Your *abilities* are the skills you already have developed. In many cases, you'll enjoy your work life more if you can take advantage of your skills. There is much satisfaction in doing something well.

Where Do You Want to Be?

Every job has a physical and an emotional environment. The *physical* environment includes the surroundings in which you work.

Identifying the kind of *emotional* environment you prefer may not be so easy. This relates to your ethics and values. You'll generally be more comfortable in a job with an emotional environment that matches your values. Would you prefer:

- An environment where people are the focus or where making the most profit is emphasized?
- A cooperative or a competitive atmosphere?
- Coworkers who share your values and work ethic?

It's a Test

Some people have more self-awareness than others. One way to identify your strengths and weaknesses is career testing.

• Work in this research laboratory could be either physical or mental. **Which would you prefer?**

If you take this type of test, you must draw your own conclusions. Don't rely solely on the results or a counselor's interpretation when you're making choices and decisions. The tests can help you and be a useful resource, but they are not a substitute for personal decision making.

A Future Designed for You

Have you ever found the perfect birthday present for a friend or family member? You matched what they wanted without a hint, because you knew them well. You'll enjoy your work and be successful if you match the type of job to who you are: your aptitudes, abilities, values, and interests. No matter how good a job or career looks to someone else, it's worthless if it doesn't fit you.

When you understand how work affects adult life, the variety, and complexity of the job market, and your personal qualities and requirements, you are exploring the factors needed to find the right job and career for you. You are on the way to increasing your chances of fulfillment and satisfaction as you look ahead to your future.

There are many aptitude, interest, and job preference surveys and inventories available. These "tests" can help you pinpoint what your interests and aptitudes are and how they fit into the job market. There is usually a fee to take them.

You may be able to take the tests through your school's counseling office. Community colleges often offer these tests to area citizens. Career counseling services or agencies may administer these tests to their clients.

REASON

Through Life's Problems

Recognize the Primary Problem

Sometimes just recognizing the primary problem is the first problem to be overcome. Can you identify what's causing the most concern in Jerome's situation below?

Jerome has had trouble sleeping at night, tossing and turning fitfully. He often wakes up suddenly, feeling panicky and having trouble catching his breath.

"What's wrong with me?" Jerome worried, sitting up in bed. "Here I am, wide awake at 2:00 A.M. again."

Turning on the lamp, Jerome saw a magazine article he had been reading before he fell asleep. The article was about ways to combat insomnia?

"Well, let's see. The authors suggest cutting out caffeine in your diet. Done that. They say to try exercising several hours before bed. I always do that, too. Stick to a consistent routine and bedtime. I do that as much as I can. Maybe it's time I go see a doctor."

Turning off the light and pulling a pillow over his head, Jerome started making a mental list of things he needed to do in the morning. Sometimes that made him sleepy.

"I'll need to go to the post office before work," he started. Jerome was working full-time at the local hardware store until his senior year of high school started in two weeks.

"Also, I need to pack for the family reunion." Jerome groaned aloud as he thought of the reunion. All of his aunts, uncles, and cousins would be there, and he knew that everyone would ask what he was planning to do after graduation.

"I don't know what I want to do after graduation! I really can't stand the thought of four more years of school right away. Mr. Hill keeps talking about me staying on at the hardware store, and taking on more of the management responsibilities. Maybe I should join the army."

Jerome's stomach started churning and his head started throbbing again. Suddenly, it came to him why he was waking up in the middle of the night, every night: he would lie in bed and worry about where he would be a year from now.

"I have myself worked up into a panic about what I am going to do after graduation!" he concluded. "Sounds like it's time to start looking at all my alternatives so I can make some decisions. Maybe then I can get some sleep."

From Your Perspective

1 What's the main problem that Jerome is facing?

2 What factors will affect how this problem will be solved?

3 When the problem is solved, what outcomes can Jerome expect?

Understanding Key Concepts

- Work is valuable because it provides income, social time with others, feelings of accomplishment, and the chance to contribute to society.
- The rapidly changing work world ensures that you will have to make changes and choices several times in your work life.
- Your physical and emotional health depend on holding a job that promotes your well-being.
- A variety of resources are available for learning more about the world of work, career clusters, and specific jobs and careers.
- Trends in the job market affect whether a particular career cluster is growing or declining.
- Understanding your characteristics and matching them with the qualities needed for a particular career cluster is the best way to find a job and career that will bring you satisfaction and fulfillment.

Checking Your Knowledge

1. Why is a strong work ethic an important ingredient for job success?
2. Describe factors that help workers feel satisfied with their jobs.
3. Identify at least five resources for researching jobs and careers. What general kind of information would you expect to find in each resource?
4. Explain how to use the U.S. Department of Education's Career Clusters to discover jobs and careers in which you might be interested.
5. What trends could affect the jobs that will be available to you in five and twenty-five years.
6. How can information about your aptitudes and abilities help you make decisions about a job or career?
7. Describe what is meant by the physical and emotional environments of work. Which would be more important to you? Why?
8. What is the role of aptitude tests and interest inventories in job and career selection?

Making TRANSITIONS

Evaluating Information

Many people are willing to give help and advice about jobs and careers. People are usually more receptive to information that fits what they already know. They often ignore evidence that contradicts their beliefs.

Imagine that you have taken an interest inventory and the career counselor is strongly suggesting a career area for you in which you have little interest. Should you ignore the counselor's advice? Accept it? Write a paragraph identifying the area and counselor's advice, and explain how you would respond to it.

STRENGTHENING *Life* SKILLS

Developing Criteria

With so much information available about jobs and careers, it is difficult to separate fact from fiction and to know what to believe. Work with a partner or a small group to develop at least five questions that would help you evaluate the accuracy and usefulness of job and career information.

Locate some information about careers, either from the library or on the Internet. Use your questions to evaluate the information you've found. Answer the following questions:

- Did your criteria cause you to question any of the information you found? Explain your answer.
- How could you use these questions in your personal job and career exploration?
- Do you feel that having the list of questions was helpful? Why or why not?

Applying Thinking Skills

1. **Predicting consequences.** What might happen in the following scenarios: A person took the first job offered regardless of what it was? Someone remained unemployed after refusing five job offers because they "weren't right"? A worker accepted a high paying job doing work he or she hated? An employee stayed in a boring job because health insurance was needed for a chronically ill child?

2. **Interpreting trends.** The average thirty-year-old today has held seven jobs. Do you think workers in your children's generation will have held, on the average, more or fewer jobs when they are thirty? Explain your reasoning.

3. **Seeing relationships.** What is the relationship between the following trends: outsourcing, working at home, and hiring temporary and part-time workers? If one of these trends were to reverse, what do you think would happen to the other trends?

Practical Applications

1. **Interviews.** Interview at least two adults, asking them to identify what they like most and least about their jobs. Record their answers. From this activity, what conclusions can you draw regarding your future career?

2. **Exploring career clusters.** List at least three jobs for each career cluster that are not listed in this text. Identify the level of training or education needed for each of the jobs you listed.

3. **Research activity.** Log on to the Internet and point your browser to at least five sites that relate to jobs and careers. Select one that you think is best. Share its address and the type of information on the site with your class.

4. **Identifying personal preferences.** Identify your job preferences regarding: working with things, people, or information; variety or predictability; physical or mental work; a relaxed or fast-paced atmosphere; indoor or outdoor work; a people or profit focus; and a cooperative or competitive environment. Identify a career cluster that would seem to fit your preferences.

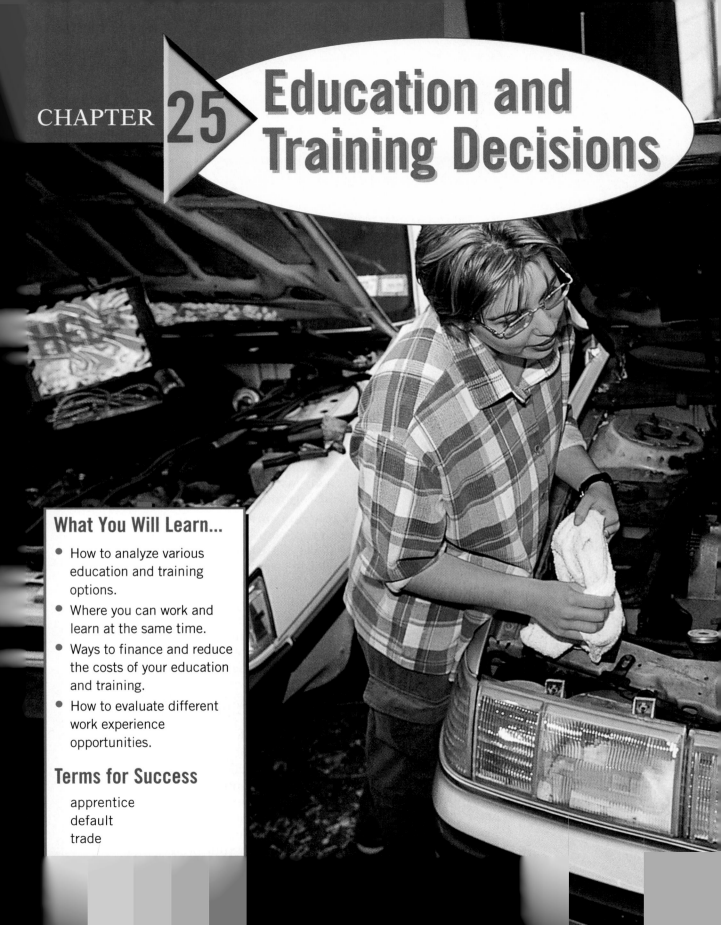

CHAPTER 25

Education and Training Decisions

What You Will Learn...

- How to analyze various education and training options.
- Where you can work and learn at the same time.
- Ways to finance and reduce the costs of your education and training.
- How to evaluate different work experience opportunities.

Terms for Success

apprentice
default
trade

Keri smiled with satisfaction as the car engine's rumble filled the garage. Like music, she thought. "You can turn it off, Brad," she called.

The garage again was quiet as Brad climbed out of the driver's seat. "That's great, but are you sure it'll start the next time? It's my mom's car, and I don't want to have to buy a new battery."

Keri shook her head. "You had some corrosion on one of the posts. I cleaned it off, so it should start fine now."

"Hey, this class is a smart idea," Brad said. "Who thought of it, anyway?"

"Mr. Peterov, our instructor—his wife, actually," Keri explained, carefully lowering the hood of the car. "She gets her hair done at a cosmetology school and suggested the school shop do the same thing with auto repair."

"Well, I'm glad she did. So are a lot of other owners of sick cars," Brad said.

Keri laughed. "So am I. Cars are very complicated today. Even the diagnostic tests are computerized. My uncle learned to fix engines by working on his friends' cars and by training on the job, but I'm using equipment here that a lot of professional garages don't even have."

"Well, I'm one happy customer," Brad grinned. "You saved me from buying a new battery, and I don't get paid 'til next Friday. Mom and I share the car to get to work, so I'm glad you found the problem."

Keri grinned. "Oh, not all the solutions are this easy, but figuring out what's the problem is half the fun. It's like solving a puzzle."

? Why do you think Brad brought his ailing car to the school auto repair shop? What are the advantages and disadvantages of on-the-job training?

Where Do You Go from Here?

With few exceptions, almost all of today's jobs call for further education or training after high school. Keri is getting practical experience along with her auto repair education. Education or training requirements differ with each profession. Some need only a certificate or license, while others require a college degree or more.

Think about an occupation that interests you. How much time and effort are required to prepare for it? How much money will it cost? This chapter helps you explore answers to questions like these. The career counselor and teachers at your school can also provide additional information about educational options available to you.

Choosing a School or College

Many communities or regions of the United States have a variety of schools and colleges that provide further education and training after high school. Depending on the career and school you choose, it can take from less than a year to ten years to finish a program of study. For most occupations, the more education and training you receive, the more career opportunities you will have.

- **Vocational-technical centers.** Training in various fields—hair care, computer programming, auto repair—can often be completed in one or two years at these centers. Flexible entrance requirements and relatively low cost attract students who can graduate with certificates or diplomas. Some vocational-technical centers provide preparation for licensing examinations.

• For most people, career training after high school is a necessity. Many students choose vocational schools or two-year colleges for their training so that they can enter the workforce earlier. What education and training options are you thinking about for your future?

- **Trade schools.** A **trade** is an occupation that requires manual or mechanical skill. Trade schools train students for specific occupations—carpentry, machining, plumbing—usually within one or two years. Because trade schools are privately run, they often are more expensive than vocational-technical centers, but some offer courses that aren't available at other schools.

- **Community and technical colleges.** Two-year degree and certificate programs in a variety of occupational areas are generally offered at these schools. Run by local, county, or state agencies, they are usually less expensive than trade schools or four-year colleges and universities. Graduates who receive a two-year associate's degree from a community or technical college can usually transfer some or all of their credits to a four-year college or university.

Refresh your Memory

Review these key terms:
- **bachelor's degree:** an academic diploma awarded to a student upon completion of a set number of credits at a four-year college or university.
- **grant:** student financial aid that does not need to be repaid.
- **lay off:** temporarily dismiss one or more employees, usually because of a company's financial circumstances.

• Colleges and universities offer academic preparation for many professions. What professions are of interest to you?

REASON Through Life's Problems

Evaluate Information

An important skill in solving problems is sorting through the multitude of information available. Note how Brianna gathers and evaluates information to find a school that will meet her needs.

Sitting cross-legged on the floor, Brianna studied the brochures, handouts, and applications spread around her. "How am I ever going to begin to sift through all this stuff?" she muttered to herself. "Deciding what school I should attend to become an R.N. sure isn't easy! I guess I'd better look at what I've gathered and then figure out if it's information I need, can use, or even if it's truthful."

Surrounding her were glossy, colorful brochures claiming that their schools were the best places for Brianna to further her education. Even more confusing were their promises of scholarships, grants, and other financial aid. Handouts from college recruiters provided such a variety of information that it was difficult for Brianna to compare colleges. The applications were similar, but not of value to her until she had narrowed down her choices to the colleges where she actually wanted to apply.

Brianna lightly hit her palm against the side of her head. "I need to think about what's important to me before I can even consider the information I have," she determined. " I know I want a small college with an R.N. program. I want to get credit for my work in the Allied Health program from the career center. Plus, I've got to have some financial aid. I'd like to take classes from professors who take an interest in their students' academic careers. It'd be fun to get involved in several student organizations. I also know I want to live far enough away from home to feel independent, but close enough to get home for a weekend.

Brianna shifted her attention back to the paper around her. "How can I be sure that the information I've gathered is accurate? I need to check out some other sources of information," Brianna concluded. "I'll see if I can find these schools' Internet sites. Tomorrow I'll make an appointment to meet with the career counselor who will be familiar with at least some of these schools. I can also look in one of those books that rank colleges. Plus I want to schedule some college visits. No brochure can tell me what I could learn by visiting the campus and talking to some of the students."

Brianna sighed, "I need to spend a lot of time looking at information and evaluating it. I sure can't analyze my alternatives unless I have the right information and know that it's accurate."

▶ From Your Perspective

1 Do you think Brianna is gathering reliable information? Why or why not?

2 Do you think Brianna has obtained enough information to solve her problem? What other sources of information could she seek?

3 What values do you think are apparent in Brianna's criteria? Which do you think she believes are most important?

• Many young adults are able to get the career training they need through the military. **How could the military help you meet your career goals?**

• **Four-year colleges and universities.** Professions that require specialized training—law, medicine, architecture, pharmacy, teaching—are offered at colleges and universities. Some students begin college unsure of what professions to enter, but usually decide after one or two years.

Learning While Earning

If you're finding it hard making a decision about education and training, you may want to think about working and learning at the same time.

• **Military service training.** All branches of the U.S. armed forces—Army, Navy, Air Force, Marine Corps, Coast Guard—offer opportunities to get paid while learning skills or trades. Enlistees can complete high school and earn college credits, as well as prepare for a career in civilian life. Training is avail-able in hundreds of different occupations and professional careers such as aeronautics, engineering, and accounting. Depending on the type of training you choose, you must pass aptitude tests and enlist for a minimum of four years of active duty.

• **Apprenticeships.** An **apprentice** is a worker who learns a skilled trade requiring two or more years of on-the-job experience and instruction. Rita is not making a high wage now, but she is developing her skills as a cabinetmaker. Later, after four to six years, she will apply to work for a custom home-builder in her community. The most popular apprenticeship programs are in the trades. Unions, state, or federal agencies regulate apprenticeships. In most apprenticeship programs, you must register with the state or federal government. At the end of the apprenticeship, you may be required to take written and practical tests before receiving a certificate or license for this trade.

• Most apprenticeships are in trades such as electricity, carpentry, or plumbing. **What trades would you consider for future employment?**

On-the-Job Training

On-the-job training, or on-site instruction in how to perform a particular job, occurs after you've been hired. Training can last from a few days, such as short periods of orientation for new employees, to two or three years. This type of training is different from an apprenticeship because there is no written agreement between the employee and the employer.

Supervisory or management training is often done on the job and may take the form of online training, informational videocassettes, or after-hours classes.

If you are interested in exploring on-the-job training, consider part-time work or employment during school vacations. Many local companies and government agencies offer part-time opportunities for people to receive training on the job. In addition, there may be openings to learn-while-you-earn in your school store or campus laboratories.

Financing Your Education and Training

If you're like many other teens, you're probably wondering how you are going to pay for your education and training. Formal education and training can be expensive. Costs may include tuition, fees, books, tools, supplies, room and board, plus transportation.

These expenditures are investments in your future. It's likely that the more education and training you have, the more money you'll be able to earn during your lifetime.

Planning is key to paying the high price of a good education. By starting to plan early—even in high school—you'll be able to afford the education and training for the career path you want to follow.

Financial Aid

State and federal agencies, corporations, various organizations, or private individuals provide aid to education in varying amounts. Financial aid includes:

- **Scholarships, grants, and awards.** These are given to students for a variety of reasons: academic achievement; leadership potential; community involvement; financial need; hobbies and affiliations; personal characteristics and special talents. Scholarships, grants, and awards do not have to be repaid, but some require you to work for several years after you have completed school as a type of repayment. Government grants are based primarily on need.

Narrowing the Field

T I P S

Comparing schools is difficult. If possible, arrange an on-site visit of two or three colleges, so you can see the campus firsthand. Some things to check are:

- **Facilities and equipment.** Are they up to date and readily available?
- **Courses and programs of study.** Will they fit my schedule? How large are the classes?
- **Graduation requirements.** How many students who enroll actually graduate and pass licensing or certification exams?
- **Housing.** Where might I live, and how much will it cost? How far away is housing from my classes?
- **Financing.** Can I get a refund if I have to drop out before I finish my course work?
- **Safety.** What measures are taken to ensure student safety?

- The amount and type of financial aid available to students varies and is generally based on a student's need and academic achievement. How would you go about seeking sources of financial aid?

Check Out Financial Aid

"How am I ever going to pay for college, Jesse? I know my parents can't afford it." Dave suddenly put down the video game controller and shook his head. "Where am I going to get the money?"

"The same way you got the money for your car," Jesse replied. "You borrow it and pay it back later."

Finacial Aid Resources

For more information on financial aid, talk with your school counselor about sources. In addition, check out the Internet for a wealth of information on student loans. You can use any major search engine with key phrases such as "financial aid," "student aid," or "scholarships" to get other information about

funding your education or training. To learn about more programs and opportunities for assistance, contact your state department of education.

Using Your Resources Wisely

1. When and how are student loans paid back? What are the penalties for late payments or defaulting on the loan?

2. If you don't have a computer at home, where can you get on the Internet?

- **Student loans.** Given by banks, these loans remain interest free as long as you are enrolled in school. You must repay the entire amount of the loan, including interest. The federal government guarantees repayment to the bank in case of **default**, or failure to repay the financial obligation. Defaulting on a student loan can damage your credit record, making you ineligible for additional student aid.

Working

Jake's goal is to earn a college degree, but now he is working at a part-time job and taking classes at the local community college. He started saving money while working during

high school. By living at home, Jake is able to put more of his income into his savings. He also indirectly saves time and money by earning course credits at the community college that can be transferred later to the university.

Many college students work on campus at jobs they found after getting information from the college's Office of Student Employment. Some of these jobs are work-study programs funded by federal and state agencies. Another alternative is to work full–time for a while, saving as much as you can to pay for education and training later.

Cut Your Costs

Regardless of the amount of funds you have available, making your money go further can help you achieve more of your goals. Some of the ways to cut education and training costs include:

- **Earning exam credits.** Take advanced placement courses while you're in high school. Some educational services give college credits to individuals who pass examinations rather than take courses. Many colleges and universities throughout the United States recognize these credits.

- **Attend a publicly-funded school.** Tuition is likely to be substantially less if you attend a college or university located in the state where you live. You'll avoid higher out-of-state tuition. By enrolling at a local community college, you may be able to live at home, thus cutting costs for housing and related expenses.

- **Complete your college degree early.** By attending school during the summer, enrolling in as many classes per semester or quarter as you can handle, and/or by earning credit for college during high school, you'll save on tuition and enter the workforce sooner. Many degrees can be finished in three-and-one-half rather than four years.

Because each person's situation is different, put your imagination and creativity to work. Think of other ways you can cut costs while receiving an education. By doing so, you can maximize the money and other resources you have available to achieve your career goals.

• One way to cut your expenses while getting your education is to share living expenses with others. What options have you considered for limiting the cost of your education?

Getting Work Experience

During summer vacation, Trina worked in a local interior design studio. Although her duties consisted mainly of answering the telephone and arranging fabric, rug, and wallpaper samples, she was able to observe what it's like to be an interior designer.

If you have the opportunity, get some work experience before finalizing your education and training plans. Experiencing a variety of real-life work situations both during and after high school can help you learn what you like to do, and what you don't. Consequently, you'll be more likely to make sound decisions about your future schooling and career goals. Some of the ways to get work experience are:

- **Part-time jobs.** By working at a variety of part-time jobs after school, on weekends, or during the summer, you can preview several occupations. Look for interesting jobs that you can do well. Part-time jobs will give you a chance to compare various work situations and job demands.
- **Work-based learning programs.** Many schools offer work-based experience that is a simulated job in a classroom setting. Others schools provide work-site learning programs on actual job locations. Students can earn class credits and a grade while learning job skills in class and on the job. Local businesses often team up with schools to provide work-based learning experience called ***internships***.

• Working at a number of part-time jobs can give you work experience and an idea of what type of job might be interesting to you as a career. At this point in your life, what type of work seems to interest you most?

- **Job shadowing.** To learn more about a certain career, try job shadowing one or more individuals. Job shadowing can provide valuable information about the kind of education and training that you need for various jobs. On your own, you might ask an employed person about his or her job.

- **Volunteer work.** Being a volunteer is another good way to get meaningful work experience and to explore careers. In Chapter 5, you studied *service learning.* Some schools give class credits for volunteer work. Most teachers and guidance counselors can refer you to organizations that need volunteers.

- **Entrepreneurship.** Start your own business. Begin by identifying a need, such as individuals who need help with lawn maintenance, animal care, moving furniture, or running errands. Then provide the service for a reasonable fee.

• Internships offer an excellent opportunity for work experience. Explore which careers offer internship experience.

Understanding Key Concepts

- Many jobs require additional education or training beyond high school. However, not every job requires a four-year college or university degree.

- In some occupational areas, the more education and training you have, the more career opportunities are likely to come your way.

- Both vocational-technical centers and trade schools train students for specific occupations.

- Community and technical colleges are less expensive than trade schools or four-year colleges and universities.

- You can find a number of opportunities to work and learn at the same time, including military service training, apprenticeships, and on-the-job training.

- Many students finance their education and training by applying for and receiving scholarships, grants, and awards or student loans.

- Ways to reduce education and training costs include earning exam credits, attending public rather than private schools, or completing your college degree early.

- Getting work experience before making final education and training plans can help you make more realistic career decisions.

Checking Your Knowledge

1. What kinds of schools are located in your community or region? Discuss the education and training they offer. Rank them according to your requirements for education and training.

2. Give two examples of professions that require one or more academic degrees from a four-year college or university.

3. Describe some ways to receive education and training at the same time. How would this cut your overall education cost?

4. Summarize options that are available to students for financing their education and training. Explain why one seems best for you.

5. What are the criteria for students to receive scholarships?

6. What are some sources of information about student financial aid?

7. What are some ways students can reduce the cost of their education and training?

8. Give some examples of how to get work experience. Why is it important to get work experience before making final education and training plans?

Making TRANSITIONS

Preliminary Observations

Acquiring more education and training means having more career opportunities from which to choose. Arrange to spend a day at an apprentice program, vocational-technical center, trade school, or one of the other kinds of education or training sites discussed in this chapter.

Write a summary of your experience based on the questions that follow:

- What did you learn about training options during your observation?
- How might you apply what you learned from this experience to your future education or training decisions?

STRENGTHENING *Life* SKILLS

Shopping for the Right School

To find a school that is right for you, research where business leaders in your community went to school. First, choose a business or profession that interests you. Contact the local chamber of commerce for names of companies in this field. Interview —by phone or face-to-face—the owners or presidents of these companies. Ask where they received their training or education. Why did they choose that school? Should they have chosen differently? Why or why not? How did their education prepare them to run a company? Compile the results of your interviews. How does this information help you choose a college?

Applying Thinking Skills

1. **Comparing and contrasting.** Think about two different occupations that interest you. Compare and contrast the kind of training and education required for each of them. What are the similarities and differences? Explain your reasoning.

2. **Recognizing assumptions.** You may have classmates who say they can't afford to go to college or vocational school. How would you respond to this assumption? What real-life examples might you give to support your position?

3. **Predicting consequences.** What positive and negative consequences might result if a young adult chose to delay his or her education or training for several years after high school?

Practical Applications

1. **Affirming yourself.** To deal with feelings of apprehension about your future, make a list of affirmations about yourself, your plans, and your future. Stress the success that you anticipate while preparing for a future career. Write a short paper explaining the ease, or difficulty, you had in making the list.

2. **Charting your options.** Imagine that you are ready to make a decision about where to go for postsecondary education. Based on your career goal, study catalogs and brochures from several schools and colleges, analyzing their courses and programs of study. Also, note the entrance requirements of each. Next, estimate the cost of attending each one for one year. Include tuition, fees, books, transportation, and—if you would be living away from home—room and board. Summarize your data in a chart, and select one of the schools as your first choice. Give reasons for your decision.

3. **Making work fun.** Many successful business empires began as the founder's hobby. One woman who enjoyed baking chocolate chip cookies built a multi-million dollar retail cookie franchise. What are your hobbies? What activities do you enjoy whenever you have extra time? Research the Internet to see how these leisure activities could be turned into a career. What additional training would you need to begin your own business venture? Which colleges or universities offer the best programs of study in your chosen area?

CHAPTER 26 Developing Job Search Skills

What You Will Learn...

- Benefits of developing a personal network.
- Places to go and tools to use when you're job hunting.
- How to develop a successful résumé, write a cover letter, and fill out an application form.
- Steps for a successful job interview.

Terms for Success

hidden job market
job lead

Kent offered his hand with a smile. "Mr. Lau? I'm Kent Shales," he said, and began to sit.

"I didn't ask you to sit down," Kent's roommate, Eli, said.

"What? Oh, yeah." Kent straightened.

"Nice to meet you, Kent. Have a seat. I've looked over your résumé. It's very impressive. Just a few questions, though. . ."

Kent listened and answered each question thoughtfully. He talked about his training, his experience and responsibilities on past jobs, and his work habits. He even pointed out his weaknesses and how he is working to improve them. Kent felt the interview was going well.

Then came the last question. "Why should I hire you?"

"Huh?"

"Don't say 'huh,' " Eli reminded him.

"What am I supposed to say?" asked Kent. "I appreciate your helping me rehearse, Eli, but what kind of question is that?"

"They ask questions like that in interviews," Eli assured him. "They want to know what you have to say for yourself."

"Well. . ." Kent fumbled, "I work hard, and I get along with people . . .. I have a way of bringing people up, especially when we've been working hard. Work shouldn't be *all* work, you know." He paused. "Is that what they want to hear? I don't like to brag about myself."

Eli smiled and wrote with an imaginary pen "Mr. Shales is genuinely enthusiastic—and modest."

How might rehearsing for an interview prepare you for a real interview?

Where Do You Find a Job?

Fear of the unknown can be frightening. Kent felt that by rehearsing for a job interview, he would be better prepared and less anxious during a real interview. Some questions are always asked at interviews. By having formulated an answer ahead of time, Kent will appear more self-confident.

It usually takes planning to find work that you enjoy and can do well. Although some people insist they got a good job simply because of luck, in most cases careful planning and research were the reasons for their successes.

Whenever you're making plans to find work, it helps to get as many leads as you can. A **job lead** is information about a possible job opening. The more leads you have, the better will be your chances of finding the work you want.

Most job leads are free, and they can be found almost anywhere there are people. Some job leads may direct you to the **hidden job market,** or sources of jobs that are less obvious to many other job seekers.

People to See

Many openings in the hidden job market aren't advertised in newspapers or listed with placement agencies. Instead, friends and acquaintances of company employees often fill these positions. For this reason, don't limit your job search to the want ads. Instead, develop your own job leads by networking.

Networking is communicating with people you know: family members, friends, teachers, classmates, neighbors, former employers, and coworkers. A network is helpful when contacts work at companies that are looking for employees.

• Many job leads are found by networking with others in a variety of situations. Why could it be to your benefit to network with others in many different situations?

The Gatekeepers

T I P S

Some employers use an assistant or a receptionist to screen phone calls and arrange appointments for them. The individual serves as a *gatekeeper*, often keeping job applicants from talking to the prospective employer.

If a gatekeeper answers the telephone, he or she probably will ask you to explain the purpose of your call. Try the following tips to get past the gatekeeper:

- Introduce yourself and, if possible, get the gatekeeper's name.
- Be honest and direct about wanting a job interview. Otherwise, you will make the gatekeeper suspicious and unlikely to help you.
- Ask the gatekeeper for help to build rapport and enlist the person's support. Give a response such as, "I sent Dr. Jones my résumé last week and would like to set up an appointment. I need only five or ten minutes. Can you help me?" If you are given the brush-off, don't force the issue. You might try again another day.

Places to Go

Where you go for job leads will depend on your community. Some places to check are:

- **School counselor's office.** The counselor's office or placement service at your school may be a good source of job leads. Information about your abilities, aptitudes, and academic records can be used to refer you to specific job openings.

• Sometimes it takes visiting several businesses to check out job leads before you find work that suits you best. **What are some things that you might do to check out job leads?**

- **Local businesses.** Visit various businesses, organizations, and agencies to ask about available jobs. You may impress a possible employer with your willingness to seek out work. The more contacts you make, the better will be your chances of finding a job.
- **Employment agencies.** An employment agency matches job hunters with available jobs. Federal and state governments operate public employment agencies, and their services are free. Privately run agencies charge a fee; this is usually a fixed amount or a percentage of your first year's salary.
- **Libraries.** Most libraries provide a variety of free job-search information, including lists of major employers in the area. Some post job openings or hold seminars to review résumés, cover letters, and interviewing techniques.

- **Chamber of Commerce.** Your chamber of commerce lists company names and addresses, and sponsors events for members to discuss issues affecting their businesses.
- **Job fairs.** Many communities have job fairs where you can learn what positions are available and what qualifications are needed.

Sharpen Your Job Search Tools

Bryan is preparing a résumé for his job search. He knows the résumé must serve as a good advertisement of who he is and what he has to offer. He hopes it will make employers want to meet him and learn more about him.

• Job fairs offer you the opportunity to meet with a varied number of employers at one time. What are the advantages and disadvantages of seeking employment at a job fair?

A résumé, cover letter, and a job application form are three tools to help you get a job.

- A résumé is a part of almost any job search, and is often the first impression an employer will have of you.
- A one-page cover letter is as important as your résumé.
- A job application form serves as a screening device.

Create a Résumé

You may be asked to include your résumé with a job application or bring it with you to an interview. If your résumé is professional and attention getting, it may secure you an interview with someone who has the power to hire you.

Follow the guidelines below to help your résumé get noticed and stand out from the crowd:

- Make sure every word is true. Focus on your skills, education, and training. Include awards, hobbies, and volunteer activities. In addition to specific duties in previous jobs, highlight your accomplishments at work. You may list references, but only with their permission, or add "References furnished upon request."
- Include basic information, such as your name, address, and telephone number. Omit personal data such as your age, height and weight, the condition of your health, and marital and parental status.
- Keep your résumé brief, accurate, and up to date—no more than one or two pages. Carefully check for errors in spelling or grammar. By creating the résumé on a computer and saving it to a personal disk, you won't have to rekey the entire document when updates are needed.
- "Customize" your résumé to use when you're applying for different jobs. Instead of distributing a single generic document, create revisions that are customized for specific job openings.

Cheaper by the Dozen?

TIPS

Sending out unsolicited or "scattershot" résumés to dozens or more potential employers isn't an efficient way to find most jobs. In fact, it is a poor substitute for personal contact, or networking. Because companies often receive hundreds of résumés for every job opening they have, many firms have formal or informal policies prohibiting responses to unsolicited inquiries, including résumés.

Refresh your Memory

Take note of these job search related terms:

- **cover letter:** A one-page letter included with your résumé, telling the employer who you are and why you are sending it.
- **references:** People who will recommend you to an employer.
- **referral:** Someone to whom you have been directed, or referred.
- **résumé:** A written summary of a person's educational background, work history, work-related personal qualifications, and other accomplishments.
- **screening stage:** A part of the hiring process when employers scan résumés and job applications to determine which to consider and which to discard.

- Your résumé should be neatly typed or computer generated, making sure that you have no errors in spelling, grammar, or usage. **What information is most important to appear on your résumé?**

is listed in chronological—or time—order, starting with the most recent first. Use the same reverse time order to list your education and other information.

- **Functional or skills oriented.** This option highlights your skills and accomplishments rather than the jobs you've held. If you have little or no work-related experience, a functional résumé may be your best choice. Certain skills or strengths—such as communication or computer skills—serve as headings. After each heading, write a description of the skill.

- **Combination.** This kind of résumé is sometimes called a "chrono-functional résumé," and is recommended by many career counselors. It showcases your skills and accomplishments while giving the reader a clear glimpse of your work history.

Write a Cover Letter

A cover letter is your first chance to make a good impression. Address it to the person responsible for hiring. The purposes of a cover letter are to:

- Tell how your job talents will benefit the company.
- Show why the employer should read your résumé.
- Ask for an interview.

Organization Is Important

How should the information in your résumé be organized—especially if you have little or no work experience? How can you present your skills, abilities, and experience to quickly attract an employer's interest? Organize your résumé according to one of the following options:

- **Chronological.** Chronological résumés are the most commonly used and the most familiar to employers. This format gives a clear overview of your work experience, as well as what you are doing and accomplishing at this stage of your life. Work experience

Electronic Résumés

Did you know that your résumé may be read by a computer—rather than by a human being? To save time and money, many companies use computers to screen résumés. First, they scan the résumés received into their computers, where they copy and store them. Then computers can do an electronic search of the résumés. This allows them to look for keywords, or nouns that describe skills or job experiences they are seeking, such as "mechanical," "interior design," or "fluent in Spanish."

To make your résumé more effective in today's electronic age, analyze the wording in job ads that relate to the job you want. Make note of words or terms that appear most often. If they apply to you, make sure these words appear in your résumé.

Voicing Your Opinion

1. *Assume you sent your résumé to a company where you intended it to be read by a human being. Instead, it was scanned through a computer programmed to look for certain keywords. Your personal qualities, volunteer activities, and list of references were never seen. How do you feel about the increasing trend toward computerized screening of résumés? Is it likely to produce the most qualified candidates? Why or why not?*

2. *Your friend showed you a résumé he is customizing for computerized screening. The résumé contains some keywords that aren't truthful reflections of his background. Should you comment on your friend's action? Why or why not?*

- Your cover letter should be short, to the point, and include three major parts:
- An *opening* that explains why you are writing. Include names of individuals from whom you learned about the job, after you have permission to use their names.
- The *body of the letter* points out specific qualities you can bring to the job. Briefly explain your current situation—whether you are working or going to school. Clarify what you're looking for, and describe the skills and experiences you have to offer the company. Use this part of the letter to call attention to one or two important points in your résumé.
- The *closing* tells how you plan to follow up this initial contact. Include your telephone number and hours when you may be reached.

A Functional Résumé

Rose Vasquez
5000 University Avenue
Austin, TX 79701

JOB OBJECTIVE

Seeking an entry-level position, with opportunities for career growth, as a Web developer/animator for a graphics or advertising firm.

SKILLS AND ABILITIES

Computer Skills: Skilled at accessing and navigating the Internet on both Macintosh and IBM-compatible computers; experience with Web graphics and animation, Windows, Quark, Java, and Perl programming.

Communication Skills: Strong skills in grammar (both English and Spanish). Served as editor of high school yearbook. Also, member of high school debate team.

Work Skills: Worked after school and on weekends in family grocery store during high school. While attending community college, worked part-time as tutor in the college computer lab. Also developed Website for the Registrar's Office at the college.

Other Skills and Abilities: Received commendations from previous employers for creativity, attention to detail, enthusiasm for work, and ability to work without supervision.

EDUCATION

Associate's Degree, Austin Community College. Diploma, Lakeview High School, Austin, Texas (graduated in top 10 percent of class).

HONORS AND MEMBERSHIPS

Editor, high school yearbook; member, high school debate team and National Honor Society.

COMMUNITY SERVICE

Volunteer, Big Sisters of Austin; designed computer interactive program for the Capital Area Children's Museum.

- A functional résumé highlights your key skills, experiences, and aptitudes. **How would you highlight your skills and abilities?**

A Cover Letter

5000 University Avenue
Austin, TX 79701
March 23, 2000

Mr. Thomas Hopkins, Personnel Dir.
Mega Graphics, Inc.
8904 6th Street
Austin, TX 79708

Dear Mr. Hopkins:

Mark Rhoden, head graphics designer at Digital Advertising, suggested that I contact you regarding an opening in your company for a junior Web developer. Please consider me an applicant for this position.

My associate's degree is in computer science, with a special emphasis in computer animation. My current position as a computer programmer has provided opportunities to develop additional skills and experience in programming and publishing.

I am especially interested in pursuing a career with Mega Graphics because of the company's reputation and experience in computer animation. I believe I can make an effective contribution to your company because of my creativity, experience, and training.

I have the interest and ability to succeed as a Web developer. Please review my enclosed résumé. It provides further details about my qualifications.

I would like to schedule an interview for this position at your convenience. I can be reached at my home telephone number (listed below) every day after 4:00 p.m.

Thank you for your time and consideration in this matter.

Sincerely,

Rose Vasquez

Rose Vasquez
555-5555

Enclosure

- A well–written cover letter makes a good first impression. How does this writer use the important elements of an effective cover letter?

Fill in an Application Form

Corinne noticed someone putting up a "help wanted" sign at a neighborhood store. "That's great," she said. "I want to get some work experience and make some money. I'll use what I've learned about getting a job to show them I'm the one they should hire."

An application form serves as a screening device and a chance to make a good first impression on the person who is hiring. Carefully read and follow the instructions. Use a pen, and print or write neatly and clearly. Answer all the questions truthfully. If a question doesn't apply to you, write "N/A" for "not applicable" or put a dash (—) in the space.

• In order to make a good first impression, scan a job application carefully and follow the instructions when filling it out. What could a poorly filled out application say to a prospective employer?

If the application asks for salary desired, write "open" or "negotiable." When asked for the date you can start, answer "upon two weeks' notice" if you are currently employed. If not, you can write "immediately," "upon graduation," or the date that you can begin.

Bring your résumé and other documents, such as your Social Security card and driver's license. If you have been granted permission to use their names, bring a list of your references and their addresses and telephone numbers.

Complete the application quickly, but accurately. Check to see that your spelling and grammar are correct. When you have finished, submit your résumé with the form.

Put Your Best Foot Forward

A job interview is a face-to-face meeting between an employer and a potential employee. It is conducted in a conversational style so that the employer can meet you as a person, not just as a name on an application form or résumé.

A job interview can mean the difference between getting a job or getting the brush-off. For this reason, you need to be well prepared before you go to an interview. Then you'll be more confident and able to demonstrate that you are the best person for the job.

Prepare Before the Interview

Does the thought of a job interview make you nervous? Are you afraid something will go wrong, and you'll fail to convince an employer to hire you? This fear is common; however, don't let it ruin your chances for the job you want. Instead, follow the steps below for a successful job interview:

• **Do your homework.** Learn as much as you can about the company, its products, services, and history. Also thoroughly research the job itself and how your skills and background qualify you for the position. If possible, talk with both former and current employees about their work with the company. Friends, neighbors, and relatives—in addition to the library, the Internet, and the local Chamber of Commerce—may be able to provide helpful information.

- **Practice your responses.** Have family members or friends conduct mock interviews, asking you questions that an employer might ask. When you answer, make a point to smile and maintain good eye contact. Afterwards, request feedback on how you did. Repeat the process until you feel comfortable being interviewed. Videotaping the sessions can help you see if you sit up straight and look alert. You can also quickly spot any nervous habits to avoid, such as twisting your hair, cracking your knuckles, or playing with coins in your pocket.

- **Dress the part.** Carefully plan what you'll wear to the interview. Your goal is to make an excellent first impression. If you can, check out the job environment to see how other workers dress. Choose similar, or slightly more formal, clothing for your interview. Try on each item of clothing—including shoes and accessories—to make sure everything fits well, feels comfortable, and is clean and neat. Shoes should be shined, and jewelry should be simple and kept to a minimum. Observe your total appearance by standing and then sitting in front of a mirror. Try to see yourself as the employer will see you. Ask yourself if the clothing sends a positive message about you and your abilities.

Be Positive During the Interview

Whether it's fair or not, first impressions are very important and hard to change. From the time you walk in the interviewer's door, judgments are made about your personality, character, and competence. For this reason, it's important that you:

- Smile and maintain eye contact.
- Stand and sit up tall.
- Appear relaxed.
- Give a firm handshake and repeat the person's name when you are introduced.

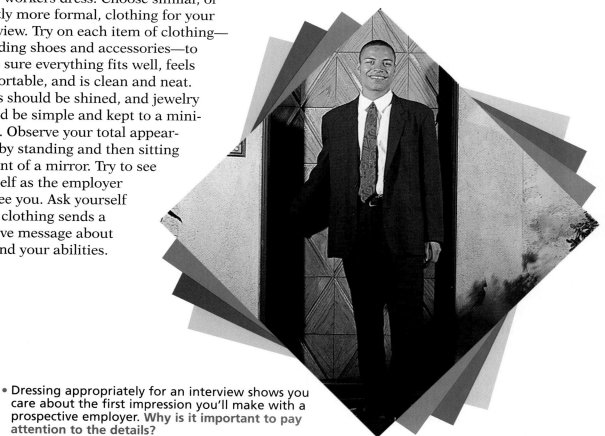

- Dressing appropriately for an interview shows you care about the first impression you'll make with a prospective employer. **Why is it important to pay attention to the details?**

Once introductions have been made, wait until you are asked before you sit down. Put your personal possessions in your lap or next to you—not on the interviewer's desk.

Interviewers often begin the session by scanning your résumé and job application. Interview success depends not only on what you say but also on how you say it. From the very first moment, try to establish rapport with the interviewer. Be friendly and keep your comments positive and enthusiastic.

Speak so you can be heard. Don't make the interviewer have to strain to understand you. Be prepared to talk about yourself—but don't pour out your life's history. The main point is to spotlight your qualifications and experience in an honest and straightforward way.

Try to relax by focusing your attention on the questions you're asked. Listen carefully, and pause before you jump in with a response. Don't interrupt the interviewer or change the subject.

Questions, Questions, Questions

An interviewer may ask questions about your education, work history, outside interests, and personal strengths and weaknesses. Although the process may seem informal and friendly, interviewers have a serious objective: to select the best person for the job. To accomplish this, they use the interview to get answers to three important questions:

- Can you do the job?
- Will you do the job?
- Can you get along with other employees?

During an interview, the employer may ask, "Do you have any questions?" Be prepared with several questions to show your interest in the company and the job. Some questions you may wish to ask are:

- What is the exact job description and its responsibilities?
- Would I work on my own or as a member of a team?

FOCUS ON ...
Getting Off on the Right Foot

Here are some helpful reminders when you're going for a job interview:

- Know the exact address and location of the interview. If necessary, make a dry run a day or so beforehand to see where it is and how long it takes to get there. Allow for rush-hour traffic, and plan to get to the site a few minutes early.
- Be conservative. Don't wear heavy makeup, perfume or cologne, or excessive hair spray or mousse. The same goes for long nails or bright nail polish.
- Bring a pen, notepad, and a copy of your résumé, even if you've already sent one. Also bring your Social Security card and driver's license.
- Arrive alone. This is not the time to bring family members or friends.
- Don't chew gum or smoke, even if you're invited to do so.
- Don't use first names unless you're requested to do so.
- Project a positive, confident image. Avoid appearing anxious, overeager, arrogant, passive, or bored.

- Whom would I report to?
- Would the skills I learn on this job prepare me for other jobs in the company?
- How is job performance measured?
- When would you want me to start work?

Many of these questions will be answered during the interview. You may want to ask other questions as they come to mind. Find out as much as possible about the position so that you can decide if it's what you want.

Don't bring up the subject of salary or benefits unless the interviewer does so. If you are offered the job, but salary or benefits haven't been mentioned, you might say, "Before I can give you my decision, I need to know the salary and benefits package you're offering."

What should you do at the end of an interview if you haven't been offered a job or told when a decision will be made? If you're unclear about what will happen next, thank the interviewer and ask if you may call about the decision in the near future. If you want the job, express your enthusiasm for the position and state that you look forward to hearing from the employer.

• Appearing confident as you enter an interview gives a positive impression to a possible employer. How could you prepare yourself and build up your confidence for an interview?

Follow Up After the Interview

Almost as soon as the interview is over, it's time to follow up. Following up an interview is as important as the preparation you did beforehand. It may help determine whether you get the job.

Start by promptly writing a thank-you letter to the interviewer. It will jog his or her mind about you as an applicant and emphasize your desire to work there. If you forgot to say something that you feel you should have said during the interview, include it in your letter. In the last paragraph, make it easy for the interviewer to reach you by including your telephone number.

Even if you decided you aren't interested in the job, send a brief thank-you letter for the time the employer took with you. In the future, this person may be someone you will want to work for, and you will have avoided creating a negative first impression of yourself.

Whether or not you are offered a job, it's helpful to evaluate your performance after every job interview. Keep a record of each interview, including names, titles, dates, and companies. Be as objective as possible, noting what went well and what you could have done better. Use the notes to prepare for future interviews.

If an employer turns you down, it's not the end of the world. Consider it a learning experience. Although it may take courage, ask the interviewer for feedback about why you weren't hired. Do you need more education and training? Does the person have suggestions to help you in your job search?

• Don't be afraid to ask questions during an interview. How might preparing several well-thought questions about a company benefit you during an interview?

REASON Through Life's Problems

Analyze Alternatives and Consequences

Carla has an appointment tomorrow for a job interview with a preschool educational service. The job involves visiting parents in their homes and helping them plan educational activities for their infants and toddlers. She needs to decide what clothing would be most appropriate for the interview. Note how Carla analyzes her alternatives and consequences.

"What in the world should I wear for this interview?" Carla wondered as she stared at the navy blue suit. "Dad is insisting that I wear this suit he bought me, but I don't know if the interviewer will be looking for professional dress, or a more casual look. I don't want to go in looking too stuffy, but I do want to make a businesslike impression."

In her employability class, her teacher always said to dress as you would for the job, or one step above that. Carla wasn't sure exactly what the dress code for the job would be, but she knew wearing a business suit would be awkward when she would be spending most of her time on the floor with young children. She would probably prefer pants for her time on home visits.

Thinking of all the possibilities, Carla tried to make up her mind what outfit would be more effective. She laid out the navy suit her dad had bought her for job interviews. It just seemed too formal for this job. Then she looked at a skirt and jacket combination, which would be a compromise between formal business attire and the corporate casual look. Finally, she looked at the pantsuit she had bought off the clearance rack last week. It looked businesslike, without being stuffy. She wanted to look approachable.

Her dad stuck his head in the door, took a look at the clothes on the bed and said, "You're not thinking of wearing anything except the suit I bought, are you? You know how important your first impression is. Nothing looks as professional as a navy blue suit."

"Dad, I'm not interviewing for an office job. I really need to think about what image I project with each of these outfits. Then I'll pick the best one for the job—meaning the interview."

► From Your Perspective

1. What other resources could Carla use to help her make her decision?

2. What other alternatives might Carla consider?

3. What values influence her choice? Her father's?

• When receiving a job offer, carefully write down all the details as the offer is made. **Why is it to your benefit to carefully consider the details of a job offer before accepting a job?**

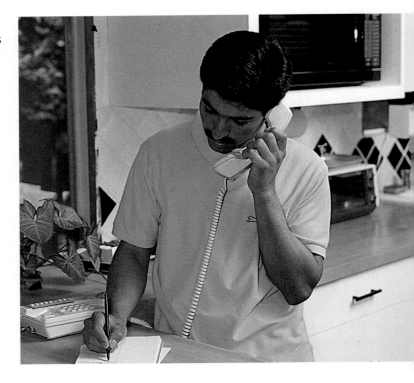

How Do You Evaluate a Job Offer?

Exactly one week after his interview, Ruben got a call from an interviewer offering him a job. He was asked to come in to discuss the position and its salary and benefits. At the close of the meeting, Ruben asked if he could take a day to decide. He wanted to analyze the offer before calling back to accept—or reject—it.

Like Ruben, you'll receive job offers and will have to decide whether or which one you will accept. Before making your final decision, consider the following factors:

- **Opportunities for training and advancement.** Does the company offer any formal training? What are your chances for advancement or promotion?

- **Lifestyle issues.** What is the work environment like? Will you have to share space? How convenient is the work location to where you live? What is the daily work schedule? Will you be expected to work overtime? To travel? If so, how often? Does the company allow time off for vacations, holidays, and illness? If so, with or without pay?

- **Benefits.** Benefits vary from company to company, and some of them may be more important to you than others. Examples include health insurance, tuition reimbursement, and childcare or eldercare. Determine the value of benefits offered before accepting a job. If it pays a higher salary but has few benefits, you may have to pay a substantial amount of money for the benefits you need.

- **Money.** Although the salary or wages offered are certainly important, the job itself is more important. It will help you establish a work history that you can use to progress up a career ladder. When deciding on a job offer, avoid setting unrealistic expectations regarding pay. Instead, consider other issues, such as advancement and training, lifestyle issues, and benefits provided. If you're offered a low salary, and you think your training and experience are worth more, counter with a somewhat higher salary that still keeps you within the range. However, avoid insisting on a high salary. In the end, it may disqualify you for the job offer.

If you decide the job is not right for you, graciously decline and thank the interviewer for the time spent with you. If you would like to work for the company, but in another position, you may add a comment such as, "If an opening comes up that requires more (or less) travel (or overtime), (or that calls for more responsibility), (or that provides more training), I would be very interested. Thanks again for your offer."

Every job you have is important in your work history. If you think a job isn't the right one for you—and that you are likely to leave it soon after starting—consider not taking it at all. Jumping quickly from job to job may jeopardize future chances to get work that you enjoy.

Résumé Pointers

Keep the following suggestions in mind when you're developing your résumé:

- Use good quality white, off-white, or ivory bond paper. Colors, other than neutral ones, and sizes, other than 8 1/2 x 11inches, are unprofessional. Avoid correction fluid or pen or pencil marks. Make sure there are no stains on the paper.

- Use a simple typeface that's easy to read. It shouldn't look like calligraphy—the typeface used for some wedding invitations.

- Make your résumé brief and easy to understand. Rather than lengthy paragraphs, use bullet points instead. Spell out abbreviations that aren't commonly used. Don't make the reader guess.

- Unless you're applying to be the company comedian, avoid humor in your résumé. Most people who read résumés aren't in the business to be entertained.

Understanding Key Concepts

● Developing a personal network is helpful in locating job leads.

● A variety of places in the community can be helpful in your job search.

● Résumés are used by employers to screen job candidates. Your résumé may be the first impression an employer will have of you.

● A résumé should be accompanied by a cover letter. The letter is successful if it interests the reader in taking a close look at your résumé.

● Applying for a job takes planning. The goal is to demonstrate that you are the best person to fill a position.

● A job interview can mean the difference between being hired or not being considered for a job.

● Following up on an interview is as important as initially preparing for it.

● Analyze a job offer to determine whether or not it is the right one for you.

Checking Your Knowledge

1. Explain why it is important to develop a personal network during your job search.

2. Give examples of people you could contact for job leads in your community.

3. What is the role of a job application form in the job search process?

4. Give examples of guidelines to follow when you're creating a résumé.

5. Which résumé option would you recommend for someone with little or no work experience? Why?

6. Summarize the three major parts of a cover letter.

7. What steps can you take to prepare for a job interview? Why is each step important?

8. What is the purpose of a job interview for the applicant? What purpose does it serve for the employer?

9. Why is it important to follow up a job interview, even if you don't want the job?

10. Summarize factors to consider when analyzing a job offer.

Making TRANSITIONS

Dealing with Inappropriate Interview Questions

Many federal, state, and local antidiscrimination statutes address questions employers can legally ask in job interviews. For example, during an interview you do not have to answer questions about your age, disabilities, children, citizenship, or HIV status.

Most employers are aware of these guidelines and follow them carefully during interviews. However, this is not always the case.

Assume you are interviewing for a job and are asked the following questions: "Do you have a disability that would interfere with your ability to perform the job?" "Have you made child-care arrangements?" "Where are your parents from?" You know these questions are not allowed, but you'd like to get the job. How might you avoid answering these questions and still put your best foot forward during the interview?

STRENGTHENING *Life* SKILLS

Using a Placement Office

Many colleges, universities, and technical schools have placement offices that help match job openings with suitable job seekers. Research the services of your community's nearest college placement office. Write or call the office to find out services that they offer students who are looking for a job or career. Write a summary of what you learned. Answer the following questions:

- How might the services of the placement office be useful to you?
- Where else might you go in your community for the same, or similar, services?

Applying Thinking Skills

1. **Comparing and contrasting.** Think about places you can go, and things you can use, in your community to get job leads. Compare and contrast their effectiveness. Defend your reasoning.

2. **Predicting consequences.** What consequences might occur in the following situations when individuals fill out and sign an application form: a job applicant failing to request people's permission before listing their names as references; an applicant listing one job he never held; and a person filling in the space "salary desired" with an amount that is double the salary she currently receives?

3. **Drawing conclusions.** What effect might an unsuccessful job interview have on an applicant? How might the experience be used to increase an individual's chances of success in the future?

Practical Applications

1. **Focusing on you.** From the "help wanted" ads in your local newspaper, select a job lead that is of interest to you. Write a letter of application for the position. Afterwards, research education and training opportunities that might enhance your chances to be considered for the job.

2. **Exchanging roles.** To prepare for future interviews, choose a partner, and take turns playing the roles of job applicant and interviewer. Later, discuss with each other the strengths and weaknesses observed during the interviews.

3. **Researching a business.** Select a company where you might like to work. Using school and community resources, research the company's history, services, and products. After studying the information, develop a list of questions to ask during a job interview at the company.

4. **Following up.** Assume you have just completed a job interview that reinforced your desire for a certain position. Write a thank-you letter to the interviewer. Share your letter with the class.

CHAPTER 27

Ensuring Workplace Success

What You Will Learn...

- Why you need workplace skills, good character, and relationship skills to succeed at work.
- Getting along with others at work involves knowing and fulfilling your role, teamwork, leadership, and courtesy.
- Continuing your training and education, having a mentor, and being a productive worker will increase your chances for advancement on the job.

Terms for Success

compensatory time
cross-functional team
functional team
workplace culture

Karin pulled into the catering shop parking lot ten minutes early. Hector was loading the van. "Ready for your first wedding?" he called.

"So ready I couldn't sleep," Karin replied. "I figured, why lie in bed and worry? I knew you'd start working before six."

Together they loaded the equipment as Hector had laid it out, in reverse order from the way it would be needed: first, dishes and table service, then warming trays, then tables. Finally, only the rolls of table covering remained.

"Those have to ride in the front seat with us," Hector explained. "We angle them like this—see? They won't fit anywhere else."

Karin frowned. "Can you see out the window?"

Hector shrugged. "Pretty well. Although shifting into reverse is kind of hard, we've managed so far. Someday, when we can buy a bigger van. . ."

Karin looked back at her car. "They'll fit in my back seat. I can follow you in my car."

Hector looked uncertainly between the two vehicles. "That would make it easier—on me," he agreed, but you'd have to drive there and back."

"I don't mind," Karin explained. "I feel like, this is my show—partly—and I want to put on a good one. I just want everything to go right."

Hector grinned. "You really are ready! Pull your car around and we'll load the table covering. Thanks. Now, if Jake will just be on time. He's supposed to be there at eight, but he always reminds me that he's not a 'morning person.' "

"Hmm. Maybe you could call him from the van on the way there," Karin suggested with a smile. "Make sure he's running on time."

Hector laughed. "Yes, a personal wake-up call from the boss. That would make a 'morning person' out of me!"

> **?** Do you know people whom you consider successful workers? Do you think of yourself as one? Why or why not? What are the qualities you need to be a successful worker?

What Makes a Successful Worker?

Being successful on the job takes hard work and sometimes going "the extra mile." Karin arrived at work early, and she was willing to make her boss's job easier by driving to their catering job.

Successful workers do more than show up and do the minimum amount of work required. They have the exact skills that are needed for their jobs. They are proactive and involved in their work, with a "can-do" attitude. The best workers get along with others and help others be successful, too.

You Measure Up

You can't be a success in the workplace unless you understand the qualities and skills that are required. Once you know what is expected on the job, you can display these traits and talents.

Employers look for workers who can get along. Do you cooperate with others and treat them fairly? Are you helpful, even when it may not be convenient for you? Are you friendly to everyone? On a new job, it's important to listen, learn, and avoid taking sides. It isn't always easy to tell who is influential.

Most employers are sympathetic to personal problems, but they expect you to keep them separate from your work life. Such problems shouldn't interfere with your work time or performance.

Appearance is important. Are you neat, clean, and dressed appropriately for your specific workplace?

Each job requires specific skills and abilities. You may need to know computer programming or accounting to get jobs in these fields. On the other hand, personal or character traits are more important to some employers. They are willing to train the right worker for the job.

• Roofing a building successfully involves knowledge and skills. Identify at least three qualities that a successful roofer would need.

Character Counts

You learned about the importance of character in Chapter 3. Moral character and ethical behavior are necessary qualities for successful workers. Employers seek these traits:

- **Reliability and dependability.** Will you be there when you are supposed to be there and do what you said you'd do? Successful workers follow through when they are given a job—they work until the job is done and take care of any loose ends.
- **Honesty.** Lying, stealing supplies, products, money, or other property belonging to your employer or coworkers will always get you in trouble.
- **Loyalty.** Loyal employees promote the best interests of their employers. Loyalty means not saying or doing things that will reflect negatively on your boss.
- **Strong work ethic.** Do you work hard, do the job right, and do your best?

The Job Measures Up

Successful workers are usually in jobs that they like and find satisfying. It's hard to be proactive, show initiative, and do your best if you don't like, or are disappointed in, your job.

You will be most successful when:

- You feel comfortable and safe in the work environment. You have the tools and equipment you need to do the job, work conditions that are safe and healthy, and there are fair, supportive policies in effect.
- You earn salaries and benefits that are appropriate for your skills. Every worker would probably prefer to earn more money. What actually happens in the workplace is that workers who have certain skills earn certain levels of pay.
- Your job allows you to do productive work you enjoy and gives you the opportunity for personal development and learning.

- Dressing appropriately for work is easy when you wear a uniform. How does appropriate dress benefit you in the workplace?

If you accept a job that is not right for you, you will find it harder to be successful. The best jobs bring out the best in you. When the job fits you, you are interested and enthusiastic. You feel like you are making an important contribution in your work.

Getting Along at Work

Most problems that people have at work are due to their relationships with other workers. Many people who leave their jobs or are fired do not lack the specific skills needed for the job. Instead, they have had difficulty in getting along with others.

When you build and maintain relationships at work, you are making an investment in your job or career. If you use relationship skills well, you will have a good chance at job success. How can you accomplish this?

- **Respect others and their qualities and personalities.** You will be more likely to get along if you appreciate peoples' differences, even when these differences cause problems.
- **Communicate effectively.** When you work with others toward common goals, you must send and receive messages accurately. Make your messages upbeat, positive, and supportive. Listening is an important skill, especially in situations where you need to know what to do.
- **Focus on effectiveness rather than personality.** One of the hardest things to do at work is to get along with people you don't really like. You have to be able to separate your personal feelings from the job requirements and appreciate the skills that the person brings to the workplace.
- **Learn to resolve workplace conflicts effectively.** If you can focus on the problem instead of your emotions, you are more apt to be thought of as a mature and professional employee. Use compromise and negotiation to help you lead the way to win-win problem solving.
- **Be a leader who promotes cooperation and teamwork.** You can help others work together toward common goals.

FOCUS ON ...

It's the Law

The federal government manages the safety of workers, through the Occupational Safety and Health Administration (OSHA). OSHA, a branch of the U.S. Department of Labor, sets standards, inspects sites, and fines companies that don't meet the standards.

A federal insurance program, *worker's compensation*, helps cover lost wages and medical expenses when workers are hurt on the job. The employer pays for this insurance.

Many state and federal laws govern work and pay. Laws set the lowest hourly wage an employer can pay workers, and an overtime wage, pay for working more than 40 hours a week. Laws also cover **compensatory time**, which is time off in exchange for working extra hours. Child labor laws regulate the minimum age for workers. Unemployment insurance helps workers who lose their jobs.

It is illegal for employers to discriminate. This means to hire, promote, or fire people because of their race, religion, nationality, gender, age, disability, or physical appearance.

Laws prohibit sexual harassment in the workplace. Sexual harassment is any unwelcome behavior of a sexual nature. It includes sexual advances or conduct that creates an intimidating, hostile, or offensive work environment.

If you feel your company or its workers are committing illegal acts, you should protect yourself. Report your concerns or complaints to the appropriate people in your company. If you don't get satisfactory answers, you can contact your local human rights office, the state agency that handles labor issues, the U.S. Department of Labor, or the U.S. Equal Employment Opportunity Commission.

Difficult People

TIPS

Every workplace seems to have a "difficult" person who makes every issue a problem and who can't get along with others. When you have to deal with a difficult person:

- **Act immediately when a problem occurs.** Using a professional manner, ask to discuss the issue right away.

- **Find a neutral site.** Can you talk over lunch?

- **Listen first.** Focus on understanding the other's position before you try to get your point across. A difficult person may just want to be heard.

- **Focus on problems, not personalities.** Don't blame—problem solve.

What's Your Role?

Every worker has important roles to play at work, or else the employer wouldn't pay to have the job done. One of your first tasks as a new worker is to figure out what your role is. Understanding your place will help you know how to act in order to do your job well.

Each workplace is different. One difference is the **workplace culture,** which is based on the values, behavior, attitudes, habits, and expectations of employees and owners. Chaney's first impression of her new job was that her coworkers were unfriendly. When she realized that competition was a big part of the workplace culture, she understood that her coworkers saw each other as competitors rather than friends.

• A strong work ethic is an asset to any worker. Write a paragraph describing how you think a person's work ethic develops.

• Company culture affects the relationships among employees. Identify three benefits to an employer of providing opportunities for employees to get to know each other better.

It will take you time to understand the culture at a new job and how to fit in. When you are in a new situation, listen, keep your eyes open, and ask questions. Until you understand the company culture, it is better to be more cautious than rash in your actions.

In most work settings, each job has a place in the hierarchy of positions. Seeing where you fit in can help you choose appropriate behavior:

- A boss or supervisor is someone to whom you report.
- Colleagues are at the same level of responsibility as you are.
- Subordinates are workers who report to you.

In each case, the company culture will probably define how you are expected to act and interact with others. Be alert to the nonverbal clues that will tell you what others expect. It will take time to learn how to be most effective.

Teamwork

Members of a sports team must work together to build a winning record. Each player has a role to play, tasks to do, and skills to learn before the team can be successful.

The team concept is becoming more common in the workplace. Working for the good of the team and cooperating to reach a common goal are just as important on the job as they are in sports.

Forming a Team

Work teams can be formed in many different ways. A **functional team** is made up of members who do similar jobs or who all work in the same department. Robert, who is a nurse, and those who work with him in the hospital intensive care unit are a functional team.

A **cross-functional team** is composed of people with different areas of expertise or from two or more departments. Robert is also on a cross-functional team that plans care for patients with long-term illnesses. This team includes Robert, a physician, a dietitian, a respiratory therapist, and a social worker.

Whatever the type of team, the activities center on reaching goals for the employer. Allie's job is in the print shop of a department store. Her team prides itself on getting materials printed correctly, on time, and economically.

Qualities of Good Team Members

Being a good team member means more than just getting along with your other team members. You must learn to work together effectively. You can do your part to build team feeling and spirit by:

- Respecting others the way you want to be respected.

- Recognizing that all team members, including yourself, have strengths and weaknesses. You can take advantage of the team's collective strengths and help make up for each other's weaknesses.
- Praising others for their contributions or efforts.
- Remaining levelheaded and calm when the inevitable conflict flares. Use your conflict resolution skills to help solve problems.
- Listening to others' ideas and positions.
- Showing genuine interest in other team members.
- Being loyal to the team by not gossiping about the company or team members.
- Focusing on cooperation and win-win solutions to problems.

• Communication is an important skill when dealing with others at work. Describe all the methods of communication that are being used in this photo.

Showing Leadership

Leadership takes time, energy, skills, and dedication. It can be learned, but it's not easy. In Chapter 5, you learned the characteristics of an effective leader. You can use these same traits on your job by using the power and abilities of others to accomplish goals. Be a good example of a loyal worker.

There are many ways to show leadership at work:

- Promote and build your team's spirit and accomplishments.
- Set an example of good work habits and ethics.

- Use and teach—by example, if nothing else—effective communication and conflict resolution skills.
- Be proactive by making things happen rather than waiting for them to happen.

Many jobs don't appear to require leadership skills. Leadership, however, can be shown in any job. Jose says, "The last job every night before we leave work is to sweep the floor. We're tired and don't always do a good job; I've been trying to make a game of it by challenging the others to a "Coin Hunt" contest. Whoever has the most dust or finds the most change on the floor wins. The games make it easier to do a job we hate." Jose showed leadership in suggesting a way to improve performance in a tedious task.

The most effective leaders, who are trusted by others, have integrity and strong moral character. They are honest, ethical, and keep the promises and agreements they make. They take responsibility for their behavior and decisions.

● Being effective team members means working well together. List five qualities that would help this team build spirit.

Fitting In

T I P S

"Fitting in" is an important skill on the job. These ideas can help:

- **Read the policy and procedures handbook.** It contains valuable information that can help you avoid mistakes.

- **Think before you speak.** This will help you avoid "foot" problems—stepping on others' toes or putting your foot in your mouth.

- **Learn the rules.** Each workplace has a culture and a personality; it takes time to figure them out.

- **Be realistic and expect the unexpected.** Don't allow yourself to get upset when unexpected things happen.

- **Don't push**—acceptance comes slowly as you show your work ethic and attitudes. Your ideas will be accepted after you have been.

- **Figure out what your boss needs and expects—and do it!** This can make your boss your biggest ally.

Friendships and Work

Work is the most likely place adults meet new people and form new friendships. While personal relationships at work can be very rewarding, they can also cause problems:

- **Conflicts.** Conflict away from work can cause friction at work and disrupt the workplace. Caitlin was furious when Morgan, one of her coworkers, borrowed and ruined her favorite sweater. How well could they work together after this experience?

- **Expectations.** Employer and role expectations can create problems. A potential trouble spot occurs if one friend is promoted and becomes the other's boss. Jason says, "When I was promoted, I became the boss of my best friend at work. It's been a bad situation—I'm not comfortable reprimanding him, so he takes advantage of me. The others don't like that, and I don't either. It's going to be our friendship or our jobs."

• Good introductions can help people feel comfortable with each other. Give three suggestions for introducing people that could help them develop rapport.

• Personal conflict in a friendship between coworkers can affect relationships and productivity at work. With your classmates, discuss why a workplace friendship can be both natural as well as a potential problem.

• **Romance.** Romantic relationships at work can be difficult. Any such relationship should be discreet, although it is best to keep work and romance separate. You should never get involved romantically with a superior or a subordinate. Sexual harassment claims or charges of preferential treatment may result.

Mind Your Manners

Common courtesy plays an important role in worker relationships. Good manners are never out of place, even in a workplace that is casual and informal. Keep these tips in mind:

• Address others with respect and dignity.
• Honor the privacy of others. This includes avoiding gossip and rumors.
• Show politeness on the telephone, no matter how much you hate being interrupted.

• Practice your introductions so that you can introduce yourself and others confidently and comfortably.
• Prepare carefully for meetings. Be on time and introduce yourself to people you don't know. Understand the issues that will be discussed. Pay attention and look interested in the proceedings. Think before you speak and when you disagree, do so tactfully and positively.

Getting Ahead

Most jobs have a probationary period, typically 30 to 90 days. This gives the employer a chance to see whether you have the skills to do the job and the ability to get along with your coworkers. At the same time, you can decide if you will be comfortable and successful in this work environment.

Opportunities for Advancement

Most people want the opportunity to advance on the job. Promotions usually bring more responsibilities, challenges, and income.

In order to be promoted, you will need to gain the attention and respect of your coworkers and boss. You must have a good relationship with your boss to advance. In making a decision, your employer will look at how you:

- Perform and produce on the job.
- Work with others.
- Deal with the stress and pressures of the workplace.
- Learn new skills and procedures.

If you have shown enthusiasm, a positive attitude, leadership skills, and loyalty to the company, you are most likely to be promoted.

Keeping up with the changes in your field or business is essential. You can update your skills through company-sponsored training, local technical or private schools, community colleges, adult education, or through seeking a college or advanced degree.

The Benefits of a Mentor

Having a mentor often helps a worker who wants to advance. A mentor is an informal teacher, usually someone older and more experienced in your field or company. Mentors can help you learn your company's culture, suggest ways you could improve your skills, and introduce you to others who can serve as resources for you.

Some workplaces have formal mentorship programs that pair up new and experienced employees. In most cases, the mentor relationship develops naturally through working together.

Changing Careers

Some people discover that their early job or career choices were not good ones. Other people decide after a few years in one type of job that they are ready for a change to something new. Workers who have been let go when a firm downsizes may not have opportunities in the same field. For whatever reason, many people decide that they want to try something new.

• Having a mentor can be a valuable way to learn what it takes to advance on the job. What are two benefits and two disadvantages of having a formal mentoring program rather than having mentorships develop informally?

Benefits Options

"Am I ever confused," said Lee. "I went in to fill out the paperwork for my new job with the county. I didn't understand any of the benefits information they told me. Which health care plan did I want? Did I want to contribute to a retirement plan? Was I interested in the child care subsidy? How did I want to use my cafeteria plan money? I didn't have a clue. The only thing I did understand was that I have unlimited free access to the workout facilities in the sheriff's department!"

Understanding Benefits

Benefits are usually part of the total compensation paid to full-time workers. Benefits average about 40 percent of an employer's payroll costs, so they are valuable. Each company's benefit plan varies depending on (1) what may be offered; (2) whether and how much the employee has to pay; and (3) whether benefits are optional or required.

A *cafeteria plan* is a system that lets employees choose the benefits they want. A worker who is covered under a spouse's health care plan may prefer disability insurance rather than duplicate medical coverage. Companies without cafeteria plans usually have set benefits for all employees.

The major types of benefits are:

- **Health Insurance.** This is the most popular benefit among employees. Several health care plans may be offered. If you understand your options, you can pick the plan that is best for your situation.

- **Retirement plans.** Companies may offer traditional pension plans or 401K savings plans. Employers, employees, or both may contribute to the plan.

- **Incentive plans.** Companies may offer bonuses for outstanding performance or profit sharing plans, in which the profit the company makes is shared with employees.

- **Other insurance.** Workers can often get economical life, disability, or legal insurance through their companies.

- **Other benefits.** Some companies provide services that make workers' lives easier, such as flexible working hours, on-site child care, auto repair, a fitness center, or food service, such as a snack bar or cafeteria.

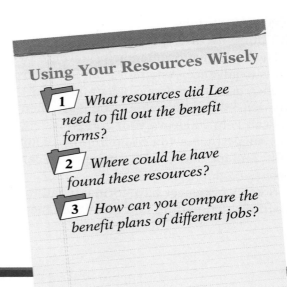

Using Your Resources Wisely

1. What resources did Lee need to fill out the benefit forms?

2. Where could he have found these resources?

3. How can you compare the benefit plans of different jobs?

Considering a new career is both exciting and frightening. Yet there are things to do that will make the process easier:

- **Learn all you can as you perform your current job.** Observe what other people do, how they interact with others, and what qualities make them valued employees.
- **Take advantage of formal learning opportunities, like training classes.** Anything you learn can be used to improve your skills and your ability to market yourself to another employer.
- **Improve your general skills.** They can often be the difference between success and failure in getting a new job.

- **Develop a portfolio of your work.** Your projects, suggestions, and reports provide concrete evidence of your capabilities to an employer.

Working for the Future

In one sense, every day you work affects your future as a worker. The work habits you develop now will be harder to change in the future. Successes build your skills and abilities. Mistakes can be learning experiences or disasters. What you do and how you handle the consequences of your actions can have a long-term impact on you both personally and as a worker.

You may hold a number of jobs in your work life. Some will be more rewarding to you than others. You will ensure your success in all of them if you prepare yourself through education and training, work well with people in a team setting, and commit yourself to doing each job competently and responsibly.

• Developing a portfolio of work can help illustrate your skills. Make a list of items that you could include in a portfolio to demonstrate your abilities.

REASON

Solving a Problem

Practical problems are complicated because they usually involve several issues. They have an impact on others, which means the decision should reflect what's right, fair, or best for everyone involved. Note the steps of the REASON process in the scenario below.

"I'm so tired of this job! Our team is not going to reach our productivity goal again. There goes my chance for a bonus check this month!" Claudia muttered to herself.

Claudia has worked at the same factory for almost two years. Her excellent job performance and near-perfect attendance has earned her the position of team leader. She is responsible for motivating five other team members into meeting their quotas every week. When they meet their quota, each member gets a bonus.

"That new guy Fred just isn't keeping up the pace," Claudia thought to herself. "He's dragging the whole team down. I just don't like his attitude. He just isn't a team player."

Claudia discussed her concerns with Greta over lunch. Greta had been a team leader for several years.

"Spend the next few days observing Fred closely," Greta suggested. "Document your concerns in writing. Then you can go to your supervisor with some specific suggestions."

The next day Claudia watched Fred closely. He came in late and went straight to this bench to work. "Why didn't he clock in?" wondered Claudia. At break time she checked Fred's time card. It said he had clocked in one-half hour earlier.

Claudia continued to watch Fred closely. Even though he worked quickly and efficiently, by early afternoon he was behind in supplying his part to the next part of the line. Claudia was shocked when Fred did not return to the line after taking a restroom break about one-half hour before quitting time. His time card at the end of the day showed a checkout time the same as everybody else's.

"It's no wonder he's always behind, if he's working an hour less than everybody else on the team," Claudia thought. She made notes on Fred's arrival and departure time the rest of the week, and found that he was consistently cheating the clock an hour every day. She saw Ethan, a member of another team, punching two time cards.

"Now what do I do?" worried Claudia. "One team member is cheating the company out of an hour every day, and another is helping him do it."

That night, Claudia took her employee handbook home. She looked up the discipline code.

"It looks like I have four choices," Claudia concluded. "I can ignore the problem. I can go to my supervisor with my documented concerns. I can talk to Fred myself, and try to convince him to quit the cheating. Or I could send an anonymous note to the supervisor telling him about what Fred is doing."

Claudia sat down at her desk and outlined her alternatives and their consequences.

"That's it," Claudia sighed. "I've got to take this to my supervisor right away. All the other alternatives have too many consequences I am not willing to accept."

"I will meet the supervisor first thing tomorrow and will show him the documentation I have gathered. I will offer to speak to Fred myself," thought Claudia, "as long as the supervisor is aware of the situation and is willing to back me up."

Several weeks later, Claudia was called into the supervisor's office and was commended on how well she had handled the situation.

Through Life's Problems

"This worked out really well," she sighed. As soon as Claudia had confronted Fred, he promised to quit cheating. He was afraid of losing his job and making Ethan lose his, too. He had been doing much better for the past several weeks, and was beginning to be one of Claudia's most productive team members. Each team member received a bonus check for the past two pay periods.

ALTERNATIVES	CONSEQUENCES FOR ME	CONSEQUENCES FOR OTHERS
1. Ignore situation.	1.a. Won't feel good about my responsibility. 1.b. Won't get bonus. 1.c. Could get in trouble for not making supervisor aware of situation. 1.d. Could lose my job for not reporting.	1.a. Company is losing money. 1.b. Other team members won't get bonuses. 1.c. Fred and Ethan could end up losing their jobs. 1.d. Fred could keep getting paid for an hour he doesn't work.
2. Talk to Fred without telling supervisor.	2.a. I'm not sure I have backing of supervisor. 2.b. Fred could get nasty, maybe retaliate. 2.c. I could lose my job.	2.a. Fred won't be sure I mean what I say. 2.b. Fred might quit cheating and suffer no consequences at all.
3. Send anonymous note.	3.a. Seems really immature. 3.b. Supervisor would not be impressed. 3.c. Would be easier.	3.a. Fred could figure out who sent the note and retaliate. 3.b. Fred would probably lose his job.
4. Talk to supervisor first, then confront Fred.	4.a. Shows supervisor I'm able to handle tough situations. 4.b. Supervisor might be upset that I hadn't reported cheating earlier.	4.a. Fred and Ethan might lose their jobs. 4.b. Fred and Ethan might stop cheating.

▶ From Your Perspective

1 What is the primary problem Claudia must deal with? Who is involved?

2 What values are involved in this situation?

3 What sources of information did Claudia use in solving her problem? Were they reliable?

4 Do you think Claudia will handle similar situations in the future in the same way? Why or why not?

Understanding Key Concepts

- To be successful, you must understand the requirements and expectations of a job and be able to meet or surpass them.
- Employers value character traits such as reliability, dependability, honesty, loyalty, and a strong work ethic.
- A job must meet your expectations in order for you to be an effective worker.
- Getting along at work requires respect for others, communication and conflict resolution skills, leadership, and appreciation of others' efforts.
- Teamwork, as seen in functional and cross-functional teams, is valuable to a productive workplace culture.
- A leader in the workplace directs others, coaches and supports, teaches, and sets an example.
- Advancement on the job is usually the result of productivity, developing new skills, showing leadership, and getting along with others.
- Mentors can help new workers advance on the job by teaching workplace and interpersonal skills.

Checking Your Knowledge

1. Why is understanding job expectations essential to workplace success?
2. Describe someone who displays the character traits desired by employers.
3. Explain why opportunities for learning and personal development can make a job more satisfying.
4. Discuss why getting along with others may be more important than specific work skills for job success.
5. Explain what is meant by workplace culture. How could it affect workers?
6. Summarize the qualities of members of an effective work team.
7. Identify at least two ways to show leadership on each of the following jobs: stock clerk; forklift driver; fast food server; retail store clerk.
8. Discuss the potential rewards and problems of developing friendships with coworkers.
9. Describe how the workplace culture could affect the manners and courtesies expected on the job.

Making
TRANSITIONS

Constructive Criticism

It's never easy to be criticized for your performance, but it happens frequently in the workplace. Constructive criticism is not meant to punish or insult a worker, but rather to help a worker improve. Your attitude toward criticism is crucial—if you view it as helpful in improving your job performance, you will benefit from it.

Imagine that you are a salesperson in a retail store. Your work supervisor has just told you that your performance is unsatisfactory because you do not get to work on time, and you have been seen being rude to customers. Your cash drawer rarely balances, and you do not keep the area around your cash register tidy. Write three questions that you could ask to identify exactly what your supervisor expects. Then write a paragraph explaining how you could use the criticism to improve so you can keep your job.

STRENGTHENING *Life* SKILLS

Making Introductions

Being able to make introductions can be an important social skill in the workplace. In making an introduction, say the name of the older person first, telling each person the name of the other. Add some information about each person so that she or he can start a conversation. For example, you might say, "Mrs. Collins, I'd like you to meet my cousin Tamara Jones. She attends North High School and is staying with me this week. Tamara, this is my neighbor Mrs. Collins. She graduated from North High School."

Form a group with two of your classmates. Practice introducing each other and see if the two people who have been introduced can start a conversation from the introduction.

When you have finished, answer the following questions:
- What types of comments or information brought about the most conversation?
- Why is practice important to make effective introductions?

Applying Thinking Skills

1. **Comparing and contrasting.** What are the similarities and differences between functional and cross-functional teams? Which do you think would be more important in the workplace? Defend your answer.

2. **Predicting consequences.** What would be the impact on employees of having a supervisor use a directive, authoritarian style of leadership? A supportive coaching style of leadership? Which would you prefer in a boss? Why?

3. **Developing criteria.** Think about the first full-time job that you would like to have when you graduate. Imagine you were going to be the supervisor of that job. How would you know when the worker has done a good job? Develop a scorecard or checklist to evaluate the performance of a worker who holds the job.

Practical Applications

1. **Personal assessment.** Using a library or the Internet, write a brief report on the personal qualities that are needed for your "dream job." Consider whether you have the qualities you've identified. If not, what could you do to acquire them?

2. **Team building observation.** Observe a team sports event and look for ways that both team members and coaches build and support team spirit. List your observations, then give one suggestion about how each team-building action you've listed about sports could be used to build team spirit in the workplace.

3. **Making decisions.** Imagine you have become a close friend with a coworker. One day your friend leaves work and says to tell the boss, if you are asked, that your friend is in another department. If your boss asks, what will you say? What personal values and ethics will affect your answer?

Glossary

A

acquired immune deficiency syndrome (AIDS): A life-threatening disease that interferes with the body's natural ability to fight infection. (12)

active listening: The listener interacts with the speaker and pays close attention to what the speaker is saying. (6)

advocates: Individuals who speak out for consumer interests. (16)

adult development: Changes in how adults think and behave as they go through different phases, such as middle age and retirement. (8)

aggressive: Messages that verbally attack, judge, and trample on the feelings of others. (6)

affirmation: Powerful expressions that smooth the way to mutual respect, understanding, and cooperation. (6)

amenities: Special features. (19)

apathy: A lack of feeling, concern, or interest in the lives of others. (4)

apprentice: A worker who learns a skilled trade requiring two or more years of on-the-job experience and instruction. (25)

assertive: Communicating directly and honestly about what you think, feel, believe, or want without showing disrespect for those of others. (6)

asset: An item of value that a person owns. (22)

attachment: The psychological and emotional ties between people in a close relationship. (8)

autonomy: Independence; freedom to enjoy time and activities away from each other. (10)

average annual expenditure: The normal amount of money spent each year by consumers. (21)

B

balance: The internal sense of steadiness that results when all parts of a person's life are in unity with what he or she values. (4)

boundaries: Limits based upon your values, goals, and priorities. (4)

C

character: Being morally strong and having the ability to think, judge, and act with maturity. (3)

collateral: Property you pledge in exchange for borrowed money. (23)

commission: A fee paid to someone for a service. (22)

commitment: A pledge to give a relationship top priority. (11)

common values: Values common to most societies and cultures. (3)

comparison shopping: Looking at quality, design, price, and warranties to compare value before you buy. (18)

compensatory time: Time off in exchange for working extra hours. (27)

context: A set of circumstances to consider. (2)

cost-per-serving: The price divided by the number of servings. (17)

cost-per-wearing: The total purchase price plus the cost of cleaning divided by the number of times you expect to wear the garment. (18)

credit bureau: A company that collects and distributes information about people's credit histories. (23)

credit report: A list of your credit use and repayment history. (23)

cross-functional team: Composed of people with different areas of expertise or from two or more different departments. (27)

D

daily values: Nutrient amounts based on recommendations of health experts. (13)

decision test: Asking yourself certain questions to determine whether or not a particular choice is ethical. (3)

default: Failure to pay a financial obligation. (25)

defense mechanism: Strategies to deal with stressful situations. (14)

depreciation: Losing value. (20)

diversify: Putting money into a variety of investments. (22)

dividends: Part of the profit from a fund or an organization. (21)

E

eating patterns: When, what, and how much people eat. (13)

engagement: A promise or intention to marry. (11)

ethics: The principles or values that guide your life. (2)

ethical choices: Choices that involve making decisions about what is fair, right, just, caring, and best for all people involved. (2)

evict: A landlord's action to force you to move out for failure to pay rent. (19)

F

freezer burn: Results when improperly stored food dries out and loses flavor and texture. (17)

fringe benefits: Income such as from sick leave, savings plans, retirement funds, or health and life insurance plans. (21)

functional team: Members who do similar jobs or who all work in the same department. (27)

G

garnishee: Money deducted from a person's paycheck and given to the winner of the lawsuit. (16)

garnishment: A legal procedure in which your employer is required to withhold part of your wages. (23)

grace period: A period of time when interest is not charged if the balance is paid in full by the end of the time. (23)

gross earnings: The amount of your paycheck, or the total wages you earned for that period, less deductions. (21)

H

health maintenance organization (HMO): A group of physicians who offer a comprehensive range of health care services for regular monthly fees. (12)

hidden job market: Sources of jobs that are less obvious to many other job seekers. (26)

human immunodeficiency virus (HIV): The virus that causes AIDS. (12)

I

interdependence: A feeling of mutual reliance with others. (1)

I-messages: Explain facts and feelings as you see them. (5)

inflation: A period of time when prices of goods and services rise sharply. (22)

J

job lead: Information about a possible job opening. (26)

job shadowing: Spending time on the job with someone who works in a career of interest to you. (24)

justification: Reasons that support your solution. (2)

L

lease: A written contract between a landlord and a renter, stating the responsibilities of both parties. (19)

lifelong learning: Taking opportunities to keep your skills and knowledge up to date throughout your life. (1)

M

marketing: The process of getting goods and services to consumers who want them. (16)

mass transit: Public transportation. (20)

maturity date: A date when the person loaning the money will receive the original amount back with interest. (22)

mediator: An impartial person who acts as a go-between for those in conflict. (7)

mentor: A guide. (4)

mobility: Geographical relocation of individuals and families due to school, work, retirement, or other factors. (9)

multipurpose garments: Garments that can be worn for more than one activity. (18)

N

network: Making contact with others. (4)

nutrient deficiency: A severe shortage of nutrients that can cause illness, infections, or other conditions later in life. (13)

nutrient-dense foods: Foods that are low or moderate in calories and rich in important nutrients. (17)

O

outsource: One company pays other companies or individuals to do certain tasks, rather than hire employees. (24)

P

passive listening: Listening quietly and attentively. (6)

persistence: Being committed to a well-reasoned solution, no matter how difficult the process may be. (2)

perspective: Looking at things from a certain point of view. (4)

physical well-being: Your health and how well you feel. (13)

platonic relationship: A relationship in which there is affection, but no romance. (10)

practical problems: Complicated situations that often include ethical choices or moral outcomes. (2)

preferred provider organization (PPO): A managed care plan in which physicians and other health care providers agree to charge less to members of the plan. (12)

pretreatment: Applying stain-removal techniques before cleaning a garment. (18)

priorities: Things most important to you. (4)

R

reciprocal relationship: A relationship in which the amount of give-and-take is equal. (5)

repetitive strain injury: A painful medical disorder caused by performing a similar activity over and over. (13)

resilience: The ability to recover from, or adjust to change or misfortune. (1)

S

safety spot: An area that provides some measure of safety from falling objects. (15)

security deposit: Money that a landlord holds as a guarantee against damages. (19)

service learning: Student action that builds on learning through community service. (4)

sexual abstinence: The decision not to engage in sexual activity. (12)

sexually transmitted diseases (STDs): Diseases passed from one person to another through sexual contact. (12)

standard: A rule, principle, or measure for testing the quality of something. (3)

staples: The basic food items you use on a regular basis, such as flour, sugar, rice, pasta, and nonfat dry milk. (17)

statement reconciliation: The process of bringing your financial account records into agreement with the statement. (22)

sticker price: Refers to the price information affixed to the vehicle window. (20)

stress management: Controlling the effect stressors have on you. (14)

stressor: A stress trigger. (14)

subletting: The process of letting someone take over a dwelling temporarily and pay the rentflusually with the landlord's approval. (19)

T

title: A legal paper that shows who owns an automobile. (20)

trade: An occupation that requires manual or mechanical skill. (25)

U

unit price: The price per ounce, quart, pound, or other unit. (17)

V

values conflict: Differences in priorities, goals, or lifestyles that clash. (9)

W

watch: A weather term than means conditions could develop into a tornado or hurricane. (15)

warning: A weather term meaning a hurricane or tornado has been sighted. (15)

wellness: A state of optimum health. (12)

win-win solution: Solution created from a collaborated effort to solve a problem so that everyone benefits. (7)

work ethic: Your choices about whether or not to work hard, do the job right, and give it your best. (24)

workplace culture: The values, behavior, attitudes, habits, and expectations of employees and the business owners. (27)

Index

A

Abilities, 449

Abstinence, 211, 509. *See also* Sexual abstinence.

Accentuating in conflict management, 116

Acceptance
in families, 141
as leadership trait, 87
in marriage, 190

Accessories, 320

Accidents. *See also* Safety
preventing home, 266-67

Acquired immune deficiency syndrome (AIDS), 175, 211, 212, 506

Active listening, 108, 506

Activities, planning creative inexpensive, 173

Adult development, 135, 506
independence in, 25-26, 140
stages of, 138-39

Adulthood, transition to, 143

Adult relationships, 152

Advancement, opportunities for, 499

Advertising, 280, 282
evaluating, 283
options in, 290

Advocates, 291, 506

Aerobic exercise, 232

Affirmations, 506
in communication, 102-3
in families, 141

Aggressive message, 103, 506

AIDS (acquired immune deficiency syndrome), 175, 211, 212, 506

Alcohol and driving, 265

Alternatives, analysis of, 44, 77, 483

Amenities, 343, 506

Amnesty International, 89

Anaerobic exercise, 232

Anger, controlling, 117

Annual Percentage Rate (APR), 425

Antitheft options for automobile, 265

Anxiety, overcoming social, 169

Apartments
disadvantages of, 345
efficiency, 335
rental agreements for, 346-47

and rights and responsibilities of renters, 347
and selecting roommate, 340-41, 344, 352, 353
technology in today's, 350

Apathy, 84, 506

Apologizing, 178

Appearance
as benefit of exercise, 228
in communication, 107

Application form, 477-78

Appreciation, showing, 145

Apprenticeships, 459, 506

Aptitudes, 449

Arbitration, 291

Asbestos, 269

Assertiveness, 103, 506
showing, 219
in stress management, 250

Assets, 398, 506

Attachment
building, 147
in families, 141-42, 506
in workplace, 146

Attitude, positive, 27

Automated teller machines (ATMs), 400

Automatic deductions from checking accounts, 384

Automobile
antitheft options for, 265
buying, 361-63, 365-70
choosing mechanic for, 367
depreciation of, 362, 507
financing, 362
gasoline for, 363
insurance for, 362-63
lemon laws for, 366
maintenance costs for, 362
safety, 264-65
title for, 370
used, 363, 366, 368-69
warranty for, 367

Autonomy, 168, 170, 506

Average annual expenditure, 385, 506

Awards, 461

Awareness, increasing, 110

B

C

P

Parenthood, desire for, and decision to have children, 194
Parenting
thinking about, 192-95
in thinking about marriage, 187
Participatory leadership, 86
Part-time jobs, 443, 464
growth in, 445
Passive listening, 108, 508
Pathogens, 211
Payee, 399
Payroll deductions, 384
Peace Corps, 89
People, meeting new, 110-11, 168-70
People with disabilities, transportation services available for, 361
Permanent insurance, 217
Persistence, 49, 87, 508
Personal fulfillment, balance in, 68
Personal identification number (PIN), 400
Personal interests in becoming volunteer, 89
Personality, 26
resilience in, 28-29
values in, 26
Personal needs, 70
Personal resources, 73
Personal safety, 258-60, 262
Personal well-being, 441
Perspective, 508
keeping healthy, 75-76
Physical activities, value of, 232
Physical environment, 449
Physical fitness, achieving, 228-35
Physical health as benefit of exercise, 228
Physical signs and effects of stress, 245-46
Physical strength as benefit of exercise, 229
Physical well-being, 236, 508
achieving, 222
improving, 252-53
Plagiarism, 62
avoiding, 62
Platonic relationship, 167-68, 508
Police, calling, 260
Policy and procedures handbook, 497
Polio, 211
Pollutants, avoiding, 268-69

Positive, accentuating, in conflict management, 117
Positive approach, 27
Positive messages, sending, 102
Possessive behavior, dealing with, 181
Practical problems, 39-40, 508
solving, 41-45
Precycling, 271
Preferred provider organization (PPO), 209, 508
Prejudice, 161
overcoming, in the workplace, 162
Premium, 208
Preparation, 90-91
Pressing, 326
Pretreatment, 323, 508
Prices, comparing, 306-7
Principal, 416
Priorities, 508
setting, 74-75
Privacy, 288
Private consumer groups, 291
Private health insurance plans, 209
Private job services or agencies, 443
Problem solving, 36-49, 502-3
and character, 54-56
communication in, 105
and conflict management, 128-29
lifelong, 49
of practical problems, 41-45
process features. See also REASON.
reasons for using, 38-40
sources of Information for, 49
using skills in, 28, 32
working with, 48-49
Professionalism at work, 154
Psychological health as benefit of exercise, 228
Public job services or agencies, 443
Publicly-funded school, 463
Public places, safety in, 259, 262
Public transportation, 359, 360-61
costs of, 373
Purchasing decisions, making, 278-82

Q

Quackery, 222
Quality of life, 83
Quantity buying discount, 285

R

Credits

Cover Design: Pudik Graphics

Cover Photography: Randall Sutter Photography

Interior Design: Greg Nettles, DesignNet

Infographic Design: Peter Getz, Circle Design and Greg Nettles, DesignNet

Chapter Opener and Unit Opener Stylist: Patricia Lipman

Arnold & Brown, 7, 24, 27, 29, 91, 100, 103, 109, 119, 125, 138, 139, 141, 144, 209, 266, 270
Roger B. Bean, 490
Marshall Berman, 17, 345, 460, 499
Ken Clubb, 32, 70, 126
Luis Delgado, 349, 351
Curt Fischer, 327, 334, 344
David R. Frazier Photolibrary, Inc.
  David Falconer, 264
  David R. Frazier, 90, 269, 470
  Trent Steffler, 346, 368-369
Tim Fuller, 296, 297, 302, 309
Ann Garvin, 223, 229, 285, 307, 322
Peter Getz, 328-329, 402-403
Grand Illusions, 463
Linda Henson, 320
International Stock
  Scott Barrow, 73
  Scott Campbell, 456
  Bob Firth, 457
  Phyllis Pacardi, 244
  Lindy Powers, 172
  Elliot V. Smith, 450
  Bill Tucker, 10, 231
Ken Lax, 12, 20-21, 22-23, 36-37, 52-53, 66-67, 80-81, 96-97, 98-99, 114-115, 132-133, 148-149, 164-165, 182-183, 200-201, 202-203, 220-221, 240-241, 256-257, 274-275, 276-277, 294-295, 312-313, 321, 332-333, 354-355, 358, 360, 374-375, 376-377, 394-395, 414-415, 434-435, 436-437, 454-455, 468-469, 488-489, 494

Lawrence Migdale, 260
Ted Mishima, 9, 40, 74, 187, 208, 226, 279, 282, 283, 289, 291, 301, 306, 308, 314, 318
Scott Pease, 322, 326, 501
Brent Phelps, 427
PhotoDisc, 42, 43, 45, 46, 47, 106, 107, 342, 343, 446-447
PhotoEdit, 268
  Bill Bachmann, 17, 127, 407
  Davis Barber, 424
  Billy E. Barnes, 152
  Robert Brenner, 362, 439
  Michelle Bridwell, 481
  Myrleen Ferguson Cate, 10, 54, 161, 236, 246, 430
  Cindy Charles, 493
  Gary Conner, 175, 184
  Deborah Davis, 407
  Mary Kate Denny, 8, 174, 356, 359, 365, 370, 378, 388, 497
  Laura Dwight, 421
  Amy Etra, 242, 348
  Tony Freeman, 5, 39, 356, 357, 378, 407, 448
  Robert W. Ginn, 249
  Spencer Grant, 85, 216, 378, 405
  Jeff Greenberg, 60, 426
  Will Hart, 464
  Bonnie Kamin, 14, 263, 410, 425
  Tom McCarthy, 150
  Michael Newman, 14, 15, 68, 75, 186, 379, 383, 384, 386, 419, 420, 423, 442, 465, 482, 491, 496, 498
  Tom Prettyman, 361
  Mark Richards, 6, 38, 92, 418, 472
  James Shaffer, 48
  Nancy Sheehan, 84
  Rhoda Sidney, 417
  Barbara Stitzer, 390
  Rudi Von Briel, 265
  David Young-Wolff, 13, 86, 101, 122, 251, 356, 378, 388, 397, 400, 428, 441, 445, 461, 484
Jennifer Leigh Sauer, 349
Gary Skillestad, 382, 399, 401
Jeff Smith, 233

Stock Market
  Peter Beck, 459
  David Burnett/Contact Press Images, 247
  Michael Kevin Daly, 9, 204
  George Disario, 215
  Anthony Edgeworth, 102
  Jon Feingersh, 15, 76, 156, 408, 438
  Mark Gamba, 69
  Charles Gupton, 88, 286
  Chris Hamilton, 82
  John Henley, 118, 207
  Bonnie Kamin, 444
  Lester Lefkowitz, 62, 89, 108, 142, 158, 305, 350, 422, 449, 475
  Rob Lewine, 151, 191
  T & D McCarthy, 169, 197, 233
  Bill Miles, 30
  Mug Shots, 11, 56, 63, 258
  Jose L. Pelaez, 5, 33, 167, 170
  Patti & Milt Putman, 243
  David Raymer, 41
  Chuck Savage, 474
  George Shelley, 6, 57
  Ariel Skelley, 193
  Joe Sohm/Chromosohm, 87
  Tom Stewart, 16, 59, 168, 195, 233
  D. R. Stoecklein, 8, 158
  Andy Washnik, 440
  Ed Wheeler, 179, 495
Jeff Stoecker, 105, 235
USDA, 225
Vote Photography, 155, 157, 166, 178, 262, 323, 324
Dana White, 7, 11, 12, 13, 16, 25, 26, 28, 55, 104, 108, 111, 116, 121, 124, 134, 135, 136, 140, 143, 145, 177, 185, 190, 196, 205, 210, 222, 227, 234, 278, 280, 284, 298, 303, 315, 316, 325, 471, 478, 479

Acknowledgement: Stephen D. Nacco, Department of Buses, MTA New York City Transit

Models and fictional names have been used to portray characters in stories and examples in this text.